Developing Mainframe
Java™ Applications

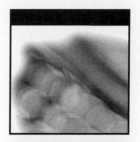

Developing Mainframe Java™ Applications

Lou Marco

Wiley Computer Publishing

John Wiley & Sons, Inc.

NEW YORK · CHICHESTER · WEINHEIM · BRISBANE · SINGAPORE · TORONTO

Publisher: Robert Ipsen
Editor: Margaret Eldridge
Assistant Editor: Adaobi Obi
Managing Editor: John Atkins
Text Design & Composition: MacAllister Publishing Services, LLC

Designations used by companies to distinguish their products are often claimed as trademarks. In all instances where John Wiley & Sons, Inc., is aware of a claim, the product names appear in initial capital or ALL CAPITAL LETTERS. Readers, however, should contact the appropriate companies for more complete information regarding trademarks and registration.

This book is printed on acid-free paper. ∞

Published by John Wiley & Sons, Inc.

Published simultaneously in Canada.

This publication is designed to provide accurate and authoritative information in regard to the subject matter covered. It is sold with the understanding that the publisher is not engaged in professional services. If professional advice or other expert assistance is required, the services of a competent professional person should be sought.

Library of Congress Cataloging-in-Publication Data:

ISBN: 0-471-41528-6

Printed in the United States of America.

10 9 8 7 6 5 4 3 2 1

Contents

Preface

Developing Mainframe Java Applications provides big iron data processors with a reference and learning tool they can use to write Java programs that run under OS/390. The thrust of the book is to describe Java in the language of the mainframe professional and to show how such professionals would develop Java applications for the IBM mainframe.

This is a "how-to" book, meant to impart rules and general techniques by drawing analogies between the familiar and the new. Scant mention is made of the technical intricacies of the Java Virtual Machine, garbage collection algorithms, "the taming of the threads," or other topics that deal with Java internals.

Who Should Read This Book?

The main audience for this book is the mainframe programmer. These programmers have years of experience on the mainframe and, although the likelihood is high that they have a wintel desktop (for email, office productivity, and mainframe terminal emulation), they may not be adept at programming on anything but a mainframe.

The book helps programmers learn Java programming, but the book has a wider audience than mainframe programmers. Systems analysts need to understand what Java is all about as well as programmers. Management, especially first and second line managers, needs an understanding of Java and a way of relating Java to their technical background.

As an aside, the book assumes that the reader has no C or C++ programming experience, which means that Java syntax, down to using curly braces, may be unfamiliar to the reader.

The Book's Organization

Part 1, "Java Fundamentals," describes Java by comparing its language features with those of third-generation procedural languages, such as COBOL and PL/I. The book describes Java as an object-oriented programming language. Part 1 concludes by showing some Java code for an application and comparing this Java code to COBOL and PL/I code that performs similar functions.

Part 1 contains chapters that discuss loops, decision constructs, declaring data, and subroutine/function (methods, really) invocation—the language of procedural programming languages. Other chapters discuss Class/Object representation, Inheritance, and Encapsulation—the language of object-oriented programming languages. After the reader completes Part 1, he or she will have a good grasp of how to use Java and how Java stacks up against familiar mainframe programming languages.

The goals of Part 1 are as follows:

- To describe Java by comparing and contrasting Java to familiar programming languages

- To introduce the Sun Java JDK so the reader can create and execute simple Java programs on his or her PC

- To explain how Java implements the object-oriented programming language metaphor, thereby showing how Java is different from PL/I, COBOL, and other languages used by the mainframe programmer

Part 2, "Java in the Mainframe Environment," describes IBM's "Java Everywhere" strategy by examining Java in the OS/390 environment. Each chapter covers how Java works with a particular brand of IBM technology, such as CICS, DB2, or VSAM. Java code exploiting IBM-specific technologies is included. The section concludes with Java code that accesses DB2 tables.

Part 2 explains shows how IBM has provided the Java programmer access to tried and true technologies. After the reader completes this section, he or she will have a good grasp of how to exploit Java in the OS/390 environment. The reader will be quite comfortable with Java; he or she knows the syntax, how Java implements the object-oriented world view (from Part 1), and how to use Java with familiar IBM technologies (Part 1).

The goals of Part 2 are as follows:

- To explain how IBM has implemented Java on its mainframe environment

- To explain how to use Java with the following IBM technologies:
  - CICS
  - IMS
  - Batch
  - VSAM
  - DB2

- To compare and contrast Java code with COBOL and PL/I code when using the previous list of technologies

- To describe IBM's JRIO classes and how the Java programmer on OS/390 uses these classes to perform record I/O

- To show application code using JDBC to access DB2 data

In the first two parts, the book shows COBOL and PL/I code that functions like the Java code in the snippets and applications. However, this approach can only take the reader so far into the world of Java. Simply put, Java is far more capable than COBOL and PL/I put together. Hence, the last section of the book describes several key features of Java that are found only in Java.

Part 3, "Java: Above and Beyond Other Programming Languages," lightly touches on several Java features and capabilities, such as applet creation, the Swing user interface classes, Java 2, Enterprise Edition (J2EE), and Remote Method Invocation (RMI).

The goals of Part 3 are to describe some of Java's unique features, including

- Applet coding

- Java Native File I/O

- Java GUI classes

- The libraries constituting the Java 2, Enterprise Edition

- The Remote Method Invocation (RMI) classes, which enable a Java programmer to execute Java programs on other machines over a network

Conventions Used in This Book

Code listings and outputs appear in a monospaced font, such as

```
public static void main( String[] args )
```

The first time a term is used in a chapter, the term is printed in *italics*.

Throughout the book, you'll find sidebar information that contains relevant information that doesn't fit into the current context. Here's what a sidebar may look like:

You'll also encounter notes that augment the material preceding the note. Here's

THIS IS HOW A SIDEBAR TITLE MAY LOOK

And here is some text explaining the sidebar title . . .

what a note may look like:

NOTE This text may explain the material immediately preceding the note.

You'll also encounter tips that offer a shortcut or a solution to a common problem that relates to the material you've just read.

TIP This text may provide a shortcut or solution to a common problem.

Acknowledgments

This work would not have been possible without the nearly infinite patience of the hard-working folk at John Wiley & Sons. Of course, kudos go to my wife who had to witness and endure some strange behaviors on my part during the completion of this work.

PART

One

Java Fundamentals

Introduction

Java Trek

You are a mainframe programmer neck deep in COBOL programming. You cannot escape the siren song of *object-oriented programming* (OOP). Every trade publication you peruse has articles from industry pundits chanting the object mantra. In an evangelical manner, these new disciples of the object faith quote chapter and verse from the missiles of Saint Booch and Saint Jacobsen. The message is clear—you must adopt the Object Tao and righteously cast out the old demons of procedural programming and structured design.

Okay, you got the calling. As a highly evolved mammal, your survival instinct kicks in. You sense that you'd better find out what this object stuff is all about. If these harbingers of the object path are correct, you could become obsolete before you become vested in your pension plan. Duly motivated, you begin your quest for the truth about object technology.

A New World of Objects

The oceans of literature and the galaxy of Web pages contain many new terms and concepts. On your own, the brave new world of object technology can be quite daunting. In this exploration, you will have an experienced guide to help you sort through the differences between mainframe programming concepts and object technology—specifically Java programming.

Object applications are not related sets of procedures acting on external data sources, but sets of communicating objects. These objects contain all their needed data and procedures. The object view of modeling software systems is based on the properties and behaviors of actual application entities. Comparatively, the old software design model of creating separate data models and structure charts seems archaic.

Reusability

The object prophets make strong claims about software reusability. On the reusability issue, the prophets speak with a single voice. They say that only by using object technology can you, the programmer, create truly reusable code.

We all know that software reusability is not a new issue. Actually, software reusability has always been the platonic ideal of programming. You've probably been very close to this ideal at times. It is possible to write reusable code with a procedural language, but the reusability is achieved in spite of, rather than because of, your programming tools and environment.

Is there really a programming environment out there somewhere that enables you to create reusable code as a rule, not as an exception? Any culture advanced enough to produce cholesterol-free eggs and breastfeeding devices for males must be advanced enough to produce this programming environment. But do object environments truly assist the programmer in writing reusable code?

Inheritance

You may have read about that wonderful property of objects called *inheritance*. With inheritance, you write code that implements some behavior for a group of similar objects, or a class. You create subclasses based on some relationship—subclass A ISA superclass of B, for example. Once done, the code that implements behaviors for the superclass is automatically known to the subclass. Yes, I said automatically known to the subclass.

Well, this certainly sounds like a feature that would help me write reusable code. Think of a bank account superclass with checking and savings account subclasses. You write code to implement the withdrawal behavior for the bank account class. This code automatically becomes known to the checking and savings account superclass. One routine, three classes. This beats the pants out of reusability in the COBOL world-copying code in a separate member of your PDS and changing a few lines. Do you see the real value in this inheritance stuff?

Encapsulation

You are likely to encounter the term *encapsulation* in any exploration of object technology. With encapsulation, the data and code that implement behaviors in application objects are hidden from other objects. The big idea is that, because other objects do not know about an object's internal data and behavior representations, these other objects cannot change these representations. In short, encapsulation provides a safety mechanism that prevents unwanted changes in an object's data.

How does this encapsulation stuff really help prevent unwanted changes? Think about the last set of COBOL modules you wrote. Let's say you coded a list of parameters in the CALL/USING statement of the calling module. Remember the unexpected behavior of the calling program? Remember trying to debug the calling program? Remember how the called program changed one of the parameters supplied in the LINKAGE section? Remember how difficult this problem was to locate? Suddenly, like the light bulb flashing over the coyote's head in those silly roadrunner cartoons, you see the beauty, majesty, and practicality of encapsulation.

The problem with the COBOL modules is that both the calling and called modules needed to know the data representation of the parameters. Because the called module knew the data representation, the module contained code that changed the parameter. At times, you count on the ability of the called COBOL module to change the parameter's value and write code to make wanted changes. Sadly, you can slip and write code that inadvertently changes passed parameters. The calling module has no knowledge of these changes and does not execute correctly.

Owing to encapsulation, an object application can never suffer this fate. What an object doesn't know, an object cannot change. Data contained on objects is safe from unwanted tampering from other objects.

Stack Class

Let's say Joe Programmer wrote a PL/I program a while back. Being a wise guy, he implemented a stack as a controlled data structure (a controlled data structure in PL/I—declared with the storage class CONTROLLED—means the PL/I program can dynamically allocate memory for the structure with the ALLOCATE statement). All routines that used the stack had this controlled structure declaration. Joe's code worked; he was immensely pleased with himself. When the team lead scheduled the code walkthrough, he couldn't wait to demonstrate his superior knowledge of the PL/I language.

Well, it turns out that Joe should have known that the project lead is not nearly as well versed in PL/I as he is. When she saw the stack and its controlled allocation, she barked, "What is this?" With pride, Joe described the intricacies of PL/I's controlled storage class. A scowl slowly spread over the project lead's face. She was clearly not impressed with Joe's code and asked him to rewrite the stack code, using a more conventional data structure. When Joe meekly asked for a suggestion, she whipped out an array representation on a white board. Joe slinked back to his cube to make the required changes.

Joe hunted down every module that accessed the stack because he had to change every one. He had to change the POP, PUSH, and ISEMPTY routines, too. What a pain. Maybe Joe should have conferred with Hagatha, the team lead, before he embarked on his coding journey.

If this application were done in an object language, Joe would need to change only the stack class. All objects communicating with the stack, being ignorant of the stack's data representation, would not have to be changed.

Another bonus—because of inheritance, all subclasses of a changed class automatically know of the change. Joe need do nothing to implement a new data representation or a behavior in the subclasses.

By now, you should be firmly convinced that this object stuff is definitely worth the admission price. This class/object representation, combined with inheritance and encapsulation, makes for powerful code. Many more object technology wonders are there to unearth—let's keep digging.

Polymorphism

What if you could send the same message to different objects and each object would invoke the appropriate behavior in response to the message? Remember that object applications are communicating objects, not separate function/module calls acting on external data sources. The term *message* makes sense in object-speak. Objects communicate by issuing messages to each other. The message invokes some behavior that you have implemented in code. The thrust of polymorphism is that each object responds to a message according to its understanding of that message.

There is practical, everyday truth in this. How do people respond to messages? Do we not respond in our own way? Don't different people (and dogs, for that matter) respond differently to the same message? When you become accustomed and attuned to this concept, the object world-view of polymorphism seems as natural and proper as wearing underwear.

You may think that object technology is recent, say 1990s, technology. However, object technology has been around since the 1970s. It may be strange to realize that object technology is older than your dog. It may be older than your significant other. It is certainly older than some of the big iron technology like DB2 and REXX that you've been using for the past 15 years.

Java and C++

By now, you have absorbed the essentials of an object system: class/object representation, encapsulation, inheritance, and polymorphism. That's good. But, as a programmer, you may be naturally curious about programming languages that implement these essentials. It seems that every programming language has an object flavor (even COBOL.) However, the most common are the C++ and Java programming languages. Let's investigate these two languages.

Your first impulse may be to rush off to a bookstore and purchase some of the uncounted number of books about these languages. Because most programming books are 40-plus dollars, a few books equate to big bucks. After all, you're a programmer, not a drug dealer or a dentist. Three books are the equivalent of food for two weeks. By now, the at-home crowd must be weary of eating beanie-weenies. Maybe you can make do without the books for now.

Internet searches reveal a wealth of links on C++ and Java. There are lots of C++ and Java source code, lots of terminology and acronyms, and lots of talk about UNIX on the net. There's little on how object technology is used by companies in certain industries—notably yours. To find out how this object–C++–Java technology is used by your industry and your company will take more research.

Perhaps a direct approach is in order. Why not talk to folks in your organization to learn if anyone in the same building is using object technology? You may meet a few object converts under your corporate roof. Perhaps some of these object practitioners can shed some interesting light on C++ and Java usage within the company.

C++

Joe, the first object practitioner you meet, uses the C++ programming language. This programmer swears with the fervor of a recent ex-smoker that any object programmer worth his salt uses C++. He gleefully takes the time to explain his ardor for C++.

Joe tells you in a pompous and annoying manner that C++ supports all the features of object programming: class/object representation, encapsulation, inheritance, and polymorphism. He explains that C++ is a hybrid object language—a language built upon an existing procedural programming language (C, in this case). He boasts that his C experience and knowledge of object concepts enabled him to start coding almost immediately.

He continues by explaining that C++ supports multiple inheritance. Multiple inheritance enables a subclass to inherit data attributes or behaviors from more than one superclass. Of course, he grins, multiple inheritance is more flexible than, and superior to, single inheritance.

Because of your hard work and research, you understand what Joe is talking about. You wax with glee as you realize that you can talk the object talk. You can't wait to walk the object walk. Impatiently, you ask him to show you some C++ code.

As your eyes scan the C++ code, your shiny, gleeful face quickly sours to a dull, woeful puss. You can't understand any of this stuff. This code could be Babylonian cuneiform writing as far as you're concerned. You can't believe that under this mess is essentially code in a procedural language.

You recall the first time you saw PL/I. You didn't understand the nuts and bolts, but you had a good understanding of what the code did. Your COBOL background was good preparation for understanding PL/I. Unfortunately, this C++ stuff looks pretty cryptic.

The C++ programmer senses your state of overall confusion and asks you how much C experience you have under your belt. There may be lots under your belt these days, but none of it is C programming experience. You're a COBOL and PL/I programmer. Remember when you had to learn pointer use in PL/I? You finally grasped that a pointer is merely a four-byte address. Joe shows you pointers to character strings, pointers to integers, and (gasp!) pointers to pointers, explaining that, although these pointers are addresses, they are all different data types. You thank the Joe for his time and mosey on to your cubie. Alone with your thoughts, the horror of learning C++ seeps in. You thought object programming would be easier than conventional procedural programming. This C++ stuff seems to be procedural programming at its worst.

At lunch, you mention to a chum that you're looking into C++ programming. This chum happens to know a thing or two about C++. He has some C++ information obtained from a vendor of Macintosh software development tools. He believes that this information is Mac-specific.But the C++ information from the Mac vendor made the stuff you gleaned from the pointer-happy programmer earlier today read like a nursery rhyme. Here's what you read:

> *When you call the function "MYSTREAM.read()", it normally returns a reference to the stream object itself, that is, . MYSTREAM. This is so you can chain these functions together, like this:*

```
MyStream.read(MyVar1).read(MyVar2).read(MyVar3)
```

> *But when you call "MYSTREAM.read()" from a function that expects an integer, the compiler performs some "sleight-of-hand" and actually returns MYSTREAM.good()" as the function result.*

So this is what the world of programming has evolved to?

Desperately, you rifle through your notes. You recall hearing through the mill that your corporate training department may be developing courses on Internet technologies. You recall the instructor of the last class you took, oh so many moons ago. Why not give her a call?

Java

Jane, a corporate instructor, is developing a course on the Java programming language. Java, she excitedly explains, is part of a suite of technologies that enable a programmer to write a program once and run it on any platform—even on the Internet. Great—you have to deal with a suite of technologies to learn and use Java. This is just what you need, right? Before you get all steamed up over technology suites and the like, your Java guide says that Java has use and value as a programming language aside and apart from Internet; Java is much more than the "Applet language of the Internet." Upon hearing this, you regain your composure.

Jane starts to talk about Java's inheritance mechanism. When you comment on C++ and its support for multiple inheritance, she audibly snickers. Jane mentions that with multiple inheritance, you have no straightforward way of knowing the origin of some inherited behavior. Her point is that an application developed with multiple inheritance may ease initial class creation and application development but could make application maintenance a nightmare. By now, you assume that Java supports single inheritance only.

However, when you point out the textbook advantages of multiple inheritance, she audibly snickers again. Your Java guide points out that she never got to explain Java's inheritance mechanism to you. She tells you that Java supports single inheritance inasmuch as every object is created from a class that has one and only one superclass. However, the Java designers were well aware of the limitations of single inheritance as well as the pitfalls of multiple inheritance. She explains that Java's inheritance mechanism is unique; a Java class has the ability to inherit behaviors from several classes but only one of these classes is the superclass. The inherited behaviors that do not belong to the superclass are defined to the class by an *interface*.

You are puzzled because this sounds like multiple inheritance. Jane explains that Java supports two separate hierarchies: a *Class* hierarchy, which defines the class/superclass relationship, and an *Interface* hierarchy, which enables a class to implement behaviors from classes not contained in the class hierarchy. In JavaSpeak, a class *extends* its superclass and (optionally) *implements* one or more interfaces.

Well, this still sounds like multiple inheritance but you get her gist: A Java class has one bonafide superclass but can implement behaviors from other classes. When you comment that a Java class can inherit method implementations from only the super-class, and the class must provide implementations for all methods used by an interface, your guide approvingly nods. She suggests that you not get hung up on the differences between a superclass and an interface yet.

Jane explains that the lazy C++ programmer could write code that doesn't do the cool object stuff, like encapsulation or inheritance. The lazy C++ programmer could write C++ code to be completely procedural. At first, you might be tempted to believe that this ability of C++ to wear two hats, so to speak, is a good thing. Yeah, but you saw C++ code, remember? C++ is not your idea of procedural programming.

Actually, she says, a common view of C++ is that C++ is a better version of C; C++ was developed to overcome the deficiencies of the C programming language (of which many exist). Now, you don't know C, and don't care to learn, but you see the wisdom of her words. You get the drift that C++ was developed from C as opposed to being developed from the ground up. C++ is a better C, not a language necessarily engineered to support object orientation.

The Java guru continues. She states that you could do procedural programming in Java, but anything of substance, like file or database I/O, requires classes and objects and inheritance—the stuff of objects. Although you could force a Java program to be procedural and not use object-oriented features, your program probably could not do anything useful.

Java is a modern language, she says. Java designers at Sun Microsystems had definite ideas in mind when Java went to the drawing board. Considering that Java was released in late 1995, you can tell that this technology is hot.

Some Java Code

Perhaps you should look at some Java code before she waxes into a Java frenzy. Jane presents an implementation of the *bubble sort* in Java as shown in Listing 1.1.

Looks like that C++ stuff you saw before. You see those ++, -- and the braces { }. At least there's a use for those braces now. For the moment, you're not impressed with the syntax of this "modern" language.

My friendly Java instructor explains that syntax is syntax; after all, isn't it all a matter of what you're used to? Of course, as a programmer, you take the time to explain that programming language syntax parallels written language inasmuch as both need to be read, written, and understandable. You take the time to explain that language replete with punctuation is more difficult to digest than language without excess punctuation. However, you are a gracious and classy person and you readily yield to your Java Guide's point about syntax.

Life, and programming, is too intense to sweat the small stuff. Jane says her time is short and she'd rather not go over too many syntax details right now; she'd rather stick to explaining Java concepts that may be daunting to a Java wannabe like you.

```java
class BubSort {                                              //1

public static void main( String args[]) {                   //2
    int  anarray[]          = {3,10,6,1,2,9} ;              //3

    sort( anarray ) ;                                       //4
    for (int idx = 0;idx < anarray.length; idx++ )
        System.out.println( anarray[ idx ] ) ;

}                                                           //5


    static void sort(int a[]) {                            //6

      for (int idx1 = a.length;  --idx1>=0; ) {
         boolean swapped = false;
         for (int idx2 = 0; idx2<idx1; idx2++) {

            if (a[idx2] > a[idx2+1]) {
                int temp      = a[idx2];
                a[idx2]       = a[idx2+1];
                a[idx2+1]     = temp;
                swapped       = true;
            }

         }
         if (!swapped)
             return ;
      }


    }                                                      //7


} //8
```

Listing 1.1   The infamous bubble sort.

She first explains that the double slashes denote a single line comment; the slash-asterisk combination denote a multi-line comment. She mentions that Java is case sensitive. That is, the variable names myPay and MYPAY are different variables. Like a chanteuse breaking into song, she starts to explain pieces of the program by the numbers. She says that even this small example contains many Java features; she has time to cover only a few points. You express your gratitude and ask her to proceed.

She explains the big picture by stating that the program has a main method that declares and initializes an array of numbers, calls a sort method, and prints out the sorted array. The sort() method implements our friend, old Mr. Bubble. Both the main()

and sort() methods are part of a class called BubSort. You may understand her reasoning; it is the way you might code an example to illustrate a sort or features of a programming language.

The Java Program-By the Numbers

She starts to discuss the numbered lines.

Line //1 is the class declaration:

```
class BubSort {
```

Every Java file containing Java source code has a class declaration. The class declaration should match the name of the dataset. In this case, the dataset name would be BubSort.java.

Line //2 is the declaration for the main() method:

```
public static void main( String args[]) {
```

Every Java application has a main() method. Now, she continues, this doesn't mean that every dataset with Java source code has a main() method. Some Java source files have support datasets. And, she adds, Java applets do not have a main() method.

Yes, applets. You recall reading about Java applets—small programs that execute within a Web page. But you withhold your questions because you're in the middle of dissecting this bubble sort.

Speaking of which, Jane returns to the explanation of line // (2). Well, those words *public static void* have meaning. She says it has to do with the visibility of the method (that's the *public* keyword)—the method does not belong to any particular object (that's the *static* keyword) and what the method does, or does not return (that's the *void* keyword).

Yes, she says—Java has keywords, or reserved words, like most programming languages.

Line //3 is a Java array declaration:

```
int       anarray[]   = {3,10,6,1,2,9} ;
```

The first keyword, *int*, is the data type of the elements of the array. You gather that the keyword *int* is short for *integer*. She tells you that you may be right, you may be wrong—it depends on what you think an integer is.

You say that the definition of an integer is operating-system dependent. On some platforms an integer is four bytes, type binary, unsigned. On other platforms, an integer is four bytes, type packed, signed. You say the *int* declaration depends on the platform you are writing Java on.

Java and Platform Independence

Well, your long-suffering and humble Java instructor certainly has a thing or two to say now. She asks you if you've read *anything* about Java. If so, she claims, you'd know that Java doesn't care for operating system particulars such as primitive data type byte sizes and formats. The *beauty* of Java is that Java was designed to be source code compatible across multiple platforms. The same Java that executes on a Wintel box will run *without modification* on a Macintosh, an IBM RS6000 running AIX, or on an IBM mainframe running OS/390.

You chortle under your breath. Seems you've heard this one before. You recall how C was the ultimate cross platform software development tool. C was the "be all, end all" of programming languages. Now, you never became proficient in C, but you work in data processing, right? If C lived up to one-tenth of its promise, you would have heard about it, right? Well, you still spent your time coding EVALUATE statements and looking at Abend-Aid dumps, right?

Apparently sensing your disbelief over her words, she explains that Java achieves this cross platform execution boast by compiling into a platform-neutral format called *bytecodes*. A platform-specific piece of software called a *Java Virtual Machine* translates the bytecodes into platform-specific machine code. Hence, the Java compiler does not have to care about operating system details; the Java Virtual Machine takes care of that. And the Java Virtual Machine is platform-specific.

You see the beauty in this approach. The Java programmer really does not have to know how big integers are or how booleans are represented on a particular platform. All the Java programmer needs to know is how big Java integers are or how Java represents booleans. The Java Virtual Machine takes care of the mundane platform-specific details.

Oh, back to the question, how large are *int* data types? She says that Java uses four byte signed binary integers.

Java Objects and Primitive Types

A typical Java declaration is the data type or *class name* followed by the variable or *object* name. In line // 3, the identifier *anarray* is the name of the declared array. My guide says that Java variables or objects can have other attributes attached to them, but for now let's keep things straightforward.

You are a bit puzzled over this "variable or object" thing. Isn't Java object-oriented? Isn't everything you use in Java an object instantiated from a class? Isn't that how this object-oriented stuff works?

She reminds you that Java is a new language. Over the years, computer scientists have learned a thing or two about programming languages. For example, a "pure object" language like Smalltalk would never, never, ever, ever permit you to use anything but objects. In Smalltalk, even the number 2 is considered an object. Some computer scientist types have concluded that this "everything is an object" approach doesn't work for some applications. A programming language runtime must keep track of memory allocated for objects (among other things). Most object languages need custom routines to compare objects for equality and to read and write objects. In short, using objects is a lot of work for a computer.

An example of an application type that is not well suited to object technology is the "number crunching" type of applications used in science labs. Remember those old Fortran programs with five nested loops? To use an object-oriented system to perform numeric calculations seems a bit wasteful of computing resources considering what the system may require to keep track of all the objects used. Of course, this is not to say that you *couldn't* code application of this type in object languages.

Java enables a programmer to use *primitive data types* instead of objects. For example, this example uses few objects. The array elements, the array indices, and the boolean flag are not objects; these program elements are variables. The array declared on line //3 is what she calls a *reference data type*.

As an aside, Java arrays are very object-like. Arrays may be assigned to variables of type Object (Object is the root class in Java, the class at the top of the hierarchy). But, she continues, Java practitioners do not consider an array an object.

You mull this over. You sort of understand that the array declaration does not declare an object. Objects use methods and there's been no talk of methods attached to this array. This array is pretty much like an array used in COBOL or PL/I.

You believe that some of this object stuff looks really good "on paper" but often fails the real world test. You've read that this object stuff is decades old. Let's face it—if this technology were so great, it would be more widespread. A mixture of old-fashioned, procedural programming and this object stuff could be just what we need in data processing, perhaps.

Possibly, says your Java guide. She continues to discuss the sort example.

Back to the Java Bubble Sort

Back to line //3. Note that this statement initializes the array. In Java, arrays start with index 0, not 1 like some programming languages. Just something to keep in mind, she quips.

Jane comments that she has to wrap this up soon; she has meetings to attend and memos to write. She starts to discuss line //4:

```
sort( anarray ) ;
```

Here's where you invoke the sort() method and pass the array argument. This is not tough, new, or strange. This is programming!

Where are the objects? Where are the classes? Java is object-oriented, right? Of course, Jane says, but we don't need object stuff to do a bubble sort. Java lets you do some things procedurally.

Take a look at line //6:

```
static void sort(int a[])
```

The sort method has a special keyword, *static*, which means that you need not attach this method to an object. Sometimes you just need a piece of code that does not depend on any particular object's data. The bubble sort is like that; the sort is entirely parameter driven. What we need is a way of telling Java that we want this method but don't want to create objects and attach the method to the object. The static keyword does just that.

She explains that if she (or anyone) needed a bubble sort, she could use the sort method in the BubSort class. First, the programmer would remove the main() method from BubSort.java; Listing 1.2 shows the new BubSort.java.

```
class BubSort {

static void sort(int a[]) {

        for (int idx1 = a.length; --idx1>=0; ) {
           boolean swapped = false;
           for (int idx2 = 0; idx2<idx1; idx2++) {

              if (a[idx2] > a[idx2+1]) {
                 int T = a[idx2];
                 a[idx2] = a[idx2+1];
                 a[idx2+1] = T;
                 swapped = true;
              }


           }
           if (!swapped) return ;
        }
     }
}
```

Listing 1.2   Bubble sort in its own class.

As you can see, the sort() method is unchanged but the class does not have a main() method. Presumably, the class that will use the sort() method has a main() method, and only one main() method per Java application is allowed.

Assuming the BubSort class is on the same directory as the UseBub class or in what Java mavens call the *classpath*, when you execute UseBub, the Java runtime will pull what UseBub needs from BubSort. In particular, UseBub needs the sort() routine. Check out the lines marked with //*** in Listing 1.3.

```
BubSort.sort( anarray ) ;
BubSort.sort( anarray2 ) ;
```

The sort() method is qualified with the class that contains the method.

You ask about the other statements in the original bubble sort program—the one from Listing 1.1. In particular, you ask about these curly braces. The rest of the numbered statements are braces that close off blocks. She explains that Java uses the curly braces as block constructs. The block construct helps to define variable visibility. Also, the block construct is required when more than one statement follows an *if* statement or a loop construct. Even a small Java program can contain numerous braces, she says.

The visibility of these variables may be defined by curly braces; variables declared within a pair of braces are known within those braces. Some cases exist where a variable is declared within a statement. In this case, that variable is visible only in that statement. She directs you to the following statement:

```
class UseBub {

static void printResults (int sorted[]) {

    for (int idx = 0; idx < sorted.length; idx++ )
       System.out.println( sorted[ idx ] ) ;

}

public static void main( String args[]) {

    int anarray[] = {3,10,6,1,2,9} ;
    BubSort.sort( anarray ) ;                        //***

    int anarray2[] = {12, 4, 35, 1, 55, 76, 3 } ;
    BubSort.sort(anarray2) ;                         //***

    printResults( anarray ) ;

    printResults( anarray2 ) ;

  }
}
```

Listing 1.3 Invoking the bubble sort from a class.

```
for (int idx = 0; idx < anarray.length; idx++ )
  System.out.println( anarray[ idx ] ) ;
```

This is a *single statement*. The variable *idx* is visible in this statement only.

She catches you staring at this statement. She catches you in mid-thought and explains that this is a looping construct that prints an array value to the default output stream. She also says that she is quickly running out of time and has to pick up the pace.

After a pregnant pause, you meekly ask her where the pointer references are. You figure that "modern" languages like C++ and Java are replete with pointers. You cite your discussion with the C++ programmer and what he told you about pointers in C++. What about pointer use in Java, you ask?

With an impish grin, she tells me that *Java does not use pointers*. No pointers? None, she answers. Java is able to do what every programming language does, and more, without the use of explicitly declared and manipulated pointers. A Java programmer cannot declare a pointer or access the starting address of a data structure in any way.

Well, well—no pointers in Java! That one statement alone is music to your code-weary ears. You start to believe that these Java engineers at Sun really know their stuff.

Meet the Sun JDK

You ask her how she compiles and links this program. She reminds you that Java compiles into a platform-neutral data format called *bytecodes*. You knowingly nod in agreement. She is using a WinTel box to compile her Java source. She tells you that the marketplace is rife with Java tools and serious Java folk have an arsenal of tools to help with Java development. For now, she explains, she'll use the standard tool suite, or Java Development Kit, available from Sun Microsystems (the developers of Java). She opens up a DOS window and compiles the program. Next, she executes the program. Figure 1.1 shows the DOS window after compiling and running the bubble sort.

The *javac* command invokes the Java compiler. In truly sparse computer geek fashion, a successful compile provides no diagnostics. A successful Java compile produces a class file—in this case, *BubSort.class*. Next, the *java* command executes the program. The java command passes the previously created class file, in Bytecode format, to the Java Virtual Machine for execution. The result of the execution is seen in the DOS window previously.

Well, well, you think. This certainly beats the pants off of submitting batch compiles and links. You enter source code in an appropriately named dataset, switch to a DOS window where you do your compiles, and repeat until you get a clean compile. Next, you execute your program in the very same window.

You note that you need a program to execute your Java program. You ask her where the executable file is produced by the linker. Actually, you ask her where and how she did the link. Your Java guide tells you that she did not link the Java code; she did not produce an executable. The java compiler, javac, produced a *class* file composed of bytecodes. The bytecodes are interpreted by the *java* command.

You ask her how much these Java tools cost—the compiler (javac), the program that executes the bytecodes (java), and the Java Virtual Machine. You would like to get a copy on your machine. When she replies that these tools are *free*, you slip off your chair. Free? How can this be? Our shop is used to paying a fortune for any software tool.

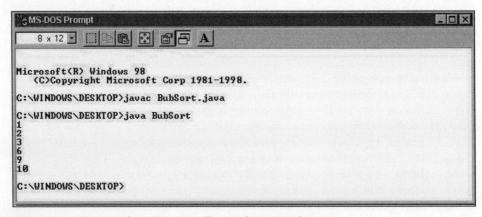

Figure 1.1   DOS window after compiling and running the sort.

My guide explains that Sun provides a base set of tools, which includes the compiler. Other vendors committed to Java provide *Java Virtual Machines*, or JVM's, bytecode interpreters, and applet viewers. She tells you that the standard *Java Development Kit*, or JDK, includes a documentation generator (javadoc), a java debugger (jdb), other tools dealing with system security (javakey), and a way of disassembling Java classes/bytecode into Java source (javap). She adds that serious Java developers have visual tools like the rest of the world and these visual tools cost money but anyone can compile and execute Java programs with the freebies included in the JDK.

You are a bit stunned over this, and, rightfully so. Now you get a glimpse into the hype, the excitement that Java has caused in the computing community. This Java stuff is the closest thing to a standard you've heard of. To top it all off, the development tools are free. Of course, you're still reeling over the phrase, "No pointers in Java."

Your very patient Java guide, and teacher, pauses once again to catch your feedback. A grin slowly washes over your face as you realize that you understand nearly everything she has said. The program you've examined makes sense in a macro sort of way. However, you're battle-hardened enough to realize that every programming language has its quirks and oddities and that the language syntax just have to be learned. In the middle of your reflections, something odd catches your eye.

You can't help notice your humble Java guide leafing through some IBM language reference manuals. When you ask her what she needs to know, she replies that she would like to know a bit more about programming language constructs in COBOL, PL/I, and REXX. She wants to compare and contrast some Java constructs with constructs from more familiar languages.

What a great idea. She likes that you find merit in her idea. She glances at the wall clock, quickly stands up, grabs a binder, and tells you she has to go. You want to show your appreciation for taking the time and energy to show you stuff. As she shrugs off your offers to buy her coffee or lunch someday, you hit upon a good idea: You tell her that you could write the sort program previously in a commonly used IBM language. She agrees that your idea has merit. You ask for a reference for Java syntax, which she gladly provides. You strut off to your designated work environment to fulfill your promise.

A PL/I Version of the Bubble Sort

You decide to have lunch at the cubie (not all that unusual, right?) and pound out some code. You wisely spend some time perusing the Java reference material. You see that the Java JDK comes with *packages*. These packages are collections of related classes that perform varied tasks from database and file I/O to mathematical computations to network data movement to graphical user interface development. You get the idea that a big part of Java software development is knowing what classes are already available for your use. The over 1,000 classes, constants, interface definitions, and exceptions available seems daunting. You put that part of the reference down for now and decide to stick with scrutinizing the syntax to create a compatible version in a procedural language.

You want to code a version of the bubble sort that does what the Java implementation previously does but in the style and flavor of a procedural language. It takes a while to dope out some of these Java constructs; the looping construct takes a bit of reading. Fortunately, you are familiar with the bubble sort—a great help when you

```
BubSort: Proc ( arg ) Options( Main ) ;
  Dcl arg          Char( 40 ) Varying ;
  Dcl anarray ( 6 )    Fixed bin( 15 ) Init( 3, 10, 6, 1, 2, 9 ) ;
  Dcl idx          Fixed bin( 15 ) Init( 0b ) ;
  Dcl arrayLength        Fixed bin( 15 ) Init( Length( anarray ) )
;
  Dcl Length        Builtin ;

  Call sort( anarray ) ;

  Do idx = 1 to arrayLength ;
     Put Skip List( anarray( idx ) ) ;
  End ;

  Sort: Proc( a ) ;
Dcl   a (*)      Fixed bin( 15 ) ;
     Dcl  arraylength Fixed bin( 15 ) Init( Length( a ) ) ;
     Dcl  idx1       Fixed bin( 15 ) Init( 0b ) ;
     Dcl  idx2       Fixed Bin( 15 ) Init( 0b ) ;
     Dcl  temp       Fixed Bin( 15 ) Init( 0b ) ;
    Dcl  swapped     Bit( 1 )      Init( '1'B ) ;    /* TRUE */

     Do idx1 = arraylength to 1 by -1 ;
       swapped      = '0'B ;        /* FALSE */
       Do idx2 = 1 to idx1 ;
         If a( idx2 ) > a ( idx2+1 ) Then
         Do ;
         temp       = a ( idx2 ) ;
         a( idx2 )   = a ( idx2 + 1 ) ;
         a ( idx2 + 1 )= temp ;
         swapped     = '1'B ;
         End ;     End ;
         if ( ^swapped )Then return ;
       End ;

  End Sort ;

End BubSort ;
```

Listing 1.4   PL/I implementation of a bubble sort.

want to code an implementation. Listing 1.4 is a PL/I implementation you've written during a greasy Tuesday taco lunch.

There is no significant difference between the Java and PL/I implementations. Both pieces of code sort the declared and initialized array and list the sorted array elements at the terminal. The PL/I code could have Begin/End block delimiters to mimic the functionality of Java's curly braces. For example, you could have coded:

```
If a( idx2 ) > a ( idx2+1 ) Then
    Begin;

        Dcl   temp   Fixed Bin( 15 ) Init( 0B ) ;

        temp        = a ( idx2 ) ;
        a( idx2 )   = a ( idx2 + 1 ) ;
        a ( idx2 + 1 )= temp ;
        swapped     = '1'B ;
    End ;
```

But you know that PL/I programmers hardly ever code in this style.

As you look at this PL/I code, you can't help but see the remarkable similarities with the Java code. You realize that, all the hype about Java aside, at the heart of this Java stuff is *Java, the programming language*. This programming language is very similar to programming languages you already know. You think about how much you've learned about Java in a few short hours; it gives you a warm feeling of satisfaction.

Meanwhile—Back at the Desk . . .

Sadly, your reality as a mainframe programmer creeps back and you check out your ever-growing, never-diminishing queue of change requests. Here's a change request to modify a report created by a COBOL application so old you can carbon-date it. As you flip through the mostly worthless documentation for this application, you can't get Java and the object worldview out of your mind. As you search the source code and compiler listings looking for variable references, you wax woefully that this application does not exploit object technology. None of this data is encapsulated or hidden in any way; every routine that accesses this data has the possibility of changing it. You need to find and analyze all references to this data across several separately compiled modules.

Oh well, someday you may get to use Java instead of coding PERFORM statements and looking at JCL job streams. In the midst of your reverie, your boss strolls by and summons you into the conference room for an impromptu staff meeting. You grab your day-timer and march quickly into the conference room; you don't want to be left standing.

Your boss announces a new strategic initiative pushed down from the rare air of executive row. The big boys approved the new customer information system. The twist is that the big boys want this system developed with object technology. Your boss asks the assemblage if anyone present knows anything about this stuff.

No sooner than the echo from your boss' mouth fades, the department loudmouth booms in obnoxiously. The loudmouth knows all about this stuff, he says. He says he's read much about C++ and that is the direction this project, nay, the whole company, should move toward. The meeting attendees seem impressed. You, of course, know better.

Opportunity Knocks

"If you want to do real object-oriented stuff, Java is the way to go," you say. You explain that Java is source code compatible across platforms. You continue by citing that Java development tools are free, including documentation generators (that seems to get everyone's attention). Also, you don't have to mess around with all those pointers because Java has no pointers.

The loudmouth barks that Java is supposed to be cool and all that but it is interpretive. "Can we take the performance hit?" The Database Administrator adds to the discussion by saying that the application will likely be I/O bound and that application execution speed may not be a bottleneck.

Attention now shifts back to you. You can't believe that everyone, including the loudmouth, is hanging on your every word. You confidently lean forward. With eyebrows triumphantly arched, you continue.

Java comes with packages, which are collections of related routines, that enable the programmer to create interface screens, read databases, and talk over the network. In addition, you cite, the industry is behind Java with the major players offering development tool suites. Java is far, far more than the "Language of the Internet." Also, Training and Development is developing an in-house course on Java programming.

You sense that your boss needs some action items for the meeting. You suggest that your boss call the manager of Training and Development to get the take on this Java versus C++ business. Your boss adjourns the meeting.

After the obligatory post-meeting chitchat with fellow wage slaves, you hunker down in your bunker, seeking variable references to this COBOL application to implement this change request. Your mind wanders. You can't help but wonder if this is the last change request for an ancient COBOL application you'll do. You understand the excitement and fervor of the object disciples in general, and the Java evangelists in particular. Can the disciples and evangelists be right? Is procedural programming a thing of the past?

The only constant in this world is change. You cannot escape the Internet and the impact Internet technologies have in business and society. Dot-coms advertise on the Super Bowl and place highway billboard ads. Business pundits talk about downsizing, outsourcing, reengineering, and the new shape of Information Systems. You hear the latest buzzwords and clichés. You hear your management buzzing with these clichés. It's pretty scary.

However, you're off to a good start. You have some understanding of the hype, the hoopla, even some of the buzzwords and clichés! Now, the time has come for you to learn how a data processor skilled in writing COBOL and PL/I programs can master Java.

In Summary

The world of Java covers every facet in data processing from client, single-user programs to large, enterprise-wide distributed systems. As you learn more and more about the brave new world, you'll encounter numerous references to odd-sounding technologies, including directory and naming services, remote method invocations, and Enterprise JavaBeans. Any understanding of these and other Java technologies start with understanding the Java programming language.

Here you are, with book in hand. You've taken a big step—but you knew that already—into a different realm. Good luck on your Java trek. If you persevere, you'll be coding Java in no time flat, and this book will help.

What Is Java?

Here, you'll read a bit about the history of Java's development, some of the guiding principles of the creators of Java (Sun Microsystems), and what may be in store for Java in the near future. This chapter touches on the similarities and differences in concept between Java and familiar mainframe programming languages. This chapter also discusses why knowing Java is a key skill for a data processor, be that data processor a programmer, analyst, project manager, or IS management.

A Brief History of Java

Sun Microsystems, a company you'll hear much of in this book, created the progenitor to Java in the old days of the early 1990s. Believe it or not, Sun initially had this idea of using what would be called Java to control household appliances. Bring on those interactive microwave ovens. Can you see the ad campaigns: "The future is bright with Sun Microsystems' programmable toasters?"

Perhaps the time is not right for smart, computer-controlled washing machines and the like. Apparently, Sun Microsystems is ahead of its time. In any event, this programming language, now dubbed Java, designed to control appliances had some interesting properties:

- Programs written in Java had to be small, or not require many resources to run. After all, you don't want to outfit your TV with many megabytes of memory, right?

■ Programs written in Java had to be put on different devices, or run on different hardware.

These two properties make Java programs ideal for running on the Web. The creators at Sun realized this and, in 1994, demonstrated Java use on the Web by writing Java programs, called *applets* that ran with a browser, also written in Java. The applet is a piece of Java code that gets downloaded to a Web page (like an image) and executed. When you leave the page by clicking on a link, the applet is terminated.

Java struck a chord with the folks at Netscape, so much that Netscape licensed Java in 1995. The world started to see Java applets appear in Web pages. Recall that the Web was still fairly new in 1995; those days, the corporate world did not allow Internet access on the job and only the enlightened few amongst us had an Internet connection at home. Even so, Sun realized that Java was a hit and cranked up their Java development efforts. Java had become worthy of coverage in several trade rags. Java usage began to spread over the Internet with applets appearing on Web page after Web page. Java version 1.0 was officially born. Java was on its way.

To encourage Java development, Sun makes its *Java Development Kit* (JDK), available at http://java.sun.com, at no charge to anyone who wants to write Java. Because Sun is the owner of Java (Java is not "open source"), you can count on the Sun JDK to work with the latest and greatest Java version. You'll read more about the JDK later and use the JDK, if you like, to compile and run some of the Java programs in this book.

Yes, this is all well and good. However, if all Java does is run in a browser window, you'd not hear a tenth of the hype and, in all likelihood, would not be reading this book. Fact is that Java is much more than the applet language of the Internet. And, in early 1997, with the release of Java version 1.1, the Java community realized that fact. The Java language itself changed very little from version 1.0 to 1.1; Java version 1.1 is a faster, more robust, and featured version of Java than version 1.0. The newer version included *application programming interfaces* (APIs) for remote access, database access, printing, encryption, and more. The JDK for this release included tools that generated documentation, a command line debugger, disassembler, and others. In short, Java version 1.1 took Java from the applet language of the Internet to a full-featured language that can be used to develop applications, on or off the Internet.

Most of the hype surrounding Java deals with the new features and capabilities arising from Java version 1.1. Java version 1.0, used for a year or two, has demonstrated its effectiveness and Sun has demonstrated a commitment to Java. The industry stood up and took notice. The big industry players began to get on board with Java. Various consortia formed in an attempt to create some sort of standards for Java technology, although some say that these consortia formed as a defense against, well, you-know-who. Software tool vendors, such as Borland, Symantec, IBM, and Sun began to offer commercial Java development tools. Companies were getting things done with Java version 1.1.

Sun's Java division pressed onward with the next release of Java, which Sun originally called Java version 1.2, officially released in late 1998, and dubbed Java 2. The leap from Java 1.1 to Java 2 is not as far as the leap from Java 1.0 to Java 1.1. However, Java 2 contains significant enhancements over Java 1.1 in the areas of event handling and user interface construction, to name a few. The JDK that supports Java 2 was called JDK 1.2.

The World of Java Today

These days, Java folk do not speak of Java *language* versions too much. Java folk speak of *platform versions*. For example, Sun has a Java *Standard* platform (J2SE for Java 2 Standard Edition), which Java savvy programmers could use to develop applets and small applications. Sun also has a Java Enterprise Platform (J2EE for Java 2 Enterprise Edition), which Java savvy programmers could use to develop large applications across a distributed (enterprise) computing environment. Also, Sun has a JDK for each platform and sets of APIs that are peculiar to each platform (or just peculiar, perhaps).

Today, the Java world is rife with acronyms, or TLAs (that's *Three Letter Acronyms*) like JSP, EJB, and RMI, to name a few. If you check out http://java.sun.com/products, you'll see dozens of acronyms—some FLA's like JNDI and JDBC, too.

Java as a programming language, apart from programming dishwashers, is five or so years old. Considering that there exists over 1,200 books on Java and the TLA's and FLA's mentioned previously is somewhat remarkable. A cursory search on the Internet for "Java Source Code" yields thousands of hits. The interested computer person could subscribe to various magazines and ezines that report on Java developments. Sun Microsystems makes available lots of Java source code. You can participate in online chats with Java experts and authors. In short, seems this is a great time to learn Java.

Java: The Programming Language

At the heart and soul of all this talk about platforms and the seemingly endless stream of TLAs and FLAs is Java, the programming language. Java has several features that make it the choice of programming languages in this heavily distributed computing environments we find are the norm these days. What are these features, you ask? Let's look at a few.

Java: The Object-Oriented Programming Language

Chapter 7, "Class and Object Representation," describes object oriented software features in general and the Java implementation of object oriented features in particular. Here, let's make a quick compare and contrast of calling COBOL modules and calling code written in Java.

When coding in COBOL or some other third generation programming language, you conceptualize your application as a set of program units often called modules. These modules interact with one another through a set of interfaces. Remember structure charts with the hollow ended and filled arrows? If this sounds like *structured programming*, you're on the money.

Structured programming stresses a separation of data from process. In theory, a piece of PL/I or COBOL code need only know the structure of data (20-byte character, for example) to act on it. The semantics of the data does not come into play at the language level. For example, a COBOL compiler and linker would not choke on the following snippet:

```
Calling Program                      Called Program 'COBEX'
01     ZIP-CODE     PIC(9)9.         LINKAGE SECTION.
       *Additional Code
CALL 'COBEX' USING ZIP-CODE.         01     SSN     PIC(9)9.
```

Because both calling and called programs are passing a nine-digit number, everything's kosher. Of course, this program will not execute properly; module COBEX is expecting a *social security number* (SSN) but is getting a nine-digit zip code.

In contrast, when coding in Java, an object oriented programming language, you conceptualize your application as a set of application units called objects. Unlike modules, an object is not separate from data-quite the contrary. An object is a happy amalgam of data and program code that acts on that data. The code that acts on the data defines the allowable operations on that data. In fact, the program code is part of the object, as much a part of the object as the data.

In an application developed with an object oriented programming language, the previous scenario with the zip code and SSN could not easily happen. You would assume that zip codes and SSNs have different semantics; an operation done on a zip code would not be likely to be done on a SSN.

In Java, (as in all object oriented programming languages) objects come from a *class*. When you call code written in Java and pass objects as arguments, the class of the argument in the calling code and the called code must match. For example, the code shown in the following simply won't fly:

```
Calling Program                      Called Program 'JavaEX'
ZipCodeClass myZip;                  void JavaEX( SSNClass aSSN) {
//Additional Code
JavaEX( myZip ) ;
```

Here, the calling routine passes an argument object of class ZipCodeClass to a routine that expects an argument object of class SSNCLass. The previous code will not compile, much less execute. Having argument mismatches caught at compile time relatively early in the software development process, bodes well for those of us who make a living by writing software.

As previously mentioned, Chapter 7 has much more to say about Java's object oriented features.

Java: The Portable Programming Language

Portability, the ability of software to execute on different platforms without source code modification, has long been a sought-after feature of many a programming language designer. Traditionally, you bust code then pass your source to a compiler that creates machine code for a particular platform. If you wanted to put your program on a different platform, you'd have to recompile your source with a compiler on the different platform, which produces machine code for that platform. After working out the subtle and not so subtle differences between the platforms, you just might get a working application.

The Java programmer does not suffer this fate. Java, you see, does not compile into machine code. Java compiles into a format called *bytecode*. The bytecode format is the same for all operating systems. You compile a Java program on a Macintosh, you get some bytecode; you compile the same Java source on a Windows or OS/390 machine, you get the same bytecode. The ten-dollar phrase is that bytecode is architecturally neutral.

How do the different operating systems understand this bytecode stuff? The answer is that the operating system needs to have a *Java virtual machine* (JVM) installed to interpret the bytecode. Sometimes the JVM is called the *Java runtime* or the *Java interpreter*. Whatever you call it, the JVM is the operating system specific software that interprets the architecturally neutral bytecode into executable code.

As you'll read later, IBM offers a Java compiler called the High Performance Java compiler that produces native OS/390 code instead of bytecode. Code produced by the High Performance Java compiler does not require a JVM for interpretation. The trade-off is that code produced by this compiler only runs on OS/390. Of course, IBM also has a Java compiler that produces bytecode and requires a JVM specific to the OS/390 platform.

Another Java feature that helps ensure that Java programs are portable across platforms is that Java does not have any platform-specific data types. Some programming languages change the size of data types depending on the operating system. For example, the C programming language uses integers of 16, 32, or 64 bits depending on the operating system. Java has one size for its data types-an integer is 32 bits in size. If you need bigger numbers, you declare a different type or class.

Remember Sun's slogan, "Write Once, Run Anywhere."

Java: The "Pointer-Less" Programming Language

Java started life as a contender for controlling appliances and rapidly evolved as a language for creating applets. Today, Java is used to create applications-both on and off the Web. The Java language supports the familiar and some unfamiliar language constructs. The familiar include loops, decision, case, and function constructs. The unfamiliar include error handling and language constructs for multitasking.

One programming language feature notably absent from Java is pointers. As you know, a pointer is a memory address, typically 4 bytes, that indicates the starting location of a data structure in memory.

The COBOL programmer typically does not use pointers much; the PL/I programmer uses pointers now and then. Hence, you may feel that the previous dissertation on the disallowance of pointer use may fall under the category of "No Big Deal." If so, read on to see why being pointerless is such a big deal.

You know the programmers who often use pointers; they can be identified by a dull haze over their faces, a nervous twitch in one of their eyes, and a strange rash. These programmers get that way by performing arithmetic on pointers to generate memory addresses, passing arrays of pointers as arguments to procedures, or (gasp!) using pointers to pointers to reference data.

You'll never see a Java programmer suffer the previous ailments for the simple reason that the Java programmer *cannot use pointers*. Put differently, the Java language does not support pointer use. You cannot declare a pointer in Java and you have no way of accessing the starting memory location of any data structure.

By eliminating pointer use, Java programs are not fodder for a host of memory related bugs. Tasks like dynamically allocating memory for various structures such as linked lists and trees are tedious, error-prone, and extremely dependent on the current execution environment. As you'll read in later chapters, Java handles memory management for you. Java detects when objects are no longer in use and automatically frees memory for later use in your program. As you've guessed, there's a ten-dollar phrase for this process—*garbage collection*.

A side effect of eliminating pointer use is that a Java program is safer than programs that use pointers. Because a Java program cannot directly access memory, a Java program (or applet) cannot use pointers to get outside a string or an array's memory. The pointerless feature of Java is a simple yet effective defense against malicious hacks wanting to do you and your precious computer harm.

While on the subject of security, Java has security-conscious features other than being pointerless. Unknown Java programs, including applets, are placed in a "sandbox" where the program can do what it will inside this box. For example, untrusted Java applets cannot access the local file system. Java has features that enforce security at the program level. You'll take a look at the Java security package, java.security, in Chapter 10, "Interfaces."

Java: The MultiThreaded Language

Most mainframe programs execute in a linear fashion, with a single flow of control. Of course, programs take branches based on inputs and various environmental conditions. However, the program itself is normally *doing one thing at any one time*. Let's call programs of this sort *singlethreaded* programs.

Most COBOL and PL/I programs are singlethreaded. PL/I has language support for multiple tasking (threading) under OS/390. However, the typical mainframe program normally does not require any sort of multiple threading mechanism. Batch jobs don't call for any sort of multithreading. Even conversational programs requiring user interaction written to execute under IMS or CICS can get away with single threading.

Web based programs can be quite the opposite. Imagine getting online, downloading a file, then clicking on a link. You notice that the browser continues your file download while displaying your newly requested page *at the same time*. We use the term *multithreaded* to describe this state of two or more processes (downloading the file and displaying the page in this case) simultaneously.

Common sense will tell you that a programming language that is used to develop Web applications should make the creation of multithreaded programs somewhat easy. Java contains a class specifically developed to ease thread use. Also, Java has the *synchronize* keyword, which helps the Java programmer control when certain pieces of code should be executed.

You'll see some examples of multithreaded code in this book.

IBM's Java Efforts

Since 1995, IBM has worked, and continues to work, closely with Sun and other industry heavies in defining and refining various Java technologies. IBM realized early in the game that Java is simply too good to ignore. IBM supplied vital input into the development of Java technologies back in the "old days" that helped make this technology suitable for enterprise application development. The result of IBM's labors is a full suite of Java development programs, support channels and tools well suited for developing enterprise class applications for OS/390 system and AS/400 systems.

Big Blue customers have a need to access years' worth of data housed on their mainframe systems with Web technologies. IBM has developed Java related technologies with this goal in mind. IBM has made several enhancements to make Java fit into its OS/390 mainframe environment. For example, IBM has Java packages-you'll read more about Java packages later-that enable a programmer to perform record based I/O, to read and write VSAM datasets and to access IMS databases. Section II, devoted entirely to accessing data using Java and IBM technologies, has material and sample code that does all of this.

IBM has its own Java development tool suite called *Visual Age for Java*, which has both a client and a server side flavor. Other IBM Java tools include a Java compiler called the High Performance Java Compiler that bypasses the interpretive/JVM execution by compiling Java source code into machine code.

For the full skinny on IBM's Java efforts, you may want to check out http://ibm.java.com.

Java versus COBOL and PL/I: A Brief Look

A respectable part of Part 1 of the book compares Java to older, procedural programming languages still in use today. Check out the following chart to see a quick look at language features and where in the book these features are covered in detail.

Here are a few words on some of these table entries:

Application structure. At a high level, a Java application is a set of files called *class* files. Each class file contains code that defines needed data and code to define objects of that class. One of these class files has a routine, or method, called *main*. The Java application works by calling code from these, and other, class files during execution. Chapter 3, "Creating Your First Java Program," where

Table 2.1   Language Features in Java versus Procedural Languages

LANGUAGE FEATURE	JAVA	COBOL	PL/I
Application structure	One or more files, one of which has a main method	One or more files containing source	One or more files, one of which has a main procedure
Variable types and typing mechanism	Primitive data types (variables) Custom data types (objects) Strong typing	Representative	Representative, some special types (file, complex, for example)
Aggregate data structures supported	Arrays	Arrays, records	Arrays, records
Arguments passed by	Internal reference (objects) Value (primitive types)	Reference	Reference, value
Variable scope	Local, class	Global to module	Local, global to module, global to program
Declared variable and object attributes	Modifiers (visibility, other)	Storage alignment	Storage class, storage alignment, others
Object support?	Yes	No	No
Pointers supported?	No	Yes	Yes
Programmer manipulation of dynamic data structures?	No. Memory management done for programmer	No features for dynamic data structures	Yes. Memory Allocate/Deallocate, and so on.

continued

Table 2.1 Language Features in Java versus Procedural Languages (*continued*)

LANGUAGE FEATURE	JAVA	COBOL	PL/I
Subprogram types	Internal and external methods (may return object, primitive type or void)	External subroutine	Internal and external subroutines and functions
Exception Handling?	Yes (throws, catch)	No	Yes (signal, on)
Multithreading language support?	Yes	No	Yes
Preprocessor, conditional compilation?	No	Some	Yes
Built-in functions?	No	No	About 100

you'll take a look at some simple Java programs, is where you'll read more about Java application structure.

Variable types and typing mechanism. Java is an object oriented programming language. In addition, Java also supports variables declared as a *primitive data type*. Java variables correspond closely with variables declared in COBOL, PL/I, and other procedural programming languages. As you'll read later, Java often treats variables differently than objects.

- Variable typing comes in four flavors: *strong, weak, none,* and *representative.* Strong typing means that variables must be of the same data type for use in expressions. Weak typing means that you can mix and match variables of different types in expressions. None (no typing) means that you don't declare variables of a type at all. Representative means that variables are declared a type that mirrors its machine representation, such as a packed number. Read Chapter 5, "Declaring and Defining Data," for more on how Java deals with declaring variables.

Aggregate data structures supported. Java supports arrays of any type or object. Java does not support record structures like you frequently use in COBOL and PL/I. However, this is not much of a hardship because Java, with its support for objects, can easily emulate record structures.

Arguments passed by. Programs can pass arguments to subprograms by *reference* or *value.* A program that passes arguments by reference passes the starting address of the variable. A program that passes arguments by value passes a copy of the variable. Several differences exist between the two passing mechanisms. The most visible and important is that a subprogram can change the value of an argument passed by reference (because the subprogram and program access the argument by its memory location) and cannot change the value of an argument passed by value (because the subprogram works with a copy of the original).

- Java uses two separate argument passing mechanisms. Java passes primitive types by value and passes objects by using an internal reference, *not an address.* Chapter 7, devoted entirely to Java's class and object representation, covers passing object references to methods in detail.

Variable scope. The scope of a declared variable defines where in the program that variable can be accessed. Java uses a related concept called variable and object *visibility* (see the following) to address variable scope. Here, we mention that Java has support for local variables and class variables. Let's defer any discussion of class variables to Chapter 7, okay?

- Local variables are declared within, and are only known within, a block of code. This code block could be a method or a "do" or "if" block. Chapter 5 has more information on local variable use.

Declared variable attributes. Some programming languages enable you to further define the qualities of a variable by supporting various attributes. For example,

PL/I supports a storage class attribute and COBOL and PL/I enable you to declare variables that line up on byte, word, or doubleword boundaries.

■ Java goes far beyond its distant procedural language cousins by supporting a variety of attributes called *modifiers* in Java-speak. Java supports a class of modifiers called *visibility* modifiers. The visibility modifier dictates where a variable or object (or method or class) can be seen. Using visibility modifiers is a topic in and of itself, which you'll read about in Chapter 7.

Java allows for other modifiers, which (you guessed it) you'll see in Chapter 7.

Object support. The line on the chart says it all.

Pointers supported. Ditto.

Programmer manipulation of dynamic data structures. Can you use dynamic data structures, such as binary trees and circular linked lists, in Java? Why, certainly. Does Java force you, the programmer, to deal with the details of allocating memory for nodes, affixing the memory to addresses, checking if the memory allocation was successful, freeing up unused nodes of your structure? Why, certainly not.

■ Java provides classes that let you use certain dynamic data structures without the muss and fuss of memory management. If you've ever had the pleasure of tending to those mundane programming details listed in the preceding paragraph, you could develop that dull haze over your face, a nervous twitch in one of your eyes, and that strange rash.

Subprogram types. The procedural terms for subprogram are subroutine and function; the object term for subprogram is method. A subroutine is a block of code that contains its own data and logic; a function is a subroutine that returns a value to the calling program. You can replace a function invocation with a variable of the function's returned data type and the code "makes sense."

■ Java is able to use methods declared internally, in the same class file, or externally, in different class files. A Java method can return pretty much anything (behave like a function) or nothing at all (behave like a subroutine).

Exception handling. Java gives you the ability to trap various conditions and (depending on the condition) affect repair or exit gracefully. Exceptions in Java are objects that contain (like other objects) data and methods. As such, exceptions can be used like objects; they can be passed as arguments to methods, for example. Chapter 12, "Exception Handling and Thread Basics," is devoted to this exciting topic of handling exceptions in Java.

Multithreaded language support. We've covered this ground earlier in this chapter. No need to be repetitious.

Preprocessor, conditional compilation. Java has no preprocessor or conditional compilation because it has no need for these features. Preprocessors and conditional compilation are mostly used to generate platform-specific code. As you know, Java has no need for such nonsense. Java doesn't need to physically include source code, like the COBOL COPY or PL/I %Include, because Java identifies files by their location in the system (this location is set by an environment variable) and the class name.

Built-in functions. A built-in function is a function that is part of the language definition. For example, PL/I has a substr function that returns part of a string, or a length function that returns the size of a string. Java does not support built-in functions per se, as part of the language definition. However, Java has methods for common classes. Java has substring and length *methods* that do the same thing as the PL/I functions cited previously.

In Summary

So, what is Java? Is Java the silver bullet we data processors have been awaiting? Will Java render the existing world of JCL job streams obsolete? Java is well accepted by major industry players. New information about Java emerges as soon as the ink dries on existing information. One thing is certain: Java is not going away anytime soon. So, perhaps a good answer to the previous question is that Java is a suite of technologies that, simply put, cannot be ignored and has to be reckoned with. Happy reckoning!

CHAPTER 3

Creating Your First Java Program

In this chapter, you'll use some of the programs available for download from the book Web site, www.wiley.com/compbooks/marco, to create a simple Java program on a wintel machine. (The software required to create a program on the mainframe is a bit too complicated for a "get up and go" exercise.) You'll make slight changes to the program and use downloaded software to execute modified versions. This chapter serves as a good segue into the next chapter.

NOTE Here, you'll use Sun's *Java Development Kit* (JDK), version 1.3. Chapter 4 describes some of the programs included with this release of the JDK. For now, the goal is to get a simple Java program up and running on your machine, learn a bit about Java by dissecting this program, and compile and run a few variations. Once you get the hang of using the JDK, you'll be ready for the rest of the chapters in this section.

Installing the JDK

Installing the Java Development Kit is fairly straightforward. Here's what you do:

- See if you have 50 MB or so to spare for the JDK installation. Truth be told, you can get away with about 30 MB. However, you'll have the option of installing a lot of *Java source code*—the source code for the Java language itself. You don't need this source to use the Java compiler or the runtime, but you might actually learn a thing or two by having the source code handy!

TIP If you have a tough time scraping 50 MB on your hard disk, perhaps its time to get rid of all those cheesy e-mail animations, electronic cards, and off-color pictures you haven't looked at for a while.

- Download the latest JDK from the Sun Java Web site http://java.sun.com/j2se.
- When you download the latest JDK version from the Sun Web site, you should check to ensure that you got the entire file. The Web site has the size of the file. After you've downloaded the JDK, check the file's size by displaying its *properties*.
- Assuming the file size found on Sun's site and the file size found by investigating the file's properties agree, just double-click the downloaded file and follow instructions. The defaults will work fine.

If the file sizes disagree, you should attempt another download. You need a working JDK to use the examples in this book; if your file sizes disagree, you'll encounter problems down the road.

Is the JDK Installed Properly?

Before you get into this chapter, you should ensure that you have correctly installed the JDK. Fortunately, this check is fairly easy. All you need to do is open a Command window (a DOS window, really) (Start Menu -> Run-Enter "Command") and type:

```
java -version
```

This command invokes the Java interpreter with an option to report the Java version installed. If you successfully installed the JDK, you may see a message similar to:

```
java version "1.3.0"
java(TM) 2 Runtime Environment,Standard Edition (build 1.3.0-C)
java HotSpot(TM) Client VM (build 1.3.0-C, mixed mode)
```

Or, you may see a message indicating a minor release, such as:

```
java version "1.2.2"
Classic VM (build JDK-1.2.2-001, native threads, symcjit)
```

If you leave out the dash in front of "version," you'll see:

```
Exception in thread "main" java.lang.NoClassDefFoundError:
version
```

Without the dash, the Java interpreter thinks you want to run a previously compiled Java program named *version.java* that compiled into *version.class*.

If you misspell "version," you'll see:

```
Unrecognized option: -voision
Could not create the Java virtual machine.
```

Just be more mindful of what you type and try again.

You *don't* want to see this:

```
Bad command or file name
```

If you do, you'll have to reinstall the JDK.

Compiling and Running the Program

Assuming you've successfully conquered the JDK installation challenge, it's time to enter a small Java program into a text editor. Java programs, like those of other programming languages, are streams of text. Any text or word processor program capable of saving your Java source as plain, old text will be fine.

You'll be entering the old, classic standby of programming language examples: HelloWorld. Open your word or text processor and enter the Java source in Listing 3.1.

Of course, you need to enter the Java code *exactly* as shown. Pay particular attention to *capitalization*. Java programmers follow naming conventions that govern capitalization; you'll read the full skinny on these conventions in Chapters 5, 6, and 7. Later in this chapter, you'll see an example of what happens when you do not pay attention to proper capitalization.

Save the file as *HelloWorld.java*. You'll see that the Java compiler cares little for the name of the source code file; the compiler, however, is really interested in the name of the *class* that you used.

Open a DOS window and check the directory referenced in the window to ensure that the directory is the same as the one where HelloWorld.java resides. Once this is done, type:

```
javac HelloWorld.java
```

```
class HelloWorld {

    public static void main(String[]commandLineArgs) {
        System.out.println("Hello World!") ;
    }

}
```

Listing 3.1   The classic HelloWorld example.

After your hard disk spits and spurts for a second or two, you will see the DOS prompt again. The Java compiler, *javac*, will not report any diagnostics if you have a successful compile. If you see any diagnostics, you've made an error. Eventually, you'll have a successful compile. To run the program, enter the following in the same DOS window:

```
java HelloWorld
```

Not surprisingly, you'll see:

```
Hello World!
```

No surprise here, right? Let's spend a bit of time on what's going on with the compile and run, followed by an examination of this tremendously exciting and complicated program you've just entered, compiled, and executed.

Figure 3.1 is a shot of a DOS window showing the execution of the Java compiler and the Java runtime.

Note the paucity of diagnostics. Remember, the invocation of the Java compiler was without options and the program merely spits out a text string. Let's face it—not much is going on here, right?

However, looks can be deceiving. The Java compiler and interpreter are extremely busy even when compiling and running an extremely simple program. You'll see this in the next section.

Compiling and Running Java Programs: A Second Look

The Java compiler, javac, located your Java source file HelloWorld.java and checked out your source for references to other Java classes. Even a program containing nothing but a method signature would require additional Java classes for a successful compile.

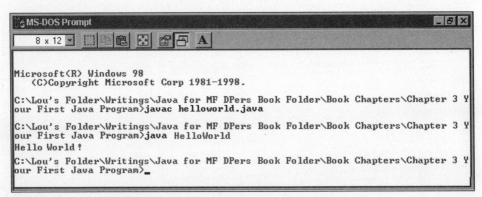

Figure 3.1 Running the HelloWorld Java program.

Anyway, the Java compiler picks up class references and makes the referenced classes available to your program.

Listing 3.2 is a compiler listing showing javac loading the classes needed for a successful compile. The invocation of the Java compiler is bolded. Note the use of the *-verbose* option to generate the list of classes loaded during the compile (yes, the leading dash is required).

Once javac finds and loads the classes you've referenced in your source, javac compiles the source into bytecode. The Java compiler doesn't care what the name of the source file is; you could have saved the file as *doodah.java* and the code would compile successfully. However, you are advised to pay close (really close!) attention to the capitalization because most Java tools pay close (really close!) attention, and as a programmer, you should be truly concerned about the behavior of the language and tools. Coming from the case-insensitive mainframe world of COBOL programming, you are hereby warned!

Running the Java compiler sans options will produce no diagnostics when the compile is successful. This is quite a change from the world of mainframe compilers! However, who in the big iron world runs compilers without options? Here, we've used the *-verbose* option to see javac loading the classes. In Chapter 4, you'll look at the rest of

```
Javac -verbose helloworld.java

[parsed HelloWorld.java in 660 ms]
[loaded C:\JDK1.2.2\JRE\lib\rt.jar(java/lang/Object.class) in 50 ms]
[checking class HelloWorld]
[loaded C:\JDK1.2.2\JRE\lib\rt.jar(java/lang/String.class) in 60 ms]
[loaded C:\JDK1.2.2\JRE\lib\rt.jar(java/io/Serializable.class) in 0
ms]
[loaded C:\JDK1.2.2\JRE\lib\rt.jar(java/lang/Comparable.class) in 0
ms]
[loaded C:\JDK1.2.2\JRE\lib\rt.jar(java/lang/System.class) in 0 ms]
[loaded C:\JDK1.2.2\JRE\lib\rt.jar(java/io/PrintStream.class) in 60
ms]
[loaded C:\JDK1.2.2\JRE\lib\rt.jar(java/io/FilterOutputStream.class)
in 0 ms]
[loaded C:\JDK1.2.2\JRE\lib\rt.jar(java/io/OutputStream.class) in 50
ms]
[loaded C:\JDK1.2.2\JRE\lib\rt.jar(java/io/IOException.class) in 0 ms]
[loaded C:\JDK1.2.2\JRE\lib\rt.jar(java/lang/Exception.class) in 0 ms]
[loaded C:\JDK1.2.2\JRE\lib\rt.jar(java/lang/Throwable.class) in 0 ms]
[wrote C:\Lou's Folder\Writings\Java for MF DPers Book Folder\Book
Chapters\Chapter 3 Your First Java Program\HelloWorld.class]
[done in 1480 ms]
```

Listing 3.2   Compiling HelloWorld.java with the -verbose option.

the options that you may use with the Java compiler on the Sun JDK. In practice, you'll use some options when you compile your Java programs.

Your source and included classes come in the Java compiler; a *class file* goes out the Java compiler. The class file is composed of the platform-neutral bytecode that you've heard so much about. This class file can run on any machine that has a Java runtime installed. The class file will reside in the same directory as the Java source unless you tell javac otherwise by using a compiler option.

When you pass this class file to the Java interpreter (or Java runtime, if you prefer), you are executing your Java program. The Java runtime looks for all of the classes requested by your program and loads them dynamically into your system's memory. Listing 3.3 is an abbreviated list of the Java runtime loading classes from the Java runtime library during the execution of HelloWorld.class.

Looks like the Java runtime is extremely busy even for a simple program! Note the bolded **Hello World!** included in Listing 3.3. That's the actual output of the program intermingled with the diagnostics.

Recall that Java is interpretive. You do not link Java programs to produce native executable code. (However, some companies, IBM for example, offer a Java compiler that produces native OS/390 code.) After a successful compile, you're ready to load and go.

Figure 3.2 shows the process in pictures.

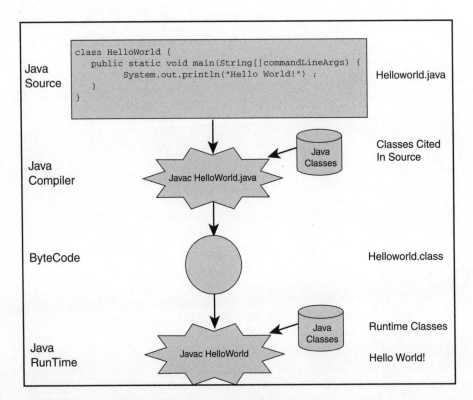

Figure 3.2   Compiling and running a Java program.

```
java -verbose HelloWorld


[Opened C:\JDK1.2.2\JRE\lib\rt.jar in 50 ms]
[Opened C:\JDK1.2.2\JRE\lib\i18n.jar in 0 ms]
[Loaded java.lang.NoClassDefFoundError from
C:\JDK1.2.2\JRE\lib\rt.jar]
[Loaded java.lang.Class from C:\JDK1.2.2\JRE\lib\rt.jar]
[Loaded java.lang.Object from C:\JDK1.2.2\JRE\lib\rt.jar]
[Loaded java.lang.Throwable from C:\JDK1.2.2\JRE\lib\rt.jar]
[Loaded java.io.Serializable from C:\JDK1.2.2\JRE\lib\rt.jar]
[Loaded java.lang.String from C:\JDK1.2.2\JRE\lib\rt.jar]
[Loaded java.lang.Comparable from C:\JDK1.2.2\JRE\lib\rt.jar]
[Loaded java.io.ObjectStreamClass from C:\JDK1.2.2\JRE\lib\rt.jar]
[Loaded java.io.ObjectStreamClass$ObjectStreamClassEntry from
C:\JDK1.2.2\JRE\lib\rt.jar]
[Loaded java.lang.ref.SoftReference from C:\JDK1.2.2\JRE\lib\rt.jar]
[Loaded java.lang.ref.Reference from C:\JDK1.2.2\JRE\lib\rt.jar]
[Loaded java.io.ObjectStreamField from C:\JDK1.2.2\JRE\lib\rt.jar]
[Loaded java.io.ObjectStreamClass$CompareClassByName from
C:\JDK1.2.2\JRE\lib\rt.jar]


(Another 100 or so classes get loaded)


[Loaded sun.net.www.URLConnection from C:\JDK1.2.2\JRE\lib\rt.jar]
[Loaded java.net.URLConnection from C:\JDK1.2.2\JRE\lib\rt.jar]
[Loaded java.net.UnknownConten Hello World!
tHandler from C:\JDK1.2.2\JRE\lib\rt.jar]
[Loaded java.net.ContentHandler from C:\JDK1.2.2\JRE\lib\rt.jar]
[Loaded sun.net.www.MessageHeader from C:\JDK1.2.2\JRE\lib\rt.jar]
[Loaded java.io.FilePermission from C:\JDK1.2.2\JRE\lib\rt.jar]
[Loaded java.io.FilePermission$1 from C:\JDK1.2.2\JRE\lib\rt.jar]
[Loaded java.lang.RuntimePermission from C:\JDK1.2.2\JRE\lib\rt.jar]
[Loaded java.lang.SecurityException from C:\JDK1.2.2\JRE\lib\rt.jar]
[Loaded java.security.cert.Certificate from
C:\JDK1.2.2\JRE\lib\rt.jar]
[Loaded [Ljava.security.cert.Certificate;]
[Loaded HelloWorld]
[Loaded java.lang.ref.Finalizer$3 from C:\JDK1.2.2\JRE\lib\rt.jar]
```

Listing 3.3 Executing HelloWorld.class with the -verbose option.

Your Java source, located in HelloWorld.java, is passed to the Java compiler (the javac program). Javac includes needed classes during the compile and produces bytecode known to your system as *helloworld.class*. This completes the compile process. To execute your program, pass the *class file* to the Java runtime (the Java program). The

Java runtime will require additional classes to successfully execute your program. These required classes are loaded dynamically during program execution. Once all required classes are brought to bear, your program successfully executes. Here, the program outputs the time-worn phrase, *Hello World!*

Notice that you must observe case sensitivity when invoking your Java program. The class name coded in your source must match the argument passed to the Java runtime program. Keep reading for more details.

Watch out for Those Class Names

Here's where the case sensitivity comes into play, big time. You want the name and the case of the class file produced by the compiler to be the same as the name of the class in your Java source. Figure 3.3 shows a screen shot of a compile and execute where this sagely advice is not heeded.

What a mess! The black text is what our "advice-ignorer" entered. Note that after this person entered

```
javac helloworld.java
```

DOS comes back with a prompt and no diagnostics; the compile was successful. However, when this is entered in the DOS window:

```
java helloworld
```

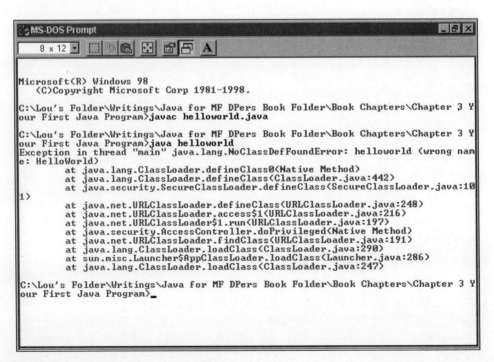

Figure 3.3 Not listening to good advice.

the Java interpreter has a thing or two to say. For now, we can concentrate on the first line of the diagnostic:

```
Exception in thread "main" java.lang.NoClassDefFoundError:
helloworld (wrong name: HelloWorld)
```

It doesn't take a rocket scientist to deduce that the Java runtime (or Java interpreter, if you prefer) reported an exception called NoClassDefFoundError and the class definition that was not found is called helloworld. The Java runtime even reported the class that should be used!

The rest of the diagnostics dumped onto the DOS window show the location (line number) of several Java classes that you didn't even realize were being used in your three-line program. Believe it or not, after you read Section I, you'll understand what this string of diagnostics mean.

What Does a Compile Error Look Like?

Good question. Face it—you want to make compile errors; the more compile errors you make, the more Java you're doing, right? Anyway, let's change your work of art above by omitting the closing quote. Here is the offending line of Java source:

```
System.out.println("Hello World!) ;
```

And the ensuing compiler output:

```
helloworld.java:5: String not terminated at end of line.
                 System.out.println("Hello World!) ;
                                                   ^
helloworld.java:6: ')' expected.
                 }
                 ^
2 errors
```

Not too shabby, right? Looks like javac is able to hone in on the problem with good accuracy. Of course, compilers have this nasty habit of cascading compile errors. That's why this faulty compile shows two compile errors where, in fact, only one true error exists.

Notice that the compiler reports on the problem source lines by number. Flipping back a page or two reveals that the Java compiler counts blank lines. Ergo, line 5 is not the fifth line of Java source; line 5 is the fifth line in the source file.

Let's Look at the HelloWorld Program

Now that you have seen what this mammoth program does, let's examine it line by line. The program is repeated in Listing 3.4 with comments as line numbers for convenience.

```
/* 1 */ class HelloWorld {
/* 2 */
/* 3 */   public static void main(String[]commandLineArgs) {
/* 4 */         System.out.println("Hello World!") ;
/* 5 */   }
/* 6 */
/* 7 */}
```

Listing 3.4   The classic HelloWorld, once more.

Note that Java can use PL/I style comments. Java supports other comment styles, which you'll read about in Chapter 6.

Every Java program consists of a group of cooperating classes. You can create (or code, if you prefer) several classes per dataset, but let's stick to creating one class per dataset for now. Line 1 shows the name of the class. Also, line 1 exhibits an opening block construct, better known by a *curly brace*; the closing block construct is on line 7. A block defines a scope where declared entities are known. In other words, entities declared between Java's block construct can be referenced and changed on any line between the curly braces. In this sense, Java's block construct is somewhat similar in function to PL/I's block constructs Begin/End and Proc/End.

Line 2 is a comment. Comments may span more than one line. As previously mentioned, Chapter 6 has the full scoop on Java comments.

A Quick Diversion into Method Headers

Line 3 is a declaration of the *main* method. Actually, this method is special because it is the main method of the class. For those of you who are familiar with PL/I, think of "Proc Options(Main)."

Every Java program has a main method as previously declared. That is, you need the words *public static void **main(String[] aLegalJavaVariableName)*** to denote this once-in-an-application main method. The bolded part, containing the method name and the argument description, is called the method's *signature*. For the main method, the italicized words are required. The word "aLegalJavaVariableName" can be any legal variable name; in our example, we've used commandLineArgs.

Figure 3.4 shows a closer look at the method header used here.

Going left to right, here's a few words describing the components of the above header.

Public is called a *visibility modifier*. In Java, you can control what classes/methods access other classes, objects, methods, and variables. The public keyword makes the method accessible to any class in your application. The main method must be declared *public*.

The *static* keyword denotes the existence of a *class method*. The object-oriented world view is that you create objects from classes (the ten-dollar word is *instantiation*, or you

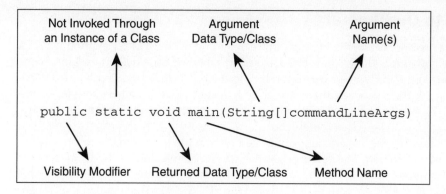

Figure 3.4   The anatomy of a method header.

instantiate an object from a class, or an object is an *instance* of a class). The classes serve as a template for similar objects. However, sometimes you need a method, but you do not want the method to come from an instance object. The main method is such a method. You can have only one main method and this method is not invoked from any instance of a class. In other words, only one version of a class method exists per class.

Methods may return a variable, an object, or nothing. Think of a PL/I function with a RETURN statement and a PROC statement listing out the returned data type. The *void* keyword means that the method does not return a variable or object. If a method does return something, this is where you would code the data type or class name corresponding to the type or class of the returned entity. The method would also contain one or more *return* statements.

Methods must have a name so make sure to give them one.

Methods, like functions and subroutines, may accept arguments. Think of the LINKAGE SECTION in COBOL, where you would define the order and type of passed arguments to subroutines. Java requires you to code the data type or class name followed by an argument name for each argument passed into the method. The main method requires a parameter list of an *array of strings*. Soon, you'll change the HelloWorld program to accept and use parameters. Java enforces type consistency; the data type or class name used in the statement that evokes the method (calls the method, so to speak) must agree with the data types and classes coded in the method's signature.

You must also supply variable names for your arguments. These names are not significant beyond the accepted Java naming conventions. They are used only in the body of the method.

This is not the full story on method headers. To keep things straightforward, a few optional keywords are omitted. Remember that the goal of this chapter is to get a simple Java program up and running and to describe what's going on with the Java compiler and runtime. You'll have more to read about signatures and naming conventions in following chapters.

Back to Our Program

Note the presence of an opening curly brace at the end of line 3. Every method requires a pair of curly braces, open and closed, to serve as method code delimiters. Line 5 contains the closing curly brace corresponding to the open curly brace on line 3. Everything sandwiched between the opening and closing brace is called the *body* of the method. As you'll see later, you'll code pairs of curly braces within methods for various programming language constructs.

Line 4 invokes the System.out.println method to write output to the console or the default output stream. The System class has several objects and methods; the println method pumps output to the default output stream. The System.out.println method does what the DISPLAY verb in COBOL and the PUT SKIP LIST statement in PL/I do. This line is the entire body of the main method.

A quick recap: Every Java program requires at least one class and one and only one main method in one and only one class. Curly braces delimit code blocks.

Let's Change the Program

Let's change the infamous HelloWorld program by allowing the program to accept a parameter and write that parameter to the default output stream. Listing 3.5 shows this change.

After a successful compile, here's how you would run the program:

```
java HelloWorld Lou
```

Here's your output:

```
Hello Lou
```

What's going on here, you ask? We've passed a parameter value, Lou, to the main method on the command line. The changed line creates an output string by concatenating the word "Hello" with the first argument passed to the method. Java uses + as

```
class HelloWorld {

    public static void main(String[]commandLineArgs) {
            /* Changed */
            System.out.println("Hello " + commandLineArgs[0]) ;
    }
}
```

Listing 3.5   The HelloWorld classic with a twist.

the string concatenation operator. Note that Java references arrays from position 0. In other words, we say that Java uses *zero-based arrays*. This is in contrast to mainframe programming languages that default to using one-based arrays.

In Summary

You've installed a JDK on your machine. You've compiled and executed some simple Java programs. You've read a bit about how Java loads classes dynamically during compile and execution. You've seen some compile and execution errors. You've also seen a method signature up close, but in brief. You've taken apart and changed a Java program. All in all, you've been pretty busy! In the next chapter, you'll read about the JDK you've just used.

The Sun Java 2 Basic JDK Tools

This chapter describes the programs, or tools, included in the Sun Java Development Kit (JDK). Some programs, like the Java compiler (javac.exe) and the Java interpreter (java.exe), you've already seen. Some programs, like the security (keytool.exe, for example) and remote invocation programs (rmic.exe), you'll see in later chapters of the book. Some programs, like idltojava.exe, are not included with the Sun JDK distribution.

Sun classifies the tools as *Basic Tools, Remote Method Invocation Tools, Internationalization Tools, Security Tools,* and *Java IDL Tools.* You'll read about the basic tools in this chapter. You'll read more about particular tools in later chapters.

Basic JDK Tools

Truth be told, you'll probably end up using tools that pack more punch than the Sun JDK tools. The professional Java crowd demands tools with graphical interfaces, screen builders, and modeling capabilities; when you join the crowd, you'll be no exception. However, as a mainframe programmer, you may be used to submitting batch compiles and not having any tools to generate documentation. The JDK tools enable interactive compiles, debugging, and documentation generation, among other things: a step up from running batch jobs, to be sure! Plus, these tools are *free, gratis,* and *on the house.* Also, the Sun JDK always works with the latest release of the JDK. So, don't dismiss these tools out of hand just yet.

You'll use these tools in Table 4.1 to code, execute, and debug applications and applets.

Here's more information on the basic JDK tools.

Appletviewer

The appletviewer tool lets you view applets without running a browser. You specify one or more options followed by one more URLs. The URLs should reference a Web page that contains a reference to the applet; if they don't, the appletviewer issues a diagnostic to that effect. Note that appletviewer does not display the Web page. The appletviewer tool uses the APPLET, EMBED, or OBJECT tags in the page to get parameter information and window size for display.

The syntax is:

```
appletviewer <options> URL₁ URL₂...URLₙ
```

If you forget the syntax, just enter *appletviewer* at the command prompt. Appletviewer will respond as follows:

```
No input files specified.
usage: appletviewer [-debug] [-J<javaflag>] [-encoding <character
encoding type> ] url|file ...
```

Table 4.2 lists the options you may pass to the appletviewer tool. All of these options are *case sensitive*. If you want to see appletviewer in action, open this folder on your desktop.

```
Jdk1.3\demo\applets\moleculeviewer
```

Table 4.1   The One-Line Descriptions

aAppletviewer	View applets in a browser-like window (but not a browser)
jar	Combines multiple files into a *Java Archive* (JAR) file
extcheck	Check if a Java Archive (JAR) conflicts with other JAR files
java	Execute Java applications (but not applets)
javac	Compile Java applications and applets
javadoc	Generate Java documentation
javah	Generate C header files for use in writing native code methods
javap	Disassemble Java source from class files
jdb	Debug Java programs and applets

Table 4.2 Appletviewer Options

-debug	Start the *Java debugger* (jdb). Later, you'll read more about jdb.
-J <somestring>	Pass <somestring> to the Java runtime. Use this option only if you truly know what you are doing as these strings impact the Java runtime environment.
- encoding <Encoding Name	The encoding scheme of the URLs passed as arguments to appletviewer.

This folder contains some sample applets and was copied onto your disk when you installed the JDK. Once this folder is open, open a DOS window. You should be in the directory corresponding to the previous folder. If not, change the directory to match this path. Enter this command at the prompt:

```
appletviewer example1.html
```

You'll see a DOS window somewhat like the one shown in Figure 4.1.

Example1.html has a reference to the applet in the form of an <applet> tag. Listing 4.1 shows the <applet> tag coded in Example1.html.

Notice that appletviewer has a menu. The applet menu includes options to reload the applet, to call Start() and Stop() methods (which are special methods in applets), and to show information about the HTML tag that references the applet.

jar

You use the jar utility to combine one or more Java class files with other files that your class files reference (such as images and sounds) into one file called a *Java Archive File*. The jar tool also compresses the files.

A common use for jar files is to package class files representing applets with other resources into one file. An applet packaged this way can be downloaded to a browser in a single request, as opposed to making the browser go back and forth to grab each file. Furthermore, because jar files are compressed, they download faster than their uncompressed brethren.

Jar files contain a *manifest* file, which contains information about the files in the archive. The jar tool automatically creates a manifest file during packaging. Optionally, you may use the *javakey* tool to provide a digital signature, thereby ensuring that the files contained in the archive were not tampered with since their creation.

Here's an overview of the syntax for jar:

```
jar <options> <manifest-file> jar-file-name <input-files>
```

The jar tool contains ten options that may be combined in various ways. Here are some examples of how jar is commonly used.

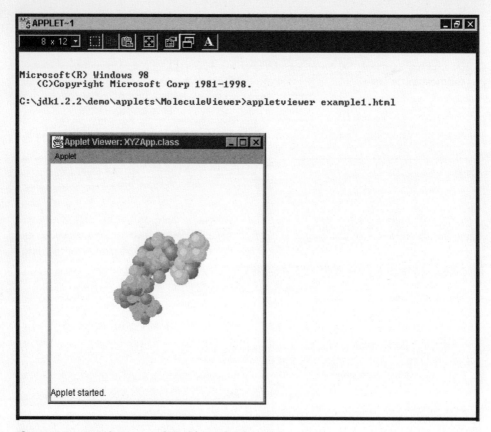

Figure 4.1 Running an applet with appletviewer.

```
<applet code=XYZApp.class width=300 height=300>
    <param name=model value=models/HyaluronicAcid.xyz>
    alt="Your browser understands the &lt;APPLET&gt; tag but isn't
        running the applet, for some reason."
    Your browser is completely ignoring the &lt;APPLET&gt; tag!
</applet>
```

Listing 4.1 Example applet tag.

This is perhaps the most common way to use jar:

```
jar cf aJarFile *.class
```

This command creates a file called aJarFile.jar from all files in the current directory with the extension "class." The *c* option directs jar to create a new archive; the *f* option tells jar the name of the new archive.

jar creates a manifest file named META-INF/MANIFEST.MF and includes this file as the first in the archive.

If you want to see what files are contained in your archive, enter this variation of the jar command:

```
jar tf aJarFile.jar
```

The *t* option tells jar to list the file names in the archive; the *f* option tells jar the name of the archive to operate on.

If you want to add a file to an existing archive, code:

```
jar uf aJarFile.jar another.class
```

The *u* option tells jar to update a jar file; the *f* option names the jar file to be updated. If you want to extract the files that make up a jar, code:

```
jar xf aJarFile.jar
```

Because jar uses the ZIP compression format, you may use any tool that operates on ZIP files to extract files from a jar archive.

Entering *jar* without parameters yields the helpful information in Listing 4.2.

One final point: The options you use with jar are *case sensitive*. Notice that –m and –M are different options.

extcheck

The extcheck utility checks extension jar files for conflicts with currently installed jar files. Extension jar files are stored in your *jre\lib\ext* directory. The extcheck utility is a good way to ensure that you don't replace a version of some needed jar file with an older version (yes, it's been known to happen!).

Extcheck uses the information in the jar's manifest file for the compare. Extcheck compares title and version information found in the manifest against the manifest files for all jars found in the extension directory. If extcheck finds any earlier (more recent) versions of the jar, it issues a nonzero return code; if not, extcheck returns zero.

Here's the syntax (this is what you would see if you entered extcheck without parameters):

```
extcheck <-verbose> aJarFile.jar
```

The sole option used with extcheck is the verbose option. Verbose lists the jar files found in the extension directory checked against the jar file argument to extcheck. Verbose will also report on the extension jars found conflicting with the jar file argument to extcheck.

```
Usage: jar {ctxu}[vfm0M] [jar-file] [manifest-file] [-C dir] files
. . .
Options:
    -c  create new archive
    -t  list table of contents for archive
    -x  extract named (or all) files from archive
    -u  update existing archive
    -v  generate verbose output on standard output
    -f  specify archive file name
    -m  include manifest information from specified manifest file
    -0  store only; use no ZIP compression
    -M  Do not create a manifest file for the entries
    -C  change to the specified directory and include the following
  file
If any file is a directory then it is processed recursively.
The manifest file name and the archive file name needs to be specified
in the same order the 'm' and 'f' flags are specified.

Example 1: to archive two class files into an archive called
classes.jar:
       jar cvf classes.jar Foo.class Bar.class
Example 2: use an existing manifest file 'mymanifest' and archive all
the files in the foo/ directory into 'classes.jar':
       jar cvfm classes.jar mymanifest -C foo/ .
```

Listing 4.2   jar command help.

java

You've already used java, the Java runtime, or Java interpreter. You use java to execute, or launch, applications from a command line. Listing 4.3 is what you'd see by entering *java* at the command line.

You can execute an application by specifying the name of a class file that contains a main() method (JAVA.EXE [-options] class [args . . .]) or by specifying a jar file containing a class with a main() method (JAVA.EXE -jar [-options] jarfile [args . . .]). So far, you've used the first syntax form for invoking the Java interpreter.

You code option flags between the java command and the class name or after the -jar flag. The args coded after the class name or the jar file name are strings passed into the main() method. (Remember main(String[] commandLineArgs) from the previous chapter?) These options are *case sensitive*. Let's take a look at these options.

The *-cp* or *-classpath* options enable you to specify a *search path* for *user written* classes (as opposed to system classes) or other files required by your application. Recall from

```
Usage: JAVA.EXE [-options] class [args . . . ]
           (to execute a class)
    or  JAVA.EXE -jar [-options] jarfile [args . . . ]
           (to execute a jar file)

where options include:
    -cp -classpath <directories and zip/jar files separated by ;>
              set search path for application classes and resources
    -D<name>=<value>
              set a system property
    -verbose[:class|gc|jni]
              enable verbose output
    -version  print product version
    -? -help  print this help message
    -X        print help on non-standard options
```

Listing 4.3   java command help.

the previous chapter that the Java interpreter loads classes dynamically as required for the proper execution of your application. Java.exe knows where to fetch these system classes. If your application requires classes that you or someone else has written, you may need to tell java.exe where to find the classes. If you put these classes in a directory that is not on the search path, you need to tell java.exe, the directory containing these classes with the -cp option. For example, to tell java.exe that you want the runtime to look in myclassdir to find user written classes, you'd invoke the interpreter as follows:

```
java -cp c:\somedir\myclassdir MyApp
```

The -D option enables you to set a system property. In the wintel environment, you set system properties by assigning an environment variable to some value. The example given in Sun's documentation is how to set the JAVA_COMPILER option to either disable a compiler (use the interpreter) or use a different compiler. Check it out:

```
java -Djava.compiler=adifferentcompiler MyApp
```

Notice the absence of a space between -D and the system property; this is no accident or typo.

The -verbose option displays information on loaded classes and other events of interest to a Java environment. You can tell what information you want by coding a suboption. Here are some examples.

```
java -verbose:class   MyApp          or
java -verbose         MyApp
```

The Java runtime will list information about the classes being dynamically loaded. You may recall from the previous chapter that you saw a partial listing of the -verbose option replete with loaded class information.

```
java -verbose:gc          MyApp
```

The Java runtime will report on garbage collection events. You may recall reading a bit about Java's ability to collect unused memory blocks using a process charmingly named *garbage collection*. If you want to know when your application is taking out the trash, use this option.

```
java -verbose:jni    MyApp
```

jni stands for *Java Native Interface*. The jni enables you to create methods in programming languages other than Java (C is the most commonly used jni language). The idea is that for some applications, performance may be key. A Java application, which is interpretive, cannot hope to match the speed of a compiled language (although the gap narrows with each new release of the JDK). Use this option if you want to know when your application is making a call to a native language program.

The *-version* option tells you what version of the JDK you're using. You may recall using this option to verify that your JDK install was correct.

The *-?* or *-help* options display the help information shown in Listing 4.3.

The *-X* option displays help information on the *nonstandard* Java runtime options. You can interpret *nonstandard* as "not as much used as standard" for the time being. Listing 4.4 shows what you'd see if you entered this command.

```
java -X
    -Xbootclasspath:<directories and zip/jar files separated by ;>
                    set search path for bootstrap classes and
                    resources
    -Xnoclassgc     disable class garbage collection
    -Xms<size>      set initial Java heap size
    -Xmx<size>      set maximum Java heap size
    -Xrs            reduce the use of OS signals
    -Xcheck:jni     perform additional checks for JNI functions
    -Xrunhprof[:help]|[:<option>=<value>,  . . . ]
                    perform heap, cpu, or monitor profiling
    -Xdebug         enable remote debugging
    -Xfuture        enable strictest checks, anticipating future
                    default
The -X options are non-standard and subject to change without notice.
```

Listing 4.4 Help screen for java -X (nonstandard options).

Here are some notes on these rarely used options.

The -*Xbootclasspath* option is similar to the -cp option except that -Xbootclasspath enables you to set the search path for *system classes*.

If a class is no longer being used, the *Java Virtual Machine* (JVM) will collect its memory. If your program creates an instance of this dropped class, Java resurrects the class. This constant purging/resurrecting could take a toll on performance. If you want to disable garbage collection for classes, perhaps to try to improve application performance, you can turn off class garbage collection with the -*Xnoclassgc* option.

-*Xrs* reduces signals sent to your application from the host operating system. You may want to tone down operating system signals during application development to simplify matters.

-*Xdebug* enables remote debugging—a handy feature where you start your application while in the debugger and issue debugging commands—even if on a different machine! You'll find further details in the section that describes the Java debugger (jdb).

The -*Xrunhprof* option enables you to peek at application profile information. Like the -X option, the -Xrunhprof option provides yet another list of suboptions. You'll see the table of options illustrated in Listing 4.5 when you enter:

```
java -Xrunhprof:help
```

For example, if you want a handle on where in your program the CPU is blowing cycles, you can receive a description of CPU usage by invoking the Java runtime with options like the example shown at the bottom of Listing 4.5.

```
Hprof usage: -Xrunhprof[:help]|[<option>=<value>, . . . ]

Option Name and Value    Description               Default
---------------------    -----------               -------
heap=dump|sites|all      heap profiling            all
cpu=samples|times|old    CPU usage                 off
monitor=y|n              monitor contention        n
format=a|b               ascii or binary output    a
file=<file>              write data to file        java.hprof(.txt for
                                                   ascii)
net=<host>:<port>        send data over a socket   write to file
depth=<size>             stack trace depth         4
cutoff=<value>           output cutoff point       0.0001
lineno=y|n               line number in traces?    y
thread=y|n               thread in traces?         n
doe=y|n                  dump on exit?             y

Example: java -Xrunhprof:cpu=samples,file=log.txt,depth=3 FooClass
```

Listing 4.5 java hprof values.

As you can see, the Java runtime certainly has a lot of options! This chapter is not the place to explore these myriad options in detail. Indeed, you should have a bit of battle-hardened Java programming experience under your belt before delving into some of these options. The good news is that most visual environments provide easy ways to turn on and view the results of these options.

One last point: the Sun JDK contains the program *javaw*, which is identical to java except that it does not open a command window. If you want to run your Java application without seeing a command window, use javaw. All the options for the java command work with javaw. For example, this command does not produce any visible output.

```
javaw -Xrunhprof:help
```

Of course, if you used java instead of javaw, you'd see Listing 4.5.

javac

javac is the Java compiler provided by Sun Microsystems. As you might imagine, the compiler has many options. Listing 4.6 shows what you'd see if you entered javac by itself on the command line.

```
Usage: javac <options> <source files>

where <options> includes:
  -g                        Generate all debugging info
  -g:none                   Generate no debugging info
  -g:{lines,vars,source}    Generate only some debugging info
  -O                        Optimize; may hinder debugging or enlarge
                            class files
  -nowarn                   Generate no warnings
  -verbose                  Output messages about what the compiler is
                            doing
  -deprecation              Output source locations where deprecated APIs
                            are used
  -classpath <path>         Specify where to find user class files
  -sourcepath <path>        Specify where to find input source files
  -bootclasspath <path>     Override location of bootstrap class files
  -extdirs <dirs>           Override location of installed extensions
  -d <directory>            Specify where to place generated class files
  -encoding <encoding>      Specify character encoding used by source
                            files
  -target <release>         Generate class files for specific VM version
```

Listing 4.6   javac help listing.

The javac program enables you to compile more than one source file per invocation. For example, you could list your Java source files one after another on the command line as follows:

```
javac JavaSrc1.java JavaSrc2.java JavaSrc3.java
```

This command would compile three Java source files and create three class files in the same directory as the source files.

If you want to compile a larger number of files, you could put the Java source code file names into a text file and direct the Java compiler to compile all the files listed in this text file. For instance, assume the file *srcs.txt* contained this information:

```
JavaSrc1.java
JavaSrc2.java
JavaSrc3.java
JavaSrc4.java
JavaSrc5.java
JavaSrc6.java
DiffSrc1.java
DiffSrc2.java
DiffSrc3.java
```

You could tell javac to compile all these files as follows:

```
javac @srcs.txt
```

It's the @ sign that makes the difference.

The *-g* options tell the java compiler to place debugging information in your byte-code. For those of you who are familiar with PL/I, this option is similar to the PL/I's *TEST(ALL,SYM)* compiler option. If you run the debugger (jdb) without first fetching debugging information with the -g option, all you'll have access to in your program is the line number and the source code. The -g option enables you to access local variable information. You can gather specific debugging information by coding the *lines, vars,* or *source* keywords to add line number, local variable, or source code debugging information, respectively. To create a lean bytecode dataset, you can turn off debugging information with the -g:none option.

The *-O* option performs certain code optimizations that improve the performance of your code at the possible expense of code size. For example, the -O option may expand small methods inside your class file (inline methods), which results in faster execution but a larger file size. One side effect of performing code optimizations is that the code is not suited to debugging because the optimized code may contain inline methods that you didn't code. In essence, using the -O option may result in a different program (but an identically functioning one—don't be alarmed!).

The *-nowarn* option suppresses warnings from the compiler. If you're supremely confident of your Java programming abilities or are sick of getting certain diagnostics, this compiler option is for you. Think of setting a COBOL compiler to suppress informational messages (return code = zero or four) and you will understand the idea of the -nowarn option.

Use the *-verbose* option to receive information on each class file loaded into your application. You've seen the -verbose option in action in the previous chapter, remember?

The *-deprecation* option lets you know where and how your program is using deprecated methods or classes. In brief, a deprecated method or class is one that was used in past releases of the JDK, but its function has been taken over by one or more recent methods. Often, your application will still work with some deprecated methods or classes. Having said that, using deprecated methods or classes is the mark of the amateur. Considering that the Java compiler can tell you where and how these deprecated methods and classes are used, you would be remiss in not trying to correct the situation.

So, should you code - *deprecation* for every compile? Well, not really. You see, the default behavior of javac is to tell you the source files that use deprecated methods or classes. Once you learn that your application uses such methods and classes, you can use the -deprecated option to hone in on the exact usage and take corrective action.

The *-classpath* option for javac serves the same function as the -cp or -classpath option for java, the runtime. In case you forgot, the -classpath option enables you to specify a search path for *user written* class files. If you don't set the CLASSPATH environment variable or you don't use the -classpath option, javac will expect any of your classes needed for this compile to reside in the current directory.

Guess what the *-sourcepath* option does? You need not have three Ph.D.'s to figure out that this option enables you to specify a search path for source files. If you do not code the -sourcepath option, javac expects to find your source in the user class file search path. In other words, using the -classpath option without using the -sourcepath option tells javac to look on this path for user class files and Java source files.

Just when you thought you've read the entire story on search paths, along comes yet another path-setting option: the *-bootclasspath* option. This option enables you to set a search path for Java system classes.

One important point regarding all these path-setting options is that these options require a semicolon-delimited list of directories, jar files, or ZIP files.

The *-extdirs* option is yet another search path setting option. This option lets you direct the Java compiler to a directory (directories) containing class files that represent system extensions. In Chapter 1, you read a bit about the *extcheck* utility. These extensions are what you would use extcheck with.

The *-target* option lets you create bytecode that is compatible or incompatible with different versions of the JVM. The default behavior of javac, version 1.2, is to generate bytecode that is compatible with version 1.1. By coding *target 1.2*, you can direct javac to generate bytecode that is incompatible with version 1.1.

The last three options discussed enable you to target Java bytecode to a different JVM. The -target option is not enough to do this. If you code the -target option without coding the -bootclassbath and -extdirs options, you may get a clean compile, but fail during execution when your bytecode loads a system class file or uses a system extension from the other (default) JVM.

The *-d* option lets you place the compiler output, or class files, into a specified directory. By default, javac places the output in the same directory as the source file. The accepted wisdom in the Java world is that you should have your class files in different directories than your source. So, get used to coding this compiler option!

Another good reason to code -d for your java compiles is that the -d option causes the directory structure of your class files to reflect your package structure. You haven't read much about packages yet. For now, think of a package as a set of related classes and other Java software constructs. Assume you've created a package *com.myPackage.MyClass* and you code the javac command as follows:

```
javac -d c:\myclassfiles MyClass.java
```

javac names the resulting class file in *c:\myclassfiles\com\mypackage\myclass.class*. The interesting and valuable feature is that javac creates all required subdirectories. Put another way, using the -d option is a smart, easy way to maintain the structure of your classes.

The *-encoding* option enables you to specify an encoding scheme. The default is whatever encoding scheme is used by your system. Unless your application has international concerns, you could probably get away with not coding this option for a long, long time.

Do you remember the section on the java runtime with the *nonstandard options*? Well, the Java compiler has a few of those as well. Listing 4.7 illustrates what you see when you enter this code at the command line:

```
javac -X
```

A few words about these options are in order.

When you code *-Xdepend*, you are telling Javac to search for and recompile Java source used in your application. If you need to recompile java source because some source kept in a different file has changed, the -Xdepend option will find and recompile the source.

Usually, javac sends error messages to whatever file or resource is mapped to *System.err*. Using *-Xstdout* directs javac error messages to *System.out*, the default output stream. Many times, System.out and System.err refer to the same stream anyway.

-Xverbosepath provides information on where javac looks for class files and other source files. When you use this option, javac responds by listing the source path and the classpath.

```
   -Xdepend          Recursively search for more recent source files to
                     recompile
   -Xstdout          Send messages to System.out
   -Xverbosepath     Describe how paths and standard extensions were
                     searched
   -J<runtime flag>  Pass argument to the java interpreter

The -X and -J options are non-standard and subject to change without
notice.
```

Listing 4.7 Nonstandard javac compiler options.

Finally, the *-J* option enables you to pass an option to the java runtime that gets invoked when you run the Java compiler. The option you pass would be one of the options described in the section "Java" above. The appletviewer tool also uses this option.

You can see that the java compiler has numerous options. Fortunately, you can get a lot done by using only a few, if any, of these options.

Javadoc

The *javadoc* tool generates documentation (yes, documentation!) in HTML format for one or more Java source files. Javadoc can accept package names, Java source code files, or both. Javadoc actually invokes part of the Java compiler to parse your Java method declarations. Because javadoc uses method headers to generate documentation, it does not even require that the methods be implemented!

Javadoc will search for all referenced and loaded classes, including system classes. Therefore, javadoc needs to locate all these classes. As you might imagine, you can code options to direct javadoc to the directories holding the required classes and packages.

Listing 4.8 is an example of a piece of Java code passed to the javadoc tool and some of what javadoc generated.

Here's the command.

```
javadoc queryBean
```

Figure 4.2 shows some of the HTML output.

Now, this is pretty good! javadoc pulls out all of those objects, provides a cross reference via hyperlinks to additional descriptions of the objects (fields), puts the descriptive portion in a frame, and slaps an index atop the page for depreciated methods, tree view, and an alphabetical index. This HTML page is one of nine (!) pages, including a *Cascading StyleSheet* (CSS) used to format the HTML pages.

Javadoc is a robust application with numerous options. Space prevents us from giving it a full treatment. To get an idea of the numerous javadoc options available, Listing 4.9 shows what you'd see if you entered this code at the command line:

```
javadoc -help
```

Although you can generate documentation with javadoc without using any options, you'll likely use several. You may use the *-sourcepath* option to tell javadoc where loaded classes reside. You'll also likely include an author tag with the *-author* option. Perhaps you'll want your own window title to appear in your HTML documents by using the *-windowtitle* option. Maybe you want a separate HTML document for each alphabetical entry (one HTML page for *A*, one for *D*, and so on) by using the *-splitindex* option.

You can use special comments with javadoc called *doc comments* to include documentation for software objects. A doc comment starts with /** and ends with */. Now, the Java compiler treats doc comments like any other comment. However, javadoc picks up on doc comments for additional processing.

```
import java.sql.*;
import java.io.*;

public class queryBean extends sqlBean
  {
  String myCustQuery = "select * from Customers where CustomerID = ";

  ResultSet myResultSet = null;
  public queryBean() {super();}

  public boolean getCustomerInfo(String custID) throws Exception
    {
    String myQuery = myCustQuery + "'" + custID + "'";

    Statement stmt = myConn.createStatement();
    myResultSet = stmt.executeQuery(myQuery);
    return (myResultSet != null);
    }

  public boolean getNextCustInfo() throws Exception
    {
    return myResultSet.next();
    }

  public String getColumn( String inCol) throws Exception
    {
    return myResultSet.getString(inCol);
    }
  }
}
```

Listing 4.8   Some Java source.

You may use *tags* to tell javadoc to include certain information, such as the author
and version, and to establish hyperlinks (think "See Also <someURL>"). For example, this doc comment contains a few tags.

```
/**   This class creates Low-Pass filters that
 *      smooth images.
 *
 *   @author <a href="http://loushomepage.html"
 *           Lou Marco </a>
 *
 *   @see <a href="http://imageenhancementinfo.html"
 *           Image Enhancement Information Site </a>
```

```
 *
 *   @see "The Big Image Book"
 */
```

Note that the comment starts with two asterisks, but ends with one—a doc comment. The @author tag adds an author entry to the HTML page. Note the use of HTML coding in the doc comment.

The @see tag displays the text "See Also" in big, bold type. When you use the @see tag, you probably want a hyperlink, so code one. The second @see tag also displays "See Also" in big, bold type. This tag does not have an accompanying hyperlink; the text in quotes is displayed under "See Also."

Today, javadoc supports 13 tags. Tomorrow, javadoc will likely support more. javadoc uses a default format for its generated HTML pages like the one in Figure 4.2 called the standard *doclet*. Looking at Listing 4.9, you see that a good chunk of javadoc options are available when you use the standard doclet. You can create your own

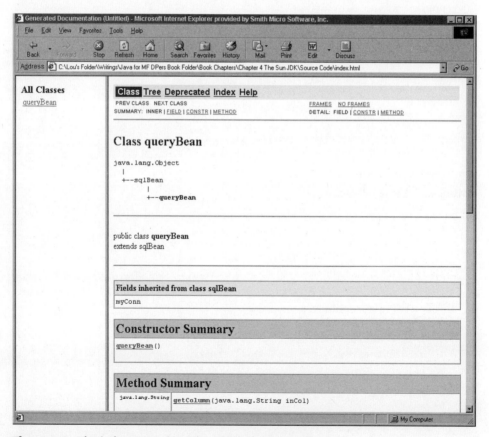

Figure 4.2   The index page of javadoc HTML documentation.

```
usage: javadoc [options] [packagenames] [sourcefiles] [classnames]
[@files]
-overview <file>           Read overview documentation from HTML file
-public                    Show only public classes and members
-protected                 Show protected/public classes and members
                           (default)
-package                   Show package/protected/public classes and
                           members
-private                   Show all classes and members
-help                      Display command line options
-doclet <class>            Generate output via alternate doclet
-docletpath <path>         Specify where to find doclet class files
-1.1                       Generate output using JDK 1.1 emulating
                           doclet
-sourcepath <pathlist>     Specify where to find source files
-classpath <pathlist>      Specify where to find user class files
-bootclasspath <pathlist>  Override location of class files loaded
                           by the bootstrap class loader
-extdirs <dirlist>         Override location of installed extensions
-verbose                   Output messages about what Javadoc is doing
-locale <name>             Locale to be used, e.g. en_US or en_US_WIN
-encoding <name>           Source file encoding name
-J<flag>                   Pass <flag> directly to the runtime system

Provided by Standard doclet:
-d <directory>             Destination directory for output files
-use                       Create class and package usage pages
-version                   Include @version paragraphs
-author                    Include @author paragraphs
-splitindex                Split index into one file per letter
-windowtitle <text>        Browser window title for the documenation
-doctitle <html-code>      Include title for the package index(first)
                           page
-header <html-code>        Include header text for each page
-footer <html-code>        Include footer text for each page
-bottom <html-code>        Include bottom text for each page
-link <url>                Create links to javadoc output at <url>
-linkoffline <url> <url2>  Link to docs at <url> using package list at
                           <url2>
-group <name> <p1>:<p2>..  Group specified packages together in
overview
                           page
-nodeprecated              Do not include @deprecated information
-nodeprecatedlist          Do not generate deprecated list
-notree                    Do not generate class hierarchy
-noindex                   Do not generate index
-nohelp                    Do not generate help link
```

Listing 4.9   The plentiful options for the javadoc tool.

```
-nonavbar                 Do not generate navigation bar
-serialwarn               Generate warning about @serial tag
-charset <charset>        Charset for cross-platform viewing of
                          generated documentation.
```

Listing 4.9 The plentiful options for the javadoc tool. (*continued*)

doclets by using Java's doclet *Application Program Interface* (API). Your doclets don't have to generate HTML; XML, RTF, or some other document format is fair game! Also, your custom doclets can use custom tags.

Here, we've only scratched the surface. Javadoc is constantly improving with each new version of the JDK. You can find out what's happening with javadoc by checking out Sun's javadoc's page at http://java.sun.com/j2se/1.3/docs/javadoc.

javah

The javah tool generates C header and source files that you use to create native methods programmed in C. These native methods written in C can communicate with your Java classes. Even though you may never code any native methods or write C code, a few words about javah are in order.

Javah generates header files (think of header files as a COBOL COPY or PL/I %Include files) containing C structs that correspond to the instance variables of the class or classes supplied as parameters (think of structs as a COBOL record variables with multiple levels). These header files are placed in the same directory from which you ran javah.

Listing 4.10 shows the list of options you can use with javah. As always, these parameters are case sensitive.

Notice the path setting options commonly used by the JDK tools.

javap

You use javap to get Java source from a class file. Now, you'll not get the code exactly as entered. You'll not get comments, but because so few programmers enter comments, you've lost little, right?

Here's a sample of what javap gives you out of the box. Refer to Listing 4.7 in our discussion of javadoc of the Java class *Vidtype*. Enter this command while at the same directory as the class file.

```
javap   Vidtype
```

Figure 4.3 shows a screen shot of what javap returns.

```
Usage: javah [options] <classes>

where [options] include:

        -help                  Print this help message
        -classpath <path>      Path from which to load classes
        -bootclasspath <path>  Path from which to load bootstrap
classes
        -d <dir>               Output directory
        -o <file>              Output file (only one of -d or -o may be
                               used)
        -jni                   Generate JNI-style header file (default)
        -old                   Generate old JDK1.0-style header file
        -stubs                 Generate a stubs file
        -version               Print version information
        -verbose               Enable verbose output
        -force                 Always write output files

<classes> are specified with their fully qualified names (for
instance, java.lang.Object).
```

Listing 4.10   javah options.

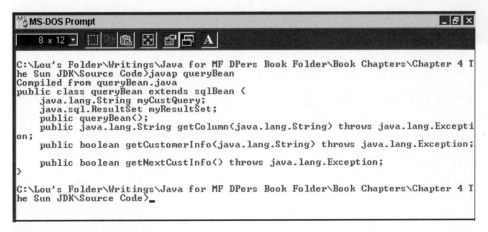

Figure 4.3   javap default output.

You may want to compare the Java source with what javap returns. Notice the absence of comments and values used for initialization.

You use javap as a quick way to see what parameters a method requires (called the *signature* of the method) or what data type/class a method returns (if any). Sometimes, entering javap <classname> is quicker than looking up the method signature on paper or by other means. Having said that, most Java-integrated development environments have method signature information a mouse click away.

Now, take a look at the Java debugger (jdb).

jdb

Jdb is a line-oriented debugger. If you've used graphical debuggers like SmartTest for COBOL or PLITEST for PL/I, you'll be disappointed with jdb. Having said that, jdb is a useful tool for finding errors in your Java programs.

The basic mode of operation is to invoke jdb for an application or applet by substituting jdb for java. In other words, instead of invoking the Java runtime with java.exe, invoke the debugger with jdb.exe. To debug applets, you need the *-debug* option of the appletviewer tool (remember?). Also, you should use the *-g* option when you compile to include all debugging information.

You know the drill, right? Listing 4.11 shows what you'll see when you enter:

Important! Note the last line of the above listing. When you are in the debugger, you can get a quick list of all jdb commands. Later, we'll do just that.

```
jdb -help
Usage: jdb <options> <class> <arguments>

where options include:
    -help               print out this message and exit
    -version            print out the build version and exit
    -host <hostname>    host machine of interpreter to attach to
    -password <psswd>   password of interpreter to attach to (from -
                        debug)
    -dbgtrace           print info for debugging jdb

options forwarded to debuggee process:
    -D<name>=<value>    set a system property
    -classpath <directories separated by ";">
                        list directories in which to look for classes
    -X<option>          non-standard debuggee VM option

<class> is the name of the class to begin debugging
<arguments> are the arguments passed to the main() method of <class>

For command help type 'help' at jdb prompt
```

Listing 4.11 jdb options.

You probably won't be doing much remote debugging, but a word or two about the *-host* and *-password* options is appropriate. You use these options when you are debugging an already started java interpretive session from afar. Whoever started the java interpretive session must use the *-Xdebug* option to generate a password. You would use this password to gain access to this session.

Note the presence of the all too familiar *-classpath* option. The *-X* option enables you to enter the same nonstandard options allowable for the java command. This makes sense because the jdb command replaces the java command; hence, the jdb command takes some of the same options as the java command.

Without further ado, Listing 4.12 lists the jdb debugging commands. To view this list, you must run jdb, then enter *help* at the jdb prompt (>).

Using jdb

Let's use jdb to debug a small program. We'll use a variation of the bubble sort implementation shown in Chapter 1 with a modification to cause an error. Listing 4.13 shows the source.

And here's the result of the execution.

```
3
1
2
6
9
10
```

Looks like we have a problem!

Let's run the program under jdb. First, compile the program with the -g option to include all debugging information.

```
javac -g BubSortMod.java
```

What follows is a sample session showing some of the debugging commands with comments in italics on what the debugging commands do. Human entries are in boldface; to the left of the boldface is the jdb prompt. You would not see these comments during debugging. Here's how you crank up the debugger.

jdb BubSortMod

```
Initializing jdb...
0xaa:class(BubSortMod)
```

Stop the program at the sort method.

```
> stop in BubSortMod.sort
Breakpoint set in BubSortMod.sort
```

```
> help
** command list **
threads [threadgroup]     -- list threads
thread <thread id>        -- set default thread
suspend [thread id(s)]    -- suspend threads (default: all)
resume [thread id(s)]     -- resume threads (default: all)
where [thread id] | all   -- dump a thread's stack
wherei [thread id] | all  -- dump a thread's stack, with pc info
threadgroups              -- list threadgroups
threadgroup <name>        -- set current threadgroup

print <id> [id(s)]        -- print object or field
dump <id> [id(s)]         -- print all object information

locals                    -- print all local variables in current
stack
                             frame

classes                   -- list currently known classes
methods <class id>        -- list a class's methods

stop in <class id>.<method>[(argument_type, . . . )] -- set a
breakpoint in
                             a method

stop at <class id>:<line> -- set a breakpoint at a line
up [n frames]             -- move up a thread's stack
down [n frames]           -- move down a thread's stack
clear <class id>.<method>[(argument_type, . . . )]   -- clear a
breakpoint
                             in a method
clear <class id>:<line>   -- clear a breakpoint at a line
step                      -- execute current line
step up                   -- execute until the current method returns
                             to its caller
stepi                     -- execute current instruction
next                      -- step one line (step OVER calls)
cont                      -- continue execution from breakpoint

catch <class id>          -- break for the specified exception
ignore <class id>         -- ignore when the specified exception

list [line number|method] -- print source code
use [source file path]    -- display or change the source path

memory                    -- report memory usage
```

Listing 4.12 jdb debugging commands.

```
gc                              -- free unused objects

load classname                  -- load Java class to be debugged
run <class> [args]              -- start execution of a loaded Java class
!!                              -- repeat last command
help (or ?)                     -- list commands
exit (or quit)                  -- exit debugger
>
```

Listing 4.12   jdb debugging commands. (*continued*)

```java
class BubSortMod {

public static void main( String args[]) {
    int anarray[] = {3,10,6,1,2,9} ;

    sort( anarray ) ;
    for (int idx = 0; idx < anarray.length; idx++ )
        System.out.println( anarray[ idx ] ) ;
    }

    static void sort(int a[]) {

    for (int idx1 = a.length; --idx1>=0; ) {
        boolean swapped = false;
        for (int idx2 = 1; idx2<idx1; idx2++) {
            if (a[idx2] > a[idx2+1]) {
                int T       = a[idx2];
                a[idx2]     = a[idx2+1];
                a[idx2+1]   = T;
                swapped     = true;
            }

        }
        if (!swapped) return ;
    }
    }
}
```

Listing 4.13   A faulty bubble sort implementation.

Continue execution until the program hits the first breakpoint.

```
> run
run BubSortMod
running ...
main[1]
Breakpoint hit: BubSortMod.sort (BubSortMod:13)
```

List out local variables and method parameters.

```
main[1] locals
Method arguments:
Local variables:
  this = BubSortMod@49bcdc7d
  a = { 3, 10, 6, ... }
```

Note that jdb does not list out the entire array. Also note that the prompt indicates the program location. Determine the array's length.

```
main[1] print a.length
a.length = 6
```

List some source code surrounding the line where jdb stopped the program.

```
main[1] list
9               }
10
11              static void sort(int a[]) {
12
13       =>     for (int idx1 = a.length; --idx1>=0; ) {
14                   boolean swapped = false;
15                   for (int idx2 = 1; idx2<idx1; idx2++) {
16                       if (a[idx2] > a[idx2+1]) {
17                           int T                = a[idx2];
```

Run the program to the next breakpoint.

```
main[1] run
run BubSortMod
running ...
main[1]
Breakpoint hit: BubSortMod.sort (BubSortMod:13)
```

Execute the program one statement at a time.

```
main[1] step
main[1]
Breakpoint hit: BubSortMod.sort (BubSortMod:14)
```

Take a look to see where we are in the program.

```
main[1] list
10
11                static void sort(int a[]) {
12
13                    for (int idx1 = a.length; --idx1>=0; ) {
14        =>            boolean swapped = false;
15                    for (int idx2 = 1; idx2<idx1; idx2++) {
16                        if (a[idx2] > a[idx2+1]) {
17                            int T                = a[idx2];
18                            a[idx2]     = a[idx2+1];
main[1] step
main[1]
Breakpoint hit: BubSortMod.sort (BubSortMod:15)
main[1] step
main[1]
Breakpoint hit: BubSortMod.sort (BubSortMod:16)
```

List the value of a variable used here.

```
main[1] print a[1]
a[1] = 10
main[1] list
12
13                    for (int idx1 = a.length; --idx1>=0; ) {
14                    boolean swapped = false;
15                    for (int idx2 = 1; idx2<idx1; idx2++) {
16        =>            if (a[idx2] > a[idx2+1]) {
17                        int T                = a[idx2];
18                        a[idx2]     = a[idx2+1];
19                        a[idx2+1]   = T;
20                        swapped     = true;
main[1] step
main[1]
Breakpoint hit: BubSortMod.sort (BubSortMod:17)
main[1] run
run BubSortMod
running ...
main[1]
Breakpoint hit: BubSortMod.sort (BubSortMod:13)
```

Check out the calling chain, or the stack trace.

```
main[1] where 1
  [1] BubSortMod.sort (BubSortMod:13)
  [2] BubSortMod.main (BubSortMod:6)
main[1] print idx1
idx1 = 5
```

Execute until the program gets to the statement immediately after the method invocation.

```
main[1] step up
main[1]
Breakpoint hit: BubSortMod.main (BubSortMod:7)
main[1] list
3           public static void main( String args[]) {
4                   int anarray[] = {3,10,6,1,2,9} ;
5
6                   sort( anarray ) ;
7        =>         for (int idx = 0; idx < anarray.length; idx++ )
8                           System.out.println( anarray[ idx ] ) ;
9                   }
10
11              static void sort(int a[]) {
```

List the array to be sorted - are we close?

```
main[1] print anarray
anarray = { 3, 1, 2, ... }
List the last array element
main[1] print anarray[5]
anarray[5] = 10
```

Note that jdb is smart enough to report on out of bounds references.

```
main[1] print anarray[6]
6 is out of bounds for { 3, 1, 2, ... }
```

Continue execution and stop at the statement immediately following the method invocation.

```
main[1] run
run BubSortMod
running ...
main[1]
Breakpoint hit: BubSortMod.sort (BubSortMod:13)
main[1] step up
main[1]
Breakpoint hit: BubSortMod.main (BubSortMod:7)
main[1] print anarray
anarray = { 3, 1, 2, ... }
```

List out the array elements not shown by the above print command.

```
main[1] print anarray[3] anarray[4] anarray[5]
anarray[3] = 6
anarray[4] = 9
anarray[5] = 10
```

Looks like the first element of the array is not "moving." Is the sort method referencing the first array element?

```
main[1] run
run BubSortMod
running ...
main[1]
Breakpoint hit: BubSortMod.sort (BubSortMod:13)
main[1] list
9               }
10
11              static void sort(int a[]) {
12
13      =>      for (int idx1 = a.length; --idx1>=0; ) {
14                  boolean swapped = false;
15                  for (int idx2 = 1; idx2<idx1; idx2++) {
16                      if (a[idx2] > a[idx2+1]) {
17                          int T               = a[idx2];
```

Check out line 15. Shouldn't the index variable idx2 start at zero? Clear out breakpoints and complete execution.

```
main[1] clear BubSortMod.sort
Breakpoint cleared at BubSortMod.sort
main[1] run
run BubSortMod
running ...
main[1] 3
1
2
6
9
10

Current thread "main" died. Execution continuing . . .
>
BubSortMod exited
```

Changing this program at line 15 to:

```
    for (int idx2 = 0; idx2<idx1; idx2++)
```

corrects the problem.

In Summary

Your quick tour of Sun's basic JDK tools is over. Hope you enjoyed the show. Part of the reason Java has, is, and will enjoy wide acceptance and success in the computing community is the availability of these and other tools. Although some may gripe about the nonvisual nature of these tools, few can argue that they do a pretty good job for free tools. These days, if you can get something that works for free, what's there to complain about?

Yes, when you get into the real world of Java development, you'll be using a visual tool suite (if not, go work for another company!). Another point worth mentioning is that the Sun JDK tools work with the latest release of Java. If you want to check out a Java feature available with the latest release, you'll have to use the Sun JDK or wait until the new Java release is supported by your tool vendor.

Declaring and Defining Data

Before you can do anything with a piece of data in Java, you have to make this piece of data known to your program. No surprise here, declaring data for use in a program is one requirement that is shared by most programming languages. Here, you'll read how to define data in Java and see how Java data declarations compare with like data declarations in COBOL and other IBM mainframe programming languages.

This chapter describes how a programmer defines data items to Java programs. Here, the comparisons between Java, COBOL, and PL/I increase. This chapter spends some time discussing strong language data typing (Java) versus weak data typing (REXX) versus representative data typing (COBOL). Java's distinction between primitive data types and reference data types is covered, as well as how the concept of primitive and reference data types are expressed in the language of the mainframe programmer. Various Java code snippets are shown here to illustrate these concepts.

Java Primitive Types

Java supports the object-oriented style of programming. Therefore, you will use objects in your Java programs. However, Java also enables you to declare variables that do not behave like objects. These variables behave like, well, variables. We Java folk say that these Java variables are declared with a *Primitive Type*. Let's defer discussion of objects to Chapter 7, "Class and Object Representation," okay?

Just what are these primitive types, anyway? Table 5.1 provides that information.

Table 5.1 Java Primitive Types

PRIMITIVE TYPE	TYPE REPRESENTS A	DEFAULT VALUE	SIZE SIZE	RANGE OF VALUES
boolean	True, false	false	1 bit	true, false
byte	Signed integer	0	8 bits	-128_{10} to 127_{10}
char	Unicode character	0	16 bits	0000_{16} to $FFFF_{16}$
double	Miniscule or gigantic number	0.0	64 bits	$4.94065645841246544 * 10^{-324}$ to $1.79769313486231570 * 10^{308}$
float	Extremely small or large number	0.0	32 bits	$1.40239846 * 10^{-45}$ to $3.40282347 * 10^{38}$
int	Signed integer	0	32 bits	-2147483648_{10} to 2147483647_{10}
long	Signed integer	0	64 bits	$-9223372036854775808_{10}$ to 9223372036854775807_{10}
short	Signed integer	0	16 bits	-32768_{10} to 32767_{10}

Java primitive data types have a fixed size regardless of the platform. Why is that, you ask? Remember, Java is platform neutral; code written on one platform must successfully execute on another platform, as long as both platforms have the same version of the Java runtime.

How do these primitive types compare to types declared in COBOL and PL/I? Table 5.2 provides that information.

Now, COBOL and PL/I declares for Java primitive types are not exact. You will learn about the differences as you read about each following primitive data type. However, you should first read a bit about this business of variable typing in general.

A Few Words on Variable Typing

You may recall some discussion from Chapter 2, "What is Java?," on variable typing. In particular, programming languages usually follow one of four variable typing classifications: *Strong, Weak, None,* and *Representative.* The typing classification governs how variables of different types may be used together in expressions.

Strong typing means that different variables used in the same expression must be of the same data type. Also, there must be a match between the data types used as arguments to a subprogram, and the parameters of that subprogram. Realize that the *lan-*

Table 5.2 Java, COBOL, and PL/I Variable Declares of Primitive Types

PRIMITIVE TYPE	JAVA DECLARE	COBOL DECLARE	PL/I DECLARE
boolean	boolean aBool ;	Can't be done!	Can't be Done! *
byte	byte aByte ;	ABYTE PIC 'X'.	Dcl aByte Fixed Bin(8) ;
char	char aChar ;	Can't be done!	Can't be done! **
double	double aDoub ;	ADOUB COMP-2	Dcl aDouble Float(64) ;
float	float afloat ;	AFLOAT COMP-1	Dcl aFloat Float(32) ;
int	int anInt ;	ANINT COMP.	Dcl anInt Fixed Bin(31) ;
long	long along ;	Can't be done!	Can't be done!
short	short aShort ;	ASHORT COMP.	Dcl aShort Fixed Bin(15) ;

* PL/I uses the BIT type to mimic booleans (Dcl aBit BIT(1)), but BITs are not Booleans.

** PL/I supports a double byte character set with the GRAPHIC attribute, but DBCS is not Unicode.

guage compiler enforces this forced matching of data types. The fact is that errors are less likely to creep into your program when you must use variables of the same type in expressions and subprogram calls; at least you'll not be combining apples and oranges in a strongly typed language. If you declare two data types as integers, you will not be able to add variables of these types together without additional coding. The Pascal family of languages (Pascal, Modula-2, and Ada) is strongly typed.

Weak typing means that you can combine variables of mostly different types in expressions. Understand that the semantics of the expression need not make sense. For example, some weakly typed programming languages enable you to add characters to numbers. Some weakly typed languages enable you to quickly get a small application up and running without the extra effort involved in enforcing variable type consistency; others are just as difficult, if not more so, than some strongly typed languages. Several flavors of BASIC and C are examples of weakly typed languages.

None, or no variable typing, or untyped, means that you don't declare variables of a type at all. You just "code and go." Untyped programming languages are often interpretive, trading ease of coding for runtime performance. Such languages are often used very effectively as scripting languages, because the success of a script rarely depends on runtime performance. REXX is an example of an untyped programming language.

Representative typing means that variables are declared to be a type that mirrors the machine representation of the data. Two often-used examples of a representative data type are *packed* and binary. In the mainframe world of OS/390, data is stored in packed format; some programming languages used on the mainframe enable for variables declared in packed format, ditto for binary data. COBOL and PL/I are the most often used programming languages that follow a representative data-typing scheme.

Variable Type Casting

One obvious question is evident: What do you do if you want to use two numeric variables of different types in the same expression when you're programming in a strongly typed language? For example, if you have a hypothetical, strongly typed language that permits declares like

```
Integer   anInteger   = 25.     -- Integer data type
Decimal   aDecimal    = 50.75.  -- Decimal data type
```

How would you perform a simple arithmetic operation like the following without generating type mismatch errors?

```
Decimal   theSum = anInteger + aDecimal.
```

The programming language could convert anInteger into an equivalent variable of type Decimal and perform the addition. However, this seems to violate the reason for having a strongly typed language in the first place, right? You want the compiler to catch what may be an oversight on your part.

Maybe you should have declared anInteger as a Decimal data type and avoided the problem. Unfortunately, you may have need of anInteger as an Integer type later on in the program. It seems silly to have two variables that represent the same thing in a program, but being of different data types. This isn't what most sane folk would call a good programming practice!

What you need is a way of explicitly coercing a variable to a different data type for a single statement. By explicitly coding some construct, you will not slip and inadvertently mix data types. In addition, you can use the same variable where you need it without having to declare copies of different data types.

The answer is to code a construct called a *cast*. Most strongly typed programming languages support this, and even some weakly typed ones as well. The common form of the cast operator is to enclose the type you need in parenthesis before the variable is declared with the "offending" type. Observe how the cast works in our hypothetical language.

```
Decimal   theSum = (Decimal)anInteger + aDecimal.
```

The cast operator does not change the variable that is being cast! What is happening previously is, for this statement only, the cast operator creates a temporary variable that has the same value as anInteger only of type Decimal. With the data types agreeing, the arithmetic can be performed.

Of course, the reason for this diatribe is that Java supports the cast operator *for primitive types* and *for objects*. Now, realize that you cannot cast any variable of a certain type to any other type; there are limits. You will read about casting rules for objects in Chapter 9, "Inheritance." In this chapter, you'll read about casting rules for primitive types.

Java Variable Typing

Right now, you are wondering, where does Java fall into this variable-typing scheme? Java has a hybrid data typing mechanism. For primitive types, Java is weakly typed for some expressions and strongly typed for others. For objects, you'll have to wait until Chapter 7 for the full explanation.

Java enables you to mix primitive, *non-boolean* types provided that the target of the expression is a data type that can contain the largest number of any components of the expression. Yes, that is quite a mouthful. Perhaps the example in Listing 5.1 will break the mouthful into bite-sized morsels.

However, the expression demonstrated in Listing 5.2 causes a Java compile error. Here is the compiler error:

```
Incompatible type for declaration. Explicit cast needed to convert
double to float.
float aFloat2 = anInt + aDoub + aByte;
                ^
```

Oddly enough, javac points to the target of the expression while saying that you need to explicitly need to cast the *double* to a float. Ergo, this change gets a successful compile:

```
float aFloat2 = anInt + (float)aDoub + aByte;
```

                         OR

```
float aFloat2 = (float)(anInt + aDoub + aByte) ;
```

```
int       anInt     = 325 ;     //Range from -2³¹ to 2³¹-1
float     aFloat    = 21.25f ; //Range a whole lot bigger
byte      aByte     = -56 ;     //Range from -128 to 127
/**
    The float variable aFloat2 can contain the largest number
    from any of the addends below.
    As an aside, notice how the floating point variable was
    initialized.
**/
float     aFloat2   = anInt + aFloat + aByte;
```

Listing 5.1 Java can deal with mixing these primitive types.

```
int         anInt      = 325 ;       //Range from -2³¹ to 2³¹-1
byte        aByte      = -56 ;       //Range from -128 to 127
double      aDoub      = 31E10d ;    //Range far bigger than
                                     //float
/**
      The float variable aFloat2 cannot contain the largest
      number from the aDoub addend below. Note that aDoub was
      initialized well within the allowable range for a Java
      float variable.

      As an aside, notice how the double variable was
      initialized.
**/
float       aFloat2    = anInt + aDoub + aByte;
```

Listing 5.2 Java cries out for a cast when mixing these primitive types.

Should the previous operand be cast, or should the target of the result of the expression to a number declared with the double primitive type be cast? You cannot intelligently answer that question without knowing the full use of these variables in a program.

In the following, more information about each of Java's primitive types is listed.

The boolean Primitive Type

Java supports a boolean data type, which has only two values: true and false. Java booleans *cannot be cast into anything*. Java booleans are not integers like they are in C, or bit switches like they are in PL/I. Hence, booleans cannot be used in any arithmetic statement in a meaningful way; javac will stop such foolish attempts.

The previous dissertation concerning casting of primitive types *does not apply to booleans*. Use Java booleans for true and false values, and forget about "boolean tricks" you used in other programming languages, like setting up multiple bit switches to represent boolean values.

Literal boolean values can only be true or false, no other options exist. In the following, the declares are listed:

```
boolean     aTrueBool  = true ;
boolean     aFalseBool = false ;
```

The char Primitive Type

You may think you know what data a variable of type *char* holds, but you're probably wrong. You'd expect a char to hold a character, which is a string of bits that represents a member of a character set, like EBCDIC or ASCII. Well, that's correct. However in Java, the character set is called *Unicode,* and each character in the Unicode character set is 16 bits, or two bytes in size. The closest available option in the mainframe world is the *Double Byte Character Set* (DBCS). Unicode is not the same as DBCS; all they share is the fact that both character sets consist of 16 bit characters.

The good news is that you need not concern yourself with Unicode if all you're working with is garden-variety ASCII or EBCDIC. Java hides the messy details of working with Unicode characters from you. Actually, the first 8 bits of the Unicode character set is the same as the Latin-I or 8-it ASCII character set.

Mainframers experienced at working with the EBCDIC character set will have to translate to ASCII, like they have always done when mainframers have needed to access any non-IBM platform.

If you have C programming experience, the following Java statement will not be surprising. If not, you'll be scratching your head.

```
int   anInt = 32 + 'a' ;   //anInt = 129
```

It seems odd to be able to add the letter 'a' to the integer 32, doesn't it? Here's another one:

```
char  aChar = 32 + 'a' ;   //aChar = '?'
```

By and large, Java treats char variables as integers. However, if you cast char variables to byte or short variables, you may get unexpected results. As you might imagine, the concept of a signed number, common for integers, is meaningless for char variables. The smart approach is to use char variables as characters and integers as numbers.

This treatment of char variables as integers is a hangover from the world of C programming. You don't have to use char variables in this way, but you should know about such usage; you will likely see it done by other Java programmers.

Character literals are either single characters between single quotes, character escape sequences, octal and hex escape sequences, and Unicode escape sequences. Check out the Java declare statements below:

```
char  aCharInQuotes   = 'a';      //Just a character in quotes
char  aCharEscSeq     = '\n';     //Escape sequence (newline)
char  aUnicodeEscSeq  = '\u10D1';//Unicode sequence (????)
```

Often-used escape sequences are shown in Table 5.3.
Ergo, the line of code,

```
System.out.println( "Hello" + '\n' + "How Are You?");
```

Table 5.3   Common Escape Sequences

ESCAPE SEQUENCE	THE CHARACTER
\n	Newline
\b	Backspace
\t	Tab
\r	Return
\\	Backslash
\'	Single Quote
\"	Double Quote

produces the following output:

```
Hello
How Are You?
```

Integer Primitive Types

In Java, you can lump together the *byte, short, int*, and *long* primitive types as integers. As you've previously read, the *char* primitive type is considered an integer by many; however, we'll not perpetuate such a consideration. All these types can be cast to one another. Unfortunately, what you see may not always be what you get. Here's an example:

```
int       anInt     = 70000;
System.out.println( (short) anInt  ) ;
/** Java Prints out 4464!!! **/
```

Here, we're casting an integer (32 bits) into a short integer (16 bits). Important things are happening here that are worthy of passing note. First, the compiler, javac, does not complain in any way, even though the initialized value of anInt exceeds the maximum value for a short integer (32767). Second, the runtime does not choke; it actually spits out a number.

The moral of the story is that you must be careful when you cast integer types. Java is very forgiving in its use of integer primitive data types. Keep in mind, or have a chart handy, of the min and max values or the bit size of the primitive integer types.

You've seen some examples of coding integer literals. In case you have a really poor retention, additional examples are listed in the following:

```
int   anInt    =    4000  ;    //Integer, 32 bits
short aShort    =    1000  ;    //Short, 16 bits
```

```
long  along    =    40001 ;    //Long, 64 bits. Note the 'l'
byte  aByte    =    40   ;      //Byte, 8 bits
```

Mainframe languages have no integer support past 32 bits; hence, Java's *long* primitive type has no direct analogue in COBOL and PL/I. If you need numbers larger than 15 digits in a COBOL program (15 significant digits), you'd have to use a floating-point data type (COMP-1 or COMP-2).

Floating Point Primitive Types

Java supports two floating point types: *float* and *double*. Although mainframe programming languages have floating point types, these types are rarely used; mainframers have access to non integers by using packed numbers, declared with a number of decimal digits. This capability goes to the heart of COBOL's representational data typing, where the mainframe contains machine instructions to manipulate packed numbers.

The COBOL programmer could declare the number 3.556 without using a floating-point type, whereas the Java programmer is required to use either a float or a double to represent such a number.

Floating-point literals are declared as follows.

```
float     afloat    = 1.0012f ;
double    aDouble    = 1.0012d ;
double    aDouble    = 1.0012  ; //d not needed for double
```

Java floating-point types have some unusual behavior. For example, check out the following line of code.

```
// Division by zero!!!!!!!!
System.out.println( aFloat/0 + "   " + -aFloat /0 ) ;
```

The output is listed in the following.

```
Infinity    -Infinity
```

Yes, you're reading this correctly. When you divide a float by zero, you get *Infinity*; when you divide a negative floating-point number by zero, you get . . . *Infinity*.

By the way, you cannot divide a number declared as an integer type by zero. You'll get the familiar, expected response.

Okay, here's another example of odd behavior. The code is:

```
float aFloat2 = 0.0f ;
System.out.println(-(aFloat - aFloat) + "   " + aFloat2/aFloat2) ;
```

The output is

```
-0.0    NaN
```

Yes, Java will generate such a thing as *negative zero*. If afloat were a variable of an integer type, Java would output 0. The "NaN" stands for "Not a Number," which is an unordered quantity that compares false to all numbers and itself.

The moral of the story is to keep an eye on those floating-point numbers; they can act in unusual ways!

Character Strings in Java

Character strings in Java are an instance of class *String*. Strings are not a primitive data type. That said, the creators of Java understood that strings are such a common and often used data structure, and that Java should make it easy for the programmer to create and use strings. Strings in Java are straightforward, as the following example shows.

```
String    aString = "Hi Ho, Cherrio!" ;
```

In other words, strings "look like" a primitive data type. Java converts all occurrences of strings into an object of class String. However, this conversion has minimal impact on the Java programmer.

The String class has an assortment of utility methods that reach into a string to pull out a substring, look for one string inside another, and determine the string's length.

Java Reference Data Types

Java draws a distinction between primitive data types and reference data types. Whereas primitive types are passed to methods by *value*, the reference types are passed by *reference*.

What is the difference? Well, when an argument is passed to a method by value, a copy of the argument variable gets shipped to the method. When an argument is passed by reference, the starting address of the argument is passed to the method. In Chapter 2, you read portions about this burning issue; you'll briefly revisit this terribly exciting topic of passing by value and by reference in Chapter 7.

The reference data types in Java are *arrays* and *objects*. In Chapter 7, you will read about objects; here, you'll read about arrays.

Java Arrays

An array is an aggregate data structure where every member of the aggregate is of the same data type, and every member of the aggregate can be referenced by an index. If you've has experience programming, you've seen arrays. That said, Java arrays have a few interesting characteristics not found in COBOL or PL/I. Let's take a look.

A few array declarations are listed in the following.

```
int        anIntArray [] = {12, 24, 36, 4 * 24, anotherInt} ;
String     aString []    = {"Hi",  "Ho", "Cherrio!"} ;
int        aTable[] []    = {
```

```
         {12, 24, 36},
         {23, -45},
         (12345}
         } ;
```

Note that the first declaration includes a calculation and a reference to another variable (let's assume this other variable exists and has a value, okay?). The array elements are separated by commas, included in curly braces.

The third declaration is an array of arrays. Note the pairs of nested curly braces. Also note the dimension of the array aTable. How many of you readers caught the first "row" of the table to have three elements, the second "row" to have two, and the third "row" to have one? Because Java implements multidimensional arrays as arrays of arrays, you do not need to have your typical rectangular arrays. Try this in COBOL or PL/I.

Notice that the third declaration is described as an "array of arrays," as opposed to a multidimensional array. What's the difference, you ask? Look at the previous declaration for aTable. ATable is not multidimensional; it is not a 2 × 3, 2 × 2, 2 × 1, or anything × anything. ATable is an array of three elements; the first element is an array of three elements, the second is an array of two elements, the third is an array of one element. The term for this sort of structure is an array of arrays. Of course, you may implement multidimensional arrays by coding a 3 X 3 or 100 X 100 X 100 array, or any array where the dimension sizes are the same. Not to make a deal about it, but Java arrays are more flexible than arrays declared in other, procedural languages that are limited to multidimensional arrays.

Another feature shared by these three declares is that all of these arrays are initialized. You cannot code

```
int        anIntArray [] ;
```

because Java would not know how much memory to allocate for the array. If you do not have initial values, you can declare your arrays as follows:

```
int        anIntArray [] = new int[200] ;
```

Here, you use the *new* operator, commonly used to create objects, to create arrays without initial values. You can declare multidimensional arrays with *new*, as shown in the following:

```
String     aStringTable[] [] [] = new String [10] [20] [200] ;
```

Actually, you could even leave out some of the dimension sizes when declaring an array. Observe the following:

```
String     aStringTable[] [] [] = new String [10] [] [] ;
```

How can this be? How can Java know how much memory to allocate for this array? Well, Java looks at this structure as a single dimensional array of 10 elements; each element is a two dimensional array.

Java also accepts this syntax:

```
int[]     anIntArray  = {12, 24, 36, 4 * 24, anotherInt} ;
String[]  aString     = {"Hi",  "Ho", "Cherrio!"} ;
int[] []  aTable      = {
                            {12, 24, 36},
                            {23, -45},
                            (12345}
                                } ;
```

Now you get the picture of a data type of an array of integers, or a data type of an array of strings. By using the concept of an array as a data type, Java enables a construct like the following:

```
int[]     anIntArray        ;//Data Type is an array of integers
anIntArray = new int[ 200 ];//Make anIntArray hold 200 integers
anIntArray = new int[ 30 ] ;//Make anIntArray hold 30 integers.
```

You know how to reference arrays, right? Probably not, because in COBOL and PL/I, arrays normally start with 1, whereas in Java, arrays start with 0. Ergo, referring to the arrays on the previous page:

```
anIntArray [ 1 ]            = 24 ;
aString [ 0 ]              = "Hi" ;
aTable[ 1 ] [ 0 ]          = 23 ;
aTable[ 2 ] [ 1 ] is out of bounds
```

If you wanted to refer to the last element in aTable, the correct reference is

```
aTable[ 2 ] [ 0 ]   = 12345 ;
```

Arrays are a big part of any programming language and Java is no exception. Java enables you to create arrays both like and unlike those in COBOL and PL/I. In Java, arrays are zero-based (a fact worth repeating).

Java Naming Conventions

Before we leave the subject of defining data, a few words about the naming of Java variables is appropriate. Java enables variables of any practical length. A Java variable does not start with a number; it starts with a lower case letter, underscore, or a dollar sign. The start of each new word is capitalized all other letters are lowercased. All but the first position of the name can be letters, numbers, and some special symbols. In addition, variable names should be nouns.

Java objects follow the same naming convention as variables of primitive types.

1. Java classes begin with a capital letter, with the start of each new word capitalized.

2. Use nouns with the occasional adjective to name Java classes, objects, and primitive variables. You remember "person, place, or thing," right?

3. Java methods follow the same naming convention as variables: Start with lower case and capitalize each word. However, Java methods should denote some sort of action, or, put differently, Java methods should contain a verb.

Pretty straightforward, right?

In Summary

The Java programming language provides support for familiar data types and data structures. The Java treatment of primitive types and data usage may seem unusual to the mainframe programmer, especially the blurring of the int and char data types. However, the similarities between the Java treatment of primitive types and the mainframe programming language treatment of most data types are more telling.

Java Language Syntax

This chapter covers the majority of Java language features and constructs, including the following:

- Assignment statements
- Operators
- Arithmetic
- Boolean
- String
- Bit
- Object
- Java Arithmetic Anomalies
- Loop constructs
- Decision statements

Every language feature is compared to identically (where possible) functioning language features of COBOL and PL/I. Also, language features present in mainframe programming languages that have no Java analogue, such as pointers, COPY/header files, and preprocessor, statements are discussed. Rounding out the chapter are discussions on the short-circuiting of boolean expressions and miscellaneous Java syntax items.

This chapter contains plenty of code and tables highlighting the similarities and differences between Java and the mainframe programming languages. You may want to enter some statements similar to the examples in a Java source file; then you should compile, execute, and observe the results.

Miscellaneous Java Syntax Items

A couple of syntax items in Java are different than more familiar mainframe programming languages. Let's discuss these items first.

Java Source Code Is Case Sensitive

Unlike COBOL, PL/I and a host of other programming languages used on the mainframe, Java, are case sensitive. Case sensitivity may be a source of frustration for the COBOL and PL/I programmer who is used to coding everything in upper case. As discussed in Chapter 5, "Declaring and Defining Data," Java programmers should follow the previously discussed naming convention for their program entities, such as variables, constants, classes, objects, and methods. You'll have no choice if you want to use an existing entity (which will occur 99.999999999999999 percent of the time); you must observe the case of the entity name in your programs. Hence, get used to being aware of the disposition of the shift key as you enter your Java source.

Java Statements Terminated by a Semicolon

Not much to add to this, right? Think COBOL with the period or PL/I with the semicolon and you will understand the idea.

Java Supports Multiple Comment Styles

In most languages, a comment is a comment is a comment. This is not so in Java, which supports three comment styles.

The first is a single-line comment that starts with a double-slash (//) and continues to the end of the line. This comment style has no closing comment delimiter.

The second example is a multi-line comment style that starts with /* and ends with */. This is the comment style used by PL/I, REXX, and C programmers. Unlike PL/I and REXX, Java will not permit you to *nest*, or place one inside another, comments.

The final example is a special, Java-only style comment that starts with /** and ends with */. This comment style is called a *doc comment*. Doc comments can be processed by a Java utility called javadoc, a program designed to generate documentation, in part, from comments written in source code. See Chapter 4, "The Sun Java 2 Basic JDK Tools," for additional information on javadoc.

Now, PL/I, REXX , and C programmers would recognize this style to be the same as the multi-line comment style. Actually, you could code this style comment in your Java programs. To put it another way, the Java compiler reads /** the same way as /*. By the way, a comment that starts with /** and ends with **/ is *not* a doc comment.

Because Java multi-line and doc comments do not nest, you should get used to coding the single-line (//) comment variety. This way, if you want to comment out blocks of code, you can do what PL/I programmers do—code a /* before the block and */ after the block.

Java Has No COPY or Include Statement

Java has no feature to bring in external source for compile, like COBOL's COPY or PL/I's %Include statement. Java counts on a strict file naming convention for Java classes. If your program needs methods or other entities from a class file, Java will be able to locate it. Java does not have to bring in the source code from other class files into your program.

Java Has No Pointers

You've read this before: Java has no pointers. Java has no support for anything related to pointers; it automatically handles referencing and dereferencing objects.

You cannot manipulate pointers or memory addresses by performing pointer arithmetic, casting objects to primitive data types, or computing or changing the byte size of any primitive object.

Fortunately, the engineers at Sun who developed Java realized that pointers, their use and especially their abuse, are a heinous source of software bugs. By eliminating pointers from the language, the creators of Java, in one fell swoop, permanently removed a persistent source of bugs.

Another factor to consider is that pointers enable a programmer to get into the bowels of a machine. The developers of Java were security conscious. Pointers and pointer arithmetic could enable a nefarious programmer to circumvent any security mechanism in place. Removing pointers strikes a blow for system security by keeping the system's internals removed from programmers.

Java Has No Preprocessor

PL/I and C programmers are familiar with a *preprocessor*. The preprocessor generates source code, which, in turn, gets passed to the particular compiler. Although COBOL's COPY statement adds source code, COBOL does not support a preprocessor.

One common reason for preprocessor use is for *conditional compilation*. Java, being platform neutral, certainly has no need for platform specifics to successfully compile.

Reserved Words Exist in Java

Like most programming languages, Java uses *reserved words*. You must use these words in their proper syntactical and semantic context. Table 6.1 shows the list of Java's reserved words.

Table 6.1   Java's Reserved Words

abstract	else	int	static
boolean	extends	interface	super
break	false	long	switch
byte	final	native	synchronized
byvalue	finally	new	this
case	float	null	throw
cast	for	operator	throws
catch	future	outer	transient
char	generic	package	true
class	Goto	private	try
const	If	protected	var
continue	implements	public	void
default	import	rest	volatile
do	inner	return	while
double	instanceof	short	

Note that *all of Java's reserved words are in lowercase.* Of course, the Java compiler (and you) recognizes a difference between the reserved word *false*, and some program entity named *False.*

Some of the reserved words have no syntactic or semantic meaning. These words are shown in Table 6.2.

Java has the audacity to reserve the previous table of words, but has no current use for them. You, however, are forbidden to use these words in your Java programs. Note that goto is a reserved word in Java, but *Java does not support a goto statement.*

The method names of Java's root class *Object* are not reserved, but these method names warrant special treatment. As you'll read in Chapter 7, "Class and Object Representation," every class inherits methods from class Object. Unless you intend to override such a method in your class, you *should not use these method names for your own methods.* Table 6.3 is the list of method names from class Object.

The more astute readers out there will take note of the use of the naming convention used in the naming of these, and other, Java methods. Yes, it's the same one discussed in Chapter 5, "Declaring and Defining Data."

If you do any REXX, you know that REXX has some so-called reserved words that aren't really reserved. For example, the word *RC*, which represents a REXX variable that holds the return code value of an operating system call, should not be used in a different context. However, the lame REXX programmer could code

Table 6.2 Java's Meaningless (for Now) Reserved Words

byvalue	generic	outer
cast	goto	rest
const	inner	var
future	operator	

Table 6.3 Java's Pseudo-Reserved Words

clone	getClass	notifyAll
equals	hashCode	toString
finalize	notify	wait

```
RC  =  "I sure am a Lame REXX Programmer!"
```

The REXX interpreter or compiler would not gag, although your fellow REXX programmers sure would.

Java, too, is forgiving on the use of these pseudo-reserved method names. For example, if you coded this method:

```
void toString( int a ) {    //toString is one of 'those' words
   int x = 5 ;
   if ( x > a )
System.out.println("Hah!") ;
}
```

or coded this variable declaration:

```
int toString = 10 ;
```

javac, the compiler, would be very forgiving; Java, the bytecode interpreter, would also be very forgiving. You would bear the brunt of all the jokes of your fellow Javaians if they caught you using these method names from class Object in a manner inconsistent with their existence. Also, you'd get no sympathy from this corner.

Java Is a Free-Form Programming Language

Back in the days when the Earth was cooling, compiler engineers thought it would be smart to make matters easier for the compiler by forcing programmers to code various things in specific columns. Those of us who remember Woodstock, remember early versions of Fortran where you had to code between columns 8 and 72. Of course, the most serious offender of the "force programmers to code in such and such column" is COBOL. There exists a nearly uncountable number of COBOL statements coded in the A and B margins.

Since Java was developed after the Cambrian Era, Java does not impose column restrictions on code. You can start and end your Java code in any column you like.

Java Assignment Statements

Assignment statements in Java have some surprises and can behave differently than assignment statements in other programming languages. Let's look at what Java assignment statements have in common with other programming languages.

Java supports the expected, usual, common, and garden-variety assignment statement:

```
aJavaVariable = aJavaExpression ;
```

where a `JavaVariable` is a previously declared variable and, well, you understand.

You have seen in the previous chapter that you can assign a value to a Java variable (or object) upon declaration. To wit:

```
char       aCharVar = 'L' ;              //Primitive Type
MyClass    anObj    = new MyClass() ; //Object
```

COBOL enables you to initialize a variable with the *Value* clause; PL/I enables you to initialize a variable with the *Init* option.

That is pretty much the entire gamut of commonality between Java assignment statements and COBOL or PL/I assignment statements. We'll have more to say about Java expressions later in this chapter.

The most dramatic difference between Java assignment statements and those used in mainframe programming languages is Java's *assignment with operator* statements. This chapter contains more information about these and the rest of Java's operators. For now, know that Java enables you to perform an operation and assign the result to a variable in one operation. Here is an example, with the promise of several more examples included in the section titled *Java Operators*:

```
int anInt  = 6 ; // Just your normal variable initialization
anInt      += 6; // Add 6 to anInt, reassign back - anInt = 12
                 // -+, *=, and others also available

anInt = anInt + 6;// Functionally equivalent to anInt += 6 ;
```

C programmers out there should be quite comfortable and familiar with the "operate and assign" family of operators.

How about another difference between Java assignment statements and COBOL and PL/I assignment statements? How do you think Java would interpret this statement?

```
int a, b ;
a = b = 7 ;
```

This assignment statement, in COBOLSpeak, is akin to a group move. In short, variables a and b have the value 7 after the assignment statement executes. In PL/I and REXX, the statement would be evaluated as follows:

```
a = (b = 7) ;
```

The variable b *would not change*. The variable b is not assigned a value; b is tested for the value 7. Only the variable a gets assigned a value of *true* (if b equals 7) *or false* (if b equals some other value).

When you read about Java's class and object representation in Chapter 7, you'll learn that assignments of objects is a bit different than assignments of variables.

Java Operators

What's a programming language without operators? You'll see that Java has several operators not found in COBOL and PL/I; here, you'll take a look at Java operators. You'll learn what operators Java have in common with COBOL and PL/I; you'll read a bit more about and see examples of the Java operators that have no counterparts in the mainframe programming world.

Do you have the Java source code window and the DOS window open? It's probably a good investment of your time to try out some of the examples as you read.

Table 6.4 shows Java's operators with their precedence ranking, their operand types, their associativity, and, of course, a brief description of the operation.

The operator's *precedence* governs when the operation is performed in relation to other operations on the same line. An operation of precedence 1, at the top of the table, is performed before a higher numbered precedence operator when both are on the same line of code. For example:

```
myMeagerPay = myTooSmallGross - shockinglyHighTaxRate *
                          mytooSmallGross ;
```

The multiplication operation is performed first, followed by the subtraction operation, and then followed by the assignment operation.

This is pretty standard stuff, right? As with other programming languages, you may use parenthesis to alter the natural order of execution as defined by the operator precedence.

```
myMeagerPay = myTooSmallGross * (1.0 - shockinglyHighTaxRate) ;
```

Table 6.4 Java Operators by Precedence

PRECEDENCE	OPERATOR	OPERAND TYPE(S)	ASSOCIATIVITY	OPERATION
1	++	Arithmetic	R-L	Unary Increment
	—	Arithmetic	R-L	Unary Decrement
	+, -	Arithmetic	R-L	Unary Plus, Unary Minus
	~	Integral	R-L	Unary Bitwise Compliment
	!	Boolean	R-L	Unary Logical Compliment
	(vartype)	Any	R-L	Type Cast
2	*, /, %	Arithmetic	L-R	Multiply, Divide, Remainder
3	+, -	Arithmetic	L-R	Addition, Subtraction
	+	String	L-R	Concatenation
4	<<	Integral	L-R	Shift Left
	>>	Integral	L-R	Shift Right, Extend Sign
	>>>	Integral	L-R	Shift Right, Zero-Fill
5	<, <=	Arithmetic	L-R	Less than, Less than or Equal to
	>, >=	Arithmetic	L-R	Greater than, Greater than or Equal to
	instanceof	Object, Type	L-R	Type/Class Compare
6	==	Primitive	L-R	Equal by Having Identical Values
	!=	Primitive	L-R	Not Equal by Having Different Values

continued

Table 6.4   Java Operators by Precedence (*continued*)

PRECEDENCE	OPERATOR	OPERAND TYPE(S)	ASSOCIATIVITY	OPERATION
	==	Object	L-R	Equal by Referring to Same Object
	!=	Object	L-R	Not Equal by Referring to Different Object
7	&	Integral	L-R	Bit AND
	&	Boolean	L-R	AND
8	^	Integral	L-R	Bit Exclusive OR (XOR)
	^	Boolean	L-R	Exclusive OR (XOR)
9	|	Integral	L-R	Bit OR
	|	Boolean	L-R	OR
10	&&	Boolean	L-R	AND (Used in Conditional Statements)
11	||	Boolean	L-R	OR (Used in Conditional Statements)
12		?:Boolean, Any, Any	R-L	Ternary (Used in Conditional Statements)
13	=	Variable, Any	R-L	Assignment
	+=, /=, %=	Variable, Any	R-L	Assignment With Operation
	+=, -=			
	<<=, >>=			
	>>>=			
	&=, ^=, !|			

The subtraction inside the pair of parenthesis is performed first, followed by the multiplication, and then followed by the assignment.

In general, Java operator precedence, first to last, is the following:

1. Increment and Decrement operators

2. Arithmetic operators

3. Compare operators

4. Boolean operators

5. Assignment operators

The operator's *associativity* governs the order of execution when two or more operators of equal precedence are on the same statement. If an operator has *Left to Right* (L-R) *associativity*, then two or more of the same precedence operators on the same line are evaluated left to right. For example, Table 6.4 states that the *addition* operator, +, has L-R associativity. Hence, the statement

```
sumof = addend1 + addend2 + addend3;
```

evaluates by first adding addend1 to addend2, then adding that sum to addend3.

Table 6.4 states that the *assignment* operator, =, has R-L associativity. Hence, the statement

```
var1=var2=var3=20;
```

evaluates by assigning 20 to var3, then assigns var3 to var2, then assigns var2 to var1.

For the most part, COBOL and PL/I, in the absence of parenthesis, use L-R associativity for same precedence operators.

You've noticed that Java has many more operators than COBOL and other mainframe programming languages. Table 6.5 shows what operations Java, COBOL, and PL/I have in common.

Let's spend some time examining Java operators not found in COBOL and other mainframe programming languages.

Java Operators not Found in Mainframe Programming Languages

The operators found in Java, but not found in COBOL or PL/I, are worthy of explanation.

Unary Increment and Decrement

Unary increment (++) and *Unary decrement* (−−) *operators* are often used in Java. These operators add or subtract 1 from a variable and assign the result back to the variable. You'll see these operators in loops where your Java code increments a loop counter.

Table 6.5 Java Operators Used in COBOL and PL/I

OPERATOR	OPERAND TYPE(S)	OPERATION	COBOL OPERATION	PL/I OPERATION
++	Arithmetic	Unary Increment	None	None
--	Arithmetic	Unary Decrement	None	None
+, -	Arithmetic	Unary Plus, Unary Minus	+, -	+, -
~	Integral	Unary Bitwise Compliment	None	None
!	Boolean	Unary Logical Compliment	NOT	^
(vartype)	Any	Type Cast	None	None
*, /, %	Arithmetic	Multiply, Divide, Remainder	*,/,None	*,/,None
+, -	Arithmetic	Addition, Subtraction	+,-	+,-
+	String	Concatenation	None	¦¦
<<	Integral	Shift Left		
>>	Integral	Shift Right, Extend Sign		
>>>	Integral	Shift Right, Zero-Fill		
<, <=	Arithmetic	Less than, Less than or Equal to	<, <=	<, <=
>, >=	Arithmetic	Greater than, Greater than or Equal to	>, >=	>, >=
instanceof	Object, Type	Type/Class Compare	None	None
==	Primitive	Equal by Having Identical Values	=	=
!=	Primitive	Not Equal by Having Different Values	NOT EQUALS	^ =

continued

Table 6.5 Java Operators Used in COBOL and PL/I (*continued*)

OPERATOR	OPERAND TYPE(S)	OPERATION	COBOL OPERATION	PL/I OPERATION
==	Object	Equal by Referring to Same Object	None	None
!=	Object	Not Equal by Referring to Different Object	None	None
&	Integral	Bit AND	None	None
&	Boolean	AND	AND	&
^	Integral	Bit Exclusive OR (XOR)	None	None
^	Boolean	Exclusive OR (XOR)	None	None
|	Integral	Bit OR	None	None
|	Boolean	OR	OR	|
&&	Boolean	AND (Used in Conditional Statements)	AND	&
||	Boolean	OR (Used in Conditional Statements)	OR	|
?:	Boolean, Any, Any	Ternary (Used in Conditional Statements)	None	None
=	Variable, Any	Assignment	=	=
+=, /=, %=	Variable, Any	Assignment With Operation	None	None
+=, -=				
<<=, >>=				
>>>=				
&=, ^=, !=				

Here are some straightforward examples:

```
int aInt = 10 ;
aInt ++ ;                // aInt equals 11 (postfix)
aInt -- ;                // aInt equals 10 (postfix)
-- aInt ;                // aInt equals 9  (prefix)
++ aInt ;                // aInt equals 10 (prefix)
```

The increment and decrement operators behave differently based on the placement of the operator. We draw a distinction between *prefix* and *postfix* increment and decrement operators. The prefix operators are placed before the variable and perform the operation before any assignment or calculation takes place; the postfix operators are placed after the variable and perform the operation after any assignment or calculation tales place. Yes, this certainly sounds like a mouthful; looking at the four examples above, you can't see any difference in the behavior of the postfix and prefix operators.

To see the difference between the behavior of the postfix and prefix operators, check this out:

```
int aInt = 10 ;
int bInt ;
bInt = aInt ++ ;         // bInt is assigned aInt's current
                         // value of 10 before aInt is incremented
                         // to 11. So aInt = 11, bInt = 10
bInt = -- aInt;          // aInt is decremented from 11 to 10,
                         // then aInt's value is assigned to bInt
                         // So aInt = 10, bInt = 10
```

The increment and decrement operators, when used in assignment statements like the previous examples, have this odd property of changing the values of variables on the right hand side of the assignment operator. To a C programmer, these operators are standard fare; to a mainframe programmer, these operators may seem unusual.

On the one hand, there is nothing forcing you to use these operators. You could add or subtract 1 from a variable using a more familiar construct. However, you can bet the ranch that you'll see these operators in someone else's Java code. You must understand the behavior of these operators.

Assignment with Operators

The assignment with operators is a shorthand way of performing an operation on a variable and assigning the new result to the same variable. Some examples are in order here:

```
int aInt = 10 ; int bInt ;
aInt *= 2 ;              // Multiply by 2 and reassign; aInt = 12
aInt += aInt ;           // Add aInt to itself and reassign.
bInt = aInt /= 2 ;       // aInt is halved to 4 then its value
                         // assigned to bInt. Recall that these
                         // operators have R-L associativity.
```

These assignments with operators can take some getting used to, especially if you chain them one after another on single statements. There is no force on Earth that can make you code with these operators. As with the increment and decrement operators, you should have a familiarity of how these operations work so you can cope with code that contains them.

Bit Operators

The bit operators perform the indicated logical operator on a binary representation of the arguments in pairs. PL/I supports bit operators whereas COBOL does not. Three examples should drive the point home:

```
int aInt = 10;          // Bit pattern: 1010
int bInt =  8;          // Bit pattern: 1000
int cInt = aInt & bInt ;// AND in pairs: 1000 = 8
cInt = aInt | bInt ;    // OR in pairs: 1010  = 10
cInt = aInt ^ bInt ;    // XOR in pairs: 0010 = 2
```

The *Exclusive OR* (XOR), returns true when only one of the arguments is true, not both.

Shift Operators

The *shift operators* also work on bit representations of integers. Also, a couple of examples should shed some insight on the workings of these operations:

```
int aInt = 10;           // Bit pattern: 1010
int bInt =  aInt << 2;// Shift left two digits to 101000, or 40
int cInt = aInt >> 2 ;// Shift left two digits to 0010, or 2
```

The Cast Operator

The *cast* operator is used to change the data type of a variable or object. In Chapter 7, you'll read about the rules governing the casting of objects. Some primitive types may be cast to different types. Java does not permit the casting of an object to a primitive type variable or the casting of a primitive type variable to an object.

If you enter this declaration,

```
float myFloat = .012 ;
```

javac will tell you that you need an explicit cast from double to float.

Some primitive types do not require an explicit cast. Chapter 5 mentions that the char data type can be used as an integer without an explicit cast. Hence, the declaration passes javac without comment:

```
int anInt = 'a' ;
```

Chapter 5 contains more information on Java primitive data types, including the integer types.

Boolean and Conditional Operators

You may be a bit befuddled and partially perplexed by the different classifications of logical operators. The *boolean operators* (&, |) and the *conditional operators* (&&, ||) both perform the logical AND and OR we've come to know and love. However, there is a sneaky difference that is illustrated by the following code:

```
int aInt = 10, bInt = 20, cInt = 0 ;
boolean aBool = ( aInt > 10 ) & ( bInt / cInt > 0 ) ;
boolean bBool = ( aInt = 10 ) | ( bInt / cInt > 0 ) ;
```

What is going to happen here? Java, in its attempt to initialize aBool, reduces aInt > 10 to false; it then figures the quotient bInt / cInt, which causes an exception—division by zero. Therefore, this code comes to a screeching, tire-smoking halt.

Well, no surprises here, right? This is the way COBOL and its mainframe kin behave. Programming languages take a dim view toward division by zero. However, there is an unspoken tale here.

If you look at the previous statement, because aInt was not greater than 10, or aInt > 10 is false, there is *no chance the expression would evaluate to true*. You see that, right? Regardless of the boolean value of the right hand side of the expression, there is *no chance the expression would evaluate to true*.

This begs the question: Why would Java even bother to evaluate the remainder of the expression when the outcome is not in doubt? The answer is simple: that is the purpose of the boolean operators. The boolean operators always evaluate each and every operation before assigning a boolean value to the target.

Now, look at the example code of assigning a value to bBool. The operation that assigns a value to bBool during initialization is the boolean OR. The first part of the expression, aInt = 10, is true; therefore, the remainder of the expression *must be true*. However, Java will evaluate the second part of the expression and, well, you know the inevitable outcome.

Now, check this out:

```
int aInt = 10, bInt = 20, cInt = 0 ;
boolean aBool = ( aInt > 10 ) && ( bInt / cInt > 0 ) ;
boolean bBool = ( aInt = 10 ) || ( bInt / cInt > 0 ) ;
```

You see the difference between this and the previous example, right? This example uses the *conditional operators*. As you've undoubtedly guessed by now, the conditional operators will suppress execution of expressions when those expressions play no part in the final outcome. Concerning the initialization of aBool, because the left part of the logical expression is false, the right part cannot contribute to the final result and is not evaluated. The right part of the initialization of bBool, too, is not evaluated, owing to the truth of the left part.

A 10-dollar phrase is used to describe the trait of the conditional operators. We in the know say that these conditional operators *short circuit* logical expression evaluation. Some programming languages (C and Ada) short circuit logical expressions. The mainframe languages (COBOL, PL/I, and REXX) do not; these languages have logical operators that behave like Java's boolean operators. Java gives you operations that enable you to short circuit or avoid short circuiting.

The String Concatenation Operator

We've already seen the *string concatenation operator* (+). This one is a breeze. The concatenation operator combines two strings into one string. Now PL/I has a concatenation operator, but COBOL does not. The examples that show Java writing output to the screen with the println() method show the use of this operator. The concatenation operator creates a long string by (pardon the pun) stringing together two strings:

```
String sVar1 = "Left", sVar2 = "Right",
SVar3 = sVar1 + sVar2 ;          // sVar3 = "LeftRight"
```

The Ternary Operator

The last new operator you'll read about in this section is the *conditional* or *ternary operator*. This operator is shorthand for an if-else construct. A basic template of this operator is:

```
logicalExpression ? valueWhenTrue : valueWhenFalse ;
```

These examples should prove to be useful:

```
int       mySalary     = 999999 ;
boolean   rUWealthy    = (mySalary > 1000000) ? true : false ;
char      uGetGovtCheese = (mySalary < 10) ? 'Y' : 'N' ;
```

The ternary operator comes in handy when assigning variables one of two values.

You see that Java has many interesting operators with interesting subtleties. There is no substitute for entering various expressions and seeing firsthand how Java behaves with your code. You'll learn all sorts of odds and ends about Java operators not mentioned here or in other books.

Speaking of interesting subtleties, let's take a look at arithmetic in Java next.

Java Arithmetic Anomalies

Many programming languages treat some aspects of arithmetic in a counterintuitive manner. Java is no exception. Here, you'll see some differences between Java and the IBM mainframe languages in the treatment of arithmetic.

Mixing Primitive Types in Arithmetic Expressions

Now, Java is considered to be a strongly typed language. However, the strong typing comes into play with reference types (objects and arrays), not with primitive data types. Look at the following statement. Any thoughts on how a strongly typed language should behave?

```
char aChar = 30 + 70 ;
```

Here, we are assigning the result of an arithmetic operation to a variable of type char. Believe it or not, javac, the Java compiler, will *not choke* on the assignment. Actually, aChar will have the value of *d*. Java performs the calculation, yielding (think fast!) 100, before interpreting 100 as an *ISO-Latin I* character and converting 100 to the letter d.

The previous assignment statement does not surprise the readership with a background in C programming. The COBOL programmer cannot get away with this. A COBOL compiler would gush up a diagnostic if a said compiler encountered the following:

```
aChar          Pic X(1)   Value( 30 + 70 ).
```

The PL/I programmer coding this statement would get a surprise:

```
Dcl  aChar     Char(1)    Init ( 30 + 70 );
```

The actual result depends on the compiler settings. aChar could have the value ' ', or could generate a diagnostic saying that "the stringsize condition would be raised" if that statement executed.

C programmers are not surprised at Java's behavior toward arithmetic being assigned to char variables. The conversion from a number to a coded representation is as old as C itself. If you want to add integers, doesn't it make sense to use int variables?

It is important to know that Java will change the type (if possible) of the result of calculations to match the type of the target variable. Put another way, Java will force the result of a computation to fit the type of the target variable. A good programmer takes steps to use variables of the same type.

It's also important to note that the previous spiel applies to computations with variables declared with *primitive types*. If you were to declare and use *objects* in your calculations, Java would expect more care. Here is an example:

```
//Primitive Data Types        Object Declaration

int  cPrim ;                   Integer cObj ;
cPrim = 'a' + 'b' ;            cObj = 'a' + 'b';
```

Java handles the assignment statement on the left as follows: Java converts the character *a* to 97 and *b* to 98 before adding the two to get (think quickly!) 195. Therefore, cPrim equals 195.

Java handles the assignment statement on the right a bit differently. The Java compiler burps, saying

```
Incompatible type for assignment. Can't convert int to
java.lang.Integer.
```

Try it. Enter similar statements and see the Java compiler tell you off.

Loss of Precision when Dividing Integers

A consequence of Java converting the result of an arithmetic operation *on primitive types* is that you may lose precision when you divide. This precision loss problem is as old as computers. You may think that as we jet-ski into the twenty-first century, we computer folk would not be plagued with such ancient problems. You may think that Java, a modern, recently created computer programming language, would not suffer from this age-old problem. You would be both right and wrong.

You would be right if you declared and used *objects*. Java would not let you get away with the mixing of object types or classes in expressions, hoping that Java would convert the result.

You would be wrong if you declared and used primitive types. Java would truncate fractional results of computations when assigning a quotient to an int variable. To wit:

```
//Primitive Data Types        Object Declaration

int    int1 = 7 ;             Integer iO1 = new Integer(7);
int    int2 = 3 ;             Integer iO2 = new Integer(3) ;
float fPrim = int1/int2;      Float afloat= new Float(iO1/iO2);
```

The code on the left, using primitive data types, compiles and executes. Here, fPrim equals *2.0* (note the .0). The code on the right, using objects, does not compile.

COBOL and PL/I fare a bit better than Java in this instance. For example,

```
*COBOL                        /* PL/I */

Int1 Pic S(9) Comp Value '7'>   Dcl Int1 Fixed Bin(15)
                                      Init(7) ;
Int2 Pic S(9) Comp Value '3'.   Dcl Int2 Fixed Bin(15)
                                      Init(3) ;
Fprim Pic S(9.999) Comp.        Dcl Fprim Fixed Dec(5,4);
Fprim = Int1 / Int2.            Fprim = Int1 / Int2 ;
* Fprim = 2.3333                /* Fprim = 2.3333 */
```

Using the previous programming languages, you need to declare the quotient with your desired precision, which cuts down on certain surprises when performing calculations. However, if you divided integers and assigned the result to an integer in COBOL or PL/I, the result would contain no fractional part.

Shoddy Floating Point
Arithmetic Results

The funny thing is, just about everyone who hasn't lived in a cave for the past few decades knows that computers can surely add up numbers. Computers can add many numbers quickly, easily, and exactly. After all, computers can't think, but they can sure crunch numbers. Well, like most generalizations, there are exceptions.

Let's take a look at some code and see these exceptions:

```
f = .125f ;  System.out.println( " f = " + f ) ; // f = 0.125
f += .125f ;  System.out.println( " f = " + f ) ; // f = 0.25
f += .125f ;  System.out.println( " f = " + f ) ; // f = 0.375
f += .125f ;  System.out.println( " f = " + f ) ; // f = 0.50
f += .125f ;  System.out.println( " f = " + f ) ; // f = 0.625
f += .125f ;  System.out.println( " f = " + f ) ; // f = 0.750
f += .125f ;  System.out.println( " f = " + f ) ; // f = 0.875
f += .125f ;  System.out.println( " f = " + f ) ; // f = 1.0
f += .125f ;  System.out.println( " f = " + f ) ; // f = 1.125
```

No surprise here, right? Let's make a minor change:

```
f = .1f ;  System.out.println( " f = " + f ) ; // f = 0.1
f += .1f ;  System.out.println( " f = " + f ) ; // f = 0.2
f += .1f ;  System.out.println( " f = " + f ) ; // f = 0.3
f += .1f ;  System.out.println( " f = " + f ) ; // f = 0.4
f += .1f ;  System.out.println( " f = " + f ) ; // f = 0.5
f += .1f ;  System.out.println( " f = " + f ) ; // f = 0.6
f += .1f ;  System.out.println( " f = " + f ) ; // f =
                                          //    0.70000005
f += .1f ;  System.out.println( " f = " + f ) ; // f = 0.8000001
f += .1f ;  System.out.println( " f = " + f ) ; // f = 0.9000001
```

Something seems a bit awry here. COBOL and PL/I behave a bit better because you typically declare the precision of your results in thee languages; also, the IBM machine instruction set includes fixed-point decimal arithmetic. For example, these statements in PL/I produce the indicated result:

```
Dcl f Fixed Dec(5,4) Init( 0.1 ) ;
f = f + .1 ;                          /* f = 0.2000 */
f = f + .1 ;                          /* f = 0.3000 */
f = f + .1 ;                          /* f = 0.4000 */
f = f + .1 ;                          /* f = 0.5000 */
f = f + .1 ;                          /* f = 0.6000 */
f = f + .1 ;                          /* f = 0.7000 */
```

Believe it or not, this precision problem with floating point numbers is experienced by nearly every programmer outside of the IBM mainframe community who uses floating point arithmetic. Floating point arithmetic is a nightmare of sorts; to hope for an exact result when using floating point is akin to hope for six good numbers in a small, state sanctioned ticket. Floating point arithmetic requires numbers being converted into a binary representation with exponents (and mantissas—remember that word from high school math?), and back again. The massive load of converting is bound to introduce inaccuracies.

As an aside, you could argue that we're comparing apples and oranges. The mainframe languages have floating point types. Why not show an example with, say, a COBOL program declaring floating point numbers and show the accuracy of COBOL's floating point arithmetic? Well, every mainframe programmer I know (and all you know, too, I'm sure) uses a fixed decimal representation for nonintegers. They have no need to use floating point because the IBM mainframe instruction set provides the tools to get accurate decimal results. Simply put, the IBM mainframer has no cause to use floating point, as opposed to fixed decimal, numbers.

If possible, try to use integer arithmetic; then, divide the result of the integer arithmetic at the end to help guard against floating point accuracy errors. To wit:

```
int     iVar = 1 ;
float   fVar = iVar / 10 ;            // fVar = 0.1
iVar++; fVar = iVar / 10 ;            // fVar = 0.2
iVar++; fVar = iVar / 10 ;            // fVar = 0.3
iVar++; fVar = iVar / 10 ;            // fVar = 0.4
```

Overflow and Keep Going

Java has an interesting habit of offering extreme forgiveness toward its primitive types. For example, when you add two integer types that exceed the range for that type, Java does not overflow, or underflow, or generate any runtime errors, as this example points out:

```
int aInt = 999999999 ;
System.out.println( aInt += 999999999 ) ;//aInt =  1999999998
System.out.println( aInt += 999999999 ) ;//aInt = -1294967299!!
System.out.println( aInt += 999999999 ) ;//aInt = -294967300!!!
```

Recall that the allowable range for int types in Java is -2^{31} to $2^{31} - 1$. The first add and assign operation yields a number within this range. However, the second one yields 2999999997, which is outside this range. Java will compile and execute these statements (try them and see). In contrast, COBOL and PL/I will generate an error when your program exceeds the numeric bounds for a variable.

The good news is that the Java engineers provided a solution to this and other problems by providing the classes *BigInteger* and *BigDecimal* in package *java.math*. These classes enable for arbitrary precision, do not overflow like variables of some of Java's primitive types do, and come with a spate of methods that handle conversions. Chapter 10, "Interfaces," has more information on the package java.math.

The moral of this tragic tale of obnoxious overflow is to be sure that your Java variables declared as an integer primitive type have plenty of room to grow.

We've yet to look at Java statements that affect the program's control flow. Java supports loops, decision statements, and case constructs. Let's now take a look at program control statements.

Java Program Control Statements

You know that a *loop* is a group of statements that either execute a fixed number of times or execute based on the value of a boolean. You also know that a *decision statement* is a two (or more) way branch that directs a program to execute statements based on the value of a boolean. I'm wagering that you know that a *case* is a construct that selects a group of statements to execute based on the value of a variable. I'll also wager that you aren't exactly sure how to code the previous three statement types in Java. For more on this, read on.

Loop Constructs

Here, you'll take a look at Java's loop constructs. Like most programming languages, Java supports an iterative loop and two forms of a conditional loop. Let's see.

The Java for Loop

The *for loop* is Java's implementation of an iterative loop. Here is the basic template:

```
for (index = startval; executioncondition; changeindex ) {
//   one or more statements that constitute the loop body
}
```

Notice the use of semicolons *inside the loop construct.*
Here is an example with a COBOL and PL/I iterative loop thrown in for comparison:

```
for (idx = 10 ;idx <= 15; idx++) {
System.out.println("Loop index is " + idx ) ;
}
```

A COBOL example follows:

```
Perform Varying Idx From 10 to 15.
    Display 'Loop Index is ', Idx.
End-Perform.
```

PL/I example:

```
Do Idx = 10 to 15;
    Put Skip List( 'Loop Index is ', Idx ) ;
End ;
```

As you can see, the Java for loop has up to four parts.

1. The Initialization Part

The *initialization* part is represented by *index = startval* in the basic template. Your for loop can initialize more than one variable by separating each variable assignment with a comma (index1 = 10, and index2 = 15). Also, you can declare variables in the initialization part. These declared variables are known only in the for loop (are *local* to the loop).

Perhaps an example will drive this point home:

```
for (int idx = 0; idx < 10; idx++ )
    System.out.println( "Inside loop " + idx  ) ;

System.out.println( "Outside loop " + idx ) ;
```

Javac responds to this code with the following diagnostic:

```
Undefined variable: idx
System.out.println( "Outside Loop " + idx ) ;
                                      ^
```

As an aside, note that this for loop does not use curly braces. Later on, you'll read more about the use of these braces in loops and decision statements. The short story is that when your program executes only one statement in a loop, your program does not need the braces surrounding that single statement.

2. The Execution Test

The execution test, represented by executioncondition, is a boolean value that governs the execution of the loop. Simply put, as long as executioncondition is true, the loop executes. Your job is to look twice to insure that executioncondition will eventually change to false, or else your loop will attain a somewhat permanent execution status.

3. The Changing of the Loop Index

The Changing of the loop index is represented by *changeindex*. In a for loop, the index is connected to the executioncondition. The usual method of changing the executioncondition is by operating on the index in the changeindex section. The examples we've seen show the use of Java's unary increment operator, which is arguably the most common use of this operator.

You can code any expression that changes the index.

4. The Loop Body

The loop body is represented by the braces and the statements between and braces. What's a loop without a loop body? The loop body is the real work of the loop and will execute as long as executecondition is true. You've figured out that you need to sandwich loop body statements between curly braces if you want these statements to execute as a unit or a block. Curly braces are Java's *block construct*. We'll meet up with the block construct many a time in this chapter.

Now, you could code an empty loop, a loop without a body. For example, if you wanted to find the first element of an array that has a certain property, you could code

```
for (int idx = 0;
     idx < myArray.length && hasTheProperty( myArray[ idx ] );
     idx++ ) ;
```

For the purposes of this somewhat contrived example, assume that the method *has-TheProperty()* returns true if the indicated array element has the property, false otherwise. You recall from Chapter 5 that Java arrays start with a zero index, right? Also, you recall from Chapter 5 the *length* property, right? Finally, you recall from this chapter why this example uses the *conditional* AND, not the *boolean* AND, right?

Note the semicolon after the previous for statement. The Java files are replete with the sad saga of programmers who mistakenly code a construct similar to the following one :

```
for (int idx = 0; idx < aNumber; idx++) ;
     { Statement₁


       Statementₙ

}
```

The semicolon—yes, the big one—after the for statement, causes Java not to associate the statements in the following braces with the for statement. In short, the previous for statement coded is an empty loop. The statements between the braces execute once. The Java compiler will not indicate the presence of an empty loop. However, if a variable declared in the for statement, like idx above, is referenced in the following block, the compiler will report that idx is an undefined variable.

It is virtually impossible to mistakenly code an empty loop in COBOL or PL/I because of the loop delimiters used in these languages. Could you see yourself coding anything like the following?

```
*COBOL                          /* PL/I */


Perform                         Do Idx = 1 to 10 ;
    idx Varying from 1 to 10.   End ;
End-Perform.
```

In brief, the Java for loop executes like its mainframe language brethren's loop. The initialization section is executed first. Next, the *executioncondition* evaluates. If true, the loop executes. After the statements in the loop body execute, the *changeindex* part executes. The cycle of executioncondition, followed by statement body execution, followed by changeindex part, continues until executioncondition is false (or a program error causes a choke).

Of course, for statements may be nested. Nested loops in Java behave like their mainframe language brethren. Nested loops are commonly used to process elements in multidimensional arrays. Most programming languages have a limit on the number of nested loops; PL/I and COBOL have a limit of 16 nested loops. Java, being interpretive, doesn't seem to care; you can code 40 plus nested loops and the compiler won't even peep. Of course, come execution time, the Java Virtual Machine and Java Runtime will be playing a different tune.

Java supports conditional loops, or loops that execute a body of statements depending on the truth value of a boolean condition. Now is the time to explore these useful constructs.

Did you catch the comment about a Java for loop having *up to four parts*? Well, you can omit parts of a for loop provided you take care of the necessary details elsewhere. Actually, Java doesn't care if you omit parts of the for loop. You, on the other hand, will probably care a great deal when your loops don't terminate or variables assume (incorrect) default values. In any event, this is a valid Java for loop:

```
int idx = 0 ;
for (; idx < 10; ) {
    // Body of the loop
    idx++ ;
}
```

Note that the index variable initialization is done when the variable is declared and the index variable increment is done inside the loop. This coding construct falls into the category of "you should know what this looks like in case you come across it."

The following will be of no surprise. Like iterative loops in most programming languages, the index variable is incremented before the test is applied. Ergo, in this code snippet:

```
int idx ;
for (idx = 0; idx < 10; idx++ ) {
    //Do something here
}
System.out.println("outside idx = " + idx ) ;
```

Java prints out 10.

The savvy programmer insures that the ignominious fate of having index variables one off by not relying on index variables for processing outside the loop. Fortunately in Java, you can easily enforce this by declaring your index variable on the for statement as described a few pages ago.

The Java while Loop

As the name implies, the Java *while* loop executes while a condition is true. In brief, the condition is first evaluated; if true, the loop body executes. Control is transferred to the while statement where the condition is reevaluated; if true, the loop body executes. This cycle of condition test/loop body execution stops when the condition becomes false.

The basic template is

```
One or more statements setting the value of aConditionIsTrue
while ( aConditionIsTrue ) {

one or more statements that constitute the loop body

    one or more statements that eventually will change the
        value of aConditionIsTrue

}
```

Syntactically, the bare-bones while loop is

```
while ( aConditionIsTrue ) { code block }
```

However, you'll rarely see while loops like the bare-bones variety. A well formed while loop can have four parts.

1. **Statements that set the initial value of the condition.** The condition in the while loop, represented by *aConditionIsTrue* in the basic template, must be true for the loop to execute. The condition is evaluated *first*. If the evaluation resolves to true, the loop body executes. Your program should have one or more statements that set the initial value of the condition. Now, these statements need not be coded immediately before the while statement, but they should be reasonably close to the while loop itself.

2. **The condition that governs the execution of the loop.** There is not much to add here. Remember that you can use either boolean or conditional operators for compound conditions.

3. **The Loop Body.** Like the for loop previously discussed, what is a loop without a loop body? If your loop body consists of more than one statement, you'll need the curly braces to form a block. Java accepts empty while loops, however, such loops will cause your program to enter a permanent state of execution. Can you figure out why?

4. **Code that eventually changes the loop condition.** Recall that a for loop has a built-in self-terminating mechanism if you code it properly. A bare-bones while loop has none; if the loop condition is true and there is no code to change the condition, *the loop will execute forever*. Because nothing you do is important enough to continue forever, you should take great pains to insure that your loops terminate.

That is why the well-formed loop has code that will, upon successive executions, change the value of the condition.

Here is an interesting and somewhat counterintuitive observation made over the coding of many while loops: The code that sets the initial value of the condition is often identical to the code that eventually changes the condition. Here is an example:

```
custName = getNextCustomerName() ;
while ( custName != null  ) {
    //Loop Body executes here

    //Get another customer
    custName = getNextCustomerName() ;
}
```

For the purposes of this example, assume that getNextCustomerName is a method that returns an object representing a customer name or null if no name is available. Note that the method invocation is used to set the initial condition and to (eventually) change the condition.

Occasionally, you can encapsulate various processing details in methods and really streamline your code. One technique is to have a method return a boolean and to use that return value as a conditional in a loop. Your opinion, please:

```
while ( weHaveaCustomerName( )  ) {
     //Loop Body executes here
}


boolean WeHaveaCustomerName( ) {

  custName = getNextCustomerName() ;
      return( custName != null ) ;
}
```

Notice that the method WeHaveaCustomerName tends to the checking for null after the invocation of method GetNextCustomerName( ). This technique works with any programming language that enables you to code functions (code that returns a single value) or methods that can return boolean values. This technique will be used quite a bit in the longer examples of the book. Alas, poor COBOL programmer, this technique is not available to you.

One point worth noting—If the code that sets the initial condition sets that condition to be false, the loop body does not execute. In our small, previous example, this makes sense; if no name is fetched, there is no need to enter the loop.

Here are the analogues in mainframe programming languages:

```
*COBOL                           /*  PL/I */

* Code that sets condition       /*Code that sets condition */
 Perform With Test Before        Do While (aConditionIsTrue);
 Until NOT aConditionIsTrue.
*   Loop Body                       /* loop Body */
*   Code that changes             /*Code that changes
*   Condition                        condition*/
 End-Perform                      End ;
```

COBOL conditional testing is based on executing statements *until* a condition *becomes* true. In COBOL, if the condition is true, the statements in the perform group do not execute, hence, the use of the NOT operator.

Let's look at a different flavor of a Java conditional loop called a *do while* loop.

The Java do while Loop

This conditional loop is very similar to the *while* loop previously described. The syntactic difference is, of course, the use of the word *do;* the operational difference is the location of the testing of the condition. Java's do while loop tests the condition at *the bottom of the loop.*

Here is the basic layout of Java's do while loop:

```
do {
   One or more statements that constitute the loop body

   One or more statements setting and eventually changing
       the value of aConditionIsTrue
}
while ( aConditionIsTrue ) ;
```

Note that you still need some code to set and change the value of the condition used to govern the loop's execution. Also, there is no hard and fast rule about the placement of the condition setting code relative to the loop body.

You see, perhaps, the most important difference between the while and do while loops, right? Once you read that the do while loop tests the condition at the bottom, it was pretty obvious. This difference is that a *do while loop must execute at least once*, whereas a *while loop may never execute at all*. This difference governs when you should use a while loop versus a do while loop.

The PL/I and COBOL analogues to Java's do while loop are shown in the following:

```
*COBOL                          /* PL/I */


Perform With Test After          Do Until
     Until NOT aConditionIsTrue.     (^aConditionIsTrue);
*   Loop Body                    /* Loop Body */
*   Code that changes            /* Code that changes
*       Condition                        Condition */
End-Perform.                     End ;
```

Note: The use of the NOT operators in each language to create an equivalent construct to Java's do while looping construct.

Interrupting the Normal Processing of Loops

In general, processing enters code blocks in loops from the to and exits from the bottom. However, Java gives you the capability to code exits from the middle, or anywhere, inside a loop. Java contains two statements that support premature loop ejection: *break* and *continue* statements.

The break Statement

You have already seen the break statement used in switch statements. You may not have guessed that break statements may also be used in loops. In a general sense, the break statement transfers the program's flow of control out of the currently executing block *as long as that block is in a loop or switch statement*. As with the switch statement, the break statement causes Java to leave the currently executing loop and pick up execution at the first statement after the loop. A simple example should suffice:

```
int idx ;
for (idx = 5; idx < someString.length; idx++ ) {
    if (idx == 7)
        break ;

    System.out.println( "Inside the Loop " + idx ) ;
}
System.out.println( "Outside the loop = " + idx ) ;
```

Well, assuming that someString has more than six characters, Java will encounter the break statement inside this loop. Once encountered, program control flow exits the loop and continues at the first statement outside the loop. Therefore, this little code snippet will produce the following output:

```
Inside the Loop 5
Inside the Loop 6
Inside the Loop 7
Outside the Loop 7
```

When you place a break statement inside nested loops, the break statement will cause program control to exit from the inner loop to the statement after, in the outer loop. Assuming the outer loop will execute, your program will enter your inner loop again. The following example shows this:

```
int aIdx, bIdx ;
for (aIdx = 5; aIdx < 7; aIdx++ ) {
    System.out.println( "Outer loop = " + aIdx ) ;
    for (bIdx = 10; bIdx < 15; bIdx++ ) {
        if (bIdx == 12)
            break ;
    System.out.println("Inner loop = " + bIdx ) ;
    }

}
```

The output follows:

```
Outer loop 5
Inner loop 10
Inner loop 11
Outer loop 6
Inner loop 10
Inner loop 11
```

The continue Statement

Another Java statement enabless a program to sidestep normal loop processing. The *continue* statement, when executed, causes the program's flow of control to go to the bottom of the loop. REXX programmers who are familiar with the REXX Iterate statement will immediately understand how to use Java's continue statement. The following shows how the continue statement acts with Java's three different loop types:

When used in *for* loops, the continue statement transfers the flow of control to the loop bottom. From the bottom, the program flow heads to the *for* statement, where the increment expression is evaluated, the test is made, and, if successful, the body of the loop executes.

When used in *while* loops, the continue statement transfers the flow of control to the loop bottom. From there, program flow heads to the top of the loop where the condition in the while statement is still true; remember—the continue statement caused your program to skip past the code in the loop that could have changed the value of the loop conditional. Hence, the continue statement in a while loop will cause the loop body to execute.

When used in *do while* loops, the continue statement causes the same result as being used in *while* loops.

Here is another way of looking at the continue statement:

```
//Using the continue Statement          Not Using Continue
for ( int a=5;  a<10;  a++){             for (int a=5;a<10; a++) {
     if (a == 8) continue ;              if (a != 8) {
//Remainder of the loop                  //Remainder of the
//body is here                           //loop body is here
}                                        }
                                         }
```

It looks a bit cleaner to use the continue statement. What do you think?

Enough about loops, okay? Next, you'll read about the terribly exciting topic of decision constructs.

Java Decision Constructs

Java decision constructs fall into two categories: *if* statements and *switch* statements. Let's examine these statements in turn.

Java if Statements

Java if statements are identical to C if statements. However, you would rather know how similar Java if statements are to COBOL or PL/I if statements. You should find this out for yourself. Here is a basic template for a Java if statement:

```
if ( aConditionIsTrue ) {
    // Execute this block of statements when condition is true
}
else {
    // Execute this block of statements when condition is false
}
```

Notice the absence of the word *then* in the construct. Notice, and remember—no *then* in Java if statements.

Of course, you realize that the *else* clause is optional. You also realize that if you want to execute only one statement after the if or else, the block brackets are not necessary.

You also realize that you can nest if statements as follows:

```
if ( aConditionIsTrue ) {
    // Execute this block of statements when aCondition is true
}
else
if (bConditionIsTrue ) {
    // Execute this block of statements when bCondition is true
}
if (cConditionIsTrue ) {
    // Execute this block of statements when cCondition is true
}
```

Remember the oddball *ternary* operator? Can you see how this operator can take the place of constructs like the following?

```
//Simple if Construct Assigning a          Ternary Operator
//Variable One of Two Values               That Does The Same Thing

if ( aConditionIsTrue )                     aVar = aConditionIsTrue
    aVar = valueA ;                          ? valueA: valueB ;
else
    aVar = valueB ;
```

You think there is a place for the ternary operator in your Java programming bag of tricks?

Java if statements behave much like COBOL and PL/I if statements. There isn't much left to add about if/else statements. You've seen them before and you'll see them again. Remember to choose the correct logical operator—the *conditional* versus the *boolean* operators to form your conditions.

Java switch *Statements*

Java supports a construct that enables your code to test a variable's value against a list of values. You can use a series of if/else statements as follows:

```
if (sysCode == 'A')          //You remember that == is the
    doAMeth() ;              //compare operator, right?
else
if (sysCode == 'B')
    doBMeth() ;
else
if (sysCode == 'C')
    doCMeth() ;
else
if (sysCode == 'D')
    doDMeth() ;
else
    doEMeth() ;
```

You've seen this sort of stuff before, right? You, of course, would never code anything so crass. You'd use a *case* construct. In COBOL, the case construct is called an *Evaluate* statement; in PL/I, the case construct is called the *Select* statement. Java's implementation of the case construct is called the *switch* statement. Listing 6.1 shows how it looks.

Well, it looks like all the ingredients for a case construct are present. The *default* option—the last option coded in the Java switch statement—is a catch all category. However, the Java switch statement has *break* statements after every option.

The Java switch statement has a couple of unexpected surprises. First of all, you need a *break* statement after each choice or Java will *fall into the other choices*. For example, without the previous break statements, all of the methods, doA through doE, would be invoked *regardless of the value of sysCode*.

When Java hits a break statement, control transfers to the first statement after the switch closing curly brace. That said, the case will sometimes occur when you may want the code in your switch statement to fall through. In other words, you may not want to code a break statement for one or more options. Let's say you want the same action(s) to take place when a variable is any one of three values. You could code your switch statement as follows:

```
switch (aVar) {
    case  val1:
    case  val2:
    case  val3:
        TakeSomeAction( aVar ) ;
        break ;
    default:
        ;
}
```

Also, notice the null statement in the default option. If you can't think of anything to code for a default, the null Java statement often fits the bill.

Another unexpected surprise, especially for a modern programming language, is the limited functionality of the switch statement. Java's switch statement can only use

JAVA

```java
switch( sysCode )
{
case 'A':
    doAMeth();
    break ;
case 'B':
    doBMeth();
    break;
case 'C':
    doCMeth();
    break;
case 'D':
    doDMeth();
    break;
default:
    doEMeth();
}
```

COBOL

```cobol
Evaluate
When SysCode = 'A'
    Perform doAMeth
    Thru   doAMeth-Exit.
When ('B')
    Perform doBMeth
    Thru   doBMeth-Exit.
When SysCode = 'C'
    Perform doCMeth
    Thru   doCMeth-Exit.
When SysCode = 'D'
    Perform doDMeth
    Thru   doDMeth-Exit.
When Other
    Perform doEMeth
    Thru   doEMeth-Exit.
End-Evaluate.
```

PL/I

```pli
Select (SysCode);
When ('A')
    Call doAMeth();
When ('B')
    Call doBMeth();
When ('C')
    Call doCMeth();
When ('D')
    Call doDMeth();
Otherwise
    Call doEMeth();
End ;
```

Listing 6.1   Case constructs in several programming languages.

values that are castable to integers. For example, if I wanted to compare a variable's value to a floating point number, I would have to use a series of nested if/elses. Java's switch statement can't cope with nonintegral values. Before you comment on the previous example shown in Listing 6.1 using characters in a Java switch statement, recall that Java treats characters as integers.

Note that you do not need to surround the statements after the *case* keyword with braces. Yes, it certainly looks strange considering that braces are used everywhere else when more than one statement is executed as a block. You could use the curly braces if you wish; javac will accept the code, but you don't have to use the braces.

Unfortunately and regrettably, the only operator allowable in the Java switch statement when comparing the variable's value is equality. For example, this PL/I Select statement has no direct Java switch statement analogue:

```
Select ;
    When ( RetirementMoney < 150000 &  Age > 40 )
          Put Skip List( 'You're running out of time') ;
    When ( RetirementMoney > 1500000 & Age > 40 )
          Put Skip List( 'Whatcher waiting for?' ) ;
    When ( RetirementMoney > 2000000 & Age > 70 )
          Put Skip List( 'Old Folk Sure Have All the Fun!' ) ;
    Otherwise
          Put Skip List( 'Get back to Work' ) ;
End ;
```

You would code if/elses to mimic this functionality in Java.

The Java switch statement is a construct of limited functionality with quirks that betray Java's C heritage. However, even with limited functionality, you'll be coding many switch statements. Remember to put in that default option; the braces to group code after each option are not required.

In Summary

You've read much in this chapter. You've read about Java's bizarre operators, the likes of which have never been seen in the mainframe world. You've read about the essentials of busting Java code—the big three statement types: assignment statements, loop statements, and decision statements. You've even learned a quirk or two about Java.

This chapter is only one of a book containing 26. You've read so much about Java. At this point, you see that despite the hype hysteria and hoopla, Java is a programming language. Subsequent chapters will deal with the object-oriented nature of Java. However, you cannot exploit Java's OO properties without an understanding of the material in this chapter.

After all, how can you write any methods unless you know how to code the big three?

CHAPTER 7

Class and Object Representation

Java's Object/Class representation, arguably the heart of any object-oriented language, is discussed in this chapter. You'll read about the makeup of a Java method, the contents of a Java class, and how to create objects from classes. Also, you'll see how to code methods, which is the meat and potatoes of implementing object behavior. Along the way, you'll read a thing or two about Java packages.

Anatomy of a Java Method

In Chapter 3, "Creating Your First Java Program," you've seen the main() method, chock full of Java keywords. In general, Figure 7.1 shows what a method header looks like.

Not shown in Figure 7.1 is the *method body*, which is responsible for implementing the behavior the method is to model.

You'll read a brief description of some keywords here and a not-so-brief description later in the chapter.

Visibility Modifiers

Java enables you to dictate what other members (methods, classes, and packages) can access or use your methods by coding an optional *visibility modifier*. The following descriptions in Table 7.1 apply to any member type (method, class, and package) declared with the modifier. At most, You can code one visibility modifier per member. Table 7.1 lists your choices.

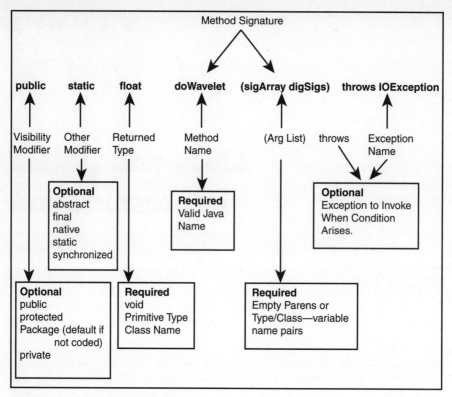

Figure 7.1 A Java method header.

Table 7.1 Visibility Modifier Overview

VISIBILITY MODIFIER	CAN BE SEEN (USED) BY:
public	Every class of your application (the world)
protected	The package (if one exists) that holds the class containing the member, the class containing the member, and all subclasses of the class containing the member
Default Package Visibility (not coded)	The package (if one exists) that holds the class containing the member and the class containing the member.
private	Every method or class within the class containing the member.

Here's the short story on when to use which visibility modifier.

- Use *public* when you want free and unfettered access to the member. Period.

- Use *protected* when you want to keep classes from changing data in the member and you want subclasses (Chapter 9, "Inheritance" explores subclasses further) to have full access to the member.

- Use the *default package visibility* (do not code a visibility modifier) if you want only the members in the package or class containing the member to have free and unfettered access.

- Use *private* when you want the only methods in the class containing the member to access the member.

You'll return to visibility modifiers in Chapter 8, "Encapsulating and Hiding Data and Methods," when you read about data hiding and encapsulation (big word!).

Other Modifiers

Java enables you to declare an additional modifier. These modifiers cannot be lumped into a single category like the visibility modifiers. As with the visibility modifiers, these other modifiers apply to classes and, sometimes, variables and methods. You may code more than one of these modifiers, at times, for the same member. Here's the list:

An *abstract* method is a method that *contains no body*; an *abstract* class contains one or more abstract methods. You'll explore abstract classes in Chapter 9.

A *final* method is one that *cannot be overridden*, a *final* class cannot be subclassed, and a *final* variable cannot be changed (constant declaration). The final modifier is the opposite of the abstract modifier. Again, you'll read more about the final modifier in Chapter 9.

A *native* method is implemented in some other programming language (usually the C programming language).

A *static* method is a method that models some behavior applicable to the class as a whole; a *static* variable is a variable that represents a property applicable to the class as a whole. You'll read more about static methods and variables in this chapter.

A *synchronized* method, class or code block (code between curly braces) causes the runtime to lock referenced objects to prevent other processes, or *threads* from changing them. Threads are discussed in Chapter 12, "Exception Handling and Thread Basics."

Returned Types Coded in Method Headers

Java methods may or may not return a value. The classical distinction in procedural programming is of a function that returns a value and a subroutine that does not. If your Java method does not explicitly return data using a *return* statement, you must code *void* in the function header. If your Java method uses a *return* statement, you must code the primitive data type or the class of the data item being returned.

Method Names and Argument Lists

A Java method name can be a string of practically any length not containing spaces and not beginning with a number. Typically, method names should be verbs that denote some action, indicative of what they do; whereas variable names should be nouns, indicative of what they are.

An Argument list, if present, is a comma delimited list of Primitive Type/Class-variable name pairs. If the method does not require an argument, you must code a pair of empty parenthesis. The variable names used in the Type/Class-name pairs have meaning only within the method. Think of these argument variables as local to the method.

As an aside, Java passes arguments of primitive types by *value* and arguments of objects by *internal reference*. The long and the short of it is that for primitive type arguments, Java passes a *copy* of the argument to the method. Therefore, the method is free to make changes to primitive type arguments and these changes will not be made to the corresponding parameters in the calling method. In contrast, for object arguments, Java passes a *reference* of the argument to the method. Therefore, if the method changes the argument object, the changes will be made to the corresponding parameter in the calling method. That's why objects in Java are also known as *reference types*.

The throws Exception-Name Option in Method Headers

Chapter 12 discusses exceptions. For now, know that a method may include an optional *throws exception-name* option, which specifies that if a coded class of exceptional condition(s) arise, the condition trickles up to an error handler, where (hopefully) you've written code to tend to the condition.

Passing by Reference and Passing by Value

Let's face it; a program written in a procedural language is a coupled collection of procedures acting independently on data in various formats. Each procedure does one of three things to a piece of data: gets it into the system, transforms the data into some other data, and gets the data out of the system. The issue is how do you, the long suffering and humble programmer, ensure that these procedures act only on the data you want to be acted on, and no other?

The nature of programming languages used in the mainframe world, with their representative typing scheme, is an accident waiting to happen. Procedures in these languages will accept any data as long as the passed data bears a resemblance to the correct parameters. Many programmers get into trouble because they may not fully understand how parameters are passed to subprograms. In other words, you can pass parameters to a subprogram with the intent of having that subprogram change the parameter value, thereby making the changed value known in the calling routine. Conversely, you can pass data to a subprogram with the intent of not changing the parameter value. The terms used to describe these mechanisms are passing parameters by *reference* and passing parameters by *value*.

You've read about these mechanisms in Chapter 2, "What is Java?"; no need to rehash the information. What needs to be said here is that Java passes arguments of primitive types by *value* and arguments of reference types by *reference*. Hence, the code snippet:

```
int aNum = 10 ;
doit( vStack, aNum ) ;
System.out.println( "aNum = " + aNum ) ;

static void doit( VectorStack aStack, int aNumber ) {
    aNumber++ ;
VectorStack.pushTheStack( aStack, "A Stack Element" );
}
```

would list aNum = 10. The value of the parameter aNum is *not* changed in the method; the method operates on a copy of the parameter. However, because the argument aStack is not a primitive type, the invocation of the method called pushTheStack() inside method doit() changes the object.

A Word or Two about Java Packages

A Java *package* is a construct that contains related classes and other Java entities. Packages have two important traits. One trait is that every method contained within has a *unique name*. Figure 7.2 shows how you name methods with packages to get this absolute uniqueness.

The first method name comes from the Java class library; the second is a method name thought up by DigVidIncLtd. Every word to the left of the *class name* is deemed to be the package name. In the case of DigVidIncLtd, their Web site is http://DigVidIncLtd. org, which is guaranteed to be unique. Hence, the method name is unique.

How do you make these methods known to your program? You need to direct your system to look on a directory (local or remote) where the desired package resides. Then you code the method name, package and all, or use the Java *import* statement. Look at the following:

```
public MyClass {
  //Java statements
  void myMethod() {
    //Java statements
    org.DigVidIncLtd.RandD.frequencyTransform.fourier(aFrame);
```

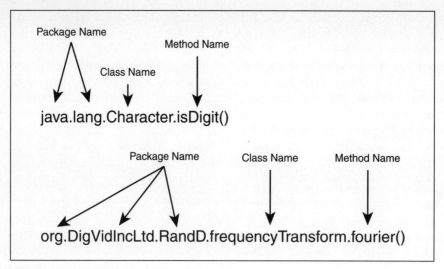

Figure 7.2   Guaranteeing unique method names.

This is what you expected, right? All you do is refer to the method name. The Java compiler and runtime are responsible for locating the package, with a little help from you.

The import Statement

As straightforward as the previous is, no true, red-blooded Java programmer would enter such a long method name. If all you need is one method from the package, well, maybe. However, if you need several, you could wear out your fingers with all that typing. Fortunately, Java provides a mechanism for dealing with this problem: the *import* statement.

The import statement merely provides a shorthand for referencing entities from packages. Take a look at Listing 7.1.

The import statement does not "bring in" any code to your program. The import statement does not behave like a COBOL COPY or PL/I %Include statement. You can have zero to many import statements. The presence or absence of import statements has no effect on your program's size or execution speed.

The difference between the two forms shown in Listing 7.1 is that the first one enables the program to use shorthand to access any class in the package, whereas the second form enables the program to use shorthand only for the named class. Understand that you can *always* code the fully qualified method name.

Some say that you should use the second form to clearly show where your classes are coming from. Sounds like good advice. Now, if you're using 15 or so classes from one package, I'm sure the Java style police aren't going to bust you for using the first

```
import org.DigVidIncLtd.RandD.* ;
//or import org.DigVidIncLtd.RandD.frequencyTransform ;

public MyClass {
  //Java statements
  void myMethod() {
    //Java statements
    frequencyTransform.fourier( aFrame );
```

Listing 7.1   Using the import statement to refer to a method in a package.

form. As a programmer who has picked up someone else's code from time to time (we all have, right?) and wished the code were better documented, you should appreciate every little mechanism provided by the environment and programming language to document things. End of editorial comment.

What is the other important trait? Package names mirror the directory where they are stored. This mirroring is partly how the Java compiler and runtime can find the package. Using our previous examples, there would be a subdirectory structure *java\lang* (UNIX), *java/lang* (Windows), or *java:lang* (Mac) within a group of directories called the *Classpath*.

The package Statement

You can (and should) group related classes into *packages*. Look, if it's good enough for the developers of Java, it's good enough for you. It's pretty easy to create a package. All you do is put your (hopefully) related classes in one source code file and code a *package* statement as the first line in the file. To wit:

```
package myPackageName ;

class MyClass1 {
/** methods, etc. for MyClass1 **/
}
public class MyClass2 {
/** Ditto **/
}
class MyClass3 {
/** Get the idea? **/
}
```

Note the absence of a curly brace; just what you see previously, okay? You can use whatever package name that will guarantee uniqueness.

One caveat—recall from the previous that the package name must reflect the actual directory structure where the file is stored. Therefore, pay heed to your package name and where you put the compiled package. Java will look along the directory structure mandated by your package name.

Here's where the visibility modifiers come in handy. If you want classes and methods coded in a package to be visible outside the package, you must remember to use the *public* visibility modifier on those classes. Now, when you use an import statement like the following:

```
import myPackageName.* ;
```

You'll import only those classes with the public modifier.

When you compile a source file with a package statement, Java creates a directory structure that mimics the package name. Compiling the previous example would create a directory called *myPackageName*. Inside the directory would be the class files MyClass1.class, MyClass2.class, and MyClass3.class.

Anatomy of a Java class

Recall that a class is a template used to create objects that have the same behavior but different properties. Every Java source code file compiles into a *class file*. Put differently, class files represent the platform-neutral bytecode you've heard so much about.

Every Java class is a subclass of class *Object*. In other words, class Object is the *root class*. The upshot of every class being a subclass of Object is that methods defined in class Object are available to each and every Java class. You'll read about the Object class, and how Java implements subclasses and implements Inheritance in Chapter 9.

Because a single Java class could be an entire application, you could find many Java software elements, or *members*, inside a class. Table 7.2 lists what you could find in a typical Java class.

Let's describe each of these members in more detail.

Constructor Methods and Instance Variables

When you create an object (instantiate the object) from a class, just what happens? In short, the created object acquires behaviors from the class (the methods) and some piece of user code imbues the object with properties (the data). Generally, the data from one object is what distinguishes it from another of the same class (of course, two identical objects could have the same data but different names, but that's why the preceding sentence began with "generally").

In Java, you can accomplish the previous by coding and invoking a *constructor method*. Let's take a look at Listing 7.2.

Before you think you are straying from a description of the items in Table 7.1, fear not. In Listing 7.2, the variables *autoName*, *modelYearYYYY*, and *retailValue* are *Instance*

Table 7.2 Class Member One-Liner Descriptions

A. Members That Are Used with Objects Instantiated from the Class

Constructor Methods	Used to implement some custom object creation process.
Instance Variables	Used to hold data that describes some property that may be unique to the object
Instance Methods	Used to implement some behavior that is usually common to all objects instantiated from the class
Finalizer Methods	Used to detach resources held by some objects that cannot be released by the system
Inner Classes	Used to create objects that are wholly contained within other objects, code blocks, or methods

B. Members That Are Used to Describe or Implement Some Behavior Peculiar to the Class

Class Variables	Used to hold data that describes some property of the class
Class Methods	Used to implement some behavior peculiar to the class as a whole
Static Blocks	Used to implement some initialization for the class
Nested Top-Level Class	Used to group related classes within the class together

Variables. These variables are present with every *instance* of class Automobile. Put differently, every object from class Automobile has the properties autoName, model YearYYYY, and retailValue.

When you create an object from class Automobile, you can provide values for these properties by invoking a *constructor method*. Note the following properties of the constructor method, shared by constructor methods, shown in Listing 7.2:

- The constructor method name is *always* the same as the class name.
- The constructor method cannot have a *return* statement.

More often than not, constructor methods have *public* visibility. You'll read more about visibility modifiers later in this chapter. For now, a member declared with public visibility means that the member can be accessed by any class in the application.

How do you create an object? You call its constructor. And, pray tell, how is that done? Well, you invoke the constructor with the *new* operator. Behold and learn in Listing 7.3.

Once the bolded statement in Listing 7.3 executes, the object myCar has its instance variables set to the values passed to the constructor. Also, any methods defined in class Automobile are now a part of the object myCar.

```
//Here is our class . . . .
public class Automobile {
    String     autoName ;
    int        modelYearYYYY ;
    /** Other variables relevant to a particular Automobile **/
    int        retailValue;
    /**  Other variables, methods, any or all of the stuff
         listed in Table 7.1 **/
/**  Here is a constructor method **/
public Automobile( String aName,
                int     aYear,
                 /**Other args for other vars **/
                int   aValue){
    autoName       =      aName ;
    modelYearYYYY =       aYear ;
    /**    Other variables relevant to an Automobile
           object set here **/
    retailValue =      aValue ;
}
}
```

Listing 7.2   A class with a constructor method.

```
public class someClass {
    //Create an object of class Automobile
    Automobile myCar = new Automobile("Rolls Royce Silver Ghost",
                                   1942,
                                   /** Other Parms **/
                                   87500 ) ;

    }
```

Listing 7.3   Invoking a constructor method.

To refer to the instance variables for a particular object, you prefix the instance variable name with that of the object. For example, to reference the value of the object created previously, you would code:

```
myCar.retailValue
```

There's more to say about constructor methods. You could have more than one constructor method for objects of the same class. Before you ask why you would want multiple constructors, first take a look at Listing 7.4 to see how you code multiple constructors.

```
/**    Here is another constructor method **/
public Automobile( String aName,
                   int     aYear,
                   /**Other args for other vars **/
                   ){
    autoName       =        aName ;
    modelYearYYYY  =        aYear ;
    /**      Other variables relevant to an Automobile
             object set here **/
    retailValue    =        0 ;

}
```

Listing 7.4 Another constructor method.

This constructor has the same name as the first. Also, you would code the second constructor in the same source file as the first. How can Java tell them apart?

You see that the *signatures* of the two constructors differ, don't you? The second constructor does not take retailValue as a parameter; the car is probably too old and not worth selling. The second constructor assigns a blue book value of 0 to all Automobiles created with this constructor.

There's *still* more to say about constructor methods. You don't have to code one, you know. The skinny is that if you don't, Java will use a default constructor with no arguments. However, most objects will require some sort of initial data, which means that you'll need a "real" constructor of some sort. The default constructor insures that every class has a constructor, although the default constructor doesn't do much.

Another point about constructors is that you cannot invoke a constructor method apart from creating an object. Too bad, because such a capability could prove useful if you needed to reinitialize an object. Perhaps in a future release.

Believe it or not, there's *still* more to say about constructors, but you'll have to wait until Chapter 9, where you read about superclasses and subclasses.

By the way, Java does not require you to code anything to destroy an object. Some programming languages (C++ comes to mind) require you to code *destructor* methods to remove unused objects, thereby reclaiming the memory for subsequent use. Java's *garbage collection* does this reclaiming for you. In short, Java's memory management keeps track of object use and destroys those objects not in use. If you had to write code to free memory by destroying objects yourself, you know what a relief it is to have the runtime do this unpleasant, error-prone task for you?

Back to the subject of creating objects, you may think that you can create an object the same way as you create a variable of a primitive data type. Why not just declare the object with the class name as the object's type, as follows?

```
Automobile someonesCar ;
```

Truth be told, you could code the previous and Java would successfully compile. However, you have not created an object from class Automobile! What you've done is create a *reference* for an object of class Automobile.

Let's step back. No, we're not splitting hairs here. A huge difference between the object and the reference to the object exists. Think of the difference between a variable and a pointer to the variable (although, as you know, Java doesn't enable the programmable use of pointers). Take a look at the code in Listing 7.5 and anticipate the output.

Class Demo1 has a main() method, so we can run this and get output. Note the use of the constructor method to create the object named *yourCar*. Seems you're riding fancy these days. Looking at line //1. You see that this statement does not use the constructor; this statement declares an *object reference* to aCar. Line // 2 *looks like* it assigns the contents of yourCar to aCar. In other words, both objects would seem to have the same data. Line // 3 changes the value of the *autoName* property of the aCar object, right? Thus, the output statements should list the autoName property values of both cars: "Dodge Stealth" and "Ford Fiesta," right?

Well, here's what's going on. While line // 2 is assigning the contents of yourCar to aCar, it is also assigning the *reference of yourCar* to the reference of aCar. Now, yourCar and aCar *reference the same object.* Along comes line // 3 to change the value of the autoName property of aCar *and yourCar*, because both names reference the same object. Now, when the output statements execute, you'll see:

```
You Drive a Ford Fiesta
The Other Car is a Ford Fiesta
```

So much for trading up!

Pop quiz: what if statement // 1 in Listing 7.5 were coded:

```
Automobile aCar = new Automobile("Buick", 1993, 3000) ;
```

```
public class Demo {
    public static void main(String[] args) {
        Automobile yourCar = new Automobile("Dodge Stealth",
                                    1999, 56500) ;
        Automobile aCar ;                     // 1
        aCar =  yourCar;                      // 2
        aCar.autoName = "Ford Fiesta" ;       // 3
        System.out.println( "You Drive a " +
                            yourCar.autoName ) ;
        System.out.println( "The Other Car is a " +
                            aCar.autoName ) ;
    }
}
```

Listing 7.5 A nasty shock!

The object aCar is now created with a "real" constructor. Would the output produced by the code in Listing 7.5 with the new line // 1 be now? If you thought that you'd be holding onto that fancy, fast Dodge Stealth, you'd be *wrong*. The behavior of the assignment of the object references on line // 2 does not change. The labels aCar and yourCar still point to the same object.

Do you recall that in Java, a string is an instance of class String? One consequence is that you cannot do what you think is obvious with strings. Listing 7.6 shows some innocent looking statements that behave in a counterintuitive manner.

Here's the output:

```
1 and 2 Equal Strings Hello There
1 and 3 Unequal Strings Hello There
```

What gives? The equality test does not compare the *contents* of the string objects; the equality test compares the *references* of the string objects. Now, Java is "smart" enough to reuse the storage allocated for string1 and string2. In essence, string1 and string2 are the *same object*. However, such is not the case for string1 and string3. Java sees the initialization of these string objects results in different strings and considers them *different objects*. However, when you change string3 to have the same *content* as string1, Java still considers them different objects. When you do the second compare, Java tells you that these string objects are, indeed, different.

Remember that Java variables declared of a primitive type behave as expected, or behave as variables from a procedural language. Java Objects, however, behave a bit differently.

A sober question is how would you assign the *contents* of one object to another of the same class but maintain the first object's reference?

```java
String   string1 = "Hello There" ;
String   string2 = "Hello There" ;
if ( string1 == string2)
    System.out.println("1 and 2 Equal Strings " + string2) ;
else
    System.out.println("1 and 2 UnEqual Strings " + string2 ) ;

String   string3 = "Hello " ;
String3  = string3 + "There"
if ( string1 == string3 )
    System.out.println("1 and 3 Equal Strings " + string3) ;
else
    System.out.println("1 and 3 Unequal Strings " + string3) ;
```

Listing 7.6 You know what will happen, right?

Instance Methods

In truth, Java provides a mechanism for assigning objects to one another by using a *clone* method in the java.lang.Object class. However, by showing different approaches to rolling your own assignment method, you will read about the different method types available to you. So, without any further ado . . .

One solution to the previous question is to code a method like the one in Listing 7.7.

You see the logic here, right? We sidestep the assignment operator that, for objects, assigns references by assigning the object properties. The *void* keyword tells Java that this method does not return a value.

Where do you put the method? You could put this method in class Automobile, under the constructor method. Listing 7.8 shows the code for class Automobile.

Coding the assignTo() method in class Automobile makes this new method part of the "template" for the class. Objects instantiated from class Automobile will have this new method as part of their behavior. Put differently, this new method is an *Instance method*.

Now, how do you use this assignTo() method? Let's look at the Demo class with a change in Listing 7.9 that answers the aforementioned question.

Well, this certainly looks good except for one small detail: The code in Listing 7.9 *will not compile*. The reason occurs because the assignTo() method, an instance method, *is not attached to an object*. Java expects an object to go along with this method. Therefore, either of the following statements will satisfy the compiler:

```
yourCar.assignTo( yourCar, aCar );
```

```
aCar.assignTo( yourCar, aCar );
```

Now, Java is able to properly reference the method and execute the statements within.

Soon, you'll see other, better ways of implementing this assignTo() method. Before you check out other ways, here's another example of an instance method. The behavior you need to implement is to determine if a particular automobile is overpriced given its retail value, name, and model year. Assume the existence of a class called *BlueBook* that has routines that return a car's blue book value based on model year and

```
void assignTo( Automobile src, Automobile tgt) {

        tgt.autoName     = src.autoName ;
        tgt.modYear      = src.modYear ;
        tgt.retailValue = src.retailValue ;
}
```

Listing 7.7 A method that assigns one car object to another.

```
public class Automobile {
    String      autoName ;
    int         modelYearYYYY ;
    /** Other variables relevant to a particular Automobile **/
    int         retailValue;

    public Automobile( String aName,
                       int     aYear,
                       /**Other args for other vars **/
                       int     aValue){
        autoName      =       aName ;
        modelYearYYYY =       aYear ;
        /**     Other variables relevant to an Automobile
                object set here **/
        retailValue       =         aValue ;
    }
    /** Assign one Automobile to another **/
void assignTo( Automobile src, Automobile tgt) {

    tgt.autoName       = src.autoName ;
    tgt.modYear        = src.modYear ;
    tgt.retailValue = src.retailValue ;
    }
}
```

Listing 7.8   The assignTo() method in class Automobile.

```
public class Demo {
    public static void main(String[] args) {
        Automobile yourCar = new Automobile("Dodge Stealth",
                                             1999, 56500) ;
        Automobile aCar new Automobile("Buick", 1993, 3000);

        assignTo( yourCar, aCar );
        aCar.autoName = "Ford Fiesta" ;
        System.out.println( "You Drive a " +
                               yourCar.autoName ) ;
        System.out.println( "The Other Car is a " +
                               aCar.autoName ) ;
    }
}
```

Listing 7.9   Problem solved?

make. Your method compares the blue book value with the retailPrice property to determine the car's "overpriced" status. Call the method *isCarOverpriced()*.

You can see that the previous method would be peculiar to each object from class Automobile, right? The data required to make this determination for each car comes from that car (and from method(s) in class BlueBook). A possible implementation is demonstrated in Listing 7.10.

Place this code in the source file for the Automobile class. Notice that the method returns a boolean, indicating whether or not the car is overpriced. Also notice the invocation of the method getBlueBookValue from class BlueBook; the method name is prefixed with the class name. You'll read more about such methods soon.

To invoke this method to determine if, say, the yourCar object is overpriced, you code:

```
yourCar.isCarOverpriced ( yourCar ) ;
```

Yes, this does work. However, a hard look at the syntax reveals the clumsiness of the solution. This invocation requires your coding a reference to the yourCar object twice: once as a prefix for the method (because it is an instance method) and once as an argument to the method. Java, a modern language, should be able to do better, right?

this—A Special Keyword

Because the previous invocation specifically calls the method belonging to object your-Car, you should not have to tell Java *again* that you want to use the yourCar object as an argument. Java gives you a way of referring to the object whose method is being invoked within the body of the method. You use the reserved Java keyword *this* to refer to the object. Take a look at Listing 7.11.

Notice the changes. You no longer need the argument because Java knows that the reserved keyword *this* refers to the object belonging to the method being invoked, or the *current object*. Now, the invocation of isCarOverpriced() becomes:

```
yourCar.isCarOverpriced( ) ;
```

Looks better, right? Of course, the reserved word *this* must be used in the body of an instance method.

```
boolean isCarOverpriced( Automobile aCar) {
  int blueBookValue =
  BlueBook.getBlueBookValue( aCar.autoName,
  aCar.modYear ) ;
  return blueBookValue < aCar.retailValue ;
  }
```

Listing 7.10 Instance method is CarOverpriced().

```
boolean isCarOverpriced( ) {

    int    blueBookValue    =
    BlueBook.getBlueBookValue( this.autoName,
                               this.modYear ) ;
    return blueBookValue < this.retailValue ;
}
```

Listing 7.11   Instance method isCarOverpriced() revisited.

```
public Automobile( String aName,
      int    aYear,
      /**Other args for other vars **/
              int    aValue){
    // Call the two-arg constructor in Listing 7.4
    this( aName, aYear ) ;
}
```

Listing 7.12   Another permitted use of *this*.

Another point about using *this*: You may code *this* on the *first statement* of a constructor to invoke another constructor. See Listing 7.12, for example.

Yes, such a construct is not too useful, but Java permits it.

Do you recall the comment about implementing the assignTo() method in a "better" way than as an instance method? Let's explore that now. Using *this*, you can recode the assignTo() method as in Listing 7.13.

Notice the use of *this* to refer to the current object. Also notice that this method has a return value: an object of class Automobile.

Now, to invoke this method, you code:

```
aCar = yourCar.assignTo() ;
```

Other ways to code assignTo exist. Let's look at them now.

Class Methods

As you know, the term *method* is a piece of code that implements some behavior. The original object-oriented languages required that only classes had methods that they passed to their instantiated objects. However, experience has shown that forcing methods to be associated with objects is limiting in some regards. Could the class *as a whole*

```
Automobile assignTo( ) {

    Automobile target = new Automobile( this.autoName,
                                        this.modYear,
                                        this.retailValue ) ;

    return target ;
}
```

Listing 7.13   assignTo() revisited.

have some behavior that demands implementation? How about some behavior that requires data from *more than one object*? Shouldn't there be a straightforward way of implementing behaviors of an entire class or more than one object?

What a coincidence! The issue of assigning object contents deals with implementing a behavior that requires data from *two* objects. Perhaps this is one of those situations that is not well served by a method that should, in theory, require data from one object.

If you think about it, why should the assignTo() method be attached to a single object? As you've seen, we could have coded the method invocation with the prefix of any Automobile object.

In addition, the assignTo() method implements what car-like behavior? I never heard of a car "assigning" itself to another car. This is not what object-oriented programming is all about. Even though the coding of the assignTo() method works, we have higher standards, don't we?

What makes more sense is to think of the assignTo() method as a utility needed for applications that use objects of class Automobile. Can we have this method available to our application by not referencing this method from an object?

Yes, we can. We can code the assignTo() method to belong to the *class* Automobile, as opposed to *objects* of class Automobile. In JavaSpeak, methods that belong to a class are called *Class Methods*.

The change needed to change assignTo() from an instance method to a class method is pretty subtle. You still code the method within the class file. Listing 7.14 shows the class method assignTo().

Notice the presence of the word *static* in the Method header. A poor choice of a word, really, to describe its purpose. Static is a hangover from the land of C and PL/I programming. When a C or PL/I programmer declares a software entity as static, she tells the compiler to allocate memory for that object, as opposed to having the runtime allocate memory during program execution. This is *not* what the keyword static means in Java.

You can think of a class member declared as static as having only one instance or occurrence. Members belonging to objects have as many copies as there are objects.

```
static void assignTo( Automobile src, Automobile tgt) {

        tgt.autoName            = src.autoName ;
        tgt.modYear             = src.modYear ;
        tgt.retailValue         = src.retailValue ;
}
```

Listing 7.14 The class method assignTo().

The assignTo() method coded in Listing 7.10 has a single occurrence. So, how is this class method invoked? Like this:

```
Automobile.assignTo( yourCar, aCar ) ;
```

You saw the previous syntax coming, right? You invoke instance methods by prefixing the method name with a particular *object*; you invoke class methods by prefixing the method name with the *class name*. Sounds simple enough.

The piece of code in Listing 7.9 that fetches the Blue Book value is a class method of BlueBook. Here it is again, with the class name bolded:

```
int   blueBookValue   =
        BlueBook.getBlueBookValue(aCar.autoName, aCar.modYear) ;
```

Oddly, Java treats class methods as belonging to *every* object instantiated from the class. This is unfortunate; such usage clouds the purpose of the class method as being a property of the class as opposed to a property of the objects from the class. Here's an example of such usage:

```
yourCar.assignTo( yourCar, aCar ) ;

aCar.assignTo( yourCar, aCar ) ;
```

This usage is the same as that for instance methods. Java accepts this syntax for class methods, bowing to the treatment of class methods belonging to every object. Looking at the two previous invocations, you'd be hard pressed to know that assignTo() is a class method. You could (likely) believe that the application has a need to include the behavior implemented by the assignTo() method to objects. Looking at the invocation prefixed by the class name, you couldn't miss the fact that assignTo() is a class method.

Why confuse the issue? If you want to use a class method, make it easier on those long-suffering programmers that will follow in your codesteps by prefixing the method name with the class name. Regardless of how you invoke a class method, you'll have only one copy in your application.

Use a class method when the desired behavior does not apply to a particular object but to the class as a whole or to multiple objects. Use a class method when the implementation of said behavior requires data from multiple objects from the same class.

Use an instance method if the behavior applies to a particular object. Use an instance method when the implementation of said behavior requires data from a single object.

Finalizer Methods

Java, as you know, reclaims memory from unused, or dead, objects by using a garbage collection scheme. If you have a need to perform some activity between the time the garbage collector recognizes an object as garbage and the time the memory for that object is reclaimed, you can code a *finalizer method*. Some resources, such as file locks, may be held even after an object representing a file is garbage collected.

All finalizer methods must have this signature:

```
protected void finalize() throws Throwable
```

When you read about threads in Chapter 11, "Java Event Handling Basics," you'll revisit finalizer methods, but not that much—you won't use them all that much.

Class Variables

Objects have behaviors that are relevant to their being implemented as instance methods. Classes have behaviors that are relevant to the class as a whole implemented as class methods. Objects have properties that describe particulars about the object stored as instance variables. Classes have properties that describe particulars about the class as a whole stored as class variables.

For example, the number of cars in class Automobile is a property of the class, not any particular object. Java provides a mechanism for declaring variables that belong to the class. All you need do is use the *static* modifier. Look at Listing 7.15.

Notice that you can use the class name to reference the variable.

Yes, this works. Do any of you astute readers see a problem with this technique? Here's a hint: The problem is not with the declaring and use of the class variable in class Automobile; the problem is in the access of this variable in class Demo.

You'll revisit this situation of improper access of class and instance variables in the next chapter.

Static Blocks

Java enables you to code blocks of code that are not part of any method. Recall that a block is one or more statements enclosed in curly braces. To code blocks that do not belong to a method, merely affix the modifier *static* to the start of the block, as follows:

```
static {
    //Some code
}
```

```
Class Automobile {
   //Other Statements
        //Here is the Class Variable
   static int    numberOfCars = 0 ;
        /**   Here is a constructor method **/
        public Automobile( String    aName,
                           int        aYear,
                           int        aValue){
        autoName    =    aName ;
        modYear     =    aYear ;
        retailValue =    aValue ;
        // Tally up the new Automobiles
        numberOfCars++ ;
       }
       //Remainder of class Automobile
      }
     Class Demo {
        //Other Statements
        System.out.println( "Number of Cars = " +
                         Automobile.numberOfCars ) ;
        //Rest of class Demo
     }
```

Listing 7.15   An example of using and referencing a class variable.

The code must be inside a class (not between a package statement and a class or between two classes) and outside all methods.

Static blocks execute only once when the class loads. You cannot invoke static code like you would a static method. Indeed, if you need to invoke the code yourself, you cannot use static code.

Static code is good for initializations when you must guarantee that some activity relevant to the class takes place only once and at the start of the class load. Also, static code can access only static, or class, variables. Although instance variables are coded outside of any methods, these variables are still off-limits to static code blocks.

Nested Top-Level Classes and Inner Classes

The last topics on Table 7.2 are the *Nested Top-Level* and *Inner Classes*. Sometimes, you may find it convenient to include one class wholly within another. The nested top-level class mechanism enables you to declare a static class within another class. You may find using a nested top-level class a handy way of organizing significant data that is tightly coupled to the enclosing class. The only requirements for a nested top-level class are that you must use the enclosing class name when referring to objects of the nested top-level class outside of the enclosing class. For example:

```
class MainClass {
    //Statements
    static class NestedClass {
        //Variables, methods, etc - same old stuff
    }
    //Reference object of NestedClass within enclosing class
    void aMethod() {
        NestedClass objNestedClass = new NestedClass() ;
    }

} // of MainClass
```

Recall that everything you code in Java has to be contained within some class. Some feel that this requirement, not specific to Java, is a flaw with object-oriented programming. If you want to code an itty-bitty utility method, you need to create a class before coding the method inside this class. Of course, to use this utility, you need to ensure that this class can be located (on the CLASSPATH) when you compile.

Inner classes help you out here. You can code a class inside an existing class. The syntax depends on the type of inner class you want. In JavaSpeak, three types of inner classes exist: Member classes, Local classes, and Anonymous classes.

You code member classes like top-level nested classes except that you omit the *static* qualifier. Thus, member classes are associated with every instance of the enclosing class. Think of objects from the member class like other members associated with objects of the enclosing class. The inner class can reference members in its enclosing class. The enclosing class needs to declare objects from the member class before using the inner class methods.

Member classes are rarely required. These classes are often a convenience. The member classes are not visible outside the enclosing class.

Here's a sample declaration and invocation of a member class:

```
class MainClass {
    //Statements
    class MemberClass {
        //Variables, methods, etc - same old stuff
    }
    //Reference object of NestedClass within enclosing class
    void aMethod() {
        MemberClass objMemberClass = new MemberClass() ;
    }

} // of MainClass
```

Local classes are another type of inner class. The difference between a member class and a local class is that a local class is *defined within a method*. The common use for a local class is to implement some behavior for a graphical interface object. An anonymous class is a refinement of the local class. This form of inner class combines the class definition with an instantiation of the class.

You'll read about local and anonymous class usage in Chapter 11 on events.

In Summary

You've read much about how Java represents objects and classes. However, the best is yet to come. In the next chapter, you'll read about that infamous object property of encapsulation. In Chapter 9, you'll read about the nefarious object property of inheritance. That will pretty much describe how Java implements the object-oriented view of programming.

CHAPTER 8

Encapsulating and Hiding Data and Methods

This chapter explores Java's technique for data hiding by way of visibility modifiers. Java code samples showing the effects of declaring objects and variables with different visibility modifiers is included. Encapsulation goes hand in hand with data hiding, and this chapter has examples of objects with protected attributes accessible by interface code only. This too is a concept that may be unfamiliar to the reader.

This chapter also includes PL/I code that, at first glance, seems to implement encapsulation. This PL/I code is compared and contrasted to Java code that successfully encapsulates object properties and behaviors. The chapter ends with a discussion on get and set methods, which enable users of your classes to have controlled access to instance variables.

Encapsulation

Encapsulation. Quite a twenty-dollar word! For our uses, encapsulation is the mechanism that prevents a variable from one class to be inadvertently modified by a method in another class. Encapsulation is a major property of object-oriented programming in general, and Java programming in particular.

Think of a class as a capsule surrounding the classes' data and methods. This capsule shields the contents of your class from outside, prying eyes. You allow access to the data and methods in the class by coding a well-defined interface. In other words, programmers do not know how you've implemented your classes and, as a consequence, cannot rely on intimate, implementation details when accessing your classes' data. In addition, you are free to change the underlying class implementation without affecting how others access your class (this is where the well-defined interface comes into play).

This capsule offers protection against data being improperly changed and methods being illegally invoked. The strength of this capsule is directly proportional to the features of the programming language that support encapsulation. Put in the language of the systems analyst, the capsule binds related data and operations that imbue data with behavior into a highly cohesive object.

As you'll read soon, Java has all the essentials to firm up that capsule wall and gives you, the humble programmer, complete control over what code can touch or access your class.

Hand in hand with encapsulation is the concept of *data hiding*. Data hiding is the strategy for implementing an encapsulation mechanism. Essentially, data hiding enables you to protect data from changes by hiding this data from unauthorized classes. Sometimes, the terms encapsulation and data hiding are used interchangeably.

Why Encapsulate and Hide Your Data and Methods?

It's all about control.

The reason you want to encapsulate your classes is to give you *control* over who, what, and where your class is accessed. Given this control, you are free to change your classes' implementation without fear of breaking existing code. In addition, you can relax, knowing that someone *cannot* mistakenly change your object's data because you have enforced access to this data by way of a well-defined interface.

Before going into the details of how to encapsulate your classes and hide your data in Java, a few words on how data can be unwittingly and erroneously changed in a Java program are in order, and what Java features help prevent such unwanted changes.

Preventing Unwarranted Changes to Your Data

Preventing unwarranted changes to your data touches on a few issues: variable scoping, the parameter passing mechanism supported by the programming language, and the features available in the programming language to hide your data and encapsulate your classes. The first two items are issues to reckon with in procedural languages as well as Java.

Variable Scoping

Variable scoping is where a variable is known in a program. If a variable is known in a program, the value of the variable can be *changed*. At times, the variable is unknowingly or mistakenly changed by a piece of code that has no business making such changes.

In COBOL, variables global to the compile unit are truly the rule; in PL/I, local variables are actually the exception. A telling clue is that compilers in these languages have options to produce variable by statement number cross-reference listings because variables can be used (and changed) on practically any statement in the compile unit. For compile units consisting of thousands of lines of source, no practical way exists for a mere mortal to keep track of what gets accessed and changed where.

Naturally, a program unit changing variables throughout its 5,000 line code is quite the mess. Commonly, COBOL and PL/I applications used in today's data intensive industries contain anywhere from 100 to 1,000 such compile units; each compile unit contains hundreds of declared variables, swimming in a sea of code.

Maybe this explains the sky-high maintenance budgets of the legacy DP shop.

Limiting variable use, or limiting the *scope* of a variable, to a subprogram makes sense because now, a mere mortal can keep up with variable changes. Now, a particular variable, more properly scoped, can be changed on, say, 100 lines as opposed to 5,000 lines. If a problem in the application can be tracked down to a compile unit, these more properly scoped variables can, in all likelihood, be removed as suspects.

Java enforces variable and object scoping with the *block* construct. You've already read that by declaring a variable or object within a pair of curly braces, the block construct, you've limited the access to that variable or object to that block. The COBOL programmer has no blocking construct; the PL/I programmer has two.

Some scoping examples follow. Any thoughts on what Java would do with the code snippet in Listing 8.1?

Notice that the loop index variable is declared within the loop. As an aside, you recall that the brackets used in the loop are optional, right? Well, here's what the Java compiler, javac, has to say about this piece of code in Listing 8.2.

Notice that the variable idx is not known outside the loop. The lingo is that the reference to the variable idx *falls outside the variable's declared scope*. Javac will not report the diagnostic by referring to scope; javac just tells you it cannot locate a definition for the referenced variable.

```
public class ScopingExample {
    public static void main(String[] args) {

        for (int idx = 0; idx < 5; idx++ ) {
            System.out.println("idx Known in loop " + idx ) ;
        }
        System.out.println("idx Known in method " + idx ) ;


    }

}
```

Listing 8.1   What will Javac and Java do?

```
ScopingExample.java:8: Undefined variable: idx
               System.out.println("idx Known in method " + idx ) ;
                                                              ^
1 error
```

Listing 8.2 Javac's response.

```
Main: Proc (aStringArgument) Options( Main ) ;
     Dcl    aStringArgument   Char( 40 ) Varying ;

     Begin ;
          Dcl      idx       Fixed Bin(31) Init( 0 ) ;
          Do idx = 0 to 5 ;
               Put Skip List ("idx known in loop " || idx ) ;
          End ;
     End ;
     Put Skip List ("idx known in method " || idx ) ;
End Main ;
```

Listing 8.3 A PL/I version of the above Java code.

As a comparison, Listing 8.3 shows how you'd code the previous (well, close enough!) in PL/I.

As an aside, PL/I will compile this example and provide a default value and data type for the variable idx referenced outside the Begin block.

One more example is demonstrated in Listing 8.4.

This main() method has two separate variables named *idx*. Each variable is defined in a separate block; therefore, each variable has its own scope. Put differently, each variable is known (and can be changed in) different parts of the program.

Now, you don't have to be especially brilliant to realize that using the same variable name in differently scoped areas of the same method is, quite frankly, the mark of the amateur.

Pop quiz: How many blocks are present in Listing 8.4? This listing has **four** blocks: the block defined for the *class*, the block defined for the *main()* method, the block defined in the *for loop*, and the block defined by the interior curly *braces*.

The previous examples showed scoping of Java primitive type variables; the same scoping rules apply to objects, or reference data types as well.

```
public class ScopingExample {

    public static void main(String[] args) {

        for (int idx = 0; idx < 5; idx++ )
            System.out.println("idx Known in loop " + idx ) ;

        {//Block defines part of the method with unique scope
            int idx = 10 ;
            if  ( idx < 20)
                System.out.println("idx Known in if stmt " +
                    idx);
        }//End of the block
    }

}
```

Listing 8.4   Another example to show Java blocks and variable scoping.

Understanding the Parameter Passing Mechanism

You've read in Chapter 7, "Class and Object Representation," that Java passes primitive types to methods *by value* and passes reference types *by reference*. Here, we mention that by not understanding the difference, you can get into a lot of trouble. COBOL and PL/I each provide mechanisms for passing parameters by value *or* by reference; Java does not. Thus, make it a point to get the passing parameters by value and by reference thing straight and understand Java's parameter passing mechanism.

How Do You Encapsulate Your Classes in Java?

As you might well imagine, the benefits of encapsulation and data hiding do not miraculously happen. You have to use the features of the programming language to *make* it happen. Java, of course, has features to enable you to encapsulate your data and methods. Your job is to use the correct Java constructs in the correct ways.

That's what this chapter is all about.

Table 8.1   Java's Visibility Modifiers

VISIBILITY MODIFIER	CAN BE SEEN (USED) BY:
public	Every class of your application (the world)
protected	The package (if one exists) that holds the class containing the member, the class containing the member, and all subclasses of the class containing the member
Default Package Visibility (not coded)	The package (if one exists) that holds the class containing the member and the class containing the member
private	Every method or class within the class containing the member

The primary Java feature you'll use in your programs to encapsulate and hide your data is the *visibility modifier*. You've read a bit about these modifiers in Chapter 7. Here, you'll delve more deeply into this vitally important Java feature.

Table 8.1 shows Java's visibility modifiers once again.

You can qualify (or modify, if you prefer) a primitive type variable, an object, a method, or a class with a visibility modifier. Here's an example from Chapter 7. Here, notice that the visibility modifiers are **bolded**. The purpose of this dissertation is to illustrate how to encapsulate items in Java. The goal is to allow access to a stack by the approved methods: popTheStack and pushTheStack. We don't care *how* these methods work or what *other* methods are needed by the stack to get the job done. All we care about is popping and pushing.

Using Visibility Modifiers

Let's see if the class with the chosen visibility modifiers in Listing 8.5 does the trick.

What follows is a short explanation on choosing the bolded visibility modifiers.

If we assume that you want other classes to access objects of class VectorStack, then you need to declare the class VectorStack *public*. Usually, you'd make the class describing a useful data structure public so others can use it.

If you do not want any users of your class to determine if a stack is empty, you declare your isStackEmpty() method as a *private* method. Now, isStackEmpty() is known *only to the methods in your class*. Notice that your popTheStack() method first invokes the isStackEmpty() method before popping. Because method isStackEmpty() has use inside your class *and nowhere else*, the method should be declared private.

Methods popTheStack() and pushTheStack() have to be accessible by any class needing a stack. Thus, the proper visibility modifier for these methods is public.

The constructor method enables users of your class to create objects from your class. Seems logical that the constructor must be declared public. Oddly, using any visibility modifier other than private works here.

Now, if you've been paying attention, you might get this question correct: What is the proper visibility modifier for the data structure that implements objects of class

```
import java.util.* ;
/** Use the methods in class Vector to implement a stack. **/
public class VectorStack{
      //Possible Stack implementation.
      //Now, the methods . . . . . . .
      static private boolean isStackEmpty( VectorStack myStack ) {

            return myStack.aStack.isEmpty() ;
      }
      static public Object popTheStack (VectorStack myStack ) {
            Object        stackElement = null ;
            if (!isStackEmpty( myStack ) ) {
                  stackElement      = myStack.aStack.lastElement();
                  myStack.aStack.removeElement( stackElement ) ;
            }
            return stackElement ;
      }
      static public void pushTheStack( VectorStack myStack,
                                       Object       myStackElement ) {
            myStack.aStack.addElement( myStackElement );
      }
      //The constructor . . . ..
      public VectorStack() {
            aStack = new Vector() ;
      }
      //Finally, the data structure
      ???   Vector aStack ;
}
```

Listing 8.5 A possible stack implementation.

VectorStack? Your first instinct may be to declare aStack, the data structure corresponding to an object of VectorStack as a public structure so other classes can access the stack. If so, your instincts are dead wrong.

Recall that the goal is to have objects of class VectorStack accessed by the classes' popTheStack() and pushTheStack() methods, none other. The idea is that a stack can only be accessed from the "top." You should not be permitted to go in the "middle" of a stack and yank out a stack element.

Let's assume you've declared aStack previously as a **public** member of class VectorStack. Take a look at the code in Listing 8.6 that uses this class.

After a successful compile, here's the output of this routine:

```
Element 4
Element 3
Element 2
```

```
public class StackWork {

public static void main( String[] args) {

    VectorStack vStack = new VectorStack(  ) ;                    //(1)

    VectorStack.pushTheStack(vStack, "Element 1") ;              //(2)
    VectorStack.pushTheStack(vStack, "Element 2") ;              //(3)
    VectorStack.pushTheStack(vStack, "Element 3") ;              //(4)
    VectorStack.pushTheStack(vStack, "Element 4") ;              //(5)

    System.out.println( VectorStack.popTheStack(vStack)) ;   //(6)
    System.out.println( VectorStack.popTheStack(vStack)) ;   //(7)

    System.out.println( vStack.aStack.elementAt(1) ) ;       //(8)


    }
}
```

Listing 8.6   Using the stack with a publicly declared data structure.

Line //(1) creates an object of class VectorStack with the *new* operator. As you know, the Java runtime will invoke the constructor method for class VectorStack in class VectorStack to create object vStack.

Lines //(2) through //(5) push an element onto the stack using the public method pushTheStack() in class VectorStack.

Lines //(6) and //(7) print out the popped stack element. Hence, you'd see the phrase "Element 4" followed by "Element 3" written to the default output stream. Again, the class uses the public method popTheStack() to access the "top" element.

Let's take a look at line //(8). This line uses a method called *elementAt()*. Now, this method is not one of the approved public methods in class VectorStack. Well, just what is this method elementAt() anyway?

Take a look at this declare in class VectorStack:

```
public   Vector aStack ;
```

This is the public declaration of the stack implementation in class VectorStack. Notice that class VectorStack implements the stack as an object of class *Vector*. Now, class Vector is a very handy class that you'll read more on in Chapter 10, "Interfaces." Without giving too much away, know that a vector in Java is a data structure that holds an array of objects that can grow or shrink in size during runtime. Class Vector is so handy that an object of class Vector has 24 public methods to add and remove elements, of which one is the elementAt() method. As the name suggests, elementAt()

returns a vector element at a given position. The pushTheStack() method added four elements to the stack; the popTheStack() element removed the "top" two elements. Thus, the stack has two elements remaining. The elementAt(1) method returns the second element in the vector (vectors are indexed from 0, like arrays). Hence, the last line of output is as shown previously, "Element 2".

So, what's going on here, anyway? Seems that we are able to access our stack with methods other than the approved public methods, pushTheStack() and popTheStack(). In JavaSpeak, we have not encapsulated the stack. Actually, as the code sits, objects instantiated from class VectorStack are *not stacks* because the operation elementAt() is not a stack operation; elementAt() is a *vector* operation.

Is this a big deal? Well, if you wanted to code an implementation of a stack and you care if you've done a good job, it sure is a big deal. After all, why go through the coding exercise of creating a stack when all you've done is hooked a few extra methods on a vector? If you wanted to create a class that has the features of class Vector with a few additional methods, you should have *subclassed* the Vector class. Chapter 9, "Inheritance," discusses how to create subclasses in particular and the object property of *Inheritance* in general.

Meanwhile, back at the ranch, you're still checking out this stack implementation. Take a look at the three following lines:

```
VectorStack vStack = new VectorStack(  ) ;                 //(1)
VectorStack.pushTheStack(vStack, "Element 1") ;           //(2)
System.out.println( vStack.aStack.elementAt(1) ) ;        //(8)
```

Notice that line //(2) using the approved public method refers to the instance of the stack, *vStack*, whereas line //(8) using the method elementAt() refers to the instance of the *vector aStack*.

How did this programmer know that objects of class VectorStack were defined in terms of objects of class Vector and that the definition relies on a vector called aStack? In the absence of any other compelling evidence, the best guess is that she looked at the code for class VectorStack. She could have run the *javap* program with the -c option to disassemble the class (read Chapter 4, "The Sun Java 2 Basic SDK Tools," to get the dope on javap).

Bottom line: The issue is not what the programmer who accesses the VectorStack class knows; the issue is the shoddiness of the code that enables a programmer to bypass the interface and directly access the underlying data structure.

You know this problem is easy to correct, right? All you need to do is declare the object of class VectorStack in Listing 8.5 as *private*, like so:

```
//Finally, the data structure
private  Vector aStack ;
```

After compiling the revised VectorStack class, you compile the code shown in Listing 8.6 and, lo and behold, Listing 8.7 is what you see.

The private visibility modifier has done its job. You cannot access the Vector object aStack used to define objects of class VectorStack. The encapsulation mechanism of Java, implemented by using visibility modifiers, will not let you. So there.

```
StackWork.java:17: Variable aStack in class VectorStack not
accessible from class StackWork.
       System.out.println( vStack.aStack.elementAt(1) ) ;
                                  ^
1 error
```

Listing 8.7   Javac tells you off.

```
StackWork.java:17: Method elementAt(int) not found
in class VectorStack.
      System.out.println( vStack.elementAt(1) ) ;

1 error
```

Listing 8.8   Do you get it now?

You may be thinking that you can fool Java by coding the invocation of elementAt() without referencing the Vector object aStack. Well, if you coded:

```
System.out.println( vStack.elementAt(1) ) ;                    //(8)
```

Listing 8.8 is what you'd see.

Now, you cannot use the elementAt() method, or any method from class Vector, in a class that accesses VectorStack because the stack representation of VectorClass objects is *invisible* to all classes but the class VectorStack.

Looks like the objective is met. The previous implementation allows access to a data structure from one location: the "top." You can only use methods to put something on and take something off. The code models the behavior of a stack, the removing of an item from the top, and the placing of an item on the top, like cafeteria trays. The code successfully encapsulates the stack and hides the internal representation from user classes.

A PL/I Example: Is This Object-Oriented Programming?

To an experienced object-oriented programmer, encapsulation is par for the course. For the mainframe data processor using procedural languages, encapsulation might sound akin to voodoo. That said, some mainframe languages have features that would seem to allow for the encapsulation of data.

Take a look at the PL/I code in Listing 8.9.

This compile unit implements a stack as controlled data structure. The code allocates memory at runtime for each stack element when required (when pushTheStack is called). Each stack element is a 32K byte varying string, which is generic as it gets in PL/I.

Listing 8.10 shows how you'd call these routines to use the stack.

So, what does this PL/I code do? The compile unit *Stack* defines a data structure and two routines to gain access to the stack: popTheStack() and pushTheStack(). The PL/I stack also uses a function, isStackEmpty(), to determine if a pop operation will be

```
Stack: Proc ;
  Dcl   popTheStack          Entry
                             Returns( Char( 32767 ) Varying ) ;
  Dcl   pushTheStack         Entry( Char (32767 ) ;
  Dcl   aStack               Char( 32767 ) Varying Controlled ;
  Dcl   Allocate             Builtin ;

  popTheStack: Entry( ) Returns( Bit( 1 ) ) ;
     Dcl   stackElement   Char( 32767 ) Varying Init( '' ) ;

     If ^stackIsEmpty() Then
     Do ;
       stackElement   = aStack ;
       Free( aStack ) ;
     End ;
     Return( StackElement ) ;

  End popTheStack ;

  pushTheStack: Entry( stackElement ) ;
     Dcl   stackElement   Char( 32767 ) Varying Init( '' ) ;

     Allocate( aStack ) ;
     aStack = stackElement ) ;

  end pushTheStack ;

  stackIsEmpty: Proc Returns( Bit( 1 ) ) ;
     Return( Allocate( aStack ) = 0 ;
  End stackIsEmpty ;

End Stack ;
```

Listing 8.9 PL/I stack implementation.

```
useTheStack: Proc Options( Main ) ;

  Dcl   popTheStack          Entry( Char (32767) Varying)
                             Returns( Char( 32767 ) Varying ) ;
  Dcl   pushTheStack         Entry( Char (32767 ) ;
  /** Put something on the Stack **/
  Call pushTheStack(" Element 1" ) ;
  Call pushTheStack(" Element 2" ) ;
  Call pushTheStack(" Element 3" ) ;
  Call pushTheStack(" Element 4" ) ;
  /** Take something off **/
  Put Skip List( popTheStack() ) ;
  Put Skip List( popTheStack() ) ;

end UseTheStack ;
```

Listing 8.10   Using the PL/I stack.

permitted. The function isStackEmpty() is hidden from users of the stack. The code in Listing 8.10 declares the stack interface routines and shows how to use these routines.

Well, well. Looks like the astute PL/I programmer can implement encapsulation by declaring a data structure, coding a well-defined interface, and hiding implementation details from users of the structure. However, one caveat exists. Do you see it?

This code does, indeed, implement *a* stack. Unfortunately, the code can use *only one stack*. Notice that the code in Listing 8.10 never refers to a stack by name. That's because the code in Listing 8.9 implements a single stack. Why bother with a name when there's only one stack to work with? In other words, the PL/I code is missing some sort of *new* operator to create a stack.

Before you think that all you need to do is declare a stack in the program shown in Listing 8.10 and modify the routines in compile unit Stack to use this declared stack, remember that once you declare the stack in Listing 8.10, you have access to the data without using the approved interface routines. Hence, you could change the routines to use more than one stack, but you'd sacrifice the benefits of encapsulation and expose the stack to whatever you could do in PL/I to the underlying data type, a string of characters. This is akin to using the elementAt() method on an object of the underlying class Vector.

If you wanted to work with two stacks in the previous Java code, all you need to do is code another object instantiation:

```
VectorStack anotherStack = new VectorStack(  ) ;
```

To use two stacks in the previous PL/I code, you'd need a copy of the Stack compile unit, say, Stack2, or you'd have to write code to empty the old stack before using the new one. The act of cleaning out a stack is not a known behavior of a stack; this is an implementation detail forced on the programmer by the limitations of the programming language.

Although PL/I has some features that allow for good procedural programming, PL/I does not implement common object-oriented features. PL/I programmers cannot implement the concept of instantiating objects from classes. That's why the previous code must reference a single stack; no language support for class creation exists.

Using Accessor (Get and Set) Methods

Data hiding means to eliminate the possibility of an unwanted change to data by removing that data from sight; you can't change what you can't see (or don't know about). Sometimes you want users of your class to have access to data in your objects or classes and, at times, change this data, but you don't want to give away the store. Put differently, you want users of your class to have *controlled* access to class and object data.

Let's say that your stack class keeps a running total of the number of objects of class String on the stack. Listing 8.11 shows a way of doing this.

To summarize the changes: Declare an *instance variable* numberStrings to hold the number of string elements. Use the *instanceof* operator to check for String elements every time pushTheStack() is invoked. Because you need users of your class to access this quantity, you declare the variable *public*.

Here's a line of code used in class StackWork (Listing 8.6) to access this quantity:

```
System.out.println( vStack.numberStrings ) ;
```

Do you see a problem? Here's a hint: Any thoughts on what will happen with the following code:

```
System.out.println( vStack.numberStrings ) ;
vStack.numberStrings = 25252 ;
System.out.println( vStack.numberStrings ) ;
```

```
   public int numberStrings = 0 ;


   static public void pushTheStack(    VectorStack myStack,
                                       Object      myStackElement ) {
        if (myStackElement instanceof String)
            myStack.numberStrings++ ;

        myStack.aStack.addElement( myStackElement );
   }
```

Listing 8.11 Changing vectorstack to track number of string elements.

The first println produces the correct number of string elements on the stack; the second produces the changed value.

Clearly, this property of the stack object should not be changed in this fashion. However, you face a dilemma: How do you allow read access to this property and prevent write access?

A related problem is how do you allow controlled write access to an object property. For example, let's say you want to give users of your VectorClass stack the ability to set the size, or set the maximum number of elements, of a stack. The caveat is that the user of the stack cannot set a stack size more than 100.

Do you see the problem? If you were to create another instance variable, say, numberStackElements, and enable the user to change it (which she must), how can you enforce the less-than-101 requirement?

The object-oriented technique for solving these dilemmas is by coding *accessor*, or *get and set methods*. The idea is to allow access to these instance variables (or properties of the object, if you prefer) by invoking *methods* as opposed to by *coding assignment statements*. The code in the get or set method enforces any restrictions on the access of the object property.

To enforce read-only access to the number of strings in the stack, you may code as in Listing 8.12.

Now, the instance variable *numberStrings* is declared as *private*. As you know, the private visibility modifier blocks any outside class from accessing the variable. The only way to read this variable is by invoking the get method, *getNumberStrings*. Here's a line of code that accesses the variable via the get method:

```
System.out.println( vStack.getNumberStrings( ) ) ;
```

Were you to try to read the value of numberStrings directly, Listing 8.13 shows what javac would tell you.

A few points about the get method are in order. Notice the name of the method, get<variableName>. This is conventional. Also notice the use of the reserved Java word, *this*, to refer to the object that invoked the method. Because this is an instance

```
private int numberStrings = 0 ;


public int getNumberStrings(  ) {

        return numberStrings ;
      //or return this.numberStrings ;
  }
```

Listing 8.12   Using a get method to read an object property.

method, you need not pass the stack as a parameter to the method. Contrast the parameterless mode of the instance method with the *class methods* pushTheStack() and popTheStack. These are class methods. Hence, you must supply the name of the object as a parameter.

Set methods follow the same principle of allowing access to an instance variable only through a method. Listing 8.14 shows how you could code a set method for the instance variable numberStackElements.

Once again, the hidden variable is declared private and the set method is declared public. We've shown a constant declaration that applies to every stack created from VectorClass. Notice that the get method has the name get<variableName>, again, by convention. Set methods do not return a value, hence, the void keyword is present on the method header. The argument is the value to use to set the instance variable. Here, this set method uses the value of the passed parameter if less than the maximum, otherwise, the maximum. Again, notice the use of the keyword *this* to refer to the object invoking the method. Here's a sample invocation:

```
vStack.setNumberStackElements( 40 ) ;
```

For instance variables declared as boolean, many use a get method named is<variableName> to retrieve the value.

```
StackWork.java:19: Variable numberStrings in class
VectorStack not accessible from class StackWork.
System.out.println( vStack.numberStrings ) ;
                    ^

1 error
```

Listing 8.13   Again, Javac tells you off.

```
private int numberStackElements ;
private final static int MAXNUMSTACKELEMENTS = 100 ;

public void setNumberStackElements( int numberElements ) {

    numberStackElements = (numberElements <= MAXNUMSTACKELEMENTS)
                          ? numberElements
                          : MAXNUMSTACKELEMENTS ;
}
```

Listing 8.14   Using a set method to write an object property.

Throughout this discussion of get and set methods, the emphasis is on instance variables. Of course, you may code get and set methods for class variables as well. However, normally an application needs access to the objects instantiated from classes as opposed to the classes themselves.

In Summary

This chapter described encapsulation, a critical feature of object-oriented programming, and how you encapsulate objects in Java. By using visibility modifiers and get/set methods, you can allow users of your classes to access needed object properties without accidentally corrupting, or changing, other properties. The result is better quality software than you could ever hope to achieve with procedural languages that lack support for encapsulation and data hiding.

Inheritance

In this chapter, you'll read about the critically important property of both object environments (in general) and Java (in particular), which is *inheritance*. This chapter begins with various comments on inheritance and a cursory examination of various inheritance hierarchies, followed by a short discussion on the merits of single versus multiple inheritance. Next, you'll see inheritance in action by a Java implementation of bank account classes. After defining the requirements for your bank accounts, you'll see the Java code that does not take advantage of inheritance, followed by Java code implementation that does.

Inheritance Defined

The simple definition of inheritance that follows belies the power of inheritance. Inheritance is a mechanism whereby one class can use the behaviors (methods) and properties (data) from other classes. Inheritance enables you to define new classes as a combination of existing classes. Additionally, you would add functionality not found in the existing classes to the new classes.

In objectspeak, a subclass *inherits* from one or more superclasses. In Javaspeak, a subclass *extends* its superclass. The astute reader notes the use of the plural in the objectspeak phrase, and the singular in the Javaspeak phrase. No, this is not accidental. Java was designed to not enable a subclass to have more than one superclass. Shortly, in this chapter, you'll read some reasons for this design decision.

The strength of inheritance is that you, the Java programmer, need do little to reuse behaviors and properties from existing classes. By using a few Java keywords here and there, you're using inheritance. You don't copy and paste code from one class to another; you reference the methods and properties in the superclass you want to use in your subclass *as if they were defined (coded) in the subclass*. Many times, if you look at the invocation (in the subclass) of inherited methods (from the superclass), you would not know that the methods are inherited.

Another way of looking at a group of subclasses and superclasses is that these classes form a hierarchy, with the superclasses on the top, and the subclasses underneath. The terms *inheritance tree* or *hierarchy tree* are aptly used to describe the inheritance relationship.

Same Classes, Different Inheritance Trees

Before you read about the Java treatment of inheritance, take a look at the two examples of hierarchy trees in Table 9.1, which are composed of real world entities. The trees show different hierarchies of the same entities. The hierarchies reflect different ways of illustrating the relationships among the same entities.

The following table shows two possible arrangements of vehicles. The first classifies vehicles by what they travel on, or in; the second classifies vehicles by what the vehicle transports. Under each hierarchy is a short list of behaviors. Think of the vehicle classifications as *classes*, and the behaviors as *methods*.

With both hierarchies, some behaviors for a vehicle are *start, stop,* and *steer*. Every vehicle has this behavior, regardless of where the vehicle travels or what the vehicle transports. If you were to model the behaviors of different vehicles, you would provide an implementation for starting, stopping, and steering a vehicle. If your implementation environment supports inheritance, you could provide implementations at the topmost entities of the hierarchy and allow the bottom entities to use all, or part of these implementations. Put differently, objects of class Cars or Space Shuttles or any other vehicle would have access to these methods.

Every operator of a land vehicle has a need to repair whatever touches the road from time-to-time, be it a tire or a tread. This repair behavior is peculiar to land vehicles because, simply put, land vehicles have tires or tread. Put another way, land vehicle objects have a property of 'have tires' or 'have treads.' By implementing a 'repair tire' behavior in an environment that supports inheritance, all land vehicles, or classes that are children of the land vehicle class, that have tires can inherit and therefore use the implementation.

When vehicles are classified according to what they transport, the behavior of repairing a tire does not fit neatly into the classification. If you need to implement a 'repair tire or tread' behavior, you *cannot take advantage of inheritance* with the second hierarchy because this hierarchy does not enable you to specify a parent class in the hierarchy as one having tires or treads. In other words, you cannot model a Passenger, Cargo, or Military Vehicle as one having tires or tread with the existing second hierarchy.

The vehicle classes used in both hierarchies are the same; they have the same attributes and behaviors. After all, that's the point of object technology—objects have a set of

Table 9.1 Two Vehicle Hierarchies

VEHICLE HIERARCHY 1	VEHICLE HIERARCHY 2

• Vehicle
  • Land Vehicle
    • Cars
    • Buses
    • Trucks
    • Tanks
    • Troop Carriers
    • Trains
  • Water Vehicles
    • Boats, Yachts
    • Sailboats
    • Cruise Ships
    • Cargo Tankers
    • Warships
    • Submarines
  • Air Vehicles
    • Planes
    • Jets
    • Gliders
    • Airships
  • Space Vehicles
    • Space Shuttles
    • Rockets
    • ICBMs
	• Vehicle
	  • Passenger Vehicles
	    • Cars
	    • Buses
	    • *Trucks*
	    • *Trains*
	    • Boats, Yachts
	    • Sailboats
	    • Cruise Ships
	    • *Planes*
	    • *Jets*
	    • Space Shuttles
	    • Gliders
	    • Airships
	  • Cargo Vehicles
	    • *Trucks*
	    • *Trains*
	    • Cargo Tankers
	    • *Planes*
	    • *Jets*
	    • Rockets
	  • Military Vehicles
	    • Tanks
	    • Troop Carriers
	    • Warships
	    • *Submarines*
	    • *Planes*
	    • *Jets*
	    • Rockets
	    • ICBMs

Some Vehicle Behaviors
  • Start, Stop, Steer
Some Land Vehicle Behaviors
  • Repair Tire or Tread
Some Water Vehicle Behaviors
  • Bail Water, Drop Anchor
Some Air Vehicle Behaviors
  • Take off, Land
Some Space Vehicle Behaviors
  • Ignite Boosters, Achieve Orbit
	Some Vehicle Behaviors
	  • Stop, Start, Steer
	Some Passenger Vehicle Behaviors
	  • Collect Fares, Confirm Destination
	Some Cargo Vehicle Behaviors
	  • *Deliver Payload*, Confirm Shipment
	Some Military Vehicle Behaviors
	  • Confirm Orders, *Deliver Payload*

properties and behaviors. These properties and behaviors doesn't change when you create different superclass/subclass hierarchies. Whether you model a truck as a child of a land vehicle or passenger vehicle, a truck has tires. Now, the problem at hand may not require you to implement a "Repair Tire" method when you classify vehicles by what they transport. If you must, you can still implement such a method. The point is that you cannot easily leverage inheritance to reuse this method when you are using the second hierarchy.

Classes often have several hierarchical relationships. Here, you've seen two possible arrangements of vehicles. You could have arranged the vehicle classes by the size of the passengers and crew, or the type of fuel used to propel the vehicle. The hierarchy you choose to create should be heavily dependent on your problem domain.

Classes at the top of a hierarchy tree are more abstract than those at the bottom. Another way of putting this is that the classes at treetop do not correspond to tangible, real world entities, whereas those classes at the bottom do. In our previous example hierarchies, the topmost class is called Vehicle. Now, vehicles have real behaviors and properties. However, real world vehicles do not come from this topmost class; they come from a bottommost class. In objectspeak, you doesn't instantiate objects from classes Vehicle or Military Vehicles; you instantiate objects from classes Tank or ICBM. In Javaspeak, class Vehicle or class Military Vehicles are *abstract* classes. The top classes exist to provide an inheritance mechanism whereby properties and behaviors may be inherited by the real world, bottommost classes. After all, cars and buses are real world things, whereas Passenger Vehicles is an abstraction.

Although the top- and mid-level classes are abstract, you'll still implement methods that correspond to the classes' behaviors. However, the logic behind coding methods for top- and mid-level classes is to make life easier for the bottom level classes. Just like life, the parents always work hard and make sacrifices for their children. The same is true with object environments and inheritance relationships among parent and child classes.

The keen reader will notice that some classes in the second hierarchy are bolded and italicized. You'll revisit these classes in the section *Single Versus Multiple Inheritance*, coming up next.

Single Versus Multiple Inheritance

The definition of inheritance, used in this chapter, allows for one or more subclasses inheriting behaviors and properties from one or more superclasses. The industry jargon for the object property of allowing a class to inherit from more than one superclass is *multiple inheritance*. You don't have to be exceedingly sharp to deduce the industry jargon of prohibiting a class from inheriting from more than one superclass.

Recall that Java does not permit a class to inherit from more than one subclass. In other words, Java permits single inheritance only. You may reasonably question the wisdom of disallowing multiple inheritance. After all, if inheriting properties and behaviors from one superclass is effective, shouldn't inheriting from more than one class be even more effective?

To shed some light on potential problems with multiple inheritance, take a look at the second hierarchy in Table 9.1. The reader will notice that some classes are bolded and italicized. These classes are repeated in the hierarchy; they have multiple super-classes. In English, a plane can transport passengers and cargo, or soldiers and armaments. Given this hierarchy, a plane class could be a child of all three superclasses.

Now, the second hierarchy shown in Table 9.1 does not reflect a multiple inheritance scenario. You could construct the hierarchy and classes such that the Plane class with a superclass of Passenger Vehicle is different than the Plane class with a superclass of Military Vehicle. Here, to draw distinctions between single and multiple inheritance, we're assuming that the plane class (and others) share properties and behaviors from multiple superclasses.

Notice that the behavior *Deliver Payload* exists for subclasses of *Cargo Vehicles* and *Military Vehicles*. You can safely assume that the implementation for the Deliver Payload behavior for a subclass of Cargo Vehicle will differ from that of a subclass of Military Vehicle. Given that objects from class Plane inherit from these two superclasses, the question arises:

Which superclass does the behavior *Deliver Payload* come from?

It turns out that no straightforward way exists for avoiding ambiguities arising from name clashes. You could change the names of the methods in the superclasses, but that seems to defeat the purpose of using an inheritance mechanism in the first place.

You can be reasonably assured that implementation for deliver payload for a cargo vehicle is somewhat different than that for a military craft. How can an object of one class intelligently use both implementations?

To avoid such ambiguities, the engineers at Sun, who developed Java, decided to forgo using multiple inheritance. Still, you can't deny that the ability to inherit from several superclasses has benefits. The Sun folk use a construct called an *Interface*. Rather than spending more time on interfaces in Java, let's defer the discussion to Chapter 10, "Interfaces."

Example of an Inheritance Tree From the Java Libraries

You will see many hierarchies of superclasses and subclasses in an object system. Nowhere is this more evident than in the Java libraries. For example, Figure 9.1 shows the hierarchy, or tree, for the Java package *java.sql* from the Sun Documentation.

You probably have a good idea of how to interpret the following hierarchy tree. The classes to the left are the parents, or the superclasses, of the classes under and to the right. For example, the class java.util.Date (second from the top) is a subclass of java.lang.Object; the class java.lang.SQLException is a subclass of java.lang.Exception.

You may be thinking that the class hierarchy shown in Figure 9.1 belies the comment regarding Java classes inheriting from (at most) one superclass. You should notice that Figure 9.1 shows class java.sql.DataTruncation as a subclass (or child) of class java.sql.SQLWarning; it also shows java.sql.SQLWarning as a child of java.sql.SQLException. You may think that class java.sql.DataTruncation has more than one superclass: the immediate parent (java.sql.SQLWarning) and the 'grandparent' (java.sql.SQLException). Well, the preceding comment on the parent/grandparent classes is, of course, true. However, when the literature speaks of a superclass/subclass relationship, the relationship is with the parent and child, not with any grandparents or grandchildren.

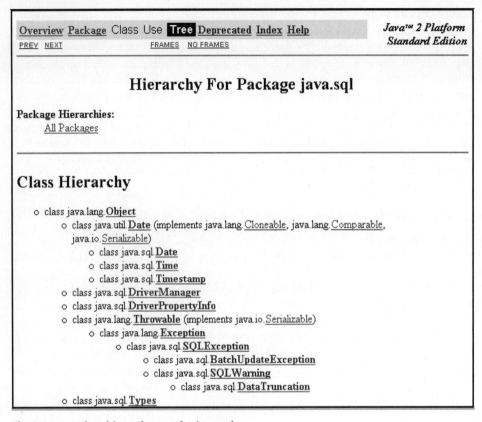

Figure 9.1 Class hierarchy tree for java.sql.

The observant reader notes that one class in this diagram *has no parent*. The class *java.lang.Object* is the ultimate parent of each and every Java class. In other words, if you were to examine each and every hierarchy for each and every package in Java (packages that are part of the Java runtime and packages created by application developers), you would find class java.lang.Object at the top of the hierarchy chain.

As a Java programmer, you will spend a great deal of time perusing class hierarchy trees. After all, you don't want to code when you can inherit, right?

An Example: Implementing Bank Accounts

Tables 9.2 and 9.3 with Listing 9.1 on the following pages show a straightforward implementation of checking and savings account behaviors that illustrate the use of inheritance in Java. The accounts have the properties and behaviors shown in Tables 9.2 and 9.3.

Table 9.2 Checking Account Properties and Behaviors

PROPERTY NAME	FORMAT
Name of Account Holder	Character String
Current Balance	Currency
Number of Withdrawals	Integer
Number of Deposits	Integer

BEHAVIOR	DESCRIPTION
Open Checking Account	Create a Checking Account given the Name of Account Holder and an initial balance. If the Name of Account is not provided, open the account for "Pete Moss."
Make a Deposit	Add the amount to be deposited to the Current Balance, generating a new value for Current Balance. Report on the status of the transaction. If successful, report the value of Current Balance and increment the number of deposits.
Make a Withdrawal	Subtract the amount to be withdrawn from the Current Balance, generating a new value for Current Balance. Report on the status of the transaction. If the transaction is successful, report on the new value of Current Balance and increment the number of withdrawals. Also, if the number of withdrawals exceeds five, report on the number of withdrawals.
Report Account Information	Display the above properties of a Checking Account.

Code for Checking and Savings Account Classes

The implementation of these methods is relatively straightforward. Listing 9.1 shows a not-too-optimal implementation. Following the Listing and an explanation of the somewhat lackluster version, you'll see a better implementation that takes advantage of inheritance and a few other Java features.

A few points about the following code are worth a comment or two. Please refer to the numbers placed conveniently to the right of the code when reading this dissertation.

Line 1 starts the constructor for the checking account class. You create objects of the checking account class by using the *new* operator, passing a name and an initial account balance.

Table 9.3 Savings Account Properties and Behaviors

PROPERTY NAME	FORMAT
Name of Account Holder	Character String
Current Balance	Currency
Number of Withdrawals	Integer
Number of Deposits	Integer

BEHAVIOR	DESCRIPTION
Open Savings Account	Create a Savings Account given the Name of Account Holder and an initial balance. If the Name of Account is not provided, open the account for "Pete Moss."
Make a Deposit	Add the amount to be deposited to the Current Balance, generating a new value for Current Balance. Report on the status of the transaction. If successful, report the value of Current Balance and increment the number of deposits. Also, if the Current Balance exceeds 1,000 dollars, add 5 percent of the amount exceeding 1,000 dollars to the Current Balance.
Make a Withdrawal	Subtract the amount to be withdrawn from the Current Balance, generating a new value for Current Balance. Report on the status of the transaction. If the transaction is successful, report on the new value of Current Balance and increment the number of withdrawals.
Report Account Information	Display the above properties of a Savings Account.

```
/**
    A far from optimal implementation of the bank account classes
    with the described properties and behaviors

    Here's the Checking Account class:
**/
class CheckingAccount
{
    String nameHolder;                    //Account owner
    Double balance ;
    int      numWithdrawals=0, numDeposits=1;
```

Listing 9.1 Implementing the checking account class.

```
        //Constructor for when we pass an account holder.
        CheckingAccount (String strAccHolder, int intDeposit) //1
        {
            //Just initialize property fields to passed values
            nameHolder       = strAccHolder;
            balance          = intDeposit;
        }
        //Constructor for Pete Moss:
        CheckingAccount (int intDeposit)                        //2
        {
            //Use Pete M. for Account Holder and the passed value
            //for initial deposit.
            NameHolder       = "Pete Moss" ;
            balance          = intDeposit;
        }
        /**
No surprise here . . . Subtract amount (passed arg) from
        Existing account balance (balance)
        **/
        public void CheckingWithdraw(double amount)             //3
        {
            String response;
            if (amount > balance)
            {
                response = "Insufficient Funds. Balance = " +
                            balance + "From Checking Account" ;
            }
            else
            {
                balance -= amount;
                numWithdrawals++;
                response = "Withdrawal Successful. Balance = " +
                            balance + "From Checking Account" ;
            }
            System.out.println( response ) ;
            //Recall requirement that if the number of withdrawals
            //exceeds 5, to report on the number of withdrawals
            //
            if (numWithdrawals > 5)
                System.out.println("Number of Withdrawals = " +
                                NumWithdrawals) ;

        }
        //Put some $$$ in
        public void CheckingDeposit(double amount)              //4
        {
            balance = balance + amount;
```

Listing 9.1 Implementing the checking account class. (continued)

```
          numDeposits++;
          System.out.println ("Deposit Successful. Balance = " +
                              Balance + "for Checking Account");
     }
     //
     //Display information on this Checking Account
     //
     public void CheckingAccountInfo()                         //5
          {
     System.out.println("Checking Account Information\n");
          System.out.println("Account Holder    : " + nameHolder);
          System.out.println("Dollars on Account: " + balance);
          System.out.println("Num Withdrawals: " +
                             numWithdrawals);
          System.out.println("Num Deposits    : " + numDeposits);
     }
 }
```

Listing 9.1   Implementing the checking account class. (continued)

Line 2 starts another constructor. This constructor causes the account holder's name to default to Pete Moss. Notice that the constructor takes one argument, the initial account balance.

Line 3 is the method header for the checking account withdrawal method. The code included in the method implements the behavior of the withdrawal action as described in Table 9.2.

Lines 4 and 5 are the method headers for the checking account deposit and display information methods, respectively.

Listing 9.2 below shows a possible Java implementation of a savings account class with the properties and behaviors described in Table 9.3.

Any similarities between the code that implements the savings account to the code that implements the checking account is not accidental. You should see that most of the code is duplicated in both classes. This sad state of affairs cries out for remedy. Fortunately, this code is Java, which means we can leverage inheritance to cut out the duplication. The next section explains this task.

Taking Advantage of Inheritance

Recall from the hierarchy trees of vehicles that the topmost classes in the tree contain behaviors common to all vehicles. Some superclasses at the middle of the hierarchy had properties (like tires and treads) common to a group of related subclasses.

```
/**
    Here's the Savings Account class.
**/
class SavingsAccount
{
    String nameHolder;                     //Account owner
    double balance ;
    int    numWithdrawals=0, numDeposits=1;
    //
    SavingsAccount (String strAccHolder, int intDeposit)     {
        nameHolder          = strAccHolder;
        balance             = intDeposit;
    }
    //
    SavingsAccount (int intDeposit)        {
        nameHolder       = "Pete Moss" ;
        balance          = intDeposit;
    }
    //
    public void SavingsWithdraw(double amount) {
        String response;
        if (amount > balance)
           response = "Insufficient Funds. Balance = " +
                          balance + "From Savings Account" ;
        else {
             balance = balance - amount;
             numWithdrawals++;
             response = "Withdrawal Successful. Balance = " +
                          balance + "From Savings Account" ;
        }
        System.out.println( response ) ;
    }
    //
    public void SavingsDeposit(double amount)      {
        balance = balance + amount;
        numDeposits++;
        //Recall the requirement that if the balance exceeds 1,000
        //this bank heaps 5% extra onto the balance.
        if (balance > 1000)
            balance += (balance - 1000) * 0.05 ;

        System.out.println ("Deposit Successful. Balance = " +
                           balance + "for Savings Account");
    }
    //
  public void SavingsAccountInfo()       {
      System.out.println("Savings Account Information\n") ;
```

Listing 9.2 Implementing the savings account class.

```
        System.out.println("Account Holder    : " + nameHolder);
        System.out.println("Dollars on Account: " + balance);
        System.out.println("Num of Withdrawals: " + numWithdrawals);
        System.out.println("Num of Deposits   : " + numDeposits);
    }
```

Listing 9.2   Implementing the savings account class. (*continued*)

A quick, but accurate, observation would be that superclasses contain properties and behaviors common to a number of subclasses.

This is also true with our checking and saving account classes. A cursory examination of the properties and behaviors of these account classes, with the goal of finding common ground, yields the the data in Table 9.4.

It looks like there is a lot of common ground here. We can leverage inheritance by taking the following steps:

1. Create a superclass containing the properties and behaviors common to both subclasses.

2. Write the code for the subclasses to reflect the differences between the subclass and superclass implementations.

Hence, without further ado, Listing 9.3 shows the code for the account classes. Now we have code for a new class: class *Account,* the superclass for classes CheckingAccount and SavingsAccount, with the code for the checking and savings account classes. This code also contains some Java constructs not peculiar to demonstrating inheritance use, but demonstrating some good coding practices. That said, some code is less than optimal; the sacrifice is made to illustrate some points about inheritance in Java.

Once again, refer to the numbered lines during the brief and informative dissertation on the code.

Line 1 is the class statement for the Account class (the superclass). The Account class ends just before line 5; the properties common to all subclasses of Account are declared here. By inheritance, any subclass has immediate and unfettered access to these properties.

Notice the class qualifier—*abstract.* By declaring the class as abstract, Java will not enable the class to be instantiated. Recall that we're interested in the checking and savings accounts; the reason for using the Account class is to take advantage of Java's inheritance mechanism. We *don't* want objects of class Account. We can lay down the law and Java will enforce it. For example, this code,

```
    Account anAcct = new Account("Lou", 250000) ;
```

will produce the following diagnostic from the Java compiler:

```
    class Account is an abstract class. It can't be instantiated.
        Account anAcct = new Account("Lou", 250000) ;
```

Table 9.4 Properties and Behaviors Common to Checking and Savings Accounts

PROPERTY NAME	FORMAT
Name of Account Holder	Character String
Current Balance	Currency
Number of Withdrawals	Integer
Number of Deposits	Integer

BEHAVIOR	DESCRIPTION
Open an Account	Create an Account given the Name of Account Holder and an initial balance. If the Name of Account is not provided, open the account for "Pete Moss."
Make a Deposit	Add the amount to be deposited to the Current Balance, generating a new value for Current Balance. Report on the status of the transaction. If successful, report the value of Current Balance and increment the number of deposits.
Make a Withdrawal	Subtract the amount to be withdrawn from the Current Balance, generating a new value for Current Balance. Report on the status of the transaction. If the transaction is successful, report on the new value of Current Balance and increment the number of withdrawals.
Report Account Information	Display the above properties of an Account.

```
Abstract class Account                                       //1
   {
      private   String nameHolder;                           //2
      private   double balance;
      private   int      withdrawals=0, deposits=1;
      //
      Account (String strAccHolder, int intDeposit) {    //3
          //Just initialize property fields to passed values
          nameHolder    = strAccHolder;
          balance    = intDeposit;
      }
      Account (int intDeposit ) {
          nameHolder   = "Pete Moss" ;
```

Listing 9.3 Bank account classes using inheritance.

```
                    balance        = intDeposit ;
            }
        public String getNameHolder() {                        //4
                return nameHolder ;
        }
        public double getBalance() {
                return balance ;
        }
        public int getWithdrawals() {
                return withdrawals ;
        }
        public int getDeposits() {
                return deposits ;
        }
        //
        public void withdraw(double amount) {
            String response;
            if (amount > balance)
                response = "Insufficient Funds. ";
            else      {
                balance = balance - amount;
                withdrawals++;
                response = "Withdrawal Successful. " ;
            }
            System.out.println( response ) ;
        }
        //
        public void deposit(double amount)         {
                balance = balance + amount;
                deposits++;
        }
        //
        public String accountInfo() {
                return ("Account Holder        : " + nameHolder + "\n" +
                        "Dollars on Account    : " + balance + "\n" +
                        "Number of Withdrawals : " + withdrawals + "\n" +
                        "Number of Deposits    : " + deposits);
        }
}                                                               //5
//
class CheckingAccount extends Account {                         //6
        CheckingAccount(String strAccHolder, int intDeposit ) {
                super( strAccHolder, intDeposit ) ;
        }

        CheckingAccount( int intDeposit ) {
                super( intDeposit ) ;
        }
```

Listing 9.3 Bank account classes using inheritance. (*continued*)

```
                                                              //7
    public void withdraw (double amount) {
        String strMsg;
                                                              //8
        super.withdraw(amount);                               //9
        strMsg = "Balance = " + getBalance() +
                " for Checking Account";
                                                              //10
        int withdrawals = getWithdrawals() ;
        if (withdrawals > 5)
            strMsg = strMsg + "\n # of Withdrawals is " +
                    withdrawals;
        System.out.println( strMsg );
    }
    public void deposit (double amount) {
      String strMsg;
      super.deposit(amount);
      System.out.println("Balance = " + getBalance() +
                        " for Checking Account");
    }
    //
    public String accountInfo() {
        String strMsg;
        strMsg = super.accountInfo();
        strMsg = "Checking Account Information\n" +
                "----------------------------\n" +
                strMsg;
        return strMsg;
    }                                                         //11
}
class SavingsAccount extends Account
{
    //
    SavingsAccount(String strAccHolder, int intDeposit )        {
        super( strAccHolder, intDeposit ) ;
    }
    SavingsAccount( int intDeposit ) {
        super( intDeposit ) ;
    }
    //
    public void savWithdraw (double amount)
    {
        String strMsg;

        withdraw(amount);
        System.out.println("Balance = " + getBalance() +
                        " for Savings Account") ;
```

Listing 9.3 Bank account classes using inheritance. (*continued*)

```
        }
    public void savDeposit (double amount) {
        String strMsg;
        double balance = getBalance() ;
        if (balance + amount > 1000)
            deposit( amount + (amount - 1000) * 0.05) ;
    else                                           //12
            deposit( amount ) ;
        System.out.println("Balance = " + getBalance() +
                        " for Savings Account" );
    }
    public String savAccountInfo() {
        String strMsg;
        strMsg = accountInfo();
        strMsg = "Savings Account Information\n" +
                "---------------------------\n" +
            strMsg;
        return strMsg;
    }
}
```

Listing 9.3   Bank account classes using inheritance. (*continued*)

You've got to love the plain English diagnostics from the Java compiler, don't you?

Line 2 starts the first constructor; the second constructor immediately follows the first. Now, as you've seen, a call to the constructor *will not* create an object of class Account. However, you'll see how the Java code uses these constructors in the CheckingAccount and SavingsAccount classes.

Line 3 starts a group of methods called *get* methods. You recall reading about get and set methods in Chapter 8, " Encapsulating and Hiding Data and Methods." Java programmers may disagree on many things, but they are nearly unanimous in agreement on declaring instance variables *private*, and using get and set methods to access the variables. The motivation is to stop code that will alter the state of an account by improperly accessing an instance variable. For example, if a class using the bank account classes had the following code,

```
CheckingAccount anAcct = new CheckingAccount("Lou", 250000) ;
anAcct.deposits      +=12 ;
```

the state of object anAcct would be inconsistent. This reference is illegal when deposits is declared private. Line 9 shows how a subclass would reference a property by using the get method.

The methods between lines 4 and 5 implement behavior that is common to the checking and savings account classes. Later in the code, you'll see references to these methods in the subclasses.

Line 5 is the class statement for the first subclass, CheckingAccount. Notice the use of the *extends* keyword. The extends keyword tells Java that the two classes named have a subclass/superclass relationship. Line 12 also uses the extends keyword.

Line 6 starts the constructors for class CheckingAccount. Notice the reference to the constructors in the superclass by using the *super* keyword. You'll see a similar reference for the other subclass after line 11.

Line 7 starts the implementation of the withdraw method for the CheckingAccount subclass. Because the name of the method found in the superclass is also withdraw, Java needs a mechanism for referring to the like-named method in the superclass. Java uses the *super* keyword for this purpose, as seen on line 8.

Because the instance variables are declared private in class Account, all other classes need to invoke the get methods to access the variable's values. Lines 9 and 10 illustrate the use of get methods for the current balance and number of withdrawals properties. The *deposit* method in class CheckingAccount uses similar constructs to get the job done.

When a subclass uses a method identically named to one in its superclass, we say that the subclass is *overriding* the superclass method. The two methods must return the same data type, an object of the same class, or void.

The methods in class SavingsAccount are *not* named identically to those in its super-class. Therefore, methods of SavingsAccount can reference superclass methods directly. Line 12 shows such a reference to the method *withdraw*. The Java runtime searches for the method declared in the containing class (SavingsAccount). Not finding the method, the Java runtime searches the superclass for the method, finds it, and executes it. The Java runtime would continue searching up the hierarchy tree looking for the method and executing the first one it finds.

At first glance, you may think that that code not relying on inheritance is shorter and simpler. Well, perhaps in this instance that is true. However, this code shows how inheritance in Java is a powerful feature that enables for true code reuse. Imagine implementing a third type of bank account, say a money market account, and using the behaviors in the parent Account class. Like the vehicles that all need to be started, stopped, and steered, bank accounts need to be opened, have money deposited, and have money withdrawn. Inheritance will certainly lighten your load.

Effects of Casting to and from Superclasses and Subclasses

Before you finish with this chapter, you need to know that you can cast to and from classes and superclasses and some of the interesting effects of such casting. As you'll read, sometimes you might see some results that seem counterintuitive.

The *only allowable* casting between objects of different classes is when these classes have a superclass/subclass relationship. For example, because class Object is the root class, or is a superclass of every Java class, the following is legal:

```
Object myObj = (Object) myChecking ;          // 1
```

Put differently, every object from any class in Java can be cast to an object of class Object.

Because class Account is the superclass of class CheckingAccount, this works, too:

```
Account myAcct = (Account) myChecking ;        // 2
```

However, this *will not* work

```
MyChecking = (SavingsAccount) mySavings ;       // 3
```

because classes CheckingAccount and SavingsAccount do not have a superclass/subclass relationship. Don't be misled because the checking and savings account classes share a superclass.

Because a child class 'belongs' to its parent in the sense that the specific (subclass) is an instance of the general (superclass), you do not need to code a cast when you assign a child to a parent. The Java assignment operator works out of the box. Hence, these statements are legal,

```
Object myObj     = myChecking ;
Account myAcct   = myChecking ;                 // 4
```

and equivalent to the cast assignments labeled // 1 and // 2. However, you cannot assign the general to the specific; a cast is required. So, you can code the following,

```
myChecking = (Account) myAcct ;                 // 5
```

but not the following:

```
myChecking = myAcct ;                           // 6
```

Looking back at line // 5, you should know that although this line shows a valid coding construct, the code *still might result in a runtime error*. For example, you might try to be sly and sneaky, and code the following:

```
Account myAcct     = myChecking ;               // 7
mySavings          = (SavingsAccount) myAcct ;
```

Your reasoning might be that this construct lets you cast a checking account into a savings account, or, to get line // 3 above to compile and execute. After all, everyone tries to outfox the compiler now and then. Well, the previous two lines compile. However, upon execution, the Java runtime issues a *ClassCastException*, which is pretty much what it sounds like.

Recall that assignment of objects in Java *does not create copies of the objects*. Java object names are a reference to the object, not the object itself. The assignment of the checking account object to one of class Account does not create a new object, just a reference to an existing one. Hence, the following code

```
Account myAcct = (Account) myChecking ;
System.out.println( "Acct Info = " + myAcct.accountInfo() );
```

will list out the account information for *myChecking*, not myAcct.

In addition, because object assignment operates on object references, you can assign and cast objects of related classes back and forth. Looking previously at line 1, you might think that when Java cast the object of subclass CheckingAccount to an object of the (most) general of Java classes, the Java environment 'lost' the subclass information. You might think this to be true, especially if you forgot that Java operates on references, not objects. Even after the assignment on line 1, *the original object still exists*. Ergo, the statements

```
Object myObj    = myChecking ;
myChecking      = (CheckingAccount) myObj ;      // 8
System.out.println( myChecking.accountInfo() ) ;
```

will list the information for the checking account. Of course, you realize that the cast coded on line // 8 is *required*.

To wrap this assignment/casting to and from subclasses and superclasses, know that you can assign a subclass instance to a superclass instance *with or without a cast*, you can assign a superclass instance to a subclass instance *with a cast*, and you cannot assign instances of unrelated classes at all, with or without a cast.

In Summary

This chapter explored the vitally important property of inheritance. You've seen how inheritance allows you to model common characteristics of several classes into a superclass. The code implementing the common characteristics can be used by child classes.

Of course code reuse saves time because you don't have to reinvent wheels, but improved system quality is another of its benefits. The reused code, presumably bug-free, should not introduce problems when incorporated into systems.

Inheritance is a feature not available to the COBOL or PL/I programmer in the mainframe shop. You, the mainframe programmer, may have to think along different lines when you write Java because inheritance is part and parcel of Java programs.

Interfaces

Chapter 9, "Inheritance," discussed the important object property of inheritance. You've read that Java supports a single inheritance scheme. You've also read a vague reference or two about a Java scheme that provides some benefits of multiple inheritance, namely *interfaces*. Now is the time to explore Java interfaces in detail.

You'll read a brief description of interfaces, followed by an explanation for how Java interfaces overcome some of the limitations of the single inheritance model. This short chapter covers the relationship between interfaces, abstract classes, and concrete classes. You'll learn how to create and implement interfaces, and see some coding examples of interfaces in use.

What Are Interfaces?

A Java interface is a collection of abstract behaviors; an object declares that it implements this. Put differently, an interface is a promise that the behaviors, or *abstract* methods, contained in the interface will be implemented by declaring objects.

The concept of a Java interface is similar to that of an API. After all, the I in API means interface, right? An API is a set of behaviors that are used by objects. When you use the *Java Database Connectivity* (JDBC) API to issue an SQL statement, you count on the JDBC API to do its job. You are ignorant of how the call is implemented. All you care about is the promise of expected behavior.

Of course, merely declaring that an object uses this or that behavior is not enough. The behaviors require an implementation. In the case of using a core, optional, or vendor API, the implementation is already coded and made available for your use. In the case of a Java interface, someone has to code the implementation. After all, it is not magic.

The relevant lingo is that a class *implements* interfaces; this is not to be confused with a subclass that *extends* a superclass. A class can extend a superclass and implement one or more interfaces. The declaration looks like this:

```
class MySubClass extends MySuperClass implements
MyInterface1,MyInterface2 { . . .
```

The implements keyword may be used apart from the extends keyword, and vice-versa.

Mainframe programmers, too, use APIs to issue SQL or create data entry screens. Mainframe APIs are like function libraries; the program issues a call to an API function and gets a result. Interfaces in Java aren't used as function libraries. Interfaces specify *what must be done*, not *how to do it*.

Why Are Interfaces Useful?

At times, Interfaces are incorrectly touted as enabling the Java programmer to take advantage of multiple inheritance. A more accurate slant is that interfaces provide the Java programmer with a mechanism to overcome some of the deficiencies of single inheritance.

One such deficiency was illustrated in Chapter 9 with the two hierarchy trees for vehicles. Using a single inheritance model, you have no easy method of implementing both trees and leveraging inheritance. You would choose one tree, implementing the methods in the other without the benefits of inheritance.

A set of interfaces defines another hierarchy separate and distinct from the inheritance hierarchy. However, interfaces are far more; interfaces enable the Java programmer to imbue objects with behaviors from several classes. When you state that your class implements an interface, you are saying that objects from your class can be used anywhere the interface is used. For example, the following declaration

```
public class Jets extends AirVehicles implements PassengerVehicles,
CargoVehicles, MilitaryVehicles { . . .
```

establishes two separate hierarchies: the Passenger/Cargo/Military vehicle hierarchy and the Land/Sea/Air/Space hierarchy. This declaration states that you can use objects from class Jets anywhere you would use a PassengerVehicle, a CargoVehicle, or a MilitaryVehicle.

Remember that with the inheritance hierarchy, the subclasses have immediate access to implementations provided in the superclass. The interface hierarchy is a different animal. Every class that implements an interface must *provide, or have access to, an implementation* of the behaviors stated in the interface. The access would be through a superclass. Put differently, if a superclass implements one or more interfaces, all subclasses therefore have access to the implementations.

Referring to the previous declaration, and to Table 9.1, class Jets would need to implement the methods CollectFares, DeliverPayload, ConfirmDestination, and so on. Now, if the following declaration existed,

```
public class Jets extends AirVehicles implements PassengerVehicles,
CargoVehicles, MilitaryVehicles { . . .
```

then class Jets would have access to the implementations of the three interfaces in class AirVehicles.

Another reason interfaces are useful is that interfaces provide a mechanism to separate implementations from classes that use the implementations. By separating the two, you can change implementations without impacting the classes that use them. As the old saying goes, the change is transparent to the user.

What About Abstract Superclasses?

Comparing interfaces to an abstract superclass is a useful comparison. Recall that an abstract class contains abstract methods, or method signatures, return types, and an optional throws clause, but with no implementation. Interfaces are similar inasmuch as an interface also contains a list of abstract methods. However, conceptual differences between the two exist.

An abstract superclass carries this overtone of "incompleteness;" the superclass requires one or more subclasses to complete it. Interfaces are not incomplete in this sense. An interface is a statement that a list of behaviors must be implemented according to a set of specifications (signatures).

The code present in the superclass places some restrictions on how the subclasses complete the implementation. Put differently, the superclass could provide a base implementation, the subclass could provide the details. The base implementation could limit subsequent subclass implementations.

For example, let's assume that our bank account hierarchy enabled for an *account identifier* property. Behaviors dealing with this property could be the following:

- Assign an account identifier.
- Retrieve account information by identifier.
- Add, Change, or Delete account by identifier.

The implementation of these behaviors could depend on the account identifier or parts of the account identifier, being a certain primitive type, like int, or object of a certain user created class. If so, method implementations in the checking and savings account subclasses must adhere to whatever constraints are placed by the selection of the underlying data type used in the superclass.

So, where is the problem? One problem could arise if there is a desire to implement this property as different data types depending on various circumstances. Perhaps one implementation of this property is best suited for in memory access, another could be best suited for disk access. The single inheritance model does not easily permit this sort of flexibility.

Creating Interfaces

The syntax for creating an interface is straightforward. Following is an example:

```
public interface PassengerVehicles {

    public double collectFares( ) ;
    public boolean confirmDestination ( Destination where ) ;
    // More method signatures here, perhaps


}
```

You code the previous interface declaration in a file named *PassengerVehicle.java* as you would with any java source. The compiler creates a class file, which is *PassengerVehicle.class*. You may pass instances of PassengerVehicles, which are arguments to methods. So far, declaring and using the interface strongly resembles declaring and using a class, right? However, differences exist, which are shown in the following:

- Interfaces are public; all the contained methods are public.

- Interfaces cannot contain "class'" variables—only variables declared *final*.

- Interfaces contain no body, only method signatures.

Let's see some sample code that ties interfaces and classes together.

Example: Implementing the Vehicle Types

Here, you'll see some code that implements the inheritance and interface hierarchies for out vehicle classes. For your convenience, Table 10.1 is a section of Table 9.1 showing parts of the vehicle hierarchies.

Table 10.1   Table 9.1 Revisited

VEHICLE HIERARCHY 1	VEHICLE HIERARCHY 2

• Vehicle
  • Land Vehicle
    • Trucks
  • Water Vehicles
    • Boats, Yachts
  • Air Vehicles
    • Jets
  • Space Vehicles
    • Rockets
	• Vehicle
	  • Passenger Vehicles
	    • Trucks
	    • Jets
	  • Cargo Vehicles
	    • Trucks
	  • Military Vehicles
	    • Tanks
	    • Jets

continues

Table 10.1   Table 9.1 Revisited (*Continued*)

VEHICLE HIERARCHY 1	VEHICLE HIERARCHY 2

• Some Vehicle Behaviors
  • Start, Stop, Steer
• Some Land Vehicle Behaviors
  • Repair Tire or Tread
• Some Air Vehicle Behaviors
  • Take Off
  • Land
	• Some Vehicle Behaviors
	  • Stop, Start, Steer
	• Some Passenger Vehicle Behaviors
	  • Collect Fares, Confirm Destination
	• Some Cargo Vehicle Behaviors
	  • Deliver Payload, Confirm Shipment
	• Some Military Vehicle Behaviors
	  • Confirm Orders, Deliver Payload

The following code shows the *inheritance* hierarchy:

```java
//The top level class
public class Vehicle {

    String vehicleName ;
    //Constructor
    Vehicle( String aName ) {
        vehicleName = aName ;
    }

    public void start( ) {
        System.out.println( vehicleName + " Has Started") ;

    }
    public void steer( ) {
        System.out.println( vehicleName + " is steered") ;

    }
    public void stop( ) {
        System.out.println( this.vehicleName + " Has Stopped") ;

    }
}

public class LandVehicles extends Vehicle{
    //Constructor
    LandVehicles (String aName ) {
        //Note reference to superclass constructor
        super( "Land Vehicle " + aName ) ;
    }

    public void repairTireorTread( ) {
```

```
              System.out.println( "Repairing Tires or Tread on " +
                        this.vehicleName ) ;


        }
public class AirVehicles extends Vehicle{

        AirVehicles (String aName ) {
            super( "Air Vehicle " + aName ) ;
        }

        public void takeOff( AirVehicles aVeh) {
            System.out.println( aVeh.vehicleName + " Taking off!!!") ;


        }
        public void land( ) {
            System.out.println( "The " + this.vehicleName +
                        " has landed") ;


        }
    }
```

Notice that the methods have implementations (or so to speak). The implementation of the takeOff() method takes an argument of class AirVehicles to reference the property; the land() method uses *this*, the implementations of start() and steer() (and others) reference the instance variable directly. The last reference is preferable to the first two.

```
interface PassengerVehicles {
        public double collectFares( );
        public boolean confirmDestination ( Destination where ) ;

}

interface CargoVehicles {
        public boolean confirmShipment( Shipment whatShipped) ;
        public void deliverPayload( ) ;

}

interface MilitaryVehicles {
        public boolean confirmOrders( Orders theOrders ) ;
        public void deliverPayload( );

}
```

These interfaces do not have the *public* visibility modifier coded. You can assume that this code appears within a class file with the public modifier. Do not expect to see any method bodies here as you did with the previous superclasses. Remember that the methods declared in the interfaces are implemented in the classes that use the interfaces.

Code for the Jet and Truck classes are listed in the following:

```
class Jets        extends   AirVehicles
         implements  PassengerVehicles, CargoVehicles, MilitaryVehicles
{
      //Constructor
      Jets (String aName ) {
         super("The Jet " + aName ) ;
      }

      public double collectFares( ) {
         System.out.println("Jet Fares Collected For " +
                   this.vehicleName ) ;
         return 1010.11 ;
      }
      public boolean confirmDestination( Destination jetDest ) {
         System.out.println("Jet Destination Confirmed For "
                   + this.vehicleName ) ;
         return( false ) ;
      }
      public void confirmShipment( ) {
         System.out.println("Jet Shipment Confirmed For "
                   + this.vehicleName ) ;
      }
      public void confirmOrders( ) {
         System.out.println("Jet Orders Confirmed For "
                   + this.vehicleName ) ;
      }
      public void deliverPayload( ) {
         System.out.println("Payload DeliveredFor "
                   + this.vehicleName ) ;
      }
      //Other methods, perhaps

}


class Trucks extends  LandVehicles
         implements PassengerVehicles, CargoVehicles, MilitaryVehicles
{
      //refer to the superclass constructor
      Trucks (String aName ) {
         super("The Truck " + aName ) ;
      }
      public double collectFares( ) {
         System.out.println("Truck Fares Collected For "
                   + this.vehicleName ) ;
         return 2323.11 ;
      }
      public boolean confirmDestination( Destination truckDest ) {
         System.out.println("Truck Destination Confirmed For "
```

```
                              + this.vehicleName ) ;
              return ( true ) ;
      }
      public void confirmShipment( ) {
          System.out.println("Truck Shipment Confirmed For "
                      + this.vehicleName ) ;
      }
      public void confirmOrders( ) {
          System.out.println("Truck Orders Confirmed For "
                      + this.vehicleName ) ;
      }
      public void deliverPayload( ) {
          System.out.println("Truck Payload Delivered For "
                      + this.vehicleName ) ;
      }
      //Other methods, perhaps
  }
```

Notice that both classes *must* provide implementations for *all* methods declared in the interfaces. Of course, you are free to declare and code other methods not defined in the interface. Here, you must use the Java reserved word *this* to refer to the object in question when you need access to instance variables.

Next, the following code refers to objects of class Jet and Truck:

```
public class VehicleExample {

    public static void main(String[] names) {

        Jets          myJet    = new Jets( names[0] ) ;
        Trucks        myTruck  = new Trucks( names[ 1 ] ) ;

        double jetFare = myJet.collectFares() ;        //1
        double truckFare = myTruck.collectFares() ;    //2

        whichPVehicle( myJet ) ;                       //3
        whichPVehicle( myTruck ) ;                     //4

    }
    static void whichPVehicle( PassengerVehicles ph ) {
        System.out.println("in Which Vehicle Routine");
        System.out.println( ph.collectFares() ) ;
    }
}
```

The main() method accepts the array of string argument, which the method uses to name the objects. Notice that both Jets and Trucks objects have their own implementation of the collectFares() method; line 1 invokes the method for class Jets, line 2 invokes the method for class Trucks.

Lines 3 and 4 show the strength of interfaces. Notice that the method *whichPVehicle*() accepts an argument of *PassengerVehicle*. However, line 3 passes an argument of class Jets. Java will allow this construct; when a class implements an interface, the class can be used anywhere the interface can be used. That is why line 4, which passes an argument of class Trucks, is also permitted.

In Summary

The importance of interfaces is to separate behaviors from classes that use the behaviors. The previous code shows how you can abstract these behaviors by referencing a class behavior through an interface. If you were to change the implementations of methods declared in interfaces, you need not change code that accesses these methods.

In the next chapter, you'll see how to use interfaces with GUI elements to handle *events*.

CHAPTER 11

Java Event-Handling Basics

In days of old, green screens were the interface between the customer and the computer, and dominated the data processing landscape. (Now, mainframe terminal emulators that run on PCs have replaced the classic green screens.) Programs had a sequential flow. Batch systems running unattended produced mountains of output. For those systems that required user inputs, the input requirements—the what, where, and when—were well defined. User inputs mostly filled out green screens and triggered transactions.

Much of the mainframe world is still like this, but with one major exception: The green screen has yielded to the personal computer as the interface between the customer and the computer. The customer entering data in a green screen uses a character-based interface; her friend down the hall entering data in a PC uses a *graphical user interface* (GUI).

Green screen inputs typically enable a customer to fill in data entry fields and press the *Enter* or a function key to accept the inputs and proceed to the next step of the application. In contrast, GUI inputs enable a customer to enter data, click buttons, invoke actions from menus, display additional windows, and so forth. As you might imagine, programming an application to accept user inputs from a green screen is vastly different than from that of a GUI.

This short chapter discusses the basics of writing Java programs to process events. After a brief discourse on events, you'll read about high-level event processing frameworks called *event models* and of course, the Java event model. To have a handle on Java event handling, you'll need a bit of background on GUI containers and interface components, which you'll also get in this chapter. You'll see some Java code that captures GUI events. This chapter closes with a summary of Java event handling.

Event Processing

At a high level, you can define an event as something that happens during the execution of a program that demands attention. For example, when your program reaches the end of a file, your program should take some action, such as closing the file. Many programs that execute in a mainframe environment handle a series of *predictable* events, especially programs that execute in batch. The handling of events is part and parcel of the programmer's job.

Notice that this description does not deal specifically with applications that accept user inputs. Chapter 12, "Exception Handling and Thread Basics," discusses the Java mechanism for handling certain events called *exceptions*. In this chapter, you'll read about how Java handles events that are created as a result of *user inputs*.

Green screen applications process user inputs in a synchronous manner; that is, the inputs come to the program as a set of well-ordered streams. The program "expects" the user inputs at certain times during its execution. Most of the time, the program will sit still and wait for users to complete their inputs, fill out data entry screens, and press ENTER or a function key to allow the program to continue execution.

The process that green screen mainframe programs use to gather user inputs is relatively straightforward: The program executes until it displays a green screen where the program patiently waits for the user to complete the screen entries and hit a *continue* or *process* key. This process is repeated until the program has all the required user inputs, after which the program executes, oblivious to the user.

In contrast, a GUI application process user inputs in an asynchronous manner. The inputs come to the program in unpredictable ways: some from clicking a button, some from entering text in a text area, and some from selecting a menu item. A GUI program has no reasonable way of knowing *ahead of time* what sort of GUI elements a user will use to provide inputs at any given time.

The unpredictability of inputs received by a GUI application demands a different process than that used for green screen applications. A GUI application has to deal with whatever is thrown its way; the application has to respond to events as they occur. The five-dollar term used to describe programming to respond to events is (not surprisingly) *event driven programming*.

One often-used scheme to implement event driven programming is to code a rather large case construct inside a conditional loop. The loop executes while user input is processed. The case construct that takes action depending on the sort of event generated is inside the loop. When no more events need to be processed, the program processes what it must in the absence of user events, otherwise it terminates. Figure 11.1 illustrates this concept.

The left column shows some of the myriad input sources available to accept inputs or those available to generate input events. Now, the program has no way of knowing which input devices will be used or what order the user will use these devices. Ergo, the computing environment, establishes an *event queue* to house generated events. The programming language has an application program interface (API) function library that can fetch these events and related information (like the source of the event) from the event queue. The conditional loop contains a case construct that invokes some user

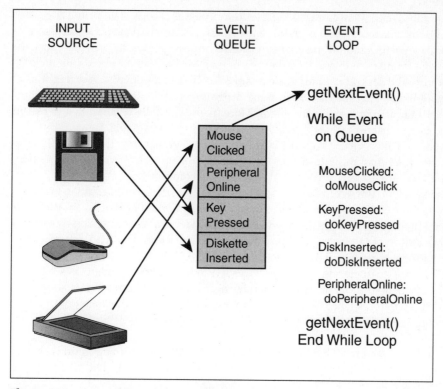

Figure 11.1 Event driven programming loop.

written routine based on the source of the event. The loop terminates when no more events need to be processed.

With the input source determined inside the case construct, each routine invoked in the case construct determines the nature of the event. For example, the *doKeyPressed* user written routine issues additional API calls to determine which keyboard character, or combination of characters, was pressed; the *doMouseClick* routine issues calls to determine what mouse button was clicked, where on the screen the mouse was clicked, and so on. If determination of the nature of the event requires additional information, the program issues additional API calls to obtain this information. If the event was generated by a mouse click, the program may need to determine just what was clicked (button, scroll bar, and so on) or where the click occurred. It's all very procedural, isn't it?

Java Graphical Interface Components

Before you read specifics about Java event handling, a few words about Java graphical interface components are in order. This topic is large enough for several chapters; the

Java interface component libraries contain hundreds of classes. The primary goal of this section is to acquaint you with some Java GUI fundamentals that are necessary to grasp Java's event handling mechanism; the secondary goal is to provide you with enough of a foundation to make further reading on Java GUI components intelligible.

Why not take several chapters to explain Java GUI components, you might ask? Well, in all likelihood, you, the mainframe programmer, will not be developing complex user interfaces in Java for the client. More likely, you'll be writing Java to use an existing user interface, such as a Web browser. Your time is valuable, right?

The basis of Java GUI components is the *Abstract Windowing Toolkit* (AWT). The AWT does more than provide classes for GUI components. However, in this section, we'll limit the discussion of AWT to AWT graphical components.

The idea behind the AWT is to provide a set of services that would enable a Java program to use the GUI and other services on the platform. In other words, an AWT button component created by a Java program running on a Wintel box is actually a Windows button, on a Macintosh it is a Mac button, and so on. The AWT relies heavily on the platform to render GUI components.

This reliance on operating system services to render GUI components is a bit troubling. Many people thought that the rendering of Java GUI components should be done with Java. In response to this line of thought, Sun created the *Swing* component set. Swing, a core library since JDK 1.2, is meant to replace the GUI components in the AWT.

Although you can mix GUI components from the AWT and Swing in one application, you are advised to follow this simple guideline: When using JDK 1.1 and prior, use AWT; when using JDK 1.2 and later, use Swing.

Using GUI components from either AWT or Swing is conceptually similar; you instantiate a Java class from the appropriate library (AWT or Swing) to create an object representing the desired graphical component. Hence, for AWT, this code creates a button:

```
import java.awt.* ;
//One of two constructors for the AWT Button class
Button myButton = new Button("Button Text") ;
```

And this code creates a Swing button:

```
import javax.swing.* ;
//One of four constructors for the Swing JButton class
JButton mySwingButton = new JButton("Button Text") ;
```

The Swing GUI component corresponding to its AWT counterpart is named *J* followed by the AWT component name.

Both AWT and Swing rely on the concept of *containers*. A container is an abstraction that holds GUI components, among other containers. You create an interface by adding GUI components to containers. Here's a code snippet that illustrates the concept:

```
//For AWT Frame Container and Button Component
import java.awt.* ;

Frame      myFrame = new Frame("My Frame") ;
Button     myButton = new Button("A Button") ;
myFrame.add( myButton ) ;
```

The idea is that the object myFrame serves as a place to put GUI components. For Swing containers and components, the mechanics are a bit different, but the idea is the same.

```
//For Swing JFrame Container and JButton Component
import javax.swing.* ;

//JFrame Is a subclass of Frame, by the way
JFrame      myJFrame = new JFrame("My Swing Frame") ;
JButton     myJButton = new JButton("A Swing Button") ;
//Panes are a Swing construct that allows for layering, transparency
MyJFrame.getContentPane().add( myJButton ) ;
```

You get the idea? Create a container and add GUI elements. Each GUI component (AWT or Swing) is an object from a class that contains properties and methods that are peculiar to the GUI component. This is all you need to know about creating GUI elements in Java in order to leap into event processing.

Java Events

As you might imagine, objects represent events in Java. Likewise, an event object has (drumroll, please) a list of properties and a set of behaviors. The Java runtime defines event classes that describe events that are generated by various input devices and various graphical components.

The parent class of all events in Java is *java.util.EventObject*. For events generated by AWT GUI components, the parent class is *java.awt.AWTEvent*. Some Swing components generate events that are represented by subclasses of EventObject.

When you click in a window created by a Java application, the Java runtime generates a window event, or an object from class *java.awt.event.WindowEvent*. When you press one or more keys, the runtime generates a keyboard event, or an object from class *java.awt.event.KeyEvent*. Sometimes such events are called low-level events.

The Java runtime defines certain event classes to capture *semantic*, or high-level events. For example, when you select a window, a list item, or some other selectable interface component, the Java runtime generates an item event in addition to the event corresponding to the particular component type selected. If needed, your Java program can respond to the high-level, meaningful event of selecting an item as opposed to dealing with the device that performed the actual selecting (the mouse).

Table 11.1 Some GUI Components with Generated Events

GUI COMPONENT	CLASSES REPRESENTING EVENTS GENERATED BY THIS COMPONENT	HOW THIS EVENT IS GENERATED
Button	ActionEvent	Clicking on a button
Check Box	ItemEvent	Selecting/deselecting an item
Combo Box	ItemEvent	Selecting/deselecting an item
List	ActionEvent ItemEvent	Double-clicking a list item Selecting/deselecting an item
Menu Item	ActionEvent	Selecting a menu item
Radio Button	ItemEvent	Selecting/deselecting an item
Scroll Bar	AdjustmentEvent	Moving a scroll bar
Text Entry Box	TextEvent ActionEvent	Changing text Finishing editing text
Window	WindowEvent	Opening/closing/ minimizing/restoring a window

Table 11.1 shows some of the Java events generated by Java graphical interface components. In other words, the table shows the classes of objects corresponding to events generated by these components.

By the way, container objects generate events from class *ContainerEvent*.

The Java Event Processing Model

The lingo used to describe how events are passed to your code that handles the events is called an *event model*. Although the model of an event loop processing events based on the event source is conceptually straightforward, the model is implemented in mostly procedural programming languages. No hint of leveraging object technology appears here. After all, you would expect Java to process events by using an object metaphor of some sort, which Java does, of course.

The event model used by Java is called the *delegation-based* model. This model enables a Java programmer to connect graphical components that generate events to the objects that handle those events. Here's the recipe of implementing the delegation-based model in Java:

1. Create an object to represent the graphical component that generates the events, which we'll call the *event source*. Add the component to a container if required.

2. Create a class to handle the generated events from the event source. The event handling class implements an interface called a *listener* in the *java.awt.event* package, which is peculiar to the graphical component.

3. Code implementations of the listener interface that implement the appropriate action in response to the generated event. Because the listener is an interface, you *must* provide implementations for all behaviors stated in the interface.

4. Delegate the code that handles the events to the component that generates them as follows:
   a. Instantiate an object of the class created in Step 2 to the component object created in Step 1.
   b. Invoke the component's *add listener* method. In Javaspeak, the invoking of the add listener method is called *registering the listener*. The add listener method, which is peculiar to each graphical component, takes the object created in Step 2 as an argument.

The event model does not dictate the exact nature of the source object. You are free to register the listener to whatever object makes sense. Usually, you'll register the listener for a component to the container holding the component. If the component is a container, you'll register the listener with the container object.

To capture events from a window, you code a class that implements the listener interface for windows, which is the *WindowListener* interface. Register the listener by invoking the window's *addWindowListener* method, passing an instance of the class that implements the WindowListener interface.

To capture events from a button, you code a class that implements the listener interface for buttons, which is the *ActionListener* interface. After you add the button object to a suitable container with the *add* method, you register the listener by invoking the button's *addActionListener* method, passing an instance of the class that implements the ActionListener interface.

Let's see some code that will bring these words to life.

THE OLD JAVA EVENT MODEL

Java 1.0 uses an event model based on an *Event* superclass and a *Component* superclass. You, the Java 1.0 programmer, would access instance variables of class Event that describe the event. Your application would code methods that override methods of class Component that handle specific events like mouseMove() and keyDown(). This chapter will not discuss the Java 1.0 event model, but you should be aware of its existence in case you run into any old Java code.

Example: Capturing Window Events

The following code creates a window and reports on various window events. This example uses Swing components. The code that uses AWT components is included as comments.

```java
import javax.swing.* ;
import java.awt.event.* ;
import java.awt.* ;

public class WindowDemo {

public static void main(String[] args) {
    //Create a container object - In this case, a window
    //This is the event source
    JFrame      myJFrame = new JFrame("My Window") ;          //1
    //These next two statements are needed to see the window
    myJFrame.setSize( 600, 600 ) ;
    myJFrame.setVisible( true ) ;
    //Create an Instance of the code that actually responds to the
//events - the event handler
    myWindowEventHandlerCode   mWEHC =
new myWindowEventHandlerCode() ;                              //4a
    //Register the event handler with the object that receives the
//events
    myJFrame.addWindowListener( mWEHC ) ;                     //4b
//
/** This is the version using AWT components

    Frame      myFrame = new Frame("My Frame") ;             //1

    myFrame.setSize(600, 600 ) ;
    myFrame.setVisible( true ) ;

    myWindowEventHandlerCode   mWEHC =                       //4a
new myWindowEventHandlerCode() ;

    myFrame.addWindowListener( mWEHC ) ;                     //4b

**/
//
class myWindowEventHandlerCode implements WindowListener{    //2

    public void windowClosing( WindowEvent we) {
        System.out.println("Bye!" ) ;
        System.exit(0) ;
    }
    public void windowActivated(WindowEvent we) {           //3
```

```
                System.out.println("Window Activated") ;
        }
        public void windowDeactivated(WindowEvent we) {          //3
                System.out.println("Window Deactivated") ;
        }
        public void windowIconified(WindowEvent we) {            //3
                System.out.println("Window Minimized/Iconified") ;
        }
        public void windowDeiconified(WindowEvent we) {          //3
                System.out.println("Window Maximized/Deconified") ;
        }
        public void windowOpened(WindowEvent we) {      }        //3

  }
```

The bolded numbers to the right of the statements correspond to the numbers shown in the previous recipe. The lines numbered 1 create a JFrame object (Swing) and a Frame object (AWT). These objects will generate the events to which the code will respond.

Line 2 is the class that contains the implementations of the response to the events capable of being generated by the objects created in lines 1. Notice that this class implements the appropriate listener interface for the event generating objects. Objects of the class created in line 2 are the event handlers. If this program created multiple JFrames and these separate JFrames required different responses to WindowEvents, you would code different class statements and provide different implementations of the WindowListener interface.

Lines 3 are the behaviors that require implementation. The only thing going on here is that in response to the event, Java writes some text to System.out. When the window is closing, Java issues a call to the System.exit() method, which stops the program.

The lines numbered 4a create an object that will respond to the generated events. Lines 4b invoke the add listener method for the JFrame (or Frame) component using the event handler object as an argument.

Figure 11.2 shows a sample execution of the program.

Of course, when you run this program, your results will differ depending on what and where you click.

One user action on a component could trigger multiple events. When you minimize, or iconify, a window, the JFrame object generates two window events: a WindowIconified event and a WindowDeselected event. This makes sense because when the window is minimized, it is also deselected.

You may be wondering just how the Java runtime knows when to fire the methods that implement the listener interface. Looking at the WindowDemo program, you can see that method invocations of say, windowActivated() or windowIconified() do not exist anywhere in the code. This is the crux of the event delegation model: The runtime delegates events to code as the events occur. The runtime knows what events go to what code by a *callback* mechanism. In other words, the event causes the runtime to call back to the code that is hooked into the listener.

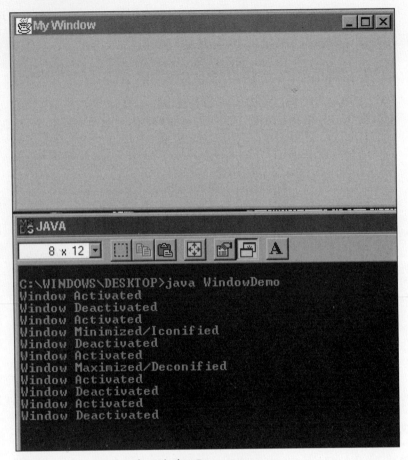

Figure 11.2   Running the WindowDemo program.

Example: Capturing Button Events

Let's look at another example. The following code shows a button added to the JFrame (or Frame) and an event listener that is hooked in to report when the button is clicked. Only the code showing the button creation, listener implementation, and listener registration is presented. The numbers in parenthesis refer to the recipe previously shown.

Create the button and add to a container (1).

```
//Swing
JButton      myJButton      = new JButton("My Button") ;
myJFrame.getContentPane().add( myJButton ) ;
//AWT
Button      myButton      = new Button("My Button")  ;
```

```
myFrame.add( myButton ) ;
```

Create a class to handle events generated by the component (2). If you look at Table 11.1, you'll note that buttons generate ActionEvents. Ergo, the event handling code, implements the ActionListener interface, as shown here:

```
//Swing and AWT
class myButtonEventHandlerCode implements ActionListener{
```

Code implementations of all behaviors required by the listener interface (3). The ActionListener interface contains only one behavior: *actionPerformed*.

```
//Swing and AWT
public void actionPerformed( ActionEvent ae) {
        System.out.println("Mouse Clicked on this button" ) ;
}
```

Delegate the event handler to the component that generates the event by instantiating an event handler object (4a)

```
//Swing and AWT
myButtonEventHandlerCode  mBEHC = new myButtonEventHandlerCode() ;
```

and invoke the component's add listener method (4b).

```
//Swing
myJButton.addActionListener( mBEHC ) ;
//AWT
myButton.addActionListener( mBEHC ) ;
```

You can skin Java events in more than one way. The next two sections show alternate coding techniques for handling events.

Variations on a Theme 1: Using Adapter Classes

A point worth mentioning is that you, the Java programmer, must provide implementations for *all* the behaviors stated in the interface. If you forgot this important fact, reread Chapter 10 "Interfaces." If you don't have the need to provide an implementation for an interface behavior, you can "dummy" it out. For an example, look at the *windowOpened()* method coded in the WindowListener interface implementation—it has no code. If you were interested in acting on only one of the window events generated, you would have to provide dummy implementations of the remaining six behaviors.

Java has several *adapter classes* that help mitigate this odd situation. An adapter class is a class of dummy methods that implement an interface. You extend the adapter class and override the dummy methods with your own. Using an adapter class, line 2 becomes:

```
class myWindowEventHandlerCode extends WindowAdapter {
```

Notice that the class definition does not implement an interface. Because the WindowAdapter class implements the WindowListener interface, the user created class extends a class. Of course, if the event handler class needs to extend a different class, you are stuck implementing the interface because as you know, a Java class can have only one superclass.

Assuming that we are interested in closing the window only, the event handler class that extends the adapter class would look like this:

```
class myWindowEventHandlerCode extends WindowAdapter{

    public void windowClosing( WindowEvent we) {
        System.out.println("Bye!" ) ;
        System.exit(0) ;
    }
}
```

Short and sweet.

Variations on a Theme 2: Using Top-Level Classes

The previous code samples show the use of a separate class that implements the listener interface or extends the adapter class. You can use just about any class to do this. Check out the following example.

```
import javax.swing.* ;
import java.awt.event.* ;
import java.awt.* ;

public class WindowDemo2 implements WindowListener {

  public static void main(String[] a) {

      JFrame      myJFrame = new JFrame("My Window") ;

    myJFrame.setSize( 400, 200 ) ;
    myJFrame.setVisible( true ) ;

      myJFrame.addWindowListener( new WindowDemo2() ) ;      //1

  }
```

```
    public void windowClosing( WindowEvent we) {
        System.out.println("Bye!" ) ;
        System.exit(0) ;
    }
    public void windowActivated(WindowEvent we) {
        System.out.println("Window Activated") ;
    }
    public void windowDeactivated(WindowEvent we) {
        System.out.println("Window Deactivated") ;
    }
    public void windowIconified(WindowEvent we) {
        System.out.println("Window Minimized/Iconified") ;
    }
    public void windowDeiconified(WindowEvent we) {
        System.out.println("Window Maximized/Deconified") ;
    }
    public void windowOpened(WindowEvent we) { }

    public void windowClosed(WindowEvent we) { }
}
```

This code shows that you may dispense with creating a separate class for the event handling code and use an existing class instead. Two points are worth noting here:

1. Because you don't have a separate class that handles the events, you would either create an instance of the top-level class and use the instance as the argument to the add listener method, or use an existing instance of the top-level class as the argument, as shown on line 1.

2. Your top-level class could extend an adapter class instead of implementing the listener interface.

If you wanted to listen for window events and button events in your top-level class, your class would implement both listeners.

Variations on a Theme 3: Using Inner Classes

In Chapter 7, "Class and Object Representation," you read a bit about *inner classes*. It turns out that the major use of inner classes is to code event handlers. Why not code your event handling code next to the code that creates the component that generates the event? This is what our add listener method looks like when an inner class represents the event handler.

```
myJButton.addActionListener( new ActionListener() {
                public void actionPerformed( ActionEvent ae) {
                    System.out.println("Mouse Clicked on this button") ;
                }
                                }
                ) ;
```

You could also use an adapter class with the inner class as follows:

```
myJFrame.addWindowListener( new WindowAdapter() {
              public void windowIconified( WindowEvent we) {
                 System.out.println("Getting Smaller Now . . . .") ;
              }
                               }
                       ) ;
```

Using inner classes works very well when the event handling code is short. However, once the event handler grows, you might find wading through the code a bit tiresome.

In Summary

In brief, Java handles events by connecting the components that generate the events to the implementation of event listeners by a callback mechanism. The event listener implementations are the methods that react to the receipt of the event.

After you've created your components and placed them in containers, you code implementations for the listeners of the components and often, the containers. The listeners are tailored to reflect the behaviors of the components and containers. Once the listeners are implemented, register them to the appropriate objects with the listener's add listener method. Once registered, your work is done. The Java runtime will dispatch the events to the appropriate event handler methods for you automatically.

You've read about the basics of Java event processing. The rest is in the details of the particular events and listener interfaces that are required to implement a full-featured GUI.

CHAPTER 12

Exception Handling and Thread Basics

In the real world, programmers must take steps to guard against occurrences that are unforeseeable, unfortunate, and avoidable. Unforeseeable occurrences often occur when customers enter bogus data or do not follow operating procedures. Unfortunate occurrences include input files containing spoiled, corrupt, or out-of-date data. Examples of avoidable occurrences include the presence of runtime errors, such as divide-by-zero and arithmetic overflows.

The bad news is that these occurrences will always be part of the programmer's world; the good news is that Java has a mechanism that helps the programmer overcome some of the ill effects that arise from these occurrences. This mechanism, called *exception handling*, is one of this chapter's subjects.

Java's language support for *multiple threads* is the other subject that is covered. A thread is a flow of program control; multiple threads mean that a single Java program may create and manage multiple program flows of control. These multiple program flows may either be used to work on different pieces of a large problem, or to keep computing resources busy. While one thread waits for, say, user inputs, another thread is busy performing some background task. As you will see, creating and managing tasks in Java is pretty straightforward once you understand the basics.

What Are Exceptions?

In plain language, an exception is some event that is not usual, normal, or anticipated. In the language of programmers, an exception means pretty much the same thing.

However, the term *exception* has a specific meaning in Java. An exception is *an instance of a class derived from class Throwable.*

This meaning tells us that exceptions are, of course, *objects*. This should not surprise you by now. After all, the heart and soul of this whole object-oriented view is to express entities as objects. In Java, entities used in your applications and system entities, such as files and exceptions, are expressed as objects.

Because exceptions are objects, each exception object has properties and behaviors. You can do object stuff with exceptions, such as create new exceptions, pass exceptions as arguments to methods, and invoke methods that implement exception behavior. In addition, Java contains custom language support for dealing with these exception objects. This language support is, of course, a topic of this chapter. Before you work on Java exception support, take a look at the Java exception hierarchy.

The Java Exception Hierarchy

The Java exception hierarchy is shown in Figure 12.1.

At the top of the chain is class Throwable. Class Throwable contains most of the methods you'll find useful, such as printing a list of the called methods (called a *stack*

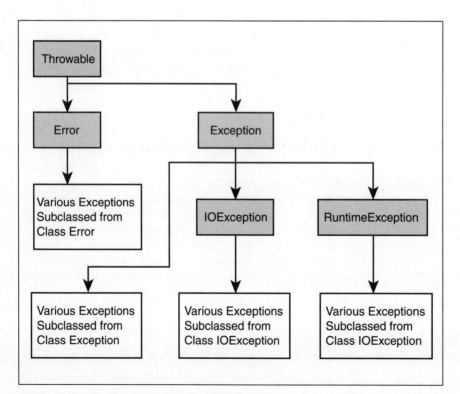

Figure 12.1 The Java Exception class hierarchy.

trace), fetching, or setting a string describing the exception. Class Throwable has two direct subclasses: Error and Exception.

Class *Error* describes exceptions that, almost always, spell certain death and doom for your program. Exceptions derived from class Error report problems with the Java Virtual Machine, such as out-of-memory or the depletion of some other system resource. There is little, if anything, you can do about such exceptions. The Java Language Specification refers to exceptions derived from class Error as *unchecked exceptions*. Fortunately, exceptions derived from class Error are rare.

Class *Exception* is where you'll spend your time catching and (hopefully) recovering from exceptional conditions. All names of each subclass of class Exception end with the word *exception*. Because most of your Java code will catch exceptions of class Exception or one of its subclasses, class Exception deserves special treatment.

The Java Exception Class

Don't get confused—this chapter, in part, talks about Java exception handling, and class Exception is one class describing exceptions. You'll know what the Java literature means by the exceptional condition and an object of class Exception.

Class Exception has about 35 subclasses, ranging from general (for example, SQLException and IOException) to specific (for example, ClassNotFoundException and ServerNotActiveException). You guessed it—the general exception classes have direct subclasses whereas the specific exception classes do not.

You could group the 35 or so subclasses of Exception into 3 categories:

1. I/O exceptions
2. Exceptions that your code should stop from occurring
3. Other exceptions not falling into the previous categories

I/O exceptions, the first category, are objects of class *IOException* or one of its subclasses. As you've deduced, exceptions in this class describe exceptions arising from I/O, such as FileNotFoundException or MalformedURLException. As a rule, you should attempt to recover from exceptions of these classes. If your program encounters a FileNotFoundException, get another (hopefully existing) file. If your program attempts to use a URL in an incorrect format, you should fix this. At the very least, your program should display informative diagnostics; try to roll the program back to a stable state and exit gracefully. Exceptions of IOException and those of its subclasses are called *checked exceptions*.

Java folk use shorthand for expressing exceptions in the second category. *Runtime* exceptions, or exceptions of class RuntimeException, or one of its direct subclasses, are exceptions that arise mostly from poor quality Java code. Now, the term runtime exception is a bit of a misnomer because all exceptions occur at runtime. Exceptions of class RuntimeException or one of its subclasses are referred to as *unchecked exceptions*. A runtime exception should *never occur* because you, the Java programmer, can write code to stop this class of exceptions from rearing their ugly heads.

Let's be honest, okay? If, while on call, you got roused from slumber at some early hour to patch a program that bombed because of a divide-by-zero, you'd be more than slightly irate, am I right? You know that a single line of code before the divide would stop the divide-by-zero from occurring. You might think that a special place exists down under (not Australia) where programmers who put this sort of code in production should go. You shudder to think what other surprises lie in store—such as accessing an array with an out-of-bounds index, or accessing an uninitialized data element.

The zerodivide and other exceptional conditions mentioned previously could have, *and should have,* never occurred. Your Java code should check your program's primitive types and objects to guard against these conditions. In other words, you should not rely on Java's exception reporting and handling mechanism to cope with exceptions of class RuntimeException and its direct subclasses.

Check for ArithmeticException by checking the divisor before performing the division. (You recall that floating point arithmetic never causes exceptions, right?) Check for ArrayIndexOutOfBoundsException by comparing the array index to the array length. Check for a ClassCastException by using the *instanceof* operator as follows:

```
MyClass anotherObject ;
If (myObject instanceof MyClass)
    anotherObject = (MyClass) myObject ;
```

Thus, you see that a little bit of caution and common sense can stop these exceptions from ever being thrown.

The exceptions falling in the third category are a hodgepodge of exceptions; you will use Java's exception handling mechanism with which to process. These exceptions are *checked exceptions.*

In short, you'll write code to handle *checked exceptions* and allow *unchecked exceptions* to pass to the Java runtime. You'll soon learn the code to write that will handle checked exceptions.

Mainframe Programming Language Exception Handling Mechanisms

The COBOL programmer handles exceptions the old-fashioned way. Assuming the program is privy to the exception(s), the program attempts the operation and, if unsuccessful, generates a code that describes the exception.

Here, the COBOL program has code to deal with the aforementioned exception before proceeding. For example, a COBOL program issuing SQL against DB2 tables must be on the lookout for a variety of exceptional conditions. Because issuing SQL generates a fixed number of return codes corresponding to a variety of conditions, the COBOL program can trap and deal with these conditions. To wit:

```
EXEC SQL.
    FETCH MYSELECTCURSOR
    INTO :HOST-VAR1, :HOST-VAR2, :HOST-VAR3
END-EXEC.
IF SQLCODE = 100 THEN
```

```
     DIAGNOSTIC = "No More Data to Process".
ELSE
IF SQLCODE < 0 THEN
     DIAGNOSTIC = "Unspecified Error".
ELSE
     PERFORM PROCESS-SELECTION THRU PROCESS-SELECTION-EXIT.
END-IF.
```

This strategy somewhat works when the program knows what exceptions can occur; however, assuming the program is ignorant of the exception(s), the program may gasp and wheeze when the exception occurs.

Sadly, the gasping and wheezing of COBOL programs is common. Yes, you can blame the programmer for this sorry state of affairs. The programmer must bear the brunt of responsibility; however, the programmer could use a bit of help. COBOL offers virtually no support for trapping and dealing with errors in a systemic manner. COBOL programs are replete with return code checking; it is the only mechanism available.

The PL/I programmer has far better language constructs for dealing with the unexpected. PL/I uses the ON block construct to trap and deal with exceptions. For example,

```
On Key( myFile )
Begin ;
     If NumberOfRetries < 4 Then
     Do ;
     Put Skip List ('Key Value ' || myKey
                    || 'Not Found In File') ;
     Put Skip List ('You Have ' || 4 - NumberOfRetries ||
                    ' Retries Left. Make Another Entry') ;
     MyKey = ReEnterKeyValue() ;
     Return ;
End ;
Else
Do ;
     Put Skip List ('You Have Exhausted Your Chances. ' ||
                    'Get Lost' ) ;
     Exit ;
End ;

End ;
/* Some PL/I Code Follows */
Read File( myFile ) Into( myStruct ) KeyFrom( myKey ) ;
```

This code snippet reads a file into a suitably declared record structure based on a key value held in variable myKey. If myKey is not present in the file's index, the Key condition is raised and the previous code block is executed. PL/I also enables the programmer to trap unspecified errors with the ON ERROR statement. Also, PL/I permits the declaration of user-defined conditions by supporting a CONDITION data type.

Actually, as you'll see, PL/I's condition trapping and handling has a passing resemblance to Java's exception handling. Now, there is no talk of exception classes and object stuff in the PL/I programmer's world. Yet, PL/I's capability to trap and deal with specific errors in different parts of the compile unit is a step in the right direction. That said, the PL/I programmer must code numerous return code checks like his or her COBOL brethren.

All programmers must be vigilant in the handling of errors. The COBOL programmer has no language features specific to error handling whereas the PL/I programmer has several. However, Java's exception handling mechanism is superior as you'll see.

The Java Exception Handling Mechanism

Java exception handling is pretty straightforward. In short, the Java programming language enables exceptions to be *thrown* and *caught*. The "throwing" of an exception is the Java way of bringing the exception to a point where the exception can be handled, whereas the "catching'" is the handling of the exception.

Throwing Exceptions

Exceptions can be thrown in one of two ways: either your code can explicitly throw the exception, or your code throws the exception in response to an event in the Java runtime. In other words, either you or the Java Virtual Machine throws the exception.

You throw an exception by coding a *throw* statement as follows,

```
throw myException ;
```

where *myException* is an object of a class that extends class Throwable.

Why would you want to throw an exception? One reason is so you can control how and when this exception gets handled. Another reason is that when you *create your own exceptions*, explicitly throwing the exception may be the only means at your disposal to manage the exception.

Creating Your Own Exception Classes

Wait a minute. Are you surprised that you can create your own exceptions? Think about it. Exceptions are objects instantiated from a subclass of Throwable. You can use the features of Java to create your own exception classes and, of course, objects from those classes. An example is listed as follows:

```
//Convert RGB Color Coordinates to H(ue)S(aturation)V(alue) Color
//Coordinates.
//Some RGB Color Values Yield Bogus HSV Values
class RGBToHSVConversionException
        extends Exception { // can extend Throwable or other
                        // exception class
```

```
       //Code Constructors..
       RGBToHSVConversionException()
              { //Default No Arg Constructor }
       RGBToHSVConversionException( String desc ) {
   //Leverage Inheritance to do the Dirty Work
   super( desc ) ;
          }


   }
```

As you see, this exception class is just like many in the Java class. Exception classes typically have two constructors: the default, no argument constructor, and one that takes a string as an argument. The string argument is a one-liner describing the nature of the exception, which you can retrieve by invoking the *getMessage()* method.

Now, back to throwing exceptions.

Throwing Exceptions—Continued

The following shows how you could throw exceptions of this (and any other) exception class:

```
class HSVVideoFrame extends VideoFrame {
     //Some code here, some code there
     anHSVCoordinate = convertRGBToHSV( anRGBCoordinate ) ;
     if ( anHSVCoordinate.hue > 360 )
         throw new
         RGBToHSVConversionException("Hue Value Out of Range");
     //Some more code
}
```

The previous code is incomplete because you'll need additional coding constructs that tell Java the nature of the exception that can be thrown. You'll see these constructs soon.

How about the cases where the Java runtime throws the exception? The JVM will throw exceptions more often than your code will. The JVM throws an exception when the exception occurs. To wit:

```
HSVCoordinate firstHSVCoordinate ;
//Some code, perhaps
if ( firstHSVCoordinate.value < 0.1 )    //OOPS!!!
     coordinateDescription = "Dark" ;
```

Assuming the first line is the only declaration of the object *firstHSVCoordinate*, the Java runtime will leave your program dangling at the end of a noose by belching out a *NullPointerException*. You can see that the object firstHSVCoordinate has no value, right? When Java reaches the *if* statement, the unhappy situation of a null object reference bears its ugly head, causing Java to throw the NullPointerException. As an aside, NullPointerException is a subclass of the exception class Runnable. Hence, the code should have checked for the validity of the object reference before making the reference.

You can throw exceptions of your making, or of a class, in one of the Java libraries by coding a throw statement. Any exceptions that you do not explicitly throw will be thrown for you by the Java runtime.

It seems that if your code is going to throw exceptions, the least your code can do is to let users of your classes know what exceptions can be thrown. Keep reading.

Declaring Potentially Thrown Exceptions

If your code explicitly throws exceptions by using one or more *throws* statements, or contains code that may cause the Java runtime to throw exceptions, you must *declare* or *catch* these exceptions. In the this section, you'll learn how to declare the exceptions.

Why declare the exceptions? By declaring in your methods that your code can, or does, throw a particular exception, you announce to the methods invoking your code that the methods must handle these exceptions. This announcement cannot be ignored. The Java compiler enforces the requirement. For example, check out the following snippet:

```
class IOExample {
private static char readIt() {

        int     anInputChar = System.in.read() ;
        return (char) anInputChar ;

}
}
```

However, javac has a thing or two to say about this code. The following shows javac's reaction:

```
C:\WINDOWS\DESKTOP>javac IOExample.java
IOExample.java:4: Exception java.io.IOException must be caught,
or it must be declared in the throws clause of this method.
        int     anInputChar = System.in.read() ;
                                          ^

1 error
```

Java is smart enough to know that the method *System.in.read()* could throw an exception of class IOException. Java also knows that this method has no code to handle this exception. Hence, Java will not let any code use this method unless the code can handle exceptions of class IOException. The following is another example of the robustness of Java at work. Java will not let exceptions declared in methods go unhandled. Java is really trying to ensure that exceptions are taken seriously.

You may wonder how Java knew that System.in.read() could throw an IOException. A cursory glance at the method header provides a clue:

```
public int read()       throws IOException
```

It looks like this read() method has a construct specifically for announcing a potentially thrown exception. Notice the choice of words in the compiler diagnostic above—declared in the *throws clause* of this method. You don't have to be a savant to pick out the throws clause in the method header for the read() method, right?

Okay, we hear what the Java compiler is saying. In response, change the code for the readIt() method to include a throws clause as follows:

```
private static char readIt() throws java.io.IOException
```

Now the code compiles without complaint. Of course you noticed that, because the method did not have an import statement; the class IOException needs a full qualification.

So far, so good. We've told the Java compiler that the method readIt() throws the exception as dictated by readIt() calling System.in.read(). Now let's use readIt() to fetch some characters from the keyboard:

```
public static String readaString() {

        String      aString = "" ;
        char        anInputChar = readIt() ;

        while (anInputChar != '\n') {
            aString = aString + anInputChar ;
            anInputChar = readIt() ;
        }

        return aString.substring(0, aString.length() - 1 ) ;
}
```

Can you guess what the Java compiler will respond with?

```
C:\WINDOWS\DESKTOP>javac IOExample.java
IOExample.java:14: Exception java.io.IOException must be caught, or it
must be declared in the throws clause of this method.
                char      anInputChar = readIt() ;
                                          ^

1 error
```

You guessed it. Java will keep you from getting away with not handling declared exceptions.

A few tidbits on declaring exceptions in a throws clause are in order. If a method can throw more than one exception, then declare the potentially thrown exception classes in the method header separated by commas. For example,

```
public void myThrowingMethod() throws IOException, InterruptedException
```

If a method declares an exception class in its throws clause, then that method can throw an exception derived from a subclass of the declared exception class as well. The System.in.read() method could throw an InterruptedIOException, a RemoteException, or an IOException.

Your rule for the day is as follows: Your methods must declare in the throws clause all the *checked exceptions* these methods throw. In other words, you need not declare exceptions derived from classes Error or RuntimeException, which, as you recall, are also known as unchecked exceptions.

You've now read about both declaring exceptions and throwing exceptions. Continue, and read how to catch exceptions.

Catching Exceptions with try/catch/finally

To catch an exception is to write a block of code that takes some action in response to the throwing of the exception. Recall that you will write code to handle checked exceptions—exceptions not belonging to classes Error or RuntimeException, or any of their subclasses. You need yet another Java language construct to handle exceptions: the *try/catch/finally blocks*.

A *try* block tells the Java compiler and runtime that an exception may be thrown by the code within the block. A *catch* block tells the Java compiler and runtime that when an exception of a given class is thrown, here is where that exception will be handled. A *finally* block is a block that gets executed under all circumstances, even if no exceptions ever get thrown.

If a method contains a try block, the method may contain zero to many catch blocks, zero, or one finally block. You cannot code a try block without *at least* one catch or one finally block. Most of the time, you'll code a try followed by one or more catch blocks.

The following is a simple example:

```
private static char readIt() {

    int      anInputChar = 0 ;

    try {
        anInputChar = System.in.read() ;
    }
    catch (IOException ioe) {
        System.out.println( "Error: " + ioe ) ;
    }
    return (char) anInputChar ;
}
```

Notice the code that could possibly cause the IOException to be thrown is included in the try block. Although the try block contains only a single line of code, the block braces are *required*. After the try statement, the catch block will catch exceptions of the specified type. You can code only one exception class in a try block. As with the try block, the curly braces are required regardless of the number of statements in the catch block.

Your catch block, if present, must immediately follow your try block. You cannot have any statements between the two blocks. You cannot code two try blocks after one another. You could code a try/catch block pair followed by another try/block pair. However, you should code one try block per method. As you've guessed by now, if your method can throw, say, exceptions from three different (and unrelated) classes, you'll usually need three catch blocks. The basic structure would be

```
try {
        //Some Java code that may throw (or cause a throwing of)
        //exception classes 1, 2 and 3
    }
    catch (ExceptionClass1 e1) {
        System.out.println( "Error: " + e1.getMessage() ) ;
        //More code, perhaps

}

catch (ExceptionClass2 e2) {
        System.out.println( "Error: " + e2.getMessage() ) ;
//More code, perhaps

}

catch (ExceptionClass3 e3) {
        System.out.println( "Error: " + e3.getMessage() ) ;
        //More code, perhaps
    }
    //Code outside try/catch blocks
```

You may code one finally block within a method. If so, the finally block must follow the catch block, if coded, or the try block, if no catch block is coded. As previously mentioned, the code within the finally block is *always* executed, even if the try or catch block has a return statement. If you want to ensure that code executes within a method, place that code inside a finally block.

In the previous example, if an exception of class ExceptionClass2 is thrown by a statement in the try block (either by a throws statement or by the Java runtime), program control transfers to the catch block for ExceptionClass2. The code in this block executes, top-down. If this block contains no transfer of control statements, such as return or System.exit() statement, *and a finally block is not present*, the program continues execution at the statement following all the catch statements labeled *Code outside try/catch blocks*. If a finally block is present, the program executes the code in this block after executing the code in the ExceptionClass2 catch block.

Variables declared within try and catch blocks are local to those blocks. Do not declare variables within a try block and expect these variables to be known in your catch and finally blocks. Of course, variables declared outside the try/catch/finally blocks, but within the method containing these blocks, are known to these blocks. Remember the variable scope visibility rule: Within a method, your program can look outside a block and know the "outside" variables, but cannot look inside a block and know the "inside" variables.

You may also pass exceptions up the calling chain (called the *stack trace*) to the method that invoked the method that threw the exception. In other words, a method does not have to handle exceptions with try/catch/finally. The method can "kick it upstairs" by enabling the calling method to handle the exception. However, you should try to handle exceptions close to where they occur. Of course, we are assuming that you know that the calling method can adequately handle the exception.

When an exception gets thrown, Java looks first in the method that threw the exception for a handler. If none is found, Java looks in the method that invoked the exception-throwing method for an exception handler, and so on. If no try/catch/finally block is found in all methods of the stack trace, then the Java runtime spits out a diagnostic, usually followed by a stack trace.

Java Exceptions Summary

- Java exceptions are objects of classes that extend Throwable.

- Unchecked exceptions are objects derived from classes Error and RuntimeException. Let the Java runtime handle these exceptions.

- You can explicitly throw exceptions with the throw statement; the Java runtime can throw exceptions, usually in response to an unfortunate and unseen circumstance.

- You must declare or catch every exception that your method throws.

- You catch exceptions with a series of try/catch/finally blocks.

- Java travels up the stack trace to search for a try/catch block that handles exceptions.

Thread Basics

In this section, you'll read an overview of Java thread support. You'll not, however, read about the full skinny on Java threads. Also, you'll read enough about Java thread support to write some straightforward multithreaded programs. Of course, after this section, you'll understand enough about Java threads to pick up the more advanced uses of threads in Java.

Most mainframe programs have a single control flow, which is governed by input states and program control statements (if/then, do/while, and so on). Let's call a program that has a single flow of control a program a *single threaded program*. All the Java programs you've seen to this point will fall into this category. Of course, we will call a program with multiple flows of control a *multithreaded program*.

Why Code Multithreaded Programs?

Multithreaded programs could maximize resource usage. Imagine, if you will, an application that presents a screen to the customer. If this application were single threaded, and as the customer hems and haws, deliberating over his or her choice of inputs, the application is dead in the water. The single thread stops at the customer's input screen, and it will stay there until the customer decides to continue. Now if this application were multithreaded, the application could be performing some useful work while the customer mulls over his or her inputs. The application could be accessing data from a previous entry, performing a database backup, or printing. The important point is that the application *need not stop.* Other threads could continue, while the thread corresponding to gathering the customer's input tends to that job.

Many programs are, and should be, written as single threaded. Many programs should be written as multithreaded programs. For example, sorting very large sets of data is a good candidate for multithreading. One thread could partition the sort job into multiple, smaller sort jobs, and assign a thread to each smaller sort. When all small sort jobs complete, one thread merges the individual results into the final sorted set. Computations involving large numbers of numbers fall into this category as well. Later, you'll see a multithreaded program that adds up 10,000,000,000 numbers.

Once you learn a few additional Java classes, you'll be able to write many multithreaded programs. Before doing so, a little groundwork is in order.

What Are Java Threads?

The short answer is that a Java thread is an *instance of class Thread* or *a subclass of Thread.* To no surprise, a Java thread is an object. You have two means at your disposal when you want to create threads:

1. You can extend the class Thread *and* override this class's *run()* method. For example,

```
class ThreadedAdd extends Thread {
public void run() {
}
}
```

2. You can implement the *Runnable* interface before providing an instance of your class that implements Runnable to the constructor for the Thread class. For example,

```
class ThreadedAdd implements Runnable {
    public void run() {      //The only method in the Runnable
interface
    }
    ThreadedAdd myAddThread = new ThreadedAdd() ;
    Thread myThread          = new Thread( myAddThread ) ; //One way
    Thread myOtherThread     = new Thread(new ThreadedAdd())
;//Another way
}
```

Think fast: If your thread class (ThreadedAdd, in this case) already extends an existing class, which way would you have to use to create threads? Of course, you remember that you must implement Runnable because Java will not permit you to have a class that extends more than one class.

Regardless of how you create the thread, you'll code the work of the thread in the run() method. You *must* code the run() method with the signature shown above. You cannot pass any arguments to run() nor can your run() method return any values.

Creating threads does not execute them. You need to keep reading to see how to execute your newly created threads.

Executing Your Threads

If you think that you need to invoke the run() method to kick off your threads, then you are half right. Your run() method *must* execute, but *you do not invoke* it. You need a bit of Java magic to invoke your run() method, thereby starting your threads. You need to invoke a method called *start()*. Once you invoke start(), the Java runtime invokes your run() method for you.

Let's back up a little. Code a run() method that does the actual work of your thread(s). Do not write any code that directly invokes run(). You invoke run by invoking start(). *You do not code a start() method.* This is the Java magic—you invoke a method you did not code in order to execute a method you did code. If this seems a bit odd, well, you have my sympathy.

Here are two steps you can take to write multithreaded programs:

1. Create a class that extends class Thread and contains an implementation of run(),

   or

   Create a class that implements the Runnable interface and contains an implementation of run().

2. Create a class that will create instances of your threads and govern the threads execution.

   If you are extending class Thread, you'll use the new operator on your thread subclass and code an invocation to subclassThreadObject.start(). If you are implementing the Runnable interface, you'll create an instance of class Thread and pass an instance of your class containing the implementation of Runnable as an argument to the thread constructor.

Let's see what this looks like by examining a multithreaded program.

Sample MultiThreaded Program

Here is a program that will add the numbers stored in an array using multiple threads. The basic idea is to slice the array up and give each thread a piece of the array. After each thread computes a partial sum, the partial sums are added together to yield a total of all the array elements.

For example, assume your array is 1,000 elements, and you'd like to use 11 threads to add all the numbers. You could have one thread as a driver of sorts (for example, thread 11) creating and executing the remaining 10 threads. As for the thread objects, we could have thread 0 (the first thread) add up array elements 0 to 100, thread 1, add up elements from 101 to 200, and so on.

Let's use the two-step recipe in the previous section, okay? First, the following shows the code for a subclass that extends Thread, or previously, number 1 :

A Subclass of Class Thread

```
class AddThreads extends Thread {                    //1
   //
   //Do not use class variables here!!! Remember----we want to access
   //the partial sums from class ThreadedAdd, which calls this
   //thread class
   //
   int     partialSum = 0 ;                          //2
   int     startIDX, endIDX ;
   //
   //Constructor. All we need is to set up the bounds for the
   //array we're gonna access.
   //
   AddThreads( int idx ) {                           //3
      int threadArrayLength     = ThreadedAdd.adders.length ;
      int arrayLength           = ThreadedAdd.addends.length ;
      startIDX = arrayLength / threadArrayLength * idx ;
      endIDX   = arrayLength / threadArrayLength * ( idx + 1 )-1 ;
   }
   //
   //Recall that threads must override the run() method of class Thread
   //when we're using this threading mechanism (as opposed to
   //implementing the Runnable interface like you MUST do with applets.
   //
   public void run() {                               //4
     //One line ought to do it!!!
     //Notice the reference to the CLASS variable addends declared
     //and initialized in class ThreadedAdd.
     //
     System.out.println("In Thread: " + getName() ) ;
     //Do the actual addition
     for (int arrIDX = startIDX; arrIDX <= endIDX; arrIDX++ )
        partialSum += ThreadedAdd.addends[ arrIDX ] ;
     System.out.println("Done with Thread: " + getName() ) ;

   } // of run() method
} // of class AddThreads
```

All right—by the numbers.

Line 1 is the method header. You know there is tasking going on when you notice that this class extends class *Thread*. This class contains the implementation of the run() method that does the work of the thread.

Line 2 shows some of the properties that objects of this class will contain. The instance variable *partialSum* holds the sum of the array piece generated by a particular thread. The instance variables *startIDX* and *endIDX* contain the start and end indices of the array this thread will access. The expression *threadArrayLength* is the number of threads created that will add up the numbers. In the method (not shown yet) that creates and starts these threads, the threads are stored as an array of subclass objects. We take care to insure that the number of threads evenly divides the number of array elements to be added by choosing appropriate numbers for both.

Line 3 starts the constructor for the subclass objects. We generate the start and end indices from an index passed from the method (not shown yet) that creates the subclass objects.

Line 4 starts the run() method. This method uses the *getName()* method to fetch the name of the thread currently executing, prints the name, and add up the numbers. A for loop adds up the array elements. When the loop is done, the method prints out the thread name.

So far, so good—we have a subclass of Thread and a run() method. Now, we need step 2, which is listed previously—a class to create and manage threads that will add the numbers. The code is show in the next section.

A Class That Creates and Manages Threads

```
public class ThreadedAdd {
    //
    //Notice that we're using CLASS variables here. No need for
    //instance variables because we're not gonna create any objects
    //for class ThreadedAdd.
    //
    static float            theSum    = 0 ;
    static float[]          addends   = new float[ 1000000 ] ;   //1
    //
    //This is an array of objects from a class that extends class Thread.
    //Objects from this class will correspond to a thread that will
    //perform the actual addition.
    //
    static AddThreads[ ] adders     = new AddThreads[ 5 ] ;          //2

    public static void main( String[] args ) {
        //Like it says........
        loadAddendArray() ;
        //
        //Create the thread objects and kick them off.
        //
        for (int tidx = 0; tidx < adders.length; tidx++ ) {
            //Yes, I know this can be done in one statement as follows:
            //addres[ tidx ] = new AddThreads( tidx ).start();
            adders[ tidx ] = new AddThreads( tidx ) ;                //3
            adders[ tidx ].start() ;
        }
        //
```

```
//Wait for all kicked threads to terminate before adding
//the partial sums.
//If we don't wait, we have no guarantee that all five threads
//will finish their tasks before we add up their (possibly)
//nonexistent or incomplete results.
//
try {
    for (int tidx = 0; tidx < adders.length; tidx++ )
        adders[ tidx ].join() ;                               //4
    }
  catch (InterruptedException ie) {
     System.out.println( "Task Interrupted" ) ;
 }
//
//Access the instance variables that hold the partial sums
//for each thread object.
//
for (int tidx = 0; tidx < adders.length; tidx++ )
    theSum += adders[ tidx ].partialSum ;
//Print the result.
System.out.println("The sum equals......" + theSum ) ;


} //of main() method
//
//Initialize array with numbers from 1 to the array size
//Might as well use a static method - no real object jazz
//required for this routine.
//
static void loadAddendArray() {                              //5
    for (int arrIDX = 0; arrIDX < addends.length; arrIDX++ )
        addends[ arrIDX ] = arrIDX + 1 ;
    } // of loadAddendArray

} //of class ThreadedAdd
```

The basic idea is to create five threads, kick them off, and wait for all five threads to complete. add up the partial sums once they complete. Hence, when the main() method executes and kicks off the five threads, there will be *six threads* executing at once. Java uses one thread for executing the main() method; the other five threads are created to do the arithmetic. The comments in the code are self-explanatory. However, some numbered lines bear additional commentary.

Line 1 is the array of numbers the program will add. If you put, say, 100 elements in the array, you'll not see any evidence of multithreading. Later, when you see the output, you'll see such evidence.

Line 2 creates an *array* of objects. Now you know that this declaration *does not create the objects*. All this array declaration does is create a reference for five objects. These objects are instances of the previous class, the class that extends class Thread. In other words, these objects are our threads that will add the array elements.

Line 3 shows the creation of the subclass objects of class Thread, and the invocation to threadObj.start(), to begin executing the threads. Remember, you code a run() method that does the work of the thread; however, you *do not* code a start() method to start the thread running. You *do not* invoke the run() method whereas you *must* invoke the start() method.

Line 4 is a method in class Thread called *join()*. The join() method instructs the Java runtime to have the thread that invoked the join() method (the thread controlling the execution of main()) wait until the thread referenced in the join() method (the threads that do the arithmetic) dies. Because the join() method is in a loop, the Java runtime will instruct the thread governing execution of the main() method to wait until all five threads complete. Like the comment says, you have no guarantee that these threads will complete at the same time or in the order they were started.

Class Thread includes methods to get or set a thread's priority, to put the thread to sleep for a specified period of time, to give up the processor to another waiting-to-execute thread, and others. Aside from run() and start(), the only other thread method used here is join().

Line 4 also shows a try/catch block. The join method throws an exception of class *InterruptedException*, which, if you've been paying attention, must be caught in this method.

Line 5 shows the array being initialized to integers 1 through the array size. This was done to check the results by using the following inductive formula:

```
Sum of numbers from 1 to N = N * ( N + 1 ) / 2
```

Now, for large array sizes, floating-point precision errors creep in; thus, the result will not be exact.

The following page shows an example of a sample output.

Figure 12.2 shows three executions of the multithreaded addition program that adds numbers ranging from one to 1,000,000. Notice how the results show evidence of concurrent threads. If this were a single-threaded program, your output would resemble the following:

```
In Thread: Thread-0
In Thread: Thread-1
In Thread: Thread-2
In Thread: Thread-3
In Thread: Thread-4
Done with Thread: Thread-0
Done with Thread: Thread-1
Done with Thread: Thread-2
Done with Thread: Thread-3
Done with Thread: Thread-4
```

However, you can see the threads completing in a different order for each execution.

Figure 12.2 Three sample executions of ThreadedAdd.

In Summary

You've read a bit about multithreading and seen Java's implementation of Threads. You've read that you create threads in Java by extending the Thread class or implementing the Runnable interface. In both cases, you must code a run() method with this signature:

```
public void run()
```

Also, you have read that your code never invokes run() directly; there is no statement invoking run(). Rather, you invoke the start() method, which kicks off the run() method. When your run() method begins execution, you are multithreading.

Again, this is not the full story. To write multithreading programs, you'll need more than a passing familiarity with the other methods in class Thread, and how to use them. However, with the explanation and the sample-threaded program, you'll be able to handle anything pertaining to Java threads that you could not have handled with time and a good resource book.

CHAPTER 13

The Training Department Class Scheduler System

In this chapter, you'll see the Java source code for a training department class scheduling system. Along the way, you'll see some code in COBOL and PL/I that provides similar functions. You'll also read about the analysis of the application, comparing and contrasting the analysis of a Java solution with the analysis of a procedural language solution.

The chapter starts by describing the high-level functionality of the application followed by some thoughts on the user interface. The chapter describes the format of the underlying data stores and the application outputs. Next, the chapter covers the processing required to produce the outputs.

So far, the application description is not specific to any programming language. Next, you'll read about Java-specific details required to implement the previous interface, outputs, and processes. You'll contrast the Java details with COBOL and PL/I details that follow.

The remainder of the chapter is the Java code that implements the application complete with comments and information on Java features not yet covered in the book. At times, you'll see COBOL and PL/I modules that implement similar application features.

The Application Defined

The purpose of the training department class scheduler is to enable students and instructors to query a set of data stores to find information about classes and courses and to update the store with new information on classes and courses. Put differently, students and instructors can find class and course information; students may enroll in courses and instructors may schedule themselves to teach classes. The application allows a fixed number of students in a class and no student may take two classes at the same time. Also, no instructor may teach two classes at the same time.

NOTE Here, a *course* is a body of instructional material on a particular topic. A *class* is a course scheduled for delivery in a room by an instructor on a given date.

The application is not particularly robust; a commercial system used to track the activities of a training department that would contain more features and functions than our application. As you read this chapter, you'll say from time to time, "Why doesn't the application do function X," or "I would have done function Y differently."

Application Options for the Students

The student will be able to perform the following activities with the application:

- List classes offered starting after a particular date
- List classes by room number
- List courses or classes by category
- List courses taken by student
- List classes with openings (available seats) starting on a particular date

Application Options for the Instructors

The application gives an instructor the same capabilities of the student plus the additional capabilities listed in the following:

- Create a new class (instructor must be teaching the new class)
- Delete an existing class (instructor must be teaching the class)
- Change an existing class (instructor must be teaching the class)
- Add or remove one or more students from a class (instructor must be teaching the class)

The User Interface

The user interface consists of entry screens and a few dialogs. The user first encounters a screen where he enters personal information. Once done, the application determines if the user is an instructor or student and displays the appropriate screen showing allowable application options. The user selects her option. Depending on the selected option, the application may display additional entry screens, perhaps to capture dates or other information required to complete the request.

The OS/390 Mainframe User Interface

Here are the user entry screens that an OS/390 mainframe user may encounter if this application were coded in a procedural language like COBOL. The entry screens are 3270 text-based ISPF entry screens.

The User Identification Screen

Figure 13.1 shows the user identification screen. Here, the user enters a name and an employee ID. The application checks the employee ID against the employee file. If the entered employee ID is on file, and the entered employee ID matches the employee name on file, the application enables the user to continue.

The Student Enter Options Screen

Figure 13.2 shows a mainframe entry screen showing the options available to a student. The options are relatively self-explanatory. The output resulting from entering options 1 or 5 is an ISPF table showing class information. We assume that the student has access to room numbers and course categories.

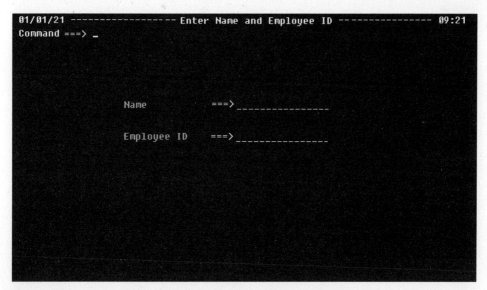

```
01/01/21 ----------------- Enter Name and Employee ID --------------- 09:21
Command ===> _




              Name           ===> _____

              Employee ID    ===> _____
```

Figure 13.1 The mainframe user identification entry screen.

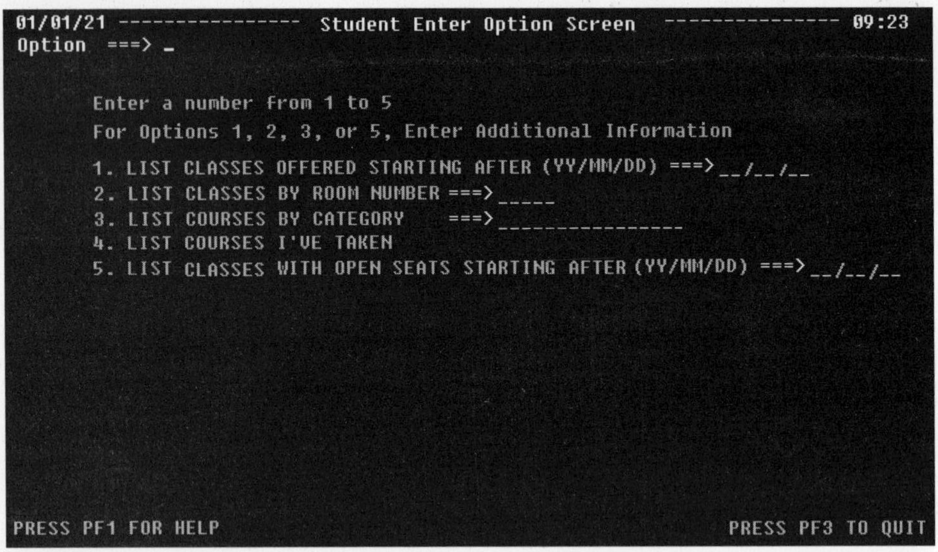

```
01/01/21 ---------------- Student Enter Option Screen  --------------- 09:23
Option ===> _


        Enter a number from 1 to 5
        For Options 1, 2, 3, or 5, Enter Additional Information

        1. LIST CLASSES OFFERED STARTING AFTER (YY/MM/DD) ===>__/__/__
        2. LIST CLASSES BY ROOM NUMBER ===>_____
        3. LIST COURSES BY CATEGORY     ===>_____
        4. LIST COURSES I'VE TAKEN
        5. LIST CLASSES WITH OPEN SEATS STARTING AFTER (YY/MM/DD) ===>__/__/__







PRESS PF1 FOR HELP                                     PRESS PF3 TO QUIT
```

Figure 13.2 The mainframe entry screen showing student options.

The Instructor Enter Options Screen

The instructor has most of the same options available to students plus the ability to create, remove, and change class information for those classes the instructor is scheduled to teach or has already taught. The result of selecting the *change student roster* option is the same list as shown in Figure 13.5.

Figure 13.3 shows the options available to an instructor.

The Instructor Create a New Class Screen

When the instructor selects option 6 from the screen shown in Figure 13.3, the instructor sees the screen shown in Figure 13.4. The entry screen shows the instructor's name by default; the instructor may change this field. The entered course ID must exist on file.

Figure 13.4 shows the entry screen for creating a new class. Here, the instructor enters particulars for the course.

The Instructor Change Existing Class Entry Screen

The change existing class screen looks the same as the screen shown in Figure 13.4, except that the input fields are prefilled with the entered class information and the

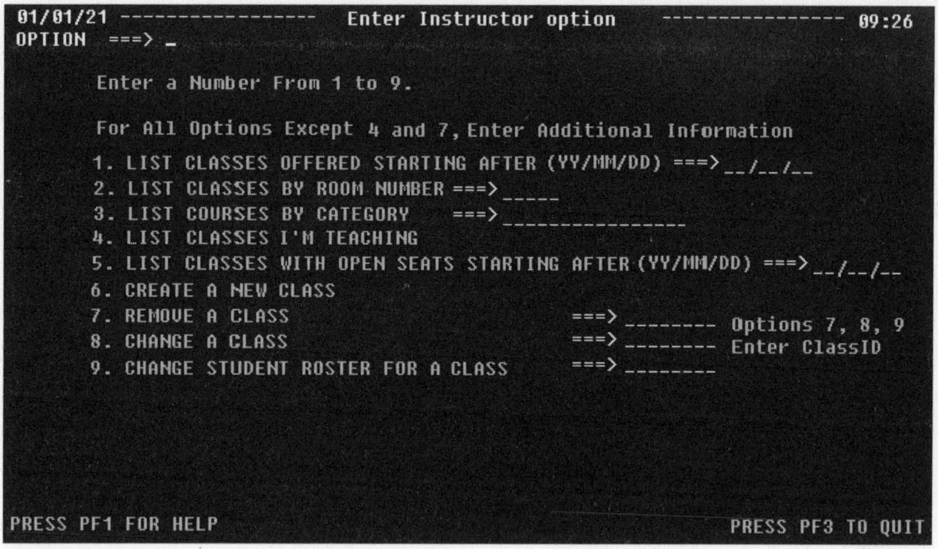

```
01/01/21 ----------------- Enter Instructor option   ---------------- 09:26
OPTION  ===> _

       Enter a Number From 1 to 9.

       For All Options Except 4 and 7, Enter Additional Information
       1. LIST CLASSES OFFERED STARTING AFTER (YY/MM/DD) ===> __/__/__
       2. LIST CLASSES BY ROOM NUMBER ===> _____
       3. LIST COURSES BY CATEGORY    ===> _____
       4. LIST CLASSES I'M TEACHING
       5. LIST CLASSES WITH OPEN SEATS STARTING AFTER (YY/MM/DD) ===> __/__/__
       6. CREATE A NEW CLASS
       7. REMOVE A CLASS                        ===> -------- Options 7, 8, 9
       8. CHANGE A CLASS                        ===> -------- Enter ClassID
       9. CHANGE STUDENT ROSTER FOR A CLASS     ===> --------




PRESS PF1 FOR HELP                                        PRESS PF3 TO QUIT
```

Figure 13.3   The mainframe entry screen showing instructor options.

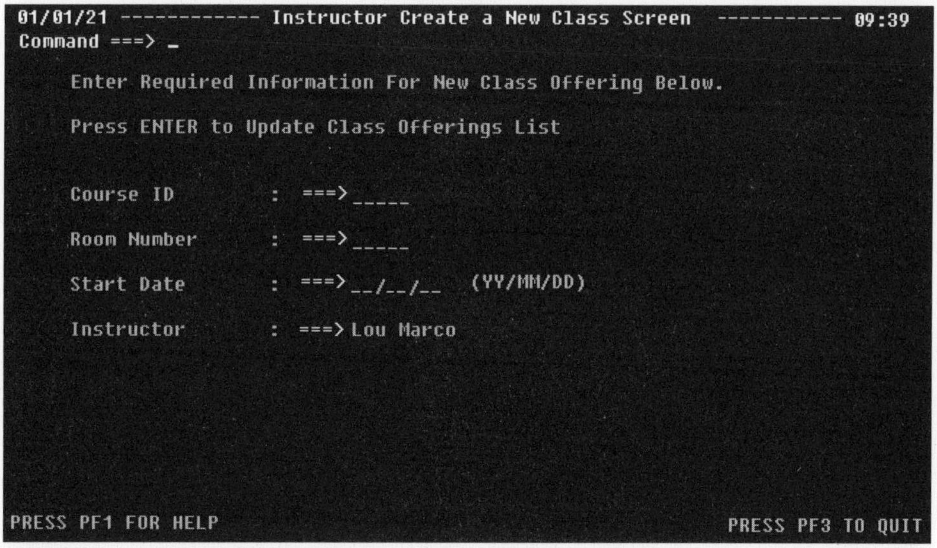

```
01/01/21 ------------ Instructor Create a New Class Screen  ----------- 09:39
Command ===> _

     Enter Required Information For New Class Offering Below.

     Press ENTER to Update Class Offerings List


     Course ID       : ===> _____

     Room Number     : ===> _____

     Start Date      : ===> __/__/__   (YY/MM/DD)

     Instructor      : ===> Lou Marco




PRESS PF1 FOR HELP                                        PRESS PF3 TO QUIT
```

Figure 13.4   The mainframe creates a new class entry screen.

instructional text reads "Enter Required Information For Clas<classID> Below," and the screen title reads "Change Information for Class <classID>," where <classID> is the class ID entered on the previous screen.

The Change Student Roster Screen

Here, the instructor has the ability to change the student roster for a class she is scheduled to teach. The processing is typical ISPF table processing—enter a code to the left of a table row that directs processing. To change an existing student, the instructor overtypes the name of an existing student. To add a student, the instructor enters A in the line command field, presses ENTER, and gets a new table row where he enters student information.

The Java User Interface

The screens are what a user may encounter if this application were coded in Java on a small machine. You'll see the Java source that created these screens later in this chapter.

This book did not cover the coding of Java user interface components yet. However, it is not possible to provide an example of a Java application without addressing the coding of user interface components to some degree. For you to see how a Java application might be put together, you need to know something about Java user interface construction. On the flip side, you'll probably not be spending too much of your time, Java-wise, coding Java user interfaces.

The approach taken in this book is to provide some exposure to coding Java user interface components without going into all the details. You'll see some input and output screen examples and the code that produces the examples. You'll read an explanation of the code that creates the examples. You will not read about most of the nuances involved in creating Java user interfaces.

```
----------------- Students Enrolled in Class ijava051 ------ Row 1 to 12 of 12
Command ===>                                               Scroll ===> CSR

       Select options: A - Add Student to Roster
                       C - Change Student
                       D - Delete Student From Roster

            or enter END command to return to previous menu

   Select      Student     Last                    First
   Code        ID          Name                    Name
     _         AX11234     Alberts                 Franklin
     _         TR12345     Bean                    Larry
     _         IV23456     Charles                 Raymond
     _         JG67890     Davis                   Jeffrey
     _         EW23409     Hadalamb                Mary
     _         HG45678     Hogg                    Ima
     _         TE45678     Knaff                   Lou
     _         UI34562     Moss                    Pete
     _         JT12765     Newby                   Mariah
     _         KL87634     Ochs                    Paul
     _         FD23412     Peters                  Peter
     _         JH34567     Quincy                  M.D.
```

Figure 13.5   The mainframe changes student roster entry screen.

The goal of this chapter is for you to see how you might code a Java application that mimics the functionality of an application developed in a procedural language on the IBM mainframe. The Java input screens were developed to be similar to the ISPF screens shown previously.

The Identify User Screen

The following screen performs the same function as the mainframe counterpart shown in Figure 13.1. The Java entry screen requires that the user click on the *submit* button whereas the mainframe entry screen requires that the user press the ENTER key after field entry.

Figure 13.6 shows the user identification screen. Here, the user enters a name and an employee ID.

The Student Enter Option Screen

With Java, we can use radio buttons to automatically enforce a mutually exclusive choice. The text fields to the right of the Student options become active when the corresponding option is selected. For example, notice that the last option is selected and the text box to the right is enabled, or can accept inputs. Were the student to click on another radio button, the corresponding text box would become enabled and the previously enabled text box becomes disabled.

The student must click on the submit button to proceed.

Figure 13.7 shows a Java entry screen showing the options available to a student.

The Java Instructor Options Entry Screen

The structure of the instructor entry screen is the same as that for the student entry screen. The similarity is mirrored in the code used to create both entry screens.

Figure 13.8 shows the options available to an instructor.

The Create a New Class Entry Screen

Figure 13.9 shows the entry screen for creating a new course. Here, the instructor enters particulars for the course. All fields require an entry.

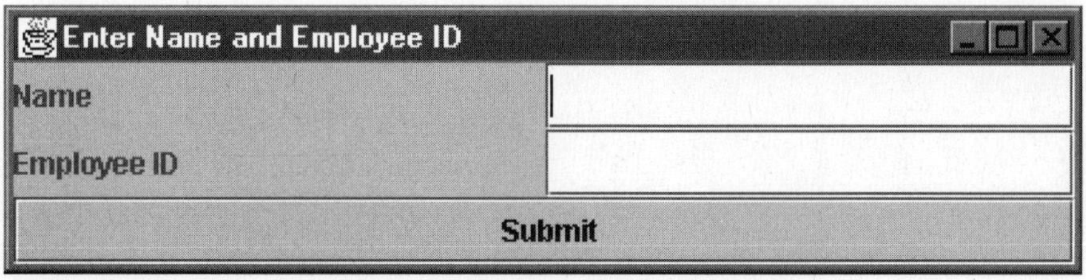

Figure 13.6 The Java small machine Identification entry screen.

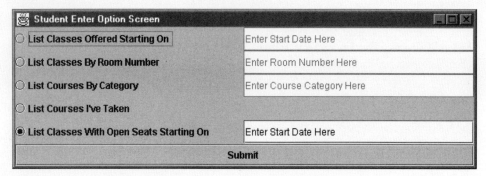

Figure 13.7   The Java small machine screen showing student options.

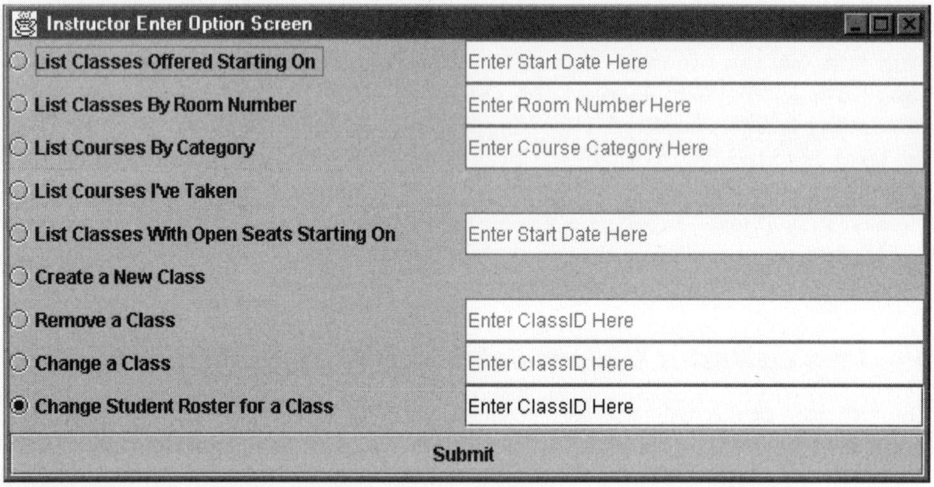

Figure 13.8   The Java small machine entry screen showing Instructor options.

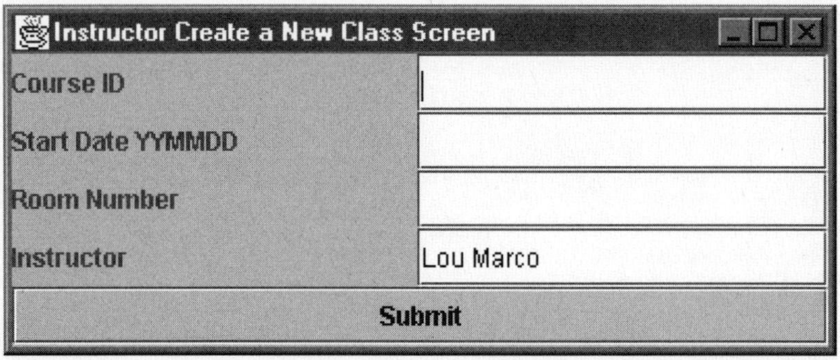

Figure 13.9   The Java small machine create a new class entry screen.

The Change Student Roster Entry Screen

This screen looks a bit different than its mainframe counterpart. Rather than have an option field to the left of each row, having a *clear* button that deletes a student does the job. Any changes the instructor makes to the roster will not take effect until the instructor clicks on the *Process Student Roster* button at the bottom of the screen.

Figure 13.10 shows the entry screen for changing the student roster for a class.

The Data Stores

In this section, you'll read a description of the files used to hold the data used by the application. The data is kept in sequential files; in Chapter 19, you'll see this application with the data stored in VSAM files and DB2 tables.

You have not read much about the Java treatment of file I/O. The case for not covering Java file I/O in detail is similar to that for not covering Java user interface component development in detail. In all likelihood, you'll spend your time writing Java programs to access databases or IBM-specific data structures, such as sequential files or VSAM datasets. Nonetheless, you deserve some exposure to Java file I/O, and here is where you'll get it.

The content and structure of the files is the same as for the procedural version of the program as for the Java version. What follows is a list of files and a brief description of each.

Select Code	Student ID	Last Name	First Name
Clear	AX11234	Albers	Franklin
Clear	TR12345	Bean	Larry
Clear	IV23456	Charles	Raymond
Clear	JG67890	Davis	Jeffrey
Clear	EW23409	Hadalamb	Mary
Clear	HG45678	Hogg	Irna
Clear	TE45678	Knaff	Lou
Clear	UI34562	Moss	Pete
Clear	JI12765	Newby	Mariah
Clear	KL87634	Ochs	Paul
Clear	FD23412	Peters	Peter
Clear	JH34567	Quincy	M.D.
Clear			
Clear			

Figure 13.10   The Java small machine change student roster entry screen.

The Course Information File

This file contains information about the courses offered by the training department. A course is a collection of material relating to a single topic. Table 13.1 shows the file layout and a description of the fields in the file.

The Class Information File

A class is a scheduled course. This file contains information on specific course offerings, or classes. Table 13.2 shows the particulars for the fields in the class information file.

The Instructor Information File

The instructor information file has personal information and classes the instructor is scheduled to teach. Table 13.3 describes the fields in the instructor information file.

The Employee Information File

This file contains information on the employees. To take a simplistic view, an employee is either an instructor or a student. To keep matters simple, this file has information relevant to the training application. Table 13.4 contains a description of this file's contents.

Application Outputs

The application produces outputs as a series of screens containing information corresponding to previous user selections. We'll look at the outputs from our mainframe version and similar outputs from our Java application. The screens that follow do not permit user inputs.

Table 13.1   Fields in the Course Information File

FIELD NAME	POSITION	DESCRIPTION
CourseID	1–5	Alpha string that identifies the course. The CourseID field is unique to each record.
Topic	5–20	Alpha string serving as a short description of the course.
Description	21–50	A longer description than the Topic field.
Prerequisites	51–70	Up to four CourseIDs that are prerequisites for this course.
Duration	71–72	Number of hours scheduled to deliver a course offering.

Table 13.2   Fields in the Class Information File

FIELD NAME	POSITION	DESCRIPTION
ClassID	1–8	Alpha string that identifies the class. The first five characters is the CourseID; the next three are numeric. The ClassID field is unique to each record.
DateOffered	9–14	A date field in YYMMDD format identifying the date the class starts.
RoomNumber	15–18	Alphanumeric string identifying the room the class is taught in.
InstructorID	19–25	Alphanumeric string identifying the instructor scheduled to teach the class.
EmployeeID	26–110	Up to 12 alphanumeric strings, each string identifying a particular student enrolled in the class. Each EmployeeID starts with two alpha characters followed by five numbers.

Table 13.3   Fields in the Instructor Information file

FIELD NAME	POSITION	DESCRIPTION
EmployeeID	1–7	A seven character string that uniquely identifies an employee. The first two characters are alpha; the remaining five are numeric.
FirstName	8–17	A 10 character field with contents that are self-explanatory.
LastName	18–27	A 10 character field with contents that are self-explanatory.
CourseIDs	28–57	Up to six CourseIDs that the instructor is qualified to teach.

OS/390 IBM Mainframe Outputs

As with the input screens, the output screens are ISPF Dialog Manager screens.

The first output screen, shown in Figure 13.11, is produced when a student requests a list of classes starting on or later than an entered date. A student would view this screen when selecting the first option from the input screen shown in Figure 13.2.

Table 13.4 Fields in the Employee Information File

FIELD NAME	POSITION	DESCRIPTION
EmployeeID	1-7	Alpha string that uniquely identifies the employee. The first two characters are alpha; the remaining five are numeric.
FirstName	8-17	A 10 character field with contents that are self-explanatory.
LastName	15-18	A 10 character field with contents that are self-explanatory.
ClassesTaken	19-65	Up to six ClassIDs of classes taken by the employee. Each ClassID is eight characters.

```
--------------- Classes Offered on or After 01/21/01 ------ Row 1 to 17 of 34
Command ===>                                                Scroll ===> CSR


   Class     Course         Instructor          Start      Room
   ID        Topic          Name                Date       Number
   ========  =============  =================   ========   ====
   iinet004  Intro Internet Lou Marco           01/02/15   r101
   pooop002  Intro to OO    I. P. Freely         01/02/15   r102
   pooop003  Intro to OO    Lou Marco           01/03/15   r103
   ijava004  Intro Java     Polly Annah         01/02/25   r101
   ijava009  Intro Java     Polly Annah         01/05/05   r105
   ivbas003  Intro to VB    Frank Furter        01/03/09   r102
   ivbas004  Intro to VB    Frank Furter        01/04/15   r105
   ivbas005  Intro to VB    Heywood Jahkikme    01/04/15   r104
   avbas008  Advanced VB    Heywood Jahkikme    01/06/21   r101
   avbas009  Advanced VB    Lou Marco           01/02/22   r102
   ajava006  Advanced Java  Lou Marco           01/03/20   r105
   ajava007  Advanced Java  Lou Marco           01/04/15   r101
   isqlp004  Intro to SQL   Frank Furter        01/01/25   r101
   isqlp005  Intro to SQL   Frank Furter        01/02/10   r103
   asqlp002  Advanced SQL   Frank Furter        01/03/20   r101
   asqlp003  Advanced SQL   Frank Furter        01/04/25   r104
   sqlpr004  SQL Programming Frank Furter        01/07/10   r105
```

Figure 13.11 The mainframe classes starting on or after an entered date.

Figure 13.12 shows a list of classes offered by room number. A student or instructor would see the following screen when selecting option 2 from the input screen shown in Figure 13.2.

Figure 13.13 shows a table of the courses by category. The user may view the following screen after selecting option 3 from the input screen shown in Figure 13.2.

Figure 13.14 shows a list of classes with open seats. The student would see this screen after selecting option 5 from the screen shown in Figure 13.2.

Figure 13.15 shows a list of classes taken by a student. The student would see this screen after selecting option 4 from the screen shown in Figure 13.2.

```
------------------- List of Classes By Room Number --------- Row 1 to 17 of 34
 Command ===> █                                          Scroll ===> CSR


    Room    Class         Course          Instructor        Start
    Number  ID            Topic           Name              Date
    ====    ========      ==============  ================   ========
    r101    iinet004      Intro Internet  Lou Marco          01/02/15
    r101    ijava004      Intro Java      Polly Annah        01/02/25
    r101    avbas008      Advanced VB     Heywood Jahkikme   01/06/21
    r101    ajava007      Advanced Java   Lou Marco          01/04/15
    r101    isqlp004      Intro to SQL    Frank Furter       01/01/25
    r101    asqlp002      Advanced SQL    Frank Furter       01/03/20
    r102    pooop002      Intro to OO     I. P. Freely       01/02/15
    r102    ivbas003      Intro to VB     Frank Furter       01/03/09
    r102    avbas009      Advanced VB     Lou Marco          01/02/22
    r103    pooop003      Intro to OO     Lou Marco          01/03/15
    r103    isqlp005      Intro to SQL    Frank Furter       01/02/10
    r104    asqlp003      Advanced SQL    Frank Furter       01/04/25
    r104    ivbas005      Intro to VB     Heywood Jahkikme   01/04/15
    r105    ijava009      Intro Java      Polly Annah        01/05/05
    r105    ivbas004      Intro to VB     Frank Furter       01/04/15
    r105    ajava006      Advanced Java   Lou Marco          01/03/20
    r105    sqlpr004      SQL Programming Frank Furter       01/07/10
```

Figure 13.12   The mainframe classes sorted by room number.

```
-------------------    List of Courses By Category   --------- Row 1 to 17 of 18
 Command ===> █                                          Scroll ===> CSR


            Course      Course
            ID          Description
            ========    ==================
            ijava       Basic Java Programming
            iinet       Basic Internet Technologies
            pooop       Object Oriented Concepts
            ivbas       Visual Basic Programming
            avbas       Visual Basic Pgming Advanced
            ajava       Advanced Java Programming
            isqlp       Simple SQL Queries
            asqlp       Not so Simple SQL
            sqlpr       SQL Programming (Java)
            javas       Intro to Java Servlets
            javac       Java for COBOL Programmers
            cobol       COBOL Programming
            vsamd       Programming with VSAM DSNs
            cplus       Programming in C++
            iproj       Project Management Basics
            aproj       Advanced Project Management
            meets       The Art of Attending Meetings
```

Figure 13.13   The mainframe list of courses by category.

The list of classes taught by an instructor screen is nearly identical to the screen shown in Figure 13.15, except that the screen title reads "Classes Taught," not "Classes Taken." An instructor would see the list of classes taught when selecting option 4 from the screen shown in Figure 13.3.

```
-------------------- Classes With Open Seats------------- Row 1 to 10 of 10
Command ===>                                              Scroll ===> CSR


Class        Course          Instructor         Start      Room    # Open
ID           Topic           Name               Date       Number  Seats
========     ==============  ================   ========   ====    ========
iinet004     Intro Internet  Lou Marco          01/02/15   r101    3
pooop002     Intro to OO     I. P. Freely       01/02/15   r102    2
pooop003     Intro to OO     Lou Marco          01/03/15   r103    4
ivbas005     Intro to VB     Heywood Jahkikme   01/04/15   r104    1
avbas008     Advanced VB     Heywood Jahkikme   01/06/21   r101    2
avbas009     Advanced VB     Lou Marco          01/02/22   r102    4
ajava006     Advanced Java   Lou Marco          01/03/20   r105    3
isqlp005     Intro to SQL    Frank Furter       01/02/10   r103    2
asqlp002     Advanced SQL    Frank Furter       01/03/20   r101    4
asqlp003     Advanced SQL    Frank Furter       01/04/25   r104    2
```

Figure 13.14   The mainframe list of classes with open seats.

```
---------------- Classes Taken by Pete Moss (UI34562) -----  Row 1 to 3 of 3
Command ===>                                                 Scroll ===> CSR


Class        Course          Instructor         Start      Room
ID           Topic           Name               Date       Number
========     ==============  ================   ========   ====
iinet004     Intro Internet  Lou Marco          01/02/15   r101
asqlp002     Advanced SQL    Frank Furter       01/03/20   r101
isqlp005     Intro to SQL    Frank Furter       01/02/10   r103
```

Figure 13.15   The mainframe list of classes taken by a student.

Java Outputs

Here, you'll see screens similar to the ones shown in Figures 13.11 through 13.15. The
screens in this section were produced with Java code. The main difference in function-

ality between the mainframe screens and the Java screens is that the user needs to hit a function key (usually PF3) on the mainframe screens to continue whereas the user needs to click a button at the bottom of the Java screen to continue.

The descriptions provided for the mainframe output screens will do for describing the Java screens. Hence, in Figures 13.16 through 13.20, we present the Java screens without additional comment.

The list of classes taught by an instructor screen is nearly identical to the screen shown in Figure 13.15, except that the screen title reads "Classes Taught," not "Classes Taken." An instructor would see the list of classes taught when selecting option 4 from the screen shown in Figure 13.3.

Putting Together the Application

This section discusses some thoughts on how this application could be constructed in a procedural, third-generation programming language and in Java. The analysis that follows is at a high level with some attention paid to details now and then.

We deliberately made the application simple. The goal is to present a problem and compare and contrast a procedural language solution to a Java solution. For example, this application uses a set of sequential files, not a database. Also, the user interface screens and outputs are hardly commercial quality. That said, you'll get a feel for the differences between putting together the application in a procedural language versus Java.

Class ID	Course Topic	Instructor	Start Date	Room #
iinet004	Intro Internet	Lou Marco	01/02/15	r101
pooop002	Intro to OO	I. P. Freely	01/02/15	r102
pooop003	Intro to OO	Lou Marco	01/03/15	r103
ijava004	Intro Java	Polly Annah	01/02/25	r101
ijava009	Intro Java	Polly Annah	01/05/05	r105
ivbas003	Intro to VB	Frank Furter	01/03/09	r102
ivbas004	Intro to VB	Frank Furter	01/04/15	r105
ivbas005	Intro to VB	Heywood Jahkikme	01/04/15	r104
avbas008	Advanced VB	Heywood Jahkikme	01/06/21	r101
avbas009	Advanced VB	Lou Marco	01/02/22	r102
ajava006	Advanced Java	Lou Marco	01/03/20	r105
ajava007	Advanced Java	Lou Marco	01/04/15	r101
isqlp004	Intro to SQL	Frank Furter	01/01/25	r101
isqlp005	Intro to SQL	Frank Furter	01/02/10	r103
asqlp002	Advanced SQL	Frank Furter	01/03/20	r101
asqlp003	Advanced SQL	Frank Furter	10/04/25	r104
sqlpr004	SQL Programming	Frank Furter	01/07/10	r105

Classes Offered on or After 01/21/01

Done Looking

Figure 13.16 The Java classes starting on or after an entered date.

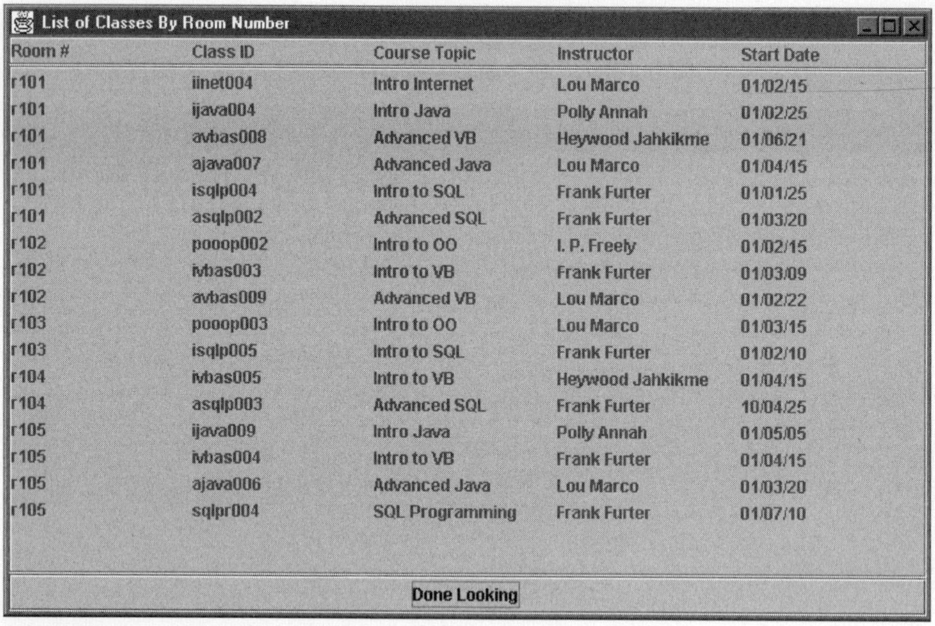

Room #	Class ID	Course Topic	Instructor	Start Date
r101	iinet004	Intro Internet	Lou Marco	01/02/15
r101	ijava004	Intro Java	Polly Annah	01/02/25
r101	avbas008	Advanced VB	Heywood Jahkikme	01/06/21
r101	ajava007	Advanced Java	Lou Marco	01/04/15
r101	isqlp004	Intro to SQL	Frank Furter	01/01/25
r101	asqlp002	Advanced SQL	Frank Furter	01/03/20
r102	pooop002	Intro to OO	I. P. Freely	01/02/15
r102	ivbas003	Intro to VB	Frank Furter	01/03/09
r102	avbas009	Advanced VB	Lou Marco	01/02/22
r103	pooop003	Intro to OO	Lou Marco	01/03/15
r103	isqlp005	Intro to SQL	Frank Furter	01/02/10
r104	ivbas005	Intro to VB	Heywood Jahkikme	01/04/15
r104	asqlp003	Advanced SQL	Frank Furter	10/04/25
r105	ijava009	Intro Java	Polly Annah	01/05/05
r105	ivbas004	Intro to VB	Frank Furter	01/04/15
r105	ajava006	Advanced Java	Lou Marco	01/03/20
r105	sqlpr004	SQL Programming	Frank Furter	01/07/10

Done Looking

Figure 13.17   The Java classes sorted by room number.

Without further ado, some thoughts on a procedural language solution follow.

A Procedural Language Solution

If you were to ask a data processor to sum up the nature of this application, she might reply that the application were a basic report-writing app. She might mention that the application follows the classic input—process—output model of the majority of data processing applications.

A data processor may create a series of flowcharts, write some pseudocode, and create a set of structure charts to describe the processes. The data processor would map processes that end up as modules on a structure chart to process boxes and decision diamonds on the flowcharts. Although we've come a long way from the days of structured design, the aforementioned tools are still used in today's data processing organizations.

Let's take a look at some flowcharts that go a long way in describing the required processes. We'll not look at all flowcharts required to describe all of the application's behavior. Later, we'll map some modules to the processes described in the flowcharts that follow and pen some pseudocode for some modules.

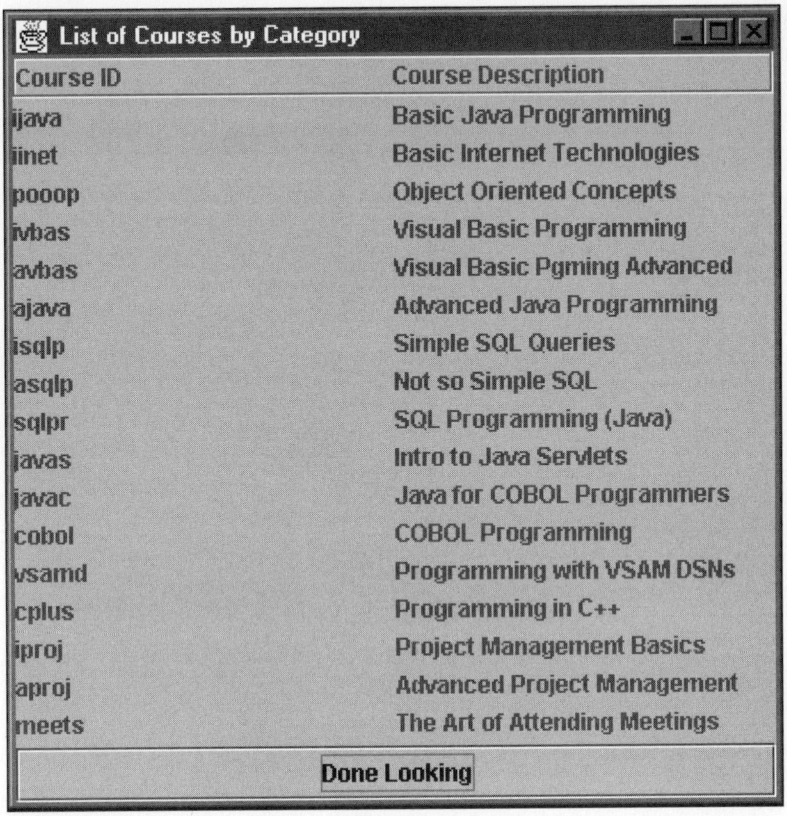

Figure 13.18   The Java list of courses by category.

Flowcharts

Figure 13.21 shows the flowchart that gets the application rolling.

After the application displays the user identification screen and accepts an employee name and employee ID, the application confirms that the name matches with the ID. If the two inputs match, the application determines if the user is an instructor or not (a student). The determination is made by examining the instructor information file; if the employee ID is found on the instructor information file, the user is deemed to be an instructor, else the user is deemed to be a student. Depending on the instructor/student qualification, the application displays the appropriate options screen.

Figure 13.22 shows a flowchart that describes the process of a student ordering the application to display a list of classes later than an entered date.

Classes With Open Seats					_ □ ×
Class ID	Course Topic	Instructor	Start Date	Room #	Open Seats
iinet004	Intro Internet	Lou Marco	01/02/15	r101	3
pooop002	Intro to OO	I. P. Freely	01/02/15	r102	2
pooop003	Intro to OO	Lou Marco	01/03/15	r103	4
ivbas005	Intro to VB	Heywood Jahkik...	01/04/15	r104	1
avbas008	Advanced VB	Heywood Jahkik...	01/06/21	r101	2
avbas009	Advanced VB	Lou Marco	01/02/22	r102	4
ajava006	Advanced Java	Lou Marco	01/03/20	r105	3
isqlp005	Intro to SQL	Frank Furter	01/02/10	r103	2
asqlp002	Advanced SQL	Frank Furter	01/03/20	r101	4
asqlp003	Advanced SQL	Frank Furter	10/04/25	r104	2
		Done Looking			

Figure 13.19 The Java list of classes with open seats.

Classes Taken By Pete Moss (UI34562)				_ □ ×
Class ID	Course Topic	Instructor	Start Date	Room #
iinet004	Intro Internet	Lou Marco	01/02/15	r101
asqlp002	Advanced SQL	Frank Furter	01/03/20	r101
isqlp005	Intro to SQL	Frank Furter	01/02/10	r103
		Done Looking		

Figure 13.20 The mainframe list of classes taken by a student.

The class information file contains a date field identifying when the class starts. The process is to read every record, comparing the date field on the record with the entered date field. If the entered date field precedes the date on record, the relevant record data

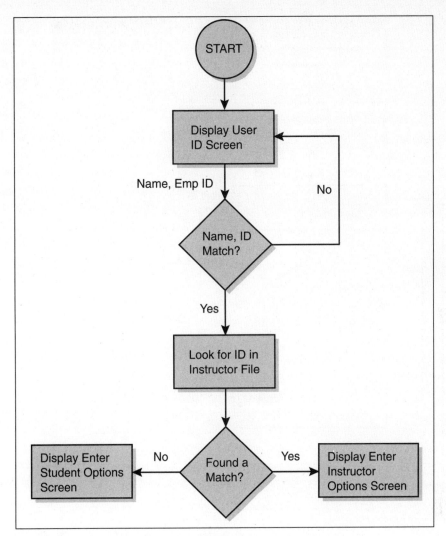

Figure 13.21 Flowchart that describes the start of the application.

is added to the structure. When the program reaches EOF, the program displays the structure with the relevant class information. The display shown in Figure 13.11 would be the resultant output.

The remaining flowcharts that describe the processes for generating the output screens would be similar to the flowchart shown in Figure 13.22. They would involve reading one or more files, comparing fields from the records against entered criteria, saving data on the records that satisfied the criteria, and displaying the results in a suitable display medium (in this case, ISPF panels).

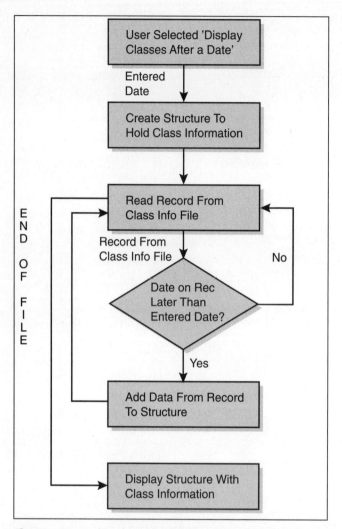

Figure 13.22 Flowchart for "display list of classes starting after a certain date" option.

Pseudocode for "Display Class List Later Than Entered Date" Option

Listing 13.1 shows an example of what may pass as pseudocode in some quarters for the flowchart shown in Figure 13.22.

Some details are omitted from the pseudocode, such as the layout of the classinfo.data record and the manner by which the entered date is fetched. Nonetheless, the pseudocode conveys the sense of the required elements of a procedural solution.

```
Display Classes After Entered Date:
   Fetch Entered Date
   Create ISPF table to hold class information
        TBCreate CLASINFO containing ClassID, Course Topic,
                Instructor Name, Start Date and Room Number
   Open File "classinfo.data"
   Read file "classinfo.data" into classinfo.data record
        at EOF, close file "classinfo.data"
        If date on classinfo.data record > Entered Date
           Then issue TBADD CLASINFO
        Else
           Read file "classinfo.data" into classinfo.data record

   Issue TBDISPL with table CLASINFO

End:
```

Listing 13.1   Pseudocode sample for flowchart in Figure 13.22

The pseudocode that describes how to generate the remaining outputs is strikingly similar to Listing 13.1. The major differences are the fields saved from the records, the files read, and the criteria used.

Features of a Procedural Language Solution

The approach taken when developing a procedural language solution is the emphasis of process over data (hence, the term *procedural language*). The flowcharts and pseudocode reveal an almost formulaic approach—read a record, compare fields, and save data. The development of code mirrors these processes.

In addition, program flow of control is sequential, top-down. Nothing happens in the program unless the code explicitly invokes a routine or "falls into" a code block.

A Java language solution contrasts with the procedural approach. Next, we'll discuss the elements of a Java language approach.

A Java Language Solution

To implement the Training Department application in Java, we must think a bit differently than our mainframe programming brethren. In Java, we'll not pay nearly as much attention to process as we would in using a procedural language. Also, we'll have to forgo the strict sequential flow of control. As you'll see, that's not the Java way, especially when dealing with user interfaces.

Let's start with basic building blocks. In a procedural language, you might start with a flowchart or pseudocode to get the ball rolling. Because Java is object-oriented, we'll have to think in terms of objects. For example, the entry screens and the output displays are *objects*. You recall that objects have an associated set of properties and behaviors. In developing our Java solution, we'll fixate on what objects will be used in our solution and the properties and behaviors of these objects.

Procedurally, a programmer thinks of programs that implement processes that read inouts and create outputs. In Java, a programmer thinks of objects that have behaviors that implement the desired processes acting on data that is the properties of objects. Ergo, a good place for a Java programmer to start in developing a solution is to determine what objects will be needed to solve the problem.

Actually, you've already seen a good number of the required Java objects—the input and output screens. These screens represent objects with properties and behaviors. Let's put a few under the microscope and see how a Java solution could be put together.

The Identify User Screen—A Java Object

You recall the user identification screen from Figure 13.6, right? Here is the screen again in case you forgot.

This screen is a Java object that has the following properties:

- The Employee Name
- The Employee ID

Now, the screen may have other properties that it requires to do its work. However, we're interested only in the screen's *public* properties. The Employee Name and Employee ID are two quantities that will be used elsewhere in the application. Any other property of the screen is relevant only to the screen and only when the screen is working.

What about the screen's behaviors? We could say that the only behaviors we are interested in is the screen's ability to capture the previous two properties and make the properties available to other objects that may need their values.

How do we go about implementing this object? As you would any other Java object; first, you create a class to serve as a template for similar typed objects. You code instance variables to represent properties and methods to represent behaviors. The properties and behaviors you want known in the rest of your application should be declared with the *public* visibility modifier. Other properties and methods may be declared private or with another modifier.

Listing 13.2 shows the Java code that represents the user identification screen.

The code shown in Listing 13.2 creates the panel shown in Figure 13.6 by using Java user interface components called *swing* components. Refer to Chapter 24 "The Java 2 Enterprise Edition Libraries," for a short discussion on using swing components to construct user interfaces. The salient point with this code is the creation of an object that encapsulates the behavior and properties required for the application.

The last routine shown in Listing 13.2 is the routine that processes the button click. Recall from Chapter 11, "Java Event Handling Basics," where you read about event

```
import java.awt.* ;
import java.awt.event.* ;
import javax.swing.* ;

public class EntryScreen extends JFrame implements ActionListener{

    String userName ;
    String userID ;

    public EntryScreen() {

        super("Enter Name and Employee ID") ;
        this.getContentPane().setLayout (new GridLayout( 3, 1) ) ;

        JPanel  userNamePanel = new JPanel( new GridLayout( 1, 2 ) ) ;
        JPanel  userIDPanel   = new JPanel( new GridLayout( 1, 2 ) ) ;

        JLabel  userNameLabel = new JLabel( "Name        " ) ;
        JLabel  userIDLabel   = new JLabel( "Employee ID " ) ;

        JTextField userNameTF = new JTextField( 20 ) ;
        JTextField userIDTF   = new JTextField(  6 ) ;

        JButton    submitBtn = new JButton(" Submit" ) ;
        submitBtn.addActionListener(this) ;

        userNamePanel.add( userNameLabel ) ;
        userNamePanel.add( userNameTF ) ;

        userIDPanel.add( userIDLabel ) ;
        userIDPanel.add( userIDTF ) ;

        this.getContentPane().add( userNamePanel) ;
        this.getContentPane().add( userIDPanel ) ;
        this.getContentPane().add( submitBtn ) ;

        addWindowListener (new WindowAdapter() {
         public void windowClosing( WindowEvent we ) {
                System.exit( 0 ) ;
         }
   } ) ;

    }
    public void actionPerformed (ActionEvent aev ) {
        userName = userNameTF.getText() ;
        userID   = userIDTF.getText() ;
        if ( ( userName.length() != 0 ) && ( userID.length() != 0 ) )
            AppUtilities.processEntries( myES, userName, userID ) ;

    }

}
```

Listing 13.2 Java code for the user Identification screen.

handling. Here, the event class for button clicks (and other GUI components, too) is ActionEvent. The listener interface is called *ActionListener* and the callback is called *ActionPerformed*. Here, the object of class EntryScreen deals with the user clicking on the Submit button. The action taken is to pass parameters to a utility routine developed to process the button click. Listing 13.3 shows the code for the method *processEntries*.

The thrust of this routine is to ensure that both user name and userID agree and to take action depending on the user being a student or an instructor. If the user is an instructor, the application creates and displays an instructor option screen, likewise for students.

Notice that a reference to the entry screen object is passed to processEntries. The reason is that when we have a bona fide employee (name and ID match), we no longer need the EntryScreen object. However, if the name and ID do not match, we want the EntryScreen object to stick around. Hence, we pass a reference and when we get a match on user name and ID, we remove the EntryScreen object.

The methods *nameAndIDMatch()* and *isAnInstructor()* are utility methods located in the same class as processEntries. The methods are static; you need not instantiate an object to use these utility methods.

```java
public static void processEntries( EntryScreen myES, String
userName, String userID ) {
     boolean processed = false ;

  //We have a live one...is this a student, an instructor or do the
number and name
     //not match?
 if ( nameAndIDMatch( userName, userID ) ) {
    myES.dispose() ;
    //If an instructor, show the Instructor choice screen
    if ( isAnInstructor( userID ) ) {
        InstructorOptionsScreen  anInstrOptionScreen =
                  new InstructorOptionsScreen() ;
            anInstrOptionScreen.show() ;
    }
     else {
          //Show the Student choice screen
          StudentOptionsScreen aStudInstrScreen =
                    new StudentOptionsScreen() ;
          aStudInstrScreen.show() ;
    }

  }

 }
```

Listing 13.3   Java code for the processEntries method.

```
public static boolean nameAndIDMatch( String empName, String empID )
{
     boolean match = false ;
 String  aLine ;
 try {
     FileReader       employeeFile =
                          new FileReader( "employeeinfo.dat" ) ;
          BufferedReader  bread         =
                          new BufferedReader( employeeFile ) ;

     while ( ( aLine = bread.readLine() ) != null ) {
           String empIDFromFile = aLine.substring(  0,  7 ) ;
           String fName         = aLine.substring(  7, 16 ) ;
           String lName         = aLine.substring( 17, 26 ) ;
           String name          = fName.trim() + " "
                                         + lName.trim() ;

           if ( empIDFromFile.equals( empID ) &&
                  name.equals( empName ) ) {
                match = true ;
                break ;
           }
 }

     bread.close() ;
 }
 catch (IOException ioe) {
             System.out.println( "Exception : "
                               + ioe.getMessage() ); } ;

 return match ;
 }
```

Listing 13.4   Java code for nameAndIDMatch method.

Listing 13.4 has the code for the *nameAndIDMatch()* method.

The code in Listing 13.4 accepts a name and ID arguments as strings, reads a file containing names and IDs, and compares the names and IDs read against the values of the arguments. If a match is found, the routine returns true.

The method has several string-handling methods from class String, such as the *trim()* and *substring()* functions. The method builds up a name form the first and last names stored on file for compare to the entered name.

The previous routine also employs Java *file I/O*. Refer to Chapter 24 for a brief dissertation on Java's file I/O capabilities.

In Summary

The thrust of this chapter is to highlight the difference in a procedural language solution and a Java (object) solution to a common data processing problem.

The procedural solution concentrates on defining the application as a separate group of modules to implement functions that operate on data. The data is analyzed and modeled separately from the modules. The flow of the system is envisioned as a well-defined sequence of actions implemented as program modules.

The Java solution concentrates on defining the application as a group of objects created from classes. The classes imbue the objects with properties and behaviors that model the essence of the application entities, such as input screens and output reports. The flow of the system is envisioned as a group of objects communication by way of a run-time event delegation model.

Java In the OS/300 Mainframe Environment

CHAPTER 14

Overview of OS/390 Java Infrastructure/Architecture

You've seen the nuts and bolts of Java programming on your Windows-based workstation. However, the reason you may have purchased this book is to learn how Java fits in with the IBM mainframe technologies you've come to know and love. This chapter provides the necessary background to prepare you to use these technologies with Java.

The chapter starts with the software requirements you'll need to write and run Java on your OS/390 system. Next, you'll read an overview of how Java works with a potpourri of IBM technologies, including DB2, CICS, IMS, and VSAM. You'll encounter some new IBM and Java terminology in this chapter as well. This chapter concludes with some references for additional reading.

Software Requirements

For you to run Java on OS/390, you'll need to enable Unix System Services, be running under *Language Environment* (LE) Release 1.5 or higher, and, of course, have a Java runtime installed. The version of the Java runtime you need to install depends on the release of OS/390 you are using.

The short story is that you'll need access to OS/390 Version 1 Release 1 or higher. However, if you can get access to OS/390 Version 1 Release 6 or higher, you'll have access to a more current JDK and some useful proprietary IBM features. Table 14.1 shows some JDK features available to various releases of OS/390 Version 1.

Table 14.1   Some Java Features Available to OS/390 by Release

FEATURE	OS/390 R1, R2, R3	OS/390 R4, R5	OS/390 R6, R7	OS/390 R8 AND ABOVE
Java 1.1	Yes	Yes	Yes	Yes
SAF/RACF Security	No	Yes	Yes	Yes
Security Migration Aid	No	No	Yes	Yes
RMI-IIOP	No	No	Yes	Yes
Swing Classes	No	No	Yes	Yes
Support for Record I/O	No	No	Yes	Yes
Java 1.2	No	No	No	No
Java 1.3	No	No	No	No

JAVA COMPILER OR JAVA INTERPRETER?

As you know, Java "compilers" generate bytecode, not native code. However, IBM has a product called the *High Performance Java Compiler (HPJ)*, which generates native OS/390 code. In the discussions that follow, we assume that you are *not* using the HPJ. Any situations that require the HPJ or require the use of the Java bytecode compiler will be cited where appropriate.

As you see, OS/390 Releases 1, 2, and 3 support Java version 1.1, Releases 6 and 7 support several features found in Java 2, such as the Swing API, and Releases 8 and above support JDK 1.3. Actually, the official Java release supported by OS/390 Version 1 Release 6 and 7 is *JDK 1.1.8* and for Releases 8 and above is *JDK 1.3.0*. The entry in Table 14.1 labeled *Support for Record I/O*, is a set of proprietary IBM classes called *JRIO*, for Java Record I/O.

Java Application Architectures

This section discusses different architectures you may implement when coding Java on OS/390. Your choices fall into one of the following categories:

- **Standalone program**. Your Java program directly communicates to some OS/390 software. You execute your Java program by invoking its main() method. The method invocation can be from a command window or a batch job.

- **Fat client**. Your Java component directly communicates to some OS/390 software, like a standalone program. However, you do not invoke a main() method; you access OS/390 software with a Java applet or servlet. This architecture is an example of a two-tiered architecture.

- **Thin client**. Your Java component communicates with some OS/390 software through some intermediate software layer. The Java components could be part of the intermediate software layer, like a servlet. This architecture is an example of a three-tiered (or N-tiered) architecture.

Java Software Components Versus Standalone Programs

Most of the examples shown and discussed in Part II of this book concentrate on both writing standalone Java programs and writing fat clients to access mainframe software and data. A good case could be made for spending more time discussing the thin client application architecture. Part III of the book spends some time discussing three- and N-tiered application architecture and the Java 2 Platform, Enterprise Edition (J2EE—refer to Chapter 2, "What is Java?" to refresh your memory).

The two- and three-tier models cited previously use Java software components as opposed to Java programs. For now, you can think of a Java software component as a piece of Java software that cannot be run as a program but performs some useful work. Put differently, the Java software component represents a tier of a multi-tiered application.

One example of such a Java software component is an *applet*, a Java software component that runs within the context of a Web browser. For the purposes of our discussion, an applet could be the implementation of the presentation tier of a multi-tiered application. The customer uses the applet to communicate with OS/390 system software to access mainframe data.

Another example is a Java *servlet*, a Java software component that runs within the context of a Web server. A servlet is an implementation of all or part of the business logic tier of a multi-tiered application. The customer does not access a servlet directly; the customer accesses the servlet typically through a Web page. The servlet performs the necessary functions of mainframe data access and passes any results back to the software components implementing the presentation layer.

Whether the mainframe data or system software access is done by a standalone Java application or a Java software component, the Java code uses a *gateway* or *connector* to access mainframe data. Think of a gateway as a software layer that provides functions to connect Java software components with existing software on an OS/390 system. Next, you'll read about gateways that enable you to access IBM system software products, like CICS and DB2.

Accessing OS/390 System Software

Here, we provide a summary of connecting to various IBM system software products. Some products, like DB2, do not require proprietary connector software. Others, like

CICS, may require proprietary connector software. Let's examine how you, the mainframe programmer, access IBM system software with Java.

Accessing DB2 with Java

Your Java programs software components can access DB2 data by using one of three methods. You can use the *Java Database Connectivity* (JDBC) API, SQLJ, or Java to invoke a DB2 stored procedures.

JDBC is industry-standard technology implemented by nearly all database vendors that enables a programmer to access data stored in relational databases. You, the mainframe Java programmer using JDBC, issue SQL calls as character-string parameters of methods in java.sql.*. You would use JDBC mostly for dynamic SQL.

SQLJ is an alternative technology that enables you to imbed SQL calls in Java programs. However, in contract to using JDBC, you would use SQLJ mostly for static SQL. Put another way, SQLJ requires the use of a preprocessor that translates the SQL calls into source code. If you've done any DB2 programming on the host in COBOL or PL/I, the aforementioned approach should sound familiar.

In Chapter 19 "Java and DB2," you'll read more about using Java to access data stored in DB2. In addition, the coding example shown in Chapter 20, "The Training Department Class Scheduler System Revisited," has additional Java code examples of DB2 data access.

Accessing CICS with Java

Your Java programs or software components can access CICS by using a custom connector called the *CICS Transaction Gateway* (CTG) or by using JCICS.

The CTG is a set of Java classes that enable your Java code to talk to CICS through the *External CICS Interface* (EXCI). CTG classes can execute over a network where the CICS servers and the clients accessing these servers can be located on different OS/390 systems. Also, the CTG classes can execute locally where the CICS servers are located on the same OS/390 system as the clients.

If you are using CICS Transaction Server Version 1.3 or later, you can access CICS transactions directly (without using a custom connector like CTG) by using JCICS. JCICS is a set of Java classes that come with CICS. You merely make these classes known to your Java development environment and code your Java/CICS programs.

In Chapter 15, "Overview of OS/390 UNIX System Services," you'll read how to access CICS transactions with Java.

Accessing IMS with Java

You have several options at your disposal to access IMS from a Java program or software component. You can use the Callable Interface, which uses the *Open Transaction Monitor Access* (OMTA) to access IMS. You can use *Advanced Peer-to-Peer Communications* (APPC). You can use a custom IMS gateway called the IMS Connector for Java (formerly called the IMS TOC Connector for Java).

You can establish both conversational and non-conversational IMS transactions from a Java client application or from a Java software component (applet, servlet).

THE JAVA NATIVE INTERFACE

Sometimes, you cannot access OS/390 resources from Java without calling a program, written in another programming language, currently on the OS/390 system. Sun provides an API, called JNI that enables you to call other, non-Java programs from Java programs. You'll see mention of JNI pop up from time-to-time in our discussion of OS/390 data access. We'll provide particulars on JNI where appropriate.

Some Java to IMS access technologies, like APPC, require the use of the *Java Native Interface* (JNI).

Chapter 15 provides additional information on IMS access with Java using the afore-mentioned products.

Running Java under MVS Batch

You have three options for running your Java programs under MVS batch. You can use the BPXBATCH utility. You could run your Java program compiled with the High Performance Compiler as an executable in an all-too-familiar JCL job. You also could run your Java program as an MVS started task.

The BPXBATCH utility enables you to run a UNIX program or script. In principle, running BPXBATCH is not that different than running a REXX EXEC under IKJEFT01 (TSO).

If you use the HPJ and linked your object code into an MVS load module, you run the Java program as you would run any COBOL program you linked.

Running your Java application as a started task is no different than running any program or script as a started task.

Chapter 16, "Java and MVS Batch," has more information on running your Java programs in MVS batch.

Accessing OS/390 Record Structures with Java

You can access stream files by using the Java base I/O classes (the java.io package). However, you, the mainframe programmer, rarely use stream I/O, right? How often do you code COBOL DISPLAY or PL/I PUT SKIP DATA statements in your production programs? What you really need to know is how to perform record I/O in Java; you need the equivalent of COBOL, PL/I READ FILE, and WRITE file statements in the Java language.

To access proprietary file structures with Java, IBM provides a custom package called Java Record I/O, or JRIO. You use JRIO to access sequential files or members of a partitioned dataset. Chapter 17, "Java Record I/O Using the JRIO Package," has details on Java record access with JRIO, including copious coding examples.

You access VSAM files with Java by using JRIO, too. JRIO supports read, append, and update record operations on random, keyed, and sequential VSAM files. You'll read the full story on Java VSAM file access with JRIO in Chapter 18, "Java COCS, and IMS." The coding example in Chapter 20 uses JRIO to access VSAM files, too.

IBM Java Development Tools

The cross platform nature of Java implies that you can develop your Java programs or software components on any hardware/software combination and upload the programs to OS/390. The reality is that you'll want your Java programs to access proprietary IBM system software. Hence, you'll need custom IBM packages representing connectors. In all likelihood, you'll not find the custom connection classes with non-IBM Java development tools.

As a mainframe COBOL or PL/I programmer, you may be accustomed to entering source code in the ISPF editor and running batch compiles. As a Java programmer, you will get accustomed to entering source code in an integrated development environment on a small machine and uploading a compiled piece of code or a software component to the host. Some of you COBOL folk with exposure to MicroFocus COBOL get the idea.

IBM has a suite of small machine development tools called the Visual Age series. IBM has Visual Age for COBOL, PL/I, C, C++, and Java. The Visual Age product has the same interface for all programming languages. Also, The Visual Age product comes in Entry, Professional, and Enterprise Editions.

IBM VisualAge for Java is a powerful rapid application development tool for building Java-compatible applications, applets, and Java software components. With the VisualAge for Java programming environment, you can build 100 percent Pure Java applications that run on any Java-compatible Virtual Machine Java Development Kit or inside any Java-enabled browser. With VisualAge for Java, you can add or change code and compile without exiting the test environment. The product includes the Visual Composition Editor and a fully integrated, repository-based environment that provides complete source and version control.

If your shop does not have, nor plans to use, IBM's Visual Age tools, do not fret. You can adapt any of the leading Java tools to use the custom IBM classes, like JRIO.

Appendix B has more information about IBM's Visual Age for Java environment, including directions on downloading a copy, and helpful tips on configuring the environment on Windows platforms, as well as information on other Java development tools.

In Summary

You see that IBM has covered the bases in providing Java access to OS/390 system software. You, the Java mainframe programmer, have the means to use Java to get to your mainframe-stored data, be it stored in a VSAM file or stored in a relational database. The next six chapters show you how.

You can reference the IBM site, www.s390.ibm.com/java/, for the most current information on OS/390 and Java. The site www-4.ibm.com/software/data/db2/ java/index.html has information on using Java with DB2. The site www.ibm.com/ developer/java/ has IBM Java information of interest to programmers. Of course, general Web searches reveal a wealth of information you might find relevant.

CHAPTER 15

Overview of OS/390 UNIX System Services

With OS/390 UNIX System Services, OS/390 and UNIX, two widely used operating systems, come together inside a single box. As previously mentioned, to use Java for OS/390, the shop needs UNIX System Services installed. It would behoove you, the IBM mainframe programmer, to know a bit about UNIX System Services, or OS/390 UNIX.

This chapter provides some information on OS/390 UNIX. We start by discussing the OS/390 command shell and methods of accessing the OS/390 shell. You'll read portions about the file system used in OS/390 UNIX, namely the *Hierarchical File System* (HFS). Lastly, you'll compare and contrast MVS concepts with those in OS/390 UNIX.

It is not the intent of this chapter to provide a comprehensive description of OS/390 UNIX System Services. Rather, the intent is to provide you, the MVS programmer, with the knowledge to use OS/390 UN IX System Services to write and execute your Java programs.

The Command Shell

The shell is a command that reads lines from either a file or the terminal, interprets them, and generally executes other commands. It is the program that is running when a user logs into the system. The shell implements a language that has flow control constructs, as well as a macro facility that provides a variety of features in addition to data storage with built-in history and line editing capabilities. It incorporates many features to aid interactive use; it's advantage is that the interpretative language is common to both interactive and non-interactive use (shell scripts). That is, commands can either be typed directly to the running shell, or they can be put into a file that can be executed directly by the shell.

Some of you stalwart MVSers may recall interacting with TSO by issuing commands at the READY prompt; using the command shell is similar.

You may wonder how you get to the OS/390 command shell in the first place. The next section discusses getting to the shell.

Accessing the Command Shell

OS/390 provides several terminal emulators that you can use to access the shells:

The TSO/E OMVS command, a 3270 terminal interface

The *rlogin* command, an asynchronous terminal interface

The *telnet* command, an asynchronous terminal interface

Your system administrator must set you up to use one of these terminal emulators. To see which terminal emulator you are set up for, you should enter the TSO command *LISTUSER* as follows:

```
LISTUSER USERNAME OMVS
```

Typical output from the LISTUSER command would be

```
UID=0000000101
HOME=/tr23790/home/loum
PROGRAM=OMVS
CPUTIMEMAX=NONE
ASSIZEMAX=NONE
FILEPROCMAX=NONE
PROCUSERMAX=NONE
THREADSMAX=NONE
MMAPAREAMAX=NONE
READY
```

The *italicized* line shows the program being used to access the shell. The default shell is accessed through the TSO OMVS command. Change the shell by entering the ALTUSER command. The following command entered at the READY prompt changes the OS/390 shell from OMVS to the OS/390 shell:

```
ALTUSER USERNAME OMVS(PROGRAM('/bin/sh'))
```

If you come from a UNIX background, you'll likely access the command shell through rlogin. If you come from an MVS background, which is a key assumption of this book, you'll likely access the shell by using the OMVS command. Let's spend some time discussing the OMVS command.

The OMVS Command

If you are not set up to use the OMVS command, you can change it by entering the *OMVS* command at the READY prompt. Figure 15.1 shows the OMVS terminal emulator with default settings.

You enter commands at the command line prefaced with = = > at the bottom of the screen. Later in this chapter, you'll read about some OS/390 UNIX commands you may enter in this screen.

The HFS File System

OS/390 UNIX files are organized in a hierarchy, as in a UNIX system. All files are members of a directory, and each directory is in turn a member of another directory at a higher level in the hierarchy. The highest level of the hierarchy is the *root* directory. A file contained within the HFS hierarchy is called an HFS file.

Figure 15.2 shows a comparison between MVS files and HFS files.

Figure 15.2 shows that the root/ directory is analogous to the MVS catalog; the root/ directory assists the file manager in locating HFS files. Each user in an HFS system is

```
IBM
Licensed Material - Property of IBM
5647-A01 (C) Copyright IBM Corp. 1993, 1998
(C) Copyright Mortice Kern Systems, Inc., 1985, 1996.
(C) Copyright Software Development Group, University of Waterloo, 1989.

All Rights Reserved.

U.S. Government users - RESTRICTED RIGHTS - Use, Duplication, or
Disclosure restricted by GSA-ADP schedule contract with IBM Corp.

IBM is a registered trademark of the IBM Corp.


$





===>
                                                       RUNNING
ESC=¢  1=Help     2=SubCmd  3=HlpRetrn  4=Top      5=Bottom  6=TSO
       7=BackScr 8=Scroll  9=NextSess 10=Refresh 11=FwdRetr12=Retrieve
```

Figure 15.1   The OMVS screen with default PFKey settings.

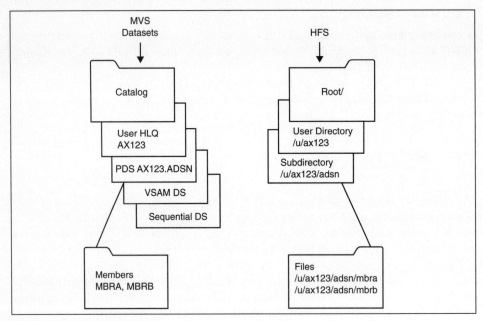

Figure 15.2   MVS datasets and HFS files compared.

assigned a *home directory*, specified by */u/*. The remaining directories *ax123* and *adsn* show one possible file organization. The files */u/ax123/adsn/mbra* and */u/ax123/ adsn/mbrb* show two files residing in the subdirectory previously shown.

In short, the directory structure used by HFS is similar to the structure used in PCs running Windows.

Working with HFS Files

This section discusses naming HFS files and shows some commands that act on HFS files.

Naming HFS Files

A filename can be up to 255 characters long. To be portable, the filename should use only the following characters:

- Uppercase or lowercase A to Z
- Numbers 0 to 9
- Period
- Underscore
- Hyphen

Do not include any nulls or slash characters in a filename. Doublebyte characters are not supported in a filename and are treated as singlebyte data. *Using doublebyte characters in a filename may cause problems.* For instance, if you use a doublebyte character in which one of the bytes is a . (dot) or / (slash), the file system treats this as a special delimiter in the pathname.

OS/390 UNIX is case-sensitive and distinguishes characters as either uppercase or lowercase. Therefore, MyFile is not the same as myfile.

A filename can include a suffix, or *extension,* that indicates its file type. An extension consists of a period () and several characters. For example, files that are Java code could have the extension .java, as in the filename myprog.java. Having groups of files with identical suffixes makes it easier to run commands against many files at once. For example, to compile all the Java programs in the current directory, you could enter

```
javac *.java
```

HFS File Commands

Table 15.1 describes some commands that act on HFS files. Some commands accept wildcard characters that enable the command to act on groups of files, like the previous example of javac command invocation.

Copying Files between UNIX Files and MVS Datasets

You can copy HFS files to MVS datasets from the OS/390 shell using the cp or mv command, or by using the following TSO commands. Some examples of using cp to copy files to and from HFS to MVS are as follows:

```
cp anhfsfile "//'myhlq.anmvsdsn'"
```

The previous command copies the file *anhfsfile* to an MVS dataset *myhlq.anmvsdsn.* Notice the use of quotes around the MVS dataset name.

```
cp -P "DSORG=PS,RECFM=FB,SPACE=(20,10)" anhfsfile "//'myhlq.anewmvsdsn'"
```

The previous command copies *anhhsfile* to a new MVS dataset *myhlq.anewmvsdsn* with the specified DCBs. Notice the -P parameter *must* be coded in uppercase.

Table 15.2 lists the TSO commands you may use to copy files to and from HFS to MVS.

Table 15.1   OS/390 UNIX File Commands

COMMAND	EXAMPLE	DESCRIPTION
ln	ln oldpath newpath	Create a *hard* link. *Oldpath* is the existing pathname; *newpath* is the new reference. Every reference to newpath is a reference to oldpath. Hard links cannot access files across file systems (in a different root structure).
	ln -s oldpath newpath	Create a *symbolic* link. A symbolic link acts like a hard link without the restriction of accessing across file systems.
	ln -e oldpath newpath	Create an *external* link. An external link may refer to an MVS dataset.
rm	rm afile bfile	Delete one or more files or links. When you delete a link, you do not affect the files, only the link(s) between them.
cp	cp filea fileb	Copy *filea* into *fileb*. If fileb does not exist, cp will create it.
mv	mv filea fileb dirA	Move one or more files to another directory.
	mv -R dirA dirB	Move all files from directory A to directory B. The -R option *must* be coded in uppercase.
diff	diff filea fileb	Compare filea and fileb.
wc	wc filea	Count the words and lines in a text file.
grep	grep aword afile	Search afile for occurrences of aword. The grep command enables for pattern searches. Patterns used by grep are not the same as wildcards used in commands. However, the concept is similar.

Comparing MVS, UNIX, and OS/390 Concepts

The following list describes platform—independent computing concepts in the language of MVS, the language of UNIX (AIX, an IBM implementation of UNIX), and OS/390 UNIX. You'll find these comparisons useful when you see how familiar concepts and properties of MVS are implemented on OS/390 with UNIX System Services.

Table 15.2 TSO Commands to Copy Files to and from HFS to MVS

TSO COMMAND	DESCRIPTION
OPUT	Puts (copies) an MVS sequential data set or partitioned data set member into the file system. You can specify text or binary data.
OPUTX	Puts (copies) a sequential data set, a data set member, an MVS partitioned data set, or a PDSE into an HFS directory. You can specify text or binary data, select code page conversion for singlebyte data, specify a copy to lowercase filenames, and append a suffix to the member names when they become filenames. OPUTX is a REXX EXEC that invokes OPUT.
OGET	Gets an HFS file and copies it into an MVS sequential data set or partitioned data set member. You can specify text or binary data, and select code page conversion for singlebyte data.
OGETX	Gets an HFS file or directory and copies it into an MVS partitioned data set, PDSE, or sequential data set. You can specify text or binary data, select code page conversion for singlebyte data, allow a copy from lowercase filenames, and delete one or all suffixes from the filenames when they become PDS member names. OGETX is a REXX EXEC that invokes OGET.
OCOPY	Copies data in either direction between an MVS data set and an HFS file, using ddnames. OCOPY can also copy within MVS (one data set to another data set) or within the shell (one file to another file). OCOPY has a CONVERT operand for converting singlebyte data from one code page to another.

Virtual Storage

Virtual (or logical) storage is a concept that, when implemented by a computer and its operating system, enables programmers to use a very large range of memory or storage addresses for stored data. The computing system maps the programmer's virtual addresses to real hardware storage addresses. Usually, the programmer is freed from having to be concerned about the availability of data storage.

On *MVS*, each user gets an *address space* of 2 gigabytes of virtual storage. Some of this storage contains common code for all users.

On *AIX UNIX*, each user gets whatever they require within the constraints of the operating system, and also the amount of real memory and storage.

On *OS/390 UNIX*, each user gets an MVS address space.

Data Storage

Data storage is what we call the physical implementation of related sets of data.

On *MVS*, data storage is named by *data sets*, sometimes, written as a single word *datasets*.

On *AIX UNIX* and *OS/390 UNIX*, data storage is named by *files*.

Configuration Data

Configuration data is a set of attributes that describe the overall behavior of the system, such as system software versions and details on various system services.

On *MVS*, configuration data is stored as members of the partitioned dataset SYS1.PARMLIB, also called the parmlib. Data in the parmlib controls the initial loading of the system as well as how MVS address spaces behave.

On *AIX UNIX*, configuration data is stored in files in the /etc directory. In addition, a utility called the Object Data Manager stores some configuration information.

On *OS/390 UNIX*, configuration data is also stored in the /etc file system.

Bit Bucket

The bit bucket, a somewhat whimsical term, is the universal data sink (originally, the mythical receptacle caught bits when they fell off the end of a register during a shift instruction). Discarded, lost, or destroyed data is said to have 'gone to the bit bucket.'

On *MVS*, the bit bucket is the DD DUMMY card.

On *AIX UNIX* and *OS/390 UNIX*, the bit bucket is a file reference called /dev/null.

Locating Data

How does a user or application locate a dataset or file? The files for an operating system are organized into a file system. Many environments, such as UNIX System Services, use a file system that consists of a hierarchy of directories. Conventional MVS, however, uses a non-hierarchical file system in which groups of data sets are referred to by their *high-level qualifier* (HLQ) specification.

On *MVS*, you locate datasets by using a catalog or a PDS directory. A catalog is a direct access dataset containing device-specific information used to locate datasets. A PDS directory is a listing of PDS member names with offsets within the PDS used to locate members.

MVS catalogs are tied into system levels. For example, a system catalog could hold information you would use to locate datasets with a system-wide high level qualifier, such as SYS1. A user catalog could hold information used to locate datasets with a user high-level qualifier.

Also, on MVS, you may use the *Volume Table of Contents* (VTOC) to list the dataset names residing on a particular direct access device. The VTOC does not contain any information on PDS members.

On *AIX UNIX* and *OS/390 UNIX*, you would navigate the directory structure of the files to locate a file. If you are familiar with Windows or DOS, you are no doubt

THE STICKY BIT

This is the bit in the mode of a UNIX file which, if set for an executable, tells the kernel to keep the code loaded in swap space even after it has finished executing on the assumption that it is likely to be used again soon. This performance optimization was included in some early versions of UNIX to save reloading of frequently used programs such as the shell from disk.

familiar with a directory file system. If so, you know how to navigate directory structures. You direct the shell to a directory with a *change directory* command and issue commands to reference files stored in that directory.

On OS/390 UNIX, the directory file system is called the *hierarchical file system* (HFS). You'll read expressions like HFS files (files stored in an HFS file system) and HFS programs (programs that access HFS files) in this and any work dealing with OS/390 UNIX System Services.

Using Shared Libraries

Shared libraries enable multiple users to access useful system resources. Every multi-user operating system enables certain libraries to be used by multiple users.

On *MVS*, the system has a common area called the *Link Pack Area* (LPA) that holds shared libraries. The LPA is available to every address space running in the system.

On *AIX UNIX* and *OS/390 UNIX*, shared libraries are loaded into the system on demand. When the first user requests use of a library, the system loads that library into memory. Subsequent users requiring access to the library may access the previously loaded copy. The operating system will purge the library when no user requires further access. OS/390 UNIX programs, with their sticky bit switched on, can access shared libraries in the LPA as well.

Data Encoding

A data encoding is a low-level representation of data. Sometimes, the term *collating sequence* is used to mean the data encoding representation. Some often-used data encodings are EBCDIC, ASCII, and Unicode.

We draw a distinction between the encoding of the data and the format of the data. For example, you can have text and binary formats with the EBCDIC encoding scheme as well as with the ASCII encoding scheme. Although both encoding schemes enable for text representation, their underlying bit patterns, or machine representations, are different.

On *MVS*, you are free to use any data encoding you wish; the applications are responsible for handling the data. However, most MVS programs expect the data to be encoded in the EBCDIC scheme. For the most part, you are safe in assuming that MVS programs use data encoded in EBCDIC.

On *AIX UNIX*, the expectation is that programs expect the data encoding to be ASCII. Of course, you can write code to use data in EBCDIC or any encoding. However, it's a safe bet that UNIX programs expect an ASCII data encoding.

On *OS/390 UNIX*, you are free to use any encoding you wish. However, IBM system software products expect data to follow the EBCDIC encoding. However, if a program coming from another UNIX environment gets ported to OS/390 UNIX, you can assume that the program to be ported uses and produces data in ASCII. If so, the ported program executing on OS/390 UNIX needs to convert the encoding from ASCII to EBCDIC. You may use the OS/390 UNIX utilities *pax* and *iconv* to convert data from ASCII to EBCDIC.

Dataset and File Formats

Some operating systems provide dataset and file formats, which are abstractions that enable an application to access data in a consistent and organized fashion.

On *MVS*, datasets may be formatted into logical records and physical records (called blocks). When an application program reads data from a file, the program may read a record of data with a record I/O statement. This I/O statement operates on a logical record. Physical records, or blocks, are what MVS uses to buffer data from storage to memory for subsequent program access.

By and large, *UNIX* and *OS/390 UNIX* do not have any real file formats or access methods. Data contained in files is a stream of bytes; any organization required by the application is enforced by the application.

Dataset Organization and Access Methods

On *MVS*, closely allied to the concept of dataset format is the concept of dataset organization. Whereas the record/block format discussed previously describes how an MVS application accesses data in a dataset, the dataset organization provides a higher-level abstraction for custom data access. Often, you'll hear MVS programmers use the term *access method* interchangeably with dataset organization.

For example, when you, the MVS programmer, perform I/O on a *sequential* dataset, you are using the *Basic Sequential Access Method* (BSAM). When you perform I/O on a VSAM dataset, you are using the *Virtual Storage Access Method*. Now, your COBOL or PL/I program issues READ FILE INTO and WRITE FILE FROM statements; these statements may perform I/O on either sequential or VSAM datasets (of course, VSAM datasets have more I/O options than BSAM datasets). The low-level system code that accesses the data is completely hidden from the program.

UNIX and *OS/390 UNIX* do not have any native support for access methods per se. File organization and access are the responsibility of the application. However, IBM has utilities that you can use to copy MVS datasets to HFS datasets to enable access by HFS programs.

Case Sensitivity

Coming from the MVS world where everything is usually coded in upper case, you may experience a few gotchas when coding in the world of OS/390 UNIX. Although you, the MVS programmer, may code your programs and issue TSO commands in upper case, MVS cares little for the case of your code. Some exceptions arise when you code JCL and runtime parameters coded on an EXEC PGM= JCL card.

In *UNIX* and *OS/390 UNIX*, case sensitivity rules the roost; nearly every command, file name, and programming language construct is case sensitive.

Supported Programming Languages

For the most part, nearly every programming language used is supported on MVS with one glaring exception, which is Java. That said, you, the MVS programmer, could code Java on OS/390 UNIX to access data resident in an MVS system. The UNIX programmer has a compiler for just about every programming language imaginable.

Operating systems typically have one or more scripting languages. You use a scripting language to control system resources, such as files or datasets, and to invoke executables. A script is a curious mix of operating system statements that may manipulate files or datasets combined with programming language constructs. An example of a typical script could be a program that checks for the existence of one or more files; if the files exist, then the script executes program X, or else the script executes program Y. Scripting languages are usually interpreted and are not processor-intensive applications.

On *MVS*, you can code TSO CLISTS, which few people use these days, and REXX EXECs.

On *AIX UNIX*, you have access to all scripting languages from MVS and AIX UNIX.

Online Help

On *MVS*, you can issue the TSO HELP command or, if within the ISPF environment, you can hit PF1 for online help. You can configure ISPF to invoke Book Manager to reference IBM programming language and system software manuals.

On *AIX UNIX* and *OS/390 UNIX*, the *man* command provides help for shell commands. In addition, you may get online help through the installed GUI. OS/390 UNIX has an interface to Book Manager via the OHELP command.

Code That Performs Work

In *MVS*, the elementary entity that performs work is called a task. MVS represents tasks by using a Task Control Block. The MVS operating system supports multiple tasks within each address space. Applications written in COBOL and PL/I usually correspond to a single task.

In *AIX UNIX* and *OS/390 UNIX*, the elementary entity that performs work is called a thread. A UNIX (AIX or OS/390) application starts a unit of work called a process, which may contain or create multiple threads. In addition, an AIX UNIX or OS/390 UNIX process can create additional processes, which, in turn, may create one or more threads.

In *MVS*, a long running task is known as a started task. A started task may execute as long as the system is active. In *AIX UNIX* and *OS/390 UNIX*, a long-running task is called a daemon; a long-running task under OS/390 may also be a started task.

Program Search Order

The program search order is the list of libraries and paths the system searches to locate executable programs.

In *MVS*, the system searches the following partitioned datasets (libraries) allocated to the following DDNAMES in the order listed: TASKLIB, STEPLIB, JOBLIB, LPALST, and LNKLST.

In *AIX UNIX*, the system searches the directories specified in the user's PATH environment variable. The value of PATH is a list of directories; the program file found in the first directory listed in the PATH is the file loaded and executed. For dynamic link libraries, the system searches a list of directories specified in the LIBPATH environment variable.

In *OS390 UNIX*, the system searches the directories specified in the user's PATH variable. However, if the program's sticky bit is switched on, the search order follows the previous rules for MVS.

Assigning Disk Storage

In *MVS*, a user assigns storage by allocating datasets. Dataset allocation can be done in the foreground by using the TSO ALLOCATE command or using dataset utilities in ISPF (which is a front end for the ALLOCATE command). MVS users may allocate disk space in batch by using DD statements in a JCL job stream.

In *AIX UNIX*, a system administrator assigns files to logical disk volumes that are mapped to physical disk volumes.

In *OS/390 UNIX*, a system administrator allocates HFS files. Also, a user may execute a shell script, REXX Exec, or a program that creates HFS files from program data.

Problem Determination

In *MVS*, you can use TSO TEST, a line-oriented debugger, or the IBM debug tool. MVS supports ABEND codes and may produce a system dump on request. Several third parties offer source level debugging tools.

In *AIX UNIX*, you have access to a range of programming debugging tools as well as system routines, such as errpt, for reporting system errors; you can also request a core dump.

In *OS/390 UNIX*, you have the same features as AIX UNIX at your disposal. You also may use the Visual Age product, which provides a source level debugger for several programming languages, including Java.

Online Execution

In *MVS*, you may log on to TSO by supplying a userID and a password. Upon logging on, the system submits a started task that represents the user logged onto the system. Each TSO user may have only one TSO session active at a given time.

The MVS user executes a program in the foreground by either entering the name of the program at the TSO "ready" prompt, or through option 6 of ISPF. The system searches the program libraries allocated to the DDNAMEs specified in the section "Program Search Order" unless the user specified the fully-qualified dataset name.

In *AIX UNIX*, users log on to the system and execute shell scripts. An AIX user may issue an rlogin or telnet command to connect to another operating system. In addition, the AIX user may enter the name of a script or executable. AIX UNIX users may have several login sessions simultaneously.

In *OS/390 UNIX*, a user may logon with the rlogin and telnet commands, then logon to TSO (MVS) and execute the OMVS command to have an MVS session. As with AIX UNIXI, OS/390 UNIX users may enter the name for a shell script or executable program.

Background Execution

In *MVS*, background program execution is done by submitting a batch file, containing JCL, to the batch environment.

In *AIX UNIX* and *OS/390 UNIX*, shell commands prefixed with both an ampersand (&) and cron command will execute in batch. In OS/390 UNIX, the BPXBATCH command enables the user to submit batch jobs and run HFS programs in JCL job streams.

Scheduling Programs for Execution

In *MVS*, a job scheduler may use a number of system utilities, such as JES or the system Automation for OS/390.

In *AIX UNIX* and *OS/390 UNIX*, the cron utility schedules programs that execute in the background. Third-party solutions for UNIX background daemons also exist.

Creating Programs

The *MVS* programmer may create a program by using a compiler with a linker or binder. The output of the binder is a load module—a member of a PDS that holds executable code.

In *AIX UNIX* or *OS/390 UNIX*, the programmer uses a compiler and a linker. Usually, a special script called a makefile is used to ensure the existence of necessary files, call the compiler, and if the return code is satisfactory, issue a call to a linker.

Editing Data

In *MVS*, the primary tool used by you, the MVS programmer, to edit data and program code is the ISPF editor.

In *AIX UNIX*, you would use one of several editors, such as vi, ed, or emacs.

In *OS/390 UNIX*, you could use the AIX UNIX editors or the edit tool. You may use a GUI-based editor called nedit, which also converts from ASCII to EBCDIC.

View and Cancel Jobs

In *MVS*, you could use SDSF or a third-party product, such as IOF, to view, purge, and cancel jobs. These tools enable you to stop a job that is currently executing or to remove a job pending execution from the job queue.

In *AIX UNIX*, you could use the ps shell to view and kill threads. To stop an online executing process, you use the Control-C key combination.

In *OS/390 UNIX*, you have the features available to both MVS and AIX UNIX to view and stop threads.

In Summary

OS/390 UNIX System Services bring together two powerful operating systems. These system services enable you, the mainframe programmer, to access MVS datasets from a UNIX environment. Since you must compile and execute your Java programs from within this environment, you need tools to access mainframe (MVS) datasets; UNIX System Services give you just that.

Java and MVS Batch

Even in this day and age of GUI applications, there will always be a need to run programs in batch. Fortunately, running Java programs in batch is not difficult. All you need to do is secure your shop's *Java Class Library* (JCL), and modify the job stream by supplying your Java program, dataset references, and other runtime and environment parameters.

This chapter provides what you, the mainframe programmer, need to know to execute a Java program in batch. You'll read about the three options that are available for batch Java program execution. For each option, you'll read about the parameters that you'll need to supply to the job stream. Along the way, you'll see which environment variables to set and how to set them in the OS/390 batch environment.

Executing Java in Batch

Three options are available to execute Java programs in batch:

1. You can execute the *Multiple Virtual Storage* (MVS) utility program *BPXBATCH*. BXBATCH enables you to run an OS/390 UNIX command or executable under MVS.

2. If you compile and link your Java program with the High Performance Compiler, you can execute your linked program as you would a COBOL or PL/I program.

3. You can run Java programs as a started task using one of the two options previously outlined.

The next sections examine these options in detail, starting with using BPXBATCH.

Running Java Programs with BPXBATCH

Because the Java interpreter runs under OS/390 UNIX system services, you can use the BPXBATCH utility to load the Java interpreter and pass the name of a Java program. You may also supply runtime parameters to the main() method of the Java program at the same time.

Listing 16.1 shows the JCL that loads BPXBATCH and runs a Java program.

This listing is an absolute minimum. BPXBATCH writes to *Hierarchical File Storage* (HFS) datasets only. (BPXBATCH can read from MVS datasets.) Hence, you can't use SYSOUT=* for the standard output streams. Some additional information on this job follows.

The Parameter Passed to BPXBATCH

This statement in Listing 16.1 is the parameter passed to BPXBATCH:

```
//      PARM='SH java javaprog parm1 parm2'
```

```
//WHOIAMA JOB (MYACCTINFO),CLASS=X,MSGCLASS=X,MSGLEVEL=(1,1),
//      REGION=16M,NOTIFY=&SYSUID
//*
//* Run Java Program with BPXBATCH
//*
//RUNJAVA EXEC PGM=BPXBATCH,
//      PARM='SH java javaprog parm1 parm2'
//STDOUT  DD  PATH='/u/homedir/stdout',
//      PATHOPTS=(OCREAT,OTRUNC,OWRONLY),
//      PATHMODE=SIRWXU
//STDERR  DD PATH='/u/homedir/stderr',
//      PATHOPTS=(OCREAT,OTRUNC,OWRONLY),
//      PATHMODE=SIRWXU
//STDENV DD PATH='/u/homedir/myenvfil'
/*
```

Listing 16.1 Running Java with BPXBATCH.

WARNING

If you misspell or omit the DDNames, STDOUT, or STDERR in your BPXBATCH job, BPXBATCH will route the output to the null and invisible output, */dev/null*.

The parameter is the standard UNIX command shell, *SH*, with the Java runtime, the name of a Java program, and any parameters the Java program requires. The Java program would contain the following constructs:

```
public class javaprog {
    public static void main( String[] args ) {
        //args[ 0 ] equals parm1, args[1] equals parm2
    }
}
```

You are not limited to passing the Java runtime interpreter to the command shell. You can pass a script that calls the Java runtime interpreter. In the script, you can set environment variables or use program logic to run different Java programs.

Standard Files Used by BPXBATCH

The filesused by BPXBATCH are STDOUT, STDERR, and STDENV.

- STDOUT is the default output file that corresponds to *System.out.print* in your Java program.
- STDERR is the error output where the Java runtime writes diagnostics-like stack traces. STDERR, if not specified in your job stream, defaults to the dataset referenced by STDOUT.
- STDENV is a file that contains options to the Java runtime, such as a classpath setting. STDENV is not required and is usually "dummied" out (DD DUMMY).

Listing 16.1 shows these files stored in a home directory, but the files can be stored anywhere the user has permission to save files.

A More Robust Job Stream for Executing BPXBATCH

In the real world, a batch job would include an IEFBR14 step at the beginning and perhaps, a step at the end to clean up or move output to another location. Listing 16.2 shows the BPXBATCH job including these steps.

The DELETE step does what you think it does; it runs IEFBR14 to delete any existing datasets that shouldn't exist for this job. The datasets in question are the standard output and standard error datasets.

```
//WHOIAMA JOB (MYACCTINFO),CLASS=X,MSGCLASS=X,MSGLEVEL=(1,1),
//    REGION=16M,NOTIFY=&SYSUID
//*
//* Run Java Program with BPXBATCH
//*
//DELETE    EXEC PGM=IEFBR14
//STDOUT    DD  PATH='/u/homedir/stdjava.out',
//              PATHOPTS=(OCREAT,OWRONLY),
//              PATHMODE=SIRWXU,
//              PATHDISP=(DELETE)
//STDERR    DD  PATH='/u/homedir/stdjava.err',
//              PATHOPTS=(OCREAT,OWRONLY),
//              PATHMODE=SIRWXU,
//              PATHDISP=(DELETE)
//*
//RUNJAVA   EXEC PGM=BPXBATCH,
//              PARM='SH java javaprog parm1 parm2'
//SYSPRINT DD  SYSOUT=*
//SYSOUT    DD  SYSOUT=*
//STDOUT    DD  PATH='/u/homedir/stdjava.out',
//              PATHOPTS=(OWRONLY,OCREAT,OTRUNC),
//              PATHMODE=SIRWXU
//STDERR    DD  PATH='/u/homedir/stdjava.err',
//              PATHOPTS=(OWRONLY,OCREAT,OTRUNC),
//              PATHMODE=SIRWXU
//STDENV    DD  DUMMY
//*
//COPYOUT   EXEC PGM=IKJEFT01,DYNAMNBR=300,COND=EVEN
//SYSTSPRT DD  SYSOUT=*
//HFSOUT    DD PATH='/u/homedir/stdjava.out'
//HFSERR    DD PATH='/u/homedir/stdjava.err'
//*Shop - specific DCBs for output files follow
//STDOUTL   DD SYSOUT=*,DCB=(RECFM=VB,LRECL=133,BLKSIZE=137)
//STDERRL   DD SYSOUT=*,DCB=(RECFM=VB,LRECL=133,BLKSIZE=137)
//SYSPRINT DD SYSOUT=*
//SYSTSIN   DD DATA
 ocopy indd(HFSOUT) outdd(STDOUTL)
 ocopy indd(HFSERR) outdd(STDERRL)
/*
```

Listing 16.2 Running Java with output redirection.

The RUNJAVA step is the same as the RUNJAVA step in Listing 16.1.

The COPYOUT step invokes TSO in the background and runs the OCOPY command to copy the data from HFS datasets to a SYSOUT dataset. You can easily code a sequential MVS or member of a partitioned dataset (PDS) for the destination of the OCOPY command.

If you're wondering why the COPYOUT step is there, sadly, it is because no symbolic temporary dataset representation is available for HFS datasets. You cannot code &&TEMP for STDOUT or STDERR datasets. Also, as previously mentioned, BPX-BATCH writes to HFS datasets only.

Compiling a Java Program in Batch

Because BPXBATCH runs OS/390 UNIX programs in batch and the Java bytecode compiler is an OS/390 UNIX program, you can compile Java programs in batch. The JCL is nearly identical to that for executing the program. The only difference is that instead of passing the *java* command to the UNIX command shell, you pass the *javac* command. You can use the job shown in Listing 16.2 and change the EXEC card of the RUNJAVA step to pass javac to compile Java programs in batch.

As previously mentioned, you can pass a shell script to the command processor to set environment variables and compiler options.

Defining Environment Variables in Batch

Whether you compile or run Java programs on a workstation or in batch, you'll need to establish the proper environment. A convenient method for establishing your Java environment for batch compiles and executions is by defining your Java environment variables in a dataset. The dataset is known to BPXBATCH jobs as DDNAME STDENV. The dataset referenced by DDNAME STDENV can be an HFS or MVS dataset (recall that BPXBATCH can *read* from MVS datasets).

BPXBATCH also accepts environment variable settings by way of an instream DD statement. For example,

```
//SYSENV DD *
    PATH==/usr/lpp/java12:/u/myhome/myprog
/*
```

Typically, you need to set the PATH and CLASSPATH environment variables. It's good practice to set the JAVA_HOME variable as well. Code the values for these environment variables in an *unnumbered* text file (turn line numbering off while editing) as name-value pairs: *environmentvarname*=varvalue. Here's how to make variable assignments for some Java environment variables in OS/390.

Assigning Environment Variables in OS/390

Here are some rules of thumb to follow when assigning Java environment variables in OS/390.

- Use a colon to separate path names.
    - Example: PATH=/usr/lpp/java12:/u/myhome/myprogs

This sets the PATH environment variable to the two directories (paths) separated by the colon. Of course, you may, and usually will, use more than two paths in an environment variable assignment.

- Environment variable names are referenced by a $ on the right-hand side of an assignment statement.

    - Example: CLASSPATH=$CLASSPATH:/u/myhome/myprogs

This sets the CLASSPATH to the existing CLASSPATH assignment and the path following the colon. Assigning an environment variable with its existing value plus additional paths is a common technique for setting environment variables.

- Most environment variables deal with paths. However, several enable the use of JAR and ZIP files in conjunction with paths.

    - Example: CLASSPATH=$CLASSPATH:/u/myhome/myprogs:/libs/tools.jar

This sets the CLASSPATH assignment to the current CLASSPATH, the path /u/myhome/myprogs, and the JAR file /libs/tools/.jar.

- You can use the values of some existing environment variables as partial paths when assigning other environment variables.

    - Example: PATH=/usr/lpp/java12:/u/myhome/myprogs:$JAVA_HOME/lib

This uses the value of JAVA_HOME to set a path that partly defines the PATH environment variable. Using an existing environment variable as part of a path works when the existing environment variable can refer to only one path, such as JAVA_HOME.

- Different products use different sets of environment variables. For example, the *Customer Information Control System* (CICS) has a set of environment variables that is unique to using Java and the CICS gateway. Using Java with DB2 requires yet another set of environment variables.

Running Compiled and Linked Java Programs

Executing Java programs compiled and linked with the *High Performance Java Compiler* (HPJC) can be done in one of two ways. If you linked your module into an HFS file, you'll use BPXBATCH. If you linked your module into an MVS dataset, you'll invoke the module directly with an EXEC PGM= JCL statement.

Listing 16.3 shows a sample job stream that runs a Java executable compiled and linked into an HFS dataset.

You'll have to code a STEPLIB DD statement in your JCL to bring in the HPJC and the IBM *Language Environment* (LE) runtime libraries. The dataset names shown here are probably not the same as those used in your installation. Notice the absence of the STDENV DD statement; you don't need one when you run Java executables.

Listing 16.4 shows a sample job stream that runs a Java executable compiled and linked into an MVS dataset.

No surprises here. Any files referenced in the program would need DD statements, of course.

```
//WHOIAMA JOB (MYACCTINFO),CLASS=X,MSGCLASS=X,MSGLEVEL=(1,1),
//     REGION=16M,NOTIFY=&SYSUID
//*
//* Run Executable Java Program with BPXBATCH
//*
//RUNJAVA EXEC PGM=BPXBATCH,
//     PARM='SH /u/homedir/javaprgs/ajavaprg'
//STEPLIB DD    DSN=HPJ.SHPJMOD,DISP=SHR
//              DD    DSN=HPJ.SHPOMOD,DISP=SHR
//              DD    DSN=CEE.SCEERUN,DISP=SHR
//STDOUT  DD  PATH='/u/homedir/stdout',
//     PATHOPTS=(OCREAT,OTRUNC,OWRONLY),
//     PATHMODE=SIRWXU
//STDERR  DD PATH='/u/homedir/stderr',
//     PATHOPTS=(OCREAT,OTRUNC,OWRONLY),
//     PATHMODE=SIRWXU
```

Listing 16.3   Running a Java executable with BPXBATCH.

```
//WHOIAMA JOB (MYACCTINFO),CLASS=X,MSGCLASS=X,MSGLEVEL=(1,1),
//     REGION=16M,NOTIFY=&SYSUID
//*
//* Run Executable Java Program From MVS Load Module DSN
//*
//RUNJAVA EXEC PGM=AJAVAPRG,
//STEPLIB DD    DSN=MYHLQ.JAVA.LOAD,DISP=SHR
//              DD    DSN=HPJ.SHPJMOD,DISP=SHR
//              DD    DSN=HPJ.SHPOMOD,DISP=SHR
//              DD    DSN=CEE.SCEERUN,DISP=SHR
//STDOUT  DD  SYSOUT=*
//STDERR DD SYSOUT=*
```

Listing 16.4   Running a Java executable as an MVS load module.

Running Java Programs as Started Tasks

You may run a Java application as an MVS started task. Note that the Java application runs under the authorization of the started task user ID, which allows you to assign specific authorities to a Java server application. In addition, your Java server runs in a familiar, "operator-friendly" environment and can be easily started, monitored, and cancelled from an MVS console.

The JCL for the started task is the same as for the batch job listing shown in Listing 16.1.

In Summary

Hopefully, you can see that running a Java program (or compiling one) in batch is not difficult. If you're not familiar with HFS dataset organization, the JCL listings included in this chapter may seem a bit strange. However, whether the datasets used by your Java programs are MVS or HFS, it all boils down to the same concepts: The OS/390 batch environment requires that certain DDNames are known to executing programs. Just make those DDNames known and the environment will do the rest.

You've also read about setting environment variables. PL/I programmers are comfortable with setting runtime environment variables; COBOL programmers are probably less comfortable. Most of the time, these environment variables will be set in script files or in SYSIN DD * JCL, so you can probably get away without being a maven on Java environment variables for now.

CHAPTER 17

Java Record I/O Using the JRIO Package

As mainframe programmers, you spend much of your time writing and maintaining programs that perform record I/O. There's one slight catch—Java has no support for record I/O. We say "slight" because the extensible nature of Java makes it possible to write Java programs that perform record I/O with a little help from our friends at IBM. The help comes in the form of a custom package called *JRIO*, for Java Record Input and Output, which is the subject of this chapter.

Here, we'll cover the particulars of using IBM's JRIO package. You'll learn where to get a copy of the required class files and see some code using the JRIO classes to perform common and useful tasks.

What Is JRIO?

JRIO is an extension library that lets Java applications access traditional OS/390 file systems in addition to the *Hierarchical File System* (HFS). JRIO makes it possible for Java applications to access records within files and to access file systems through native methods. You do not have to write any code using the *Java Native Interface* (JNI) to use JRIO.

Recall that java.io, the base I/O package from Sun, provides *byte-oriented* or *field-oriented* access to files. JRIO is a class library that provides *record-oriented* access. JRIO uses separate interfaces for representing files and directories. JRIO also provides interfaces and classes for binary record-oriented operations and supports text only fields within binary record files.

JRIO provides access methods to read, write, or update sequential BSAM, random access, and keyed access files that are supported. In addition, Java programs using JRIO can access VSAM datasets, a PDS directory, and the system catalog.

JRIO enables you to access VSAM datasets in entry sequence order, by accessing a unique, primary key, or by accessing an alternate index. Directory and catalog operations supported by JRIO are listing the high level qualifiers in the system catalog, listing the datasets starting with a qualifier, and listing the members of a PDS.

JRIO is part of Java for OS/390. You can download the JDK for OS/390 from www.s390.ibm.com/java. JRIO is installed when you install the downloaded JDK.

Contents of the JRIO Package

This section describes the list of interfaces, related classes, constants, and exceptions available in the JRIO package *com.ibm.recordio*. You can divide the elements in JRIO among elements dealing with HFS files, OS/390 non VSAM files, and OS/390 VSAM files.

Let's take a look at the interfaces provided by JRIO.

JRIO Interfaces

JRIO provides Java interfaces that allow you to access directory information as well as perform record IO on common IBM data structures. The sections that follow provide details on the JRIO interfaces.

IDirectory

The *IDirectory* interface defines the operations on a directory, such as getting attributes, listing contents, creating new directories, and deleting or renaming existing directories. The related class, Directory, acts as a handler class when instances are created using the new() operator. The Directory class also provides several getInstanceOf() static factory methods that return references to concrete classes.

WHAT IS A FACTORY?

A *factory* is an object that creates or locates other objects. Objects are usually created with the new operator, which is analogous to having a static (factory) method on the object's class object. Often such static methods are named *getInstanceOf()* or *newInstance()*. This enables users of an interface to obtain instances of objects that implement the desired interface, without knowing or specifying the concrete class of the object. This enables a *runtime* choice of which implementation to use, based on the particulars of the environment, user inputs, or other factors.

IRecordFile

The *IRecordFile* interface defines the operations on a file, such as getting and setting attributes, creating new files, and deleting or renaming existing files. The related class, RecordFile, acts as a handle class when instances are created using new() operator. The RecordFile class also provides several getInstanceOf() static factory methods that return references to concrete classes.

IRecord

The IRecord interface defines the operations on the Record class, which is a wrapper for a byte array. An object of type *byte[]* is the simplest form of a record. The Record class provides field navigation by name or field index and also provides field-level type conversion. The record streams and random and keyed access files support reading and writing IRecords. IRecord and Record are part of the IBM VisualAge for Java Record Framework com.ibm.record package. This package is included with Java for OS/390.

NOTE Although the record streams and the random access and keyed access files all support reading and writing byte arrays, the application must handle any field navigation, type conversion, and exceptions arising from invalid conversions.

IFileInputRecordStream

The *IFileInputRecordStream* interface extends the InputRecordStream interface. Both interfaces define the sequential file input operations for record files, basically read and close. The related class, FileInputRecordStream, acts as a handler class when instances are created using the new() operator.

FileInputRecordStream also provides several getInstanceOf() static factory methods that return references to concrete classes. FileInputRecordStream extends the abstract class Input Record Stream. FileInputRecordStream is similar to FileInputStream in the java.io package. InputRecordStream is similar to InputStream in the java.io package.

IFileOutputRecordStream

The IFileOutputRecordStream interface extends the IOutputRecordStream interface. Both interfaces define the sequential file output operations for record files, including write, flush, and close. The related class, FileOutputRecordStream, acts as a handle class when instances are created using the new() operator.

FileOutputRecordStream also provides several getInstanceOf() static factory methods that return references to concrete classes. FileOutputRecordStream extends the abstract class OutputRecordStream. FileOutputRecordStream is similar to FileOutputStream in the java.io package. OutputRecordStream is similar to OutputStream in the java.io package.

IRandomAccessRecordFile

The *IRandomAccessRecordFile* interface defines the random access operations for record files, such as relative positioning, seeking, reading, writing, and closing. The related class, RandomAccessRecordFile, acts as a handle class when instances are created using new() operator. RandomAccessRecordFile also provides several getInstanceOf (. . .) static factory methods that return references to concrete classes.

IKeyedAccessRecordFile

The *IKeyedAccessRecordFile* interface defines the keyed access operations for record files, such as positioning by key, reading, writing, updating, deleting records, getting related index files, and closing. The related class, KeyedAccessRecordFile, acts as a handler class when instances are created using the new() operator.

KeyedAccessRecordFile also provides several getInstanceOf(. . .) static factory methods that return references to concrete classes. KeyedAccessRecordFile is somewhat similar to RandomAccessFile in the java.io package, but it introduces new, key-related positioning functions and the ability to logically delete records. Its function is somewhat similar to the java.util.Properties class. It lets you store and retrieve records by using a key.

IKeyDescriptor and IKey

The *IKey* interface defines the operations for a key, such as getting the bytes from the key and comparing this key's value with another key's value. The related class, Key, is a simple wrapper for a byte array (that is, it is not a handler class). It does provide a utility method, named getKey(), to create a key wrapper object from bytes extracted from another key or from a record when you provide the offset and length of the key bytes in the record.

An object of class Key does not contain its offsets or its length. However, an object of class KeyDescriptor contains the offset and length attributes needed to extract the key from a record, but does not contain the key's actual data.

The next section has information on the constants used by classes in JRIO.

JRIO Constants

JRIO constants are static variables in interface *com.ibm.recordio.IConstants*. Table 17.1 shows the JRIO constants used by classes that implement the *IRecord interface*, their values, the JRIO classes that you'll use these constants in, and a short description.

Table 17.2 shows the JRIO constants representing file attributes used by the *listDetailed()* method of the class *Directory*. ListDetailed() returns an array of file names and file attributes. The class Directory implements the *IDirectory* interface.

Listing 17.1 shows how to use the listDetailed() method.

The next section has some information on exceptions thrown by methods from JRIO classes.

Table 17.1 JRIO Constants Used in Classes that Implement IRecord

CONSTANT NAME	VALUE	USED IN CLASSES	DESCRIPTION
JRIO_DEFAULT_RECORD_FORMAT	String = "FB"	RecordFile	Default file record format RandomAccessRecordFile
JRIO_DEFAULT_RECORD_LENGTH	int = 80	RecordFile	Default LRECL RandomAccessRecordFile KeyedAccessRecordFile
JRIO_FIXED_MODE	String = "FB"	RecordFile	Represents Fixed Blocked RECFM RandomAccessRecordFile
JRIO_MAX_RECORD_LENGTH	int = 32760	RecordFile	The largest LRECL possible RandomAccessRecordFile
JRIO_MIN_RECORD_LENGTH	int = 1	RecordFile	The smallest LRECL possible RandomAccessRecordFile
JRIO_READ_EOF	int = -1	FileInputRecordStream	End of file marker RandomAccessRecordFile KeyedAccessRecordFile
JRIO_READ_MODE	String = "r"	RandomAccessRecordFile	Random access read only mode KeyedAccessRecordFile
JRIO_READ_WRITE_MODE	String = "rw"	RandomAccessRecordFile	Random read-write access mode KeyedAccessRecordFile
JRIO_VARIABLE_MODE	String = "vb"	RecordFile	Represents variable blocked RECFM RandomAccessRecordFile

Table 17.2   JRIO Constants Used by listDetailed() from Class Directory

CONSTANT NAME	VALUE	DESCRIPTION
JRIO_DIR_ENTRY_POSIX	byte = 0	File entry is a POSIX file
JRIO_DIR_ENTRY_CATALOG	byte = 1	File entry came from a catalog
JRIO_DIR_ENTRY_HLQ	byte = 2	File entry came from a High Level Qualifier
JRIO_DIR_ENTRY_PDS	byte = 3	File entry came from a PDS directory
JRIO_DIR_ENTRY_TYPE_BYTE_SIZE	byte = 1	Size of a directory entry identifier

```
static final String myHLQ = "//TR23790" ;
//Get a reference to the Directory (an HLQ In this case)
Directory myDSNsDir = Directory new( myHLQ ) ;
//Fetch dataset names from HLQ directory object
byte[] [] myDSNs = myDSNsDir.listDetailed() ;
//This will hold an Individual dataset name
String aDSN ;
//This will always be JRIO_DIR_ENTRY_HLQ (2) in this example
byte dsnEntryType ;
for (int i = 0; i < myDSNs.length; i++ ) {
    aDSN = "" ;
    //Access the first byte of the returned byte array
    dsnSource = myDSNs[ i ] [ 0 ] ;
    //Create a dataset name as a string from the bytes returned from
    //listDetails()
    for (int j = 1; j < myDSNs[ i ].length ; j++ )
        aDSN = aDSN + (char)myDSNs[ i ][ j ] ;
    //List dataset name to standard output
    System.out.println( "DSN = " + aDSN ) ;
}
```

Listing 17.1   listDetailed() example

JRIO Exceptions

Methods from classes derived from JRIO throw some Java exceptions as well as some exceptions unique to JRIO. Of the exceptions unique to JRIO, you can group them into *common exceptions* and *keyed access exceptions*. The common exceptions are thrown by a variety of methods that operate on keyed and non-keyed datasets and directories whereas keyed access exceptions are thrown by methods that operate on keyed datasets only.

The following general Java exceptions in the java.io package are thrown by many methods of JRIO: FileNotFoundException, IOException, IllegalArgumentException, IllegalStateException, and SecurityException.

Short descriptions of the JRIO-specific exceptions follow, starting with those exceptions common to methods that operate on both VSAM and non-VSAM files and directories.

Common JRIO Exceptions

JRIO methods throw two common exceptions: *RecordIOException* and *RecordIORuntimeException*.

RecordIOException

RecordIOException is a subclass of the Java exception class java.io.IOException that distinguishes I/O exceptions detected when using JRIO methods. RecordIOException is a *checked* exception, which means that your application code must explicitly handle it. The method that throws the exception can use a try-catch block to handle the exception or pass the exception to the calling method by declaring the exception in the method header.

RecordIORuntimeException

RecordIORuntimeException is a subclass of the Java exception class java.lang.RuntimeException that distinguishes runtime exceptions detected within JRIO. RecordIORuntimeException is an unchecked exception, which the application methods need not catch nor declare in a throws clause.

> **NOTE** Recall that your application normally can't do anything about unchecked exceptions except, perhaps, report on them and gracefully exit. If your application catches unchecked exceptions, you'll use *System.exit(0)* to stop your application. If you let the JVM handle the unchecked expression, the JVM will stop your application and generate a stack trace.

JRIO Exceptions Unique to Keyed File Processing

The exceptions described in this section are specific to keyed file access. They are all subclasses of com.ibm.recordio.RecordIOException. Methods of class KeyedAccessRecordFile can throw these exceptions. Like RecordIOException, they are also checked exceptions. Some of these exceptions are a result of programming or input errors; some could result from normal processing.

DuplicateKeyException

DuplicateKeyException exception is thrown when your application calls a write or update method that uses a new record containing a key that violates uniqueness in a unique key index of a cluster. DuplicateKeyException usually indicates an application logic error or bad input data. It is hard to imagine a situation where the generation of a duplicate key results from normal or expected application behavior.

IllegalKeyChangeException

IllegalKeyChangeException exception is thrown when your application calls an update method that uses a key to locate a record to update and then tries to change the field containing the key. Your application cannot change the field containing the key used to locate a record. You may be able to change keys in other fields. However, this could cause a DuplicateKeyException.

KeyNotFoundException

KeyNotFoundException is thrown when your application calls the *positionForward(keyFile, thisKey)* method and the method cannot locate a record in keyFile containing the key with value thisKey. The method positionForward() does not perform a read operation; the method moves the cursor to the record with the key value specified in its argument. The similar method *positionForwardGE(key)* does not throw this exception, but positions to the next higher key if the specified key is not found. The next read could get an End-Of-File indication if no more keys in this index exist.

MissingPriorReadException

MissingPriorReadException is thrown when your application calls either deleteRecord (aRecordFile) or update (aRecordFile, aRecord) and the previous operation is not a successful read of the record to delete or update. Put simply, your call to deleteRecord or update has no record to delete or update.

Now that you've read a bit about the JRIO interfaces, classes, constants, and exceptions, you can check out some Java that uses JRIO. The next section provides some coding examples of JRIO in action.

Using JRIO

Here, we present code samples illustrating key concepts of using the JRIO API. The code samples are not complete programs; their purpose is to impart a flavor of using JRIO. Before we jump into the code samples, a few words on dataset and directory naming conventions, required import statements, and JRIO record representation are called for.

Directory and Dataset Naming Conventions

JRIO routines expect directory and dataset names to be strings that begin with //. Therefore, all datasets with the high level qualifier TR23790 would be accessed through a directory object "//TR23790". A PDS directory is the name of the PDS dataset, such as "//TR23790.MYPDS.LIB". The slash-string "//" represents the root of all high level qualifiers.

Aside from starting the strings with double slashes, dataset names known to JRIO methods are like dataset names used in a JCL job stream. A non-VSAM dataset name understood by JRIO could be "//TR23790.MYFLATFILE.DATA". A member of a PDS is named as you'd expect, "//TR23790.MYPDS.LIB(MYMEM)". A sequential VSAM dataset name could be "//MYHLQ.VSAMSEQ.ESDS" and a keyed VSAM dataset name could be "//YOURHLQ.VSAMKEY.KSDS".

> **NOTE** You can use JRIO methods to create a non-VSAM dataset. However, you cannot use JRIO methods to create a VSAM dataset. You *must* use IDCAMS, usually in a JCL job stream, to create a VSAM dataset before you can access the dataset with JRIO. Later, you'll see a code snippet using JRIO methods that create a non-VSAM dataset.

For HFS datasets, you'll code a path string like "/homedir/hfsDsn.data". Where "//" represents the root of all high level qualifiers for non-HFS files, a single slash, "/", represents the root of HFS files.

import Statements Needed for JRIO

As previously mentioned, JRIO is in the extension com.ibm.recordio. Hence, the import statement:

```
import com.ibm.recordio.* ;
```

is required. However, you'll also need to import the base Java IO library as well. If you want to use custom record classes as opposed to byte arrays to represent your record structures, you'll need the com.ibm.record package as well. You could, of course, import specific public classes and interfaces if you like. If you want to "code and go," you'll need the three import statements shown in the following to start using JRIO:

```
import com.ibm.recordio.* ;
import com.ibm.record.* ;
import java.io.* ;
```

Representing Record Structures

You have two choices when implementing record structures in Java for use with JRIO: as *byte arrays* and as a *record framework objects.* This section provides details on these alternatives.

Representing Records as Byte Arrays

A simple way to implement records is to use a byte array. You can think of a byte array as an array of characters. By now you know that an array of characters is not a Java string, although in COBOL and PL/I, an array of characters is pretty much the same thing as a string. You may be tempted to implement your record structures as byte arrays because of the familiarity you have with using arrays of characters as strings.

When you use a byte array to represent a record, your application must know each field offset, length, and type in order to access a field. In addition, your application is responsible for converting a field to whatever data type is needed at the time, and back to a byte array, if necessary. This isn't COBOL or PL/I, where you can establish a record structure as a mixture of representative data types, code your application to read a record into the record structure knowing that the runtime will store characters as characters, packed numbers as packed, and so on (as long as the record structure agrees with the record contents, of course). All this accessing by offset and length and converting from one data type to the other and back sounds like a lot of work. You'll see some examples of accessing fields in a record represented as a byte array later in this chapter.

You create a byte array representing a record using the *new*() operator as follows:

```
//LRECLMYDSN is the logical record length of a dataset.
byte[ ] myRec = new byte[ LRECLMYDSN ];
//You could use the JRIO_MAX_RECORD_LENGTH from interface IConstants
//if you want your byte array to hold a record from any file.
byte[ ] anyRec = new byte[JRIO_MAX_RECORD_LENGTH];
```

Remember that with the byte array representation, your application is responsible for keeping track of all the data types, offsets, and field lengths. Doesn't sound very much like object orientation, does it?

If the previous dissertation on using byte arrays to represent records sounds unappealing, fear not. You have another choice. You can represent your records as record framework objects. It is not by coincidence that the subject of record framework representation is the topic of the next section.

Representing Records as Record Framework Objects

Another way to implement records is as record framework objects. The record framework provides the capability of creating a JavaBean, which encapsulates a record by providing accessors (get and set methods) to the fields of a record. The record framework runtime handles any data conversion on the fields by managing a set of metadata that describe each field offset, length, and type. The record framework provides classes with operations that use this metadata that assist in locating and converting fields to and from bytes when accessing a field. In short, the record framework does all the dirty work you read in the previous section, work you would have to do when you use a byte array to represent a record to JRIO.

Worthy of mention is that the record framework *does not perform any I/O*. Not to belabor the obvious, but file I/O is performed by JRIO, not the record framework. The record framework provides a representation of a record that enables a Java application access to the record fields without the hassles associated with byte array representation.

You do not need to use the record framework classes in order to JRIO. However, you would be remiss in your professional responsibility not to investigate using the record framework instead of using detail-laden, error-prone byte arrays.

You create a record object with the *new()* operator. However, you need to create an instance of the record type and a record object as an object of the record type. In practice, you would code a class that contains the constructors, and the get and set methods for all the fields.

```
//Create an instance of the record type.
//MyRecordType Is a class that Implements IRecordType
IRecordType myRecType = new MyRecordType();
//Create an Instance of a record of a particular type
//myRecord Is a method that creates an Instance of myRec.
//myRec must be from a class that Implements the IRecord Interface.
IRecord myRec = myRecType.myRecord();
```

The record framework classes are in the package *com.ibm.record*. You get this package with JRIO. You could code all the accessor methods, complete with the required data conversions, by hand. A better strategy would be to acquire a tool that helps you take advantage of the labor-saving features of the record framework. Such a tool exists, the Visual Age for Java, Enterprise Edition. Perhaps a word or two on this flavor of the Visual Age product is in order here.

Visual Age for Java, Enterprise Edition, and the Record Framework

The VisualAge for Java Enterprise Edition Record Framework is a collection of predefined classes of objects that work together to handle record-oriented data in Java. The record framework enables you to create a JavaBean. Think of a JavaBean, or bean, as a class that contains no public instance variables—only public accessor methods (get and set methods, remember?). In a bean that corresponds to a record structure, the bean has accessor methods for the record fields. Hence, when your Java program needs to access a field on the record, your program would invoke an accessor method. Any data conversions required are handled by methods, usually the accessor methods.

The Record Framework is provided with JRIO to make it easier for Java applications to access fields within records. The Visual Age for Java Enterprise Edition for the workstation (NT, OS/2, Windows 95, 98, and 2000, AIX) has tools that enable the programmer to create record beans without requiring any knowledge of the Record Framework or even writing a single line of code. The tools are contained in the *Enterprise Access Builder* (EAB) feature of the product. There is an importer (that imports COBOL source code to create a record bean) and a Record Editor (that enables the programmer to create, manipulate, or examine records graphically. Currently, support only exists for C, COBOL, and 3270 records, but the advanced programmer can extend the Record Framework to support other types of records. The records generated by tools provide access to the fields of a record as properties of the generated record bean.

NOTE Sadly, Visual Age for Java Enterprise Edition is not a free download (although Visual Age for Java Developers Edition is).

JRIO Coding Examples

Here, you'll see JRIO code that performs common file I/O actions. The following list shows the actions covered in this section.

- Adding Records
  - Add a record to a file output record stream
  - Add a record to a keyed access record file
  - Add a record to a random access record file
- Determine the existence of a file or directory
  - Check the existence of a directory
  - Check the existence of a file
- Create a directory or non-VSAM file
  - Create a directory
  - Create a record file
  - Create a temporary directory
  - Create a temporary record file
  - Create (define) a key
- Locate a record
  - Locate a record by key in a keyed access record file
  - Position to a record in a random access record file
- Read a record
  - Read a record from a file input record stream
  - Read a record from a keyed access record file
  - Read a record from a random access record file
- Delete items
  - Delete a directory
  - Delete a record file
  - Delete a record from a keyed access record file
- Fetching Encoded Data From and Setting Encoded Data to Fields
- Update a record in a keyed access record file
- Compare two keys

Adding Records With JRIO

The following examples illustrate using JRIO to add records. The examples *do not show* how the records get data (this section has examples of how to load fields with different types of data). Also, the examples *do not show* exception handling or recovery code.

Append a Record to a File Output Record Stream

The JRIO methods used in the following block are the constructors for the classes that implement the JRIO record interfaces.

```
//RecordFile Is a class that Implements IRecordFile.
//Note the double-slashes for the file name.
//Think of the object of IRecordFile as being Instantiated from
//what we would call the file name.
//
IRecordFile myRecFile = new RecordFile("//MYHLQ.FLATFILE.DATA");
//Dataname declares for a PDS member and a HFS dataset follow.
//   myRecFile = new RecordFile("//MYHLQ.PDSFILE.LIB(MEMBER)");
//Note the single-slash for the HFS dataset name.
//   myRecFile = new RecordFile("/u/lou/myRecordFile");
//The first block that follows shows the record represented
//as an array of bytes. In this case, we need a Stream writer
//
IFileOutputRecordStream myOutStream = null;
//The true parm In the second argument tells Java to append subsequent
//output to the end of the stream.
//
myOutStream = FileOutputRecordStream.getInstanceOf(myRecFile, true);
//
byte[ ] byteRecRepresentation = new byte[JRIO_MAX_RECORD_LENGTH];
//You would have code that sets the byte array elements to values
//corresponding to the fields In the record
//
//Notice that we are not writing directly to the IRecordFile
//object. We are writing to the stream which has an association
//with the IRecordFile object.
//
myOutStream.write(byteRecRepresentation);
```

Here is some code that shows the record framework representation of the record.

```
IRecordFile myRecFile = new RecordFile("//MYHLQ.FLATFILE.DATA");
IFileOutputRecordStream myOutStream = null;
myOutStream = FileOutputRecordStream.getInstanceOf(myRecFile, true);
//MyRecordType Is an Implementation of IRecordType corresponding to
//the particulars of the record structure.
//
IRecordType myRecType = new MyRecordType();
IRecord myRecord = myRecType.newRecord ();
//You would have code that sets the fields In myRecord to values
//corresponding to the fields In the record
//
myOutStream.write(myRecord);
```

Append a Record to a Keyed Access Record File

The JRIO methods used in the following are the constructors for the classes that implement the record and keyed file interfaces.

```
//You need an Instance of a IRecordFile which corresponds to the
//file name, or what some think of as the 'real' file object
IRecordFile myRecFile =
            RecordFile.getInstanceOf("//MYHLQ.VSAM.KSDS.CLUSTER");
//Here you define the type of record file created In the previous
//statement. Recall that the constants come from the IConstants
//Interface.
//
IKeyedAccessRecordFile myKeyedFile =
            new KeyedAccessRecordFile(myRecFile,
                                      JRIO_READ_WRITE_MODE);
//Here's the byte array representation
//
byte[ ] byteRecRepresentation = new byte[JRIO_MAX_RECORD_LENGTH];
//Set the contents of the record and write the byte array out.
//
myKeyedFile.write(byteRecRepresentation);
```

Here are the few lines showing the write operation with a record framework representation.

```
//This seems more straightforward than the byte array representation
//right?
IRecordType myKeyedRecType = new MyRecordType();
IRecord myRecord = myKeyedRecType.newKeyedRecord();
//Set the contents of the record
myKeyedRecType.write(myRecord);
```

Append a Record to a Random Access Record File

The JRIO methods used in the following are the constructors for the classes that implement the record and random file interfaces.

```
IRecordFile myRecFile = null;
//Here we are using an HFS file. Note the object creation
//strategy - a bit different than the ones shown In the preceding
examples.
//You can use any of the create record file object statements
//for any record file object.
//
myRecFile = new RecordFile("/u/lou/myRecordFile");
//Again - one statement creates a IRecordFile object
//corresponding to the 'real' file and another object corresponding
//to the 'type' of file we are going to use.
//
IRandomAccessRecordFile myRandomFile = null;
myRandomFile = new RandomAccessRecordFile(myRecFile,
                                          JRIO_READ_WRITE_MODE);
//Move the cursor to the end of the file, or the start
//of the last record.
```

```
//
myRandomFile.positionLast();
//You've seen this before...
//
byte[ ] byteRecRepresentation = new byte[JRIO_MAX_RECORD_LENGTH];
//Set the contents of the record and write the byte array out.
//
myRandomFile.write(bytes);
```

As with the preceding examples, here is the code for the record representation.

```
IRecordType myRandomRecType = new MyRecordType();
IRecord myRecord = myRandomRecType.newRandomRecord();
//Set the contents of the record
myRandomRecType.write(myRecord);
```

Determine the Existence of a File or Directory

The following examples illustrate using JRIO to check if various items exist.

Check the Existence of a Directory

To check the existence of some JRIO object, use the *exists()* method as shown in the following.

```
IDirectory myDir = new Directory("//MYHLQ.PDSFILE.LIB");
//Here's code to create an HFS directory
//  IDirectory myDir = new Directory("/u/lou/myHFSDir");
//The getAbsolutePath() method returns a String representing
//(you guessed it) the path of the object
//If you're really with it, you'd figure that the exists() method
//returns a boolean  - true If the object exists, false if not.
if ( myDir.exists() )
    System.out.println("dir = " + myDir.getAbsolutePath() +
                       " exists");
```

Check the Existence of a File

```
IRecordFile myRecFile = new RecordFile("//MYHLQ.FLATFILE.DATA");
    //Here are file declares for a PDS member and an HFS dataset.
    //
    //  IRecordFile myRecFile = new
    RecordFile("//MYHLQ.PDSFILE.LIB(MEMBER)");
    //  IRecordFile myRecFile = new RecordFile("/u/lou/myHFSFil");
    //
    //You've seen this before, right?
    //
    if ( myRecFile.exists() )
        System.out.println("myRecFile = " + myRecFile.getAbsolutePath()
```

```
                                              + " exists." ) ;
```

Create a Directory or Non-VSAM File

Recall that you must use IDCAMS to create VSAM files. In other words, you won't see JRIO methods that create VSAM files.

Create a Directory

Use the *mkDir()* method to create a directory object as shown in the following. The mkDir() method uses the default attributes when creating a new directory. For example, your shop may use a default of 96 directory blocks for a PDS space allocation. The following code also shows use of the *mkdirLike()* method that creates a new directory based on the attributes of an existing one.

```
IDirectory myDir, yourDir;
//Create an HFS Directory
myDir = new Directory("/u/lou/myHFSDir");
if ( myDir.mkDir() )
   System.out.println("HFS Directory " +
                      myDir. getAbsolutePath() +
                      " Created" ) ;
//Create a PDS Directory
myDir = new Directory("//MYHLQ.PDSFILE.LIB");
if ( myDir.mkDir() )
   System.out.println("PDS Directory " +
                      myDir. getAbsolutePath() +
                      " Created" ) ;
//Create a PDS directory with the same space attributes
//as an existing PDS directory
myDir = new Directory("//MYHLQ.PDSFILE2.LIB");
yourDir = new Directory("//YOURHLQ.PDSFILE.LIB");
if ( myDir.mkdirLike( yourDir ) )
    System.out.println(" dir = " + dir.getAbsolutePath() +
                       " like = " + yourDir.getAbsolutePath() +
                       " created " ) ;
```

Create a Non-VSAM Record File

The following code shows using the *createFile()* method to create an HFS file and a sequential file. The createfile() method uses the default space and DSN attributes. Also shown is the use of the *createFileLike()* method that does what you expect—creates a file based with the attributes of an existing file.

```
IRecordFile myRecFile, yourRecFile;
//Set the name of the file - an HFS file here
myRecFile = new RecordFile("/u/lou/myHFSFil");
//Create using createFile()
if (myRecFile.createFile() )
```

```
      System.err.println("HFS Record File located at "+
                          myRecFile.getAbsolutePath()+ " created" ) ;
//Creating a sequential (flat) file Is just as straightforward.
//The methods In the JRIO package hide the details of creating
//an HFS file versus creating an MVS sequential file.
//The constructor below allocates the named dataset with an
//LRECL of 160 with a fixed record format.
myRecFile = new RecordFile("//MYHLQ.FLATFILE.DATA",
                            160,
                            JRIO_FIXED_MODE);
if (myRecFile.createFile() )
    System.err.println("Sequential Record File located at "+
                        myRecFile.getAbsolutePath()+ " created" ) ;
//Last but not least, create a sequential file like an
//existing file
yourRecFile = new RecordFile("//YOURHLQ.FLATFILE.DATA");
myRecFile   = new RecordFile("//MYHLQ.ANOTHER.FLATFILE.DATA");
if (myRecFile.createFileLike(yourRecFile) )
    System.err.println("Sequential Record File located at " +
                        myRecFile.getAbsolutePath() +
                        " with the same attributes as " +
                        yourRecFile.getAbsolutePath() + " created") ;
```

Create a Temporary Directory

You use the same JRIO methods, *mkDir()* or *mkdirLike()*, to create a temporary directory as you would to create a permanent one. The following code shows removing the temporary directory in a *finally* block. You recall from Chapter 11, "Java Event-Handling Basics," that a finally block is always executed, even when no exceptions are thrown. Using a finally block is a handy way of ensuring that code tasked with the removal of a temporary directory (or file, for that matter) will be executed.

Because the methods mkDir() and mkdirLike() do not throw any exceptions, you'll not code a catch clause; there's nothing to catch.

One additional caveat is that you'll check to ensure that the directory is non-null before deletion. The call to delete() will fail if the directory is not empty.

```
IDirectory myDir = null;
//Encase the JRIO method calls within a try block.
try {
  myDir = new Directory("//MYHLQ.TEMPPDS.LIB");
  if ( myDir.mkdir() )
    System.out.println("Directory Located at " +
                        myDir.getAbsolutePath()+ " created " ) ;
  //Do whatever you need to do with this directory (i.e.,
  //create files)
  //If any code you place here throws exceptions, catch
  //them with a catch clause
}
finally {
```

```
    if(myDir != null)
    //If you've created any files In the temp directory, remove them
    //Time to delete the directory
    if ( myDir.delete() )
        System.out.println("Directory Located at " +
myDir.getAbsolutePath()+ " deleted") ;
    }
```

Create a Temporary Record File

As with creating a temporary directory, you'll not write different JRIO calls to create a temporary file as to create a permanent file. You'll need code that attempts to remove the temporary dataset, again, like working with a temporary directory.

JRIO methods that write data and position cursors throw IOExceptions. When you code such methods, you'll need a catch clause to trap and deal with such exceptions. Also, your file must be closed before you attempt deletion. In Java, you don't explicitly open files and streams but you *must* close them.

Objects instantiated from class RecordFile are, essentially, *datasets*. After a successful creation of RecordFile objects, you create File objects, which are, essentially, DDNames. You code JRIO read and write operations as methods invoked from File objects, like you would code a READ FILE statement in COBOL or WRITE FILE FROM statement in PL/I.

```
//Recall that when working with files, you create a dataset with a
//name and optional attributes. This call to new()uses an
//LRECL = 100.
//Think ALLOCATE DSN here.
IRecordFile myTempFile = new
            RecordFile("//MYHLQ.TEMPRANDOM.DATA", 100 );
//Next, create the file that you'll reading and writing to.
//Think DDNAME here.
IRandomAccessRecordFile myRandomAccessFile =
        new RandomAccessRecordFile(myTempFile);
//Do stuff with your newly created file (I.e., write data to It)
try {
  myRandomAccessFile.write(...);
  myRandomAccessFile.positionFirst(...);
  myRandomAccessFile.read(...)
}
//JRIO methods that read, position the cursor and write to record
//files throw checked exceptions that must be caught or
//otherwise handled.
catch(IOException ioe) {
  ioe.printStackTrace(); //Whatever...
}
//This code always gets executed.
finally
{
  if (myTempFile!= null)
      try {
```

```
            myRandomAccessFile.close();
        }
        catch(IOException ioe) {
            //Do something, stack trace, whatever...
        }
    if (myTempFile!= null)
        try { myTempFile.delete(); }
        catch(IOException ioe) {
            //Do something, stack trace, whatever...
        }
}
```

Create (Define) a Key

The code that follows shows how you'd use the constructor for the Key class to create objects of class Key. The constructor takes a byte array as an argument. The JRIO method *getBytes()* is a useful method that generates a byte array from a string or Key object.

```
Key k1 = new Key( "10101".getBytes() );
Key k2 = new Key( "ABC".getBytes() );
//If you have unprintable characters, you can create your
//byte array as shown below
byte[ ] myByteArray = {
(byte) 0xCA, (byte) 0xFE, (byte) 0xBA, (byte) 0xBE,
};
Key k3 = new Key( myByteArray );
```

Locating and Reading Records with JRIO

The next group of code snippets shows how to use JRIO to locate and read records.

Locate a Record by Key in a Keyed Access
Record File

JRIO has methods to locate a record based on the value of a supplied key. The following code shows you how to use these methods. Locate and position methods for keyed files search the *index* of the file, not the file itself. If the key is not found in the index, the position cursor does not change.

```
IKeyedAccessRecordFile myKeyedFile =
            new KeyedAccessRecordFile("//MYHLQ.KEYED.KSDS",
                                JRIO_READ_MODE);
//
IRecordFile myIndex = myKeyedFile.getPrimaryIndex();
//Assume myKey Is an object of class Key with a value
//Find the first reference to the key In the Index
myKeyedFile.positionForward(myIndex, myKey);
//Now you can read the record...
```

Position to a Record in a Random Access Record File

The following code shows more JRIO record locate methods. Record searches by key may fail because the key is not contained in the index; record searches by position (aside from generating an IO exception) will not fail.

JRIO has methods that position the read cursor relative to the current cursor position or absolute to the beginning of the file. Relative positioning methods include positionNext() and positionPrev(). Absolute positioning methods use a *record index* as an argument; the first record is referenced by an index value of zero. Hence, to reference the Ith record in a random access record file, you would look for the I—1 th record.

The code snippet shows the invocation of read() methods. We don't have to worry about EOF because we are reading a record after positioning the file to the desired record.

```
IRandomAccessRecordFile myRandomFile =
new RandomAccessRecordFile("//MYHLQ.VSAM.KSDS",
                           JRIO_READ_MODE);
//recBuffer holds the data read from the file.
byte[]recBuffer = byte[ 200 ] ; //LRECL = 200
//The cursor begins life at the first record. Performing a read()
//without positioning the cursor gets the first record In the file.
myRandomFile.read(recBuffer);
//The positionLast() method advances the read cursor after the last
//record. Hence, to read the last record In the file, you need to
//'back up' one record after advancing to the end of the file.
myRandomFile.positionLast();
//'Back up' one record
myRandomFile.positionPrev();
//Read the last record
myRandomFile.read(recBuffer);
//You can position the read cursor forwards and backwards. However,
//you cannot go two or more records back with one method
//Invocation.
//Position the read cursor to the beginning of the file.
myRandomFile.positionFirst();
//Skip to the next record
myRandomFile.positionNext();
//Read the second record.
myRandomFile.read(recBuffer);
//Move the read cursor to the 6th record (remember that record
//references are zero-based!)
myRandomFile.seek(5L);    //Note the use of primitive type long
//Read the sixth record
myRandomFile.read(recBuffer);
myRandomFile.close();
```

Read All Records from a File Input Record Stream

The short story is that you code a loop reading one record at a time until you reach the end of file. In other words, nothing new except for the use of JRIO methods to perform the reading.

You can read a record into a byte array or a record, depending on the record representation coded. The following code shows reading into both representations.

When you read into a byte array, you could code the size of the byte array equal to the LRECL of the file or equal to the constant JRIO_MAX_RECORD_LENGTH. You don't want the byte array size less than the file's LRECL; you'll read only the number of bytes equal to the size of the byte array. In addition, you'll not receive any warning that your read operation did not fetch the entire record. In the case of coding, the byte array size equal to JRIO_MAX_RECORD_LENGTH, the read() method will read a number of bytes equal to the LRECL of the file. Coding an array size of JRIO_MAX_RECORD_LENGTH removes the need to hardcode LRECLs in your applications.

```
//You read from the myFileInputStream regardless of the record
//representation (byte array or custom record)
IFileInputRecordStream myFileInputStream =
     new FileInputRecordStream("//MYHLQ.FLATFILE.DATA");
//This Is the byte array record representation
byte[ ] recBuffer = new byte[ JRIO_MAX_RECORD_LENGTH ];
//
//This continuous looping structure Is familiar to mainframe
programmers.
//COBOL programs have record structures with 77 levels coded to
//detect EOF. PL/I programs use ON ENDFILE conditions to catch EOF.
//Loop until you break
for(;;)
{
  int bytesRead = myFileInputStream.read(recBuffer);
  if (bytesRead != JRIO_READ_EOF)
  {
    //Process the record just read
  }
  else
    break;
}
myFileInputStream.close();
```

The code that follows shows a different looping structure.

```
int bytesRead = myFileInputStream.read(recBuffer);
while (bytesRead != JRIO_READ_EOF) {
   //Process the record just read
   bytesRead = myFileInputStream.read(recBuffer);
}
```

Here's an example using a record representation from the JRIO record framework. The read() method returns the number of records read either 1 or 1 (JRIO_READ_EOF).

```
//The method getCustomRecordType() Is coded In my custom class that
//Implements the particulars of the record and the record field's
//get and set methods.
IRecordType myCustomRecType = myRecRepresentation.getCustomRecordType();
CustomRecord myCustomRecord = (CustomRecord)
myCustomRecType.newRecord();
int recsRead = myFileInputStream.read( myCustomRecord );
while (recsRead!= JRIO_READ_EOF) {
   //Process the record just read
   recsRead = myFileInputStream.read( myCustomRecord );
}
```

Read a Record from a Keyed Access Record File

The particulars of reading from a keyed file versus a sequential file deal with the establishment of the appropriate keyed dataset structures. The methodology for performing the I/O is the same regardless of the underlying dataset organization. That's part of the power of an object-oriented programming language like Java.

The following code shows the continuous loop shown previously. However, because the code searches for records with a matching key, the code does not examine every record in the file. For keyed files, you can search for records using either the primary index or an alternate index (assuming the dataset has an alternate index). In practice, the search for a record by primary index would not be contained within a loop, because primary indices contain unique keys. The loop structure for record searches in keyed access files is more appropriate for datasets containing an alternate index.

You can use the code in the section that reads all records from a file input stream to read all records from a keyed file sequentially. Put differently, if you want to process all records in a keyed file, you need not access them by key values. You can access the records sequentially using the code, with appropriate changes to the file objects, shown in the previous section.

```
IKeyedAccessRecordFile myKeyedFile =
      new KeyedAccessRecordFile("//MYHLQ.VSAMDATA.KSDS");
IRecordFile myPrimaryIDX = myKeyedFile.getPrimaryIndex();
//Byte array representation of the record follows
byte[ ] recBuffer = new byte[JRIO_MAX_RECORD_LENGTH];
//Assume the key has a value.
myKeyedFile.positionForward(key);
//Do the read Into the buffer
bytesRead = myKeyedFile.read(myPrimaryIDX, recBuffer);
if ( bytesRead != JRIO_READ_EOF )
   //Record found...process
```

The code that follows shows record access and input by using an alternate index. Note that the method *getAlternateIndex()* requires the name (the path, really) of the alternate index file whereas the method *getPrimaryIndex()* does not require any arguments.

```
myKeyedFile.positionForward(key);
IRecordFile myAlternateIDX =
    myKeyedFile.getAlternateIndex("//MYHLQ.ALTERNATE.AIX",
                                  JRIO_READ_MODE);
byte[ ] recBuffer = new byte[JRIO_MAX_RECORD_LENGTH];
int bytesRead = myKeyedFile.read(myAlternateIDX, recBuffer);
while (bytesRead != JRIO_READ_EOF) {
   //Record found...process
   //Read the next record with the matching key
   bytesRead = myKeyedFile.read(myAlternateIDX, recBuffer);
}
myKeyedFile.close();
```

Read a Record from a Random Access Record File

The code seeks out a particular record then reads that record. The code is conceptually the same as searching for a record by primary key followed by a read. As in the case of sequential reads from a keyed file, you can use the code in the "read all records" section to access and read all records from a random file.

```
IRandomAccessRecordFile myRandomFile =
    new RandomAccessRecordFile("//MYHLQ.RANDOM.DATA");
//You've seen this before...
byte[ ] recBuffer = new byte[JRIO_MAX_RECORD_LENGTH];
//recNumWeWant is the record number we're looking for.
myRandomFile.seek( recNumWeWant );
int bytesRead = myRandomFile.read( recBuffer );
if (bytesRead != JRIO_READ_EOF) {
   //Record found and read - process It
}
myRandomFile.close();
```

Deleting Directories, Files, and Records with JRIO

The next group of code snippets show delete actions.

Delete a Directory

Before deleting a directory, you check if the directory is non null, as the following code shows. You must remove any files in the directory or the call to delete() will fail.

```
IDirectory myDir;
//Do stuff with this directory...
if ( myDir != null ) {
   System.out.print(" Directory Located at "+ myDir.getAbsolutePath() );
```

```
//Remove files In the directory before directory deletion
if ( myDir.delete() )
   System.out.println(" Is deleted" ) ;
else
   System.out.println(" Is not deleted" ) ;
}
```

Delete a Record File

Deleting a file is a single JRIO method call. However, you must have permission to delete a file. The Java Security manager, called from your OS/390 system, will check permissions by invoking the file's checkDelete() (not a JRIO method!) method.

```
IRecordFile myRecordFile;
//Do stuff with the record file.
try {
  if ( myRecordFile.delete() )
     System.out.println("File Located at " +
                        myRecordFile.getAbsolutePath() +
                        " deleted" ) ;
  else
     System.out.println("File Located at " +
                        myRecordFile.getAbsolutePath() +
                        " not deleted" ) ;
}
catch (SecurityException sex) {
     System.out.println("You do not have permission to delete " +
                        myRecordFile.getAbsolutePath() ) ;
}
```

Delete a Record from a Keyed Access Record File

You must read a record from a keyed file before you can perform operations on the record, such as update or delete. The following code does not show any record read operation(). As with the previous delete record example, the Security manager checks for user permissions before enabling any record or file operations. The following code does not show catching any security exceptions that may be thrown.

```
IKeyedAccessRecordFile myKeyedFile =
     new KeyedAccessRecordFile("//MYHLQ.VSAM.KSDS",
                        JRIO_READ_WRITE_MODE);
//Need an Index to access the file, right?
IRecordFile index = myKeyedFile.getPrimaryIndex();
//Do stuff with the keyed file (I.e., read, update, delete records)
//The deleteRecord call removes the last record read
myKeyedFile.deleteRecord(index);
//Close the file to make
myKeyedFile.close();
```

Fetching Encoded Data from and Setting Data to Fields

Sometimes your records contain raw data encoded in ASCII, EBCDIC, or some other encoding. The technique for extracting such data is to issue a call to the String constructor with four arguments:

```
AString = new String( byteArray, fieldOffset, fieldLength, Encoding );
```

The byteArray is your record, the field offset is zero-based, the field length is, of course, the length of the field, and the encoding is a string that describes the character encoding. If you are using a record framework representation, you'll have get methods for your record fields; the get methods would contain code that implements the previous technique.

Table 17.3 shows some of the more common character encodings and the values of the argument strings.

The following code shows extracting an EBCDIC field from a record represented as an array of bytes.

```
//Assume the record Is laid out as follows:
//    Field 1 = "2A"
//    Field 2 = "4B"
//    Field 3 = "6C"
//Here's what this record looks like
//byte[ ] myEBCDICRec = {
//                          (byte) 0xF2, (byte) 0XC1,
//                          (byte) 0XF4, (byte) 0XC2,
//                          (byte) 0XF6, (byte) 0XC3
//                      } ;
//We want to access Field 2.
String field2 = new String(myEBCDICRec,    //Record Byte array
                    2          ,    //First array element of
                                    //field
                    2          ,    //Field 2 length
                    "Cp1047");       //Value representing
                                    //EBCDIC
```

Table 17.3 Character Encoding Values for the String Constructor

ENCODING	VALUE FOR STRING CONSTRUCTOR
8859_1	ASCII (ISO Latin-1)
Cp1047	EBCDIC
UnicodeBig	Unicode
UTF8	UTF-8

For other encodings, merely change the value of the fourth argument in the String constructor and you're all set.

As for setting the value of a record field to an encoded value, the short story is to use a call to method *getBytes()*. The getBytes() method from class String converts a string into a byte array according to a character encoding scheme passed as an argument. The values of the character encoding are listed in Table 17.3. Sure sounds like what we need here, doesn't it? Here's a code sample:

```
//Once again, assume the record Is laid out as follows:
//   Field 1 = "2A"
//   Field 2 = "4B"
//   Field 3 = "6C"
//The code below changes Field 2 to "AB"
//myASCIIRec Is the byte array representation of a record.
final int FIELDOFFSET = 2;
String newASCIIValue = "AB";
//Create a byte array holding the new field 2 value
byte[ ] newField2Bytes =
        newASCIIValue.getBytes("8859_1");
//We need the field offsets to put the data Into the record.
//So, put the data back In!
for(int i = 0; i < newField2Bytes.length; ++i)
   myASCIIRec [FIELDOFFSET + i] = newField2Bytes [i];
```

Update a Record in a Keyed Access Record File

Updating a record involves one method invocation (you guessed it—update()). However, you can update only the last record read. Hence, your application must read a record prior to issuing the call to update(). The following code shows the way. Obviously, the file *must* be opened for read-write mode. Not so obvious is that you must access the record-to-be-updated by using an index.

The update() method throws JRIO-specific exceptions that arise when code changes key fields improperly.

```
IKeyedAccessRecordFile myKeyedFile =
      new KeyedAccessRecordFile("//MYHLQ.MYKEYED.FILE",
                              JRIO_READ_WRITE_MODE);
//Need an Index for the update call. Here, we're using the primary
//Index
IRecordFile primIDX = myKeyedFile.getPrimaryIndex();
//You could use a record representation or a byte representation
myKeyedFile.read(primIDX, recBuffer);
//Code to change non-key fields follows
//
//Update the record.
myKeyedFile.update(primIDX, recBuffer);
myKeyedFile.close();
```

Compare Two Keys

Comparing keys is a common operation. The JRIO *Key* class has its own *equals()* and *compareTo()* methods. In Java, objects are compared by reference but the methods in class Key compare by value.

Given the key declarations in the following:

```
Key k1 = new Key("1A".getBytes());
Key k2 = new Key("2A".getBytes());
Key k3 = new Key("2A".getBytes());
```

Key k1 is not equal to keys k2 and k3. Keys k2 and k3, although different objects, are equal.

In Summary

The one striking difference between the mainframe data processor's applications and those of her small machine counterparts is the overwhelming amount of record I/O performed by the mainframe data processor. A programming environment without support for record I/O is of little use to the mainframe programmer. With JRIO, the mainframe programmer can use Java to access familiar and useful IBM dataset structures.

Here, you've seen code snippets using JRIO to perform useful tasks. The next chapter shows additional and more fully featured JRIO code.

Java, CICS, and IMS

CICS and IMS are two of the most widely used products in the IBM OS/390 mainframe shop. For Java technology to be a force in mainframe processing, you, the mainframe programmer, must have the ability to write Java applications using CICS transactions, and IMS applications using Java.

This chapter covers how to access CICS transactions with Java by using the CICS Transaction Gateway and a set of Java classes called JCICS. We'll also look at the IBM IMS Connector for Java products, which supports communications with IMS between one or more TCP/IP clients and one or more IMS systems.

Java and CICS

As previously mentioned, the Java CICS programmer has two options: the *CICS Transaction Gateway* (CTG) and the JCICS classes. These are not either-or choices; you'll see that you may use JCICS classes to write Java code that invokes CICS transactions through the Transaction Gateway. First, let's look at the Transaction Gateway.

The CICS Transaction Gateway

The IBM *CICS Transaction Gateway* (CTG) for OS/390 provides access from Web browsers and network computers to applications running on a CICS Transaction Server in a two-tier configuration. It replaces the CICS Gateway for Java (MVS), which was shipped as a component of the CICS Transaction Server for OS/390 1.2.

The CTG for OS/390 runs in the same operating environment as the CICS Transaction Server for OS/390, using the UNIX System Services of the OS/390 Operating System. It is supported with the CICS Transaction Server for OS/390 1.2 and 1.3. It provides an API that enables Java applets and Java servlets to communicate using the CICS *External Call Interface* (ECI). The CTG for OS/390 converts this ECI communication to access the CICS Transaction Server for OS/390 using the *External CICS Interface* (EXCI). Unlike the CTG supported in other platforms, the CTG for OS/390 can only route ECI requests and not the *External Presentation Interface* (EPI) requests.

CTGs on other platforms can access multiple CICS servers; however, the CTG for OS/390 can only access the CICS Transaction Server for OS/390.

The JVM and CICS Execution Environment

The JVM used in CICS uses the open TCB provided by the CICS *Open Transaction Environment* (OTE). The OTE enhances CICS internal architecture to enable specified user tasks to run under their own *task control block* (TCB), the open TCB. The open TCB that CICS uses to run the JVM is called J8 TCB. The J8 TCB uses the MVS *Language Environment* (LE) services, rather than CICS LE services because CICS LE does not support threading. In addition, each J8 TCB is set up to run as an MVS UNIX System Services process, which is required by the JVM on OS/390.

Each Java program requiring services runs under its own J8 TCB with its own JVM. The JVM cannot be reused. It is created, used, and destroyed only for the Java program that requires the JVM.

An open TCB is assigned to a CICS task for the life of the CICS task. No subdispatching of other CICS tasks takes place under the open TCB. The execution of the JVM must not impact the main CICS workload, so it runs at a lower priority than the main CICS TCB.

An MVS JVM requires significant storage above and below the line outside the CICS DSAs. In practice, currently, no more than 30 JVMs can be active at any one time.

The good news is that you, the Java CICS programmer, need not be too concerned with these details. When you write a Java CICS application, you typically require only one JVM. The system programmers should configure the CICS gateway to make the required memory for the JVM above and below the line available to your application program.

Changes to Your JCL for Java
CICS Execution

You, or some other party responsible for maintaining JCL, must make a few changes to run Java with CICS. To run with only JVM (bytecode) support, put the MVS LE executable SCEERUN in the CICS STEPLIB or MVS LINKLIST. To run with JVM support and CICS LE support, you (or this other person) should put SCEERUN in the CICS STEPLIB or MVS LINKLIST and put SCEECICS followed by SCEERUN in DFHRPL.

In addition, two DD cards are needed in the CICS startup JCL:

```
DFHCJVM DD DUMMY
```

and

```
DFHJVM DD DSN=CICSTS13.CICS.SDFHENV
```

The environment variables that control the JVM initialization are supplied in the SDFHENV PDS. The member DFHJVMEV contains default values and should be copied and tailored to your desired values. The default name of the copied member is DFHJVM.

DFHCJVM is a standard batch C program using the MVS Language Environment. The job of DFHCJVM is to create a Java Virtual Machine whenever a Java program consisting of bytecode (as opposed to executable code created by the High Performance Java Compiler) is loaded. It is loaded during CICS initialization as part of the CICS nucleus. The program uses the DFHCJVM DDname for STDIN rather than the SYSIN DDname.

CTG Modes of Operation

The gateway classes have two modes of operation: *Network mode* and *Local mode*. In Network mode, the gateway must be customized to listen on a TCP/IP port. The CTG can be activated as a started task or from a UNIX Systems Services command line. Requests arriving over the network can then be serviced by the gateway and connections can be made to CICS servers.

Application programmers in the mainframe environment rarely are responsible for configuring network devices. Let's face it—the application programmer's job is tough enough without having to configure networked resources. Usually, the job of configuring the gateway is delegated to a separate team within the organization.

In Local mode, no customization is required. The gateway classes can be used directly in Java code and connections can be made locally to CICS servers running on the same OS/390 system. CICS support for transactions written in Java is included in the base product and no specific installation is required.

More good news—you, the Java CICS programmer, need not be too concerned about the configuration (Network mode) or lack of configuration (Local mode).

Java CICS Processing Flow

Here are the typical steps required to use the CICS Transaction Gateway in a Web-based application:

1. A URL is invoked from the browser with input parameters.

2. The Web server loads the servlet if it is not already loaded and invokes the servlet *service()* method.

3. In the initialization process (*init* method), the servlet creates a local logical connection to the CICS Transaction Gateway. In the termination process (*destroy()* method), the servlet closes the logical connection to the CICS Transaction Gateway.

4. In the *service()* method, the servlet sends a request to the CICS Transaction Gateway using the ECI API.

5. The CTG calls CICS transaction services locally using EXCI.

6. A JCICS Java program retrieves data through the CICS COMMAREA.

Actually, the previous steps are not peculiar to Java CICS programs. They may describe a CICS transaction written in any programming language supported by CICS, such as COBOL, PL/I, or C.

Figure 18.1 shows the connection between the relevant pieces in the CICS and Web server environments that typically make up a three-tier Java CICS application.

EXCI is the *External CICS Interface* and ECI is the *CICS External Call Interface*.

Writing a CTG Application

Take the following steps to implement a CICS Transaction Gateway application:

1. Import the required Java CICS package com.ibm.ctg.client.*;.

2. Create the connection to CTG for OS/390. The class that represents the logical connection between a Java program and the CICS Transaction Gateway for OS/390 is called JavaGateway:

   ```
   JavaGateway jgConnection = new JavaGateway();
   ```

This is the default constructor that creates a blank JavaGateway object. You must set the relevant attributes to define the kind of connection you are using. For now, assume you'll set up a local connection. Here's the code to set up the JavaGateway object *jgConnection* to use a local connection:

```
try{
jgConnection.setURL("local:");
```

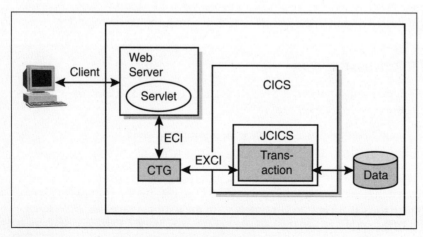

Figure 18.1 Java CICS application environment.

```
}catch(java.io.IOExceptoin e){
//Deal with the exception
e.printStackTrace();
}
```

The *setURL()* method in class JavaGateway determines whether the connection is local or network-based.

3. Open the connection by coding the following:

```
try{
jgConnection.open();
}catch (java.io.IOException e){
//Deal with the exception
e.printStackTrace();
}
```

4. Initialize the CICS COMMAREA.

The ECI interface sends data to the CICS Transaction Server program and receives data from it through the CICS COMMAREA. A COMMAREA is an array of bytes that may contain different data types such as characters, binary numbers, or packed decimal numbers. To work with the COMMAREA, you can manipulate it one byte at a time or you can access the contents of the COMMAREA using the IBM Java Record Framework to access fields as objects (refer to Chapter 17, "Java Record I/O Using the JRIO Package"). The following code shows a method, initCommArea(), which initializes a byte array with the data to be sent. This is the code of the initCommArea() method:

```
public byte[] initCommArea(int size , String data)
{
//build a temporal byte array
byte [] dataBytes = data.getBytes();
//Create new commArea long enough to store the request and to store
the reply
byte []theCommArea=new byte[size];
//Copy input data into the commArea
System.arraycopy(dataBytes,0,theCommArea,0,dataBytes.length);
//Fill the rest of commArea bytes with 0
int c = dataBytes.length;
while (c < size) theCommArea[c++]=0;
return theCommArea;
}
```

This method returns a byte array with the request data contents. Keep in mind that the byte array commArea is an input/output field. Its length must be large enough to store the request and the reply. However, the size of the COMMAREA may not exceed 64K.

5. Initialize the COMMAREA by invoking the previous method:

```
byte []commArea = initCommArea(2048,data);
```

6. Create a request. You may create a synchronous or asynchronous request. Here you'll see how to create a synchronous request. A synchronous request causes the runtime to wait until the request is completed before proceeding. The class that represents an ECI request is ECIRequest. Here is a code sample:

```
ECIRequest eciRequest = new ECIRequest(
CICS_APPLID, //CICS Region Name
null,        //UserID
null,        //Password
programName, //CICS Target Program Name
commArea,    //COMMAREA Byte Array to hold Request results
ECIRequest.ECI_NO_EXTEND,  //ECI_NO_EXTEND to tell CICS extended
units of work are not supported
ECIRequest.ECI_LUW_NEW);   //This value Is Ignored for non extended
units of work
```

Flow the request to the CICS transaction server. Here's an example invocation:

```
try{
jgConnection.flow(eciRequest);
}catch (java.io.IOException e){
//Deal with the exception
e.printStackTrace();
}
```

7. Process the reply from the CICS server. The reply attributes are contained in the ECIRequest object (property COMMAREA) used to make the synchronous request. If the transaction originated from a Java servlet, the servlet could format an HTML or XML page containing the data for the reply.

8. Close the connection to the CICS Transaction Gateway. Here's a code sample:

```
try{
jgConnection.close();
}catch (java.io.IOException e){
//Deal with the exception
e.printStackTrace();
}
```

The methods in class JavaGateway are straightforward: setURL(), open(), flow(), and close(). Each method should be contained within a try/catch block.

Writing a JCICS program using COMMAREA

This section shows a sample program that receives data and sends back the reply through the COMMAREA. A COMMAREA is an array of bytes that may contain different data types such as character, binary number, or packed decimal numbers. To work with the COMMAREA, you can manipulate it one byte at a time or you can access the contents of COMMAREA using the IBM Java Record Framework to access fields as objects.

The class that represents the COMMAREA is *CommAreaHolder*. The actual COMMAREA is an instance variable of type byte[] with the name value. The reason for this extra holder class is that a COMMAREA is used both for input and output, so the extra level of indirection is needed as Java only passes arguments by value. On input, value contains the COMMAREA that is being passed into the program. The program returns a COMMAREA by setting value to a new byte[] that it has constructed.

Listing 18.1 shows a CICS program using the JCICS classes to receive data from the COMMAREA.

The parameter *ca* of class *CommAreaHolder* will hold the input and output of the main() method. Notice the property *value* of the argument of the main() method. This property represents the byte array that will hold the data returning from the COMMAREA.

Java and IMS

As earlier mentioned, IBM supports Java access to IMS by means of a proprietary product called IMS Connect for Java. IMS Connector for Java provides a way to create Java applications that can access IMS transactions. With additional support from the IBM WebSphere Studio and IBM WebSphere Application Server, you can build and run Java servlets that access your transactions from Web sites.

```
public static void main(CommAreaHolder ca) {
String caString = new String (ca.value); [2]
int receivedLength = caString.length();
System.out.println("String size we get from CommArea : " +
receivedLength
);
System.out.println("String that we get from CommArea : " + caString
);
//Write the commarea back to ctg
String sCommAreaResponse = ( "Message received: "+caString);
System.out.println("Reply commArea set to : "+ sCommAreaResponse);
//Create reply that includes message received and date
String dateString = (new java.util.Date()).toString();
String sCommAreaResponse = ( "Message received. Date: "+dateString);
ca.value = sCommAreaResponse.getBytes();
return;
}
```

Listing 18.1 Receiving data from the COMMAREA.

You will not configure IMS Connector for Java. The IMS Connector for Java is a piece of system software and it is they who will tend to installation and tuning.

What Is IMS Connect for Java?

IMS Connector for Java provides a Common Connector Framework-compliant Java interface to IMS Connect. IMS Connector for Java is a class library that consists of two packages: *com.ibm.connector.imstoc* and *com.ibm.imstoc*. All of the classes in the com.ibm .imstoc package and many of the classes in the com.ibm.connector.imstoc package are support classes that are not used by application developers during the development of applications that use IMS Connector for Java.

Prerequisites for Running IMS Connect for Java

A prerequisite to using IMS Connector for Java is IMS Connect (formerly called IMS TCP/IP OTMA Connection, or simply ITOC). IMS Connect enables client applications to send messages to IMS TM through the IMS *Open Transaction Manager Access* (OTMA) interface, providing connections to IMS transactions from a variety of platforms, including both workstation and mainframe products. IMS Connect will provide enhancements in usability, performance, and SMP installability. Before you attempt to run a Java application program or servlet that uses IMS Connector for Java, Version 3.5, be sure that the following products are installed on the target host machine.

IMS Connector for Java Concepts

This section provides an overview of some of the concepts and terminology needed to understand IMS Connector for Java, and it includes

- MFS formatting
- Java classes provided with IMS Connector for Java
- IMS messages
- IMS message formats
- IMS logon information
- Synchronization levels
- Connection management
- IMS conversations

MFS Formatting

Transaction input and output messages that are provided to IMS through IBM's *Open Transaction Manager Access* (OTMA) bypass online MFS processing. MFS is the online processing component in IMS that performs message formatting, such as field padding, truncation, justification, and the insertion of literal data in messages.

Java Classes Provided with IMS Connector for Java

IMS Connector for Java provides a number of Java beans to aid you in building Java programs and servlets. All of these beans are in the IMS Connector for Java package *com.ibm.connector.imstoc*. You can combine these beans into a composite bean that accesses an IMS transaction. IMS Connector for Java includes the following documented classes:

- IMSConnectionSpec: The IMSConnectionSpec bean provides information about the connection between a Java program and an IMS Connect host component, as well as information about connection management. The IMSConnectionSpec host name and port properties are specific to IMS Connector for Java, while the other properties are inherited from the Common Connector Framework interface com.ibm.connector.ConnectionSpecManagementProperties.

- IMSConvContext: The IMSConvContext bean is used to comply with the IMS Connect requirement that the same connection is used for all iterations of an IMS conversation. A connection is a communications link, a socket in the case of TCP/IP, and is analogous to the phone line that connects two telephones during a telephone conversation. IMS Connector for Java includes this class in its programming model for use by conversational Web applications. A Java application or servlet should create a single instance of the IMSConvContext class at the start of a conversation and associate this single instance with the connection used for the conversation. This ensures that the connection will be preserved for the lifetime of the IMS conversation and that the CCF ConnectionManager will always return the same connection for each iteration of the IMS Conversation.

- IMSConvHttpSessionCleanup: IMS Connector for Java includes the class IMSConvHttpSessionCleanup in its programming model for use by conversational Web applications only. This class implements the HttpSessionBindingListener interface and is used to capture the unbound event of an HttpSession object during an active conversation, and to then perform appropriate cleanup.

- IMSInteractionSpec: The IMSInteractionSpec bean provides information about the interaction between a Java program and a datastore. Interaction properties include

  - *ConvTerminated*, set to TRUE if the host IMS application program ends the IMS conversation. The Java application program checks the value of this property to determine whether or not the conversation has been terminated by the host.

  - *Datastore name*, the name of the target IMS datastore that is defined in the IMS Connect configuration file.

  - *LTERM name*, used to override the LTERM name in the IMS application program I/O PCB. The override is used if the client does not want to override the LTERM name in the I/O PCB with the transaction pipe.

  - *Map name* (or the MFS MOD name), which is the name provided by an IMS application program when returning the output of a transaction. It can also be provided by IMS when returning a status message, such as the output from a /DIS command, or an error message.

- *Mode*, or the type of interaction to be carried out between the Java program and the IMS datastore. The modes that are currently supported include MODE_SEND_RECEIVE, MODE_ACK, MODE_NACK, and MODE_END_CONVERSATION.

- *Synchronization level*, or what specifies the transaction synchronization level—the way in which the client (a Java application or servlet) and server transaction program (for example, an IMS application program) interact with respect to transaction output messages. Stated simply, the synchronization level determines whether or not transaction output messages must be acknowledged, that is, accepted (ACK) or rejected (NACK), by the client.

- DFSMsg: The DFSMsg bean represents IMS status or error messages that are returned to a Java application or servlet in response to a command or a transaction. These messages typically begin with the characters DFS. Often, DFS messages are returned to a Java application or servlet. Some DFS messages indicate error situations, while others are returned as the output of IMS commands. In all cases, because OTMA is used to return the message, MFS formatting is not performed. However, IMS includes an MFS MOD name (map name) with DFS messages. IMS Connector for Java checks the MOD name field of messages that it receives from IMS Connect. If the MOD has one of the following names, the message is processed as a DFS message. If the name is not listed in the following list, it is processed as transaction output.

IMS Messages

The messages sent to IMS or received from IMS by a Java application or servlet using IMS Connector for Java can be any of the following:

- IMS transaction input messages
- IMS transaction output messages
- IMS status or error messages (also called DFS messages)
- IMS commands
- IMS command output messages
- IMS Connector for Java is primarily designed to handle the first three types of messages.

IMS Message Format

Message segments that are sent to and received from IMS transactions always begin with a two-byte segment length field (called LL), followed by a two-byte field that contains IMS information (called ZZ). The two-byte segment length field represents the length of the entire message segment, including the LL and ZZ fields. The data of the message segment follows the LL and ZZ fields. In the case of the first segment of the transaction's input message, up to the first n+1 bytes of the data portion of the segment contain the n-byte transaction code, followed by a blank.

IMS Logon Information

The IMS logon information (user ID, password, and group name) provided to the run-time context of a Java application or servlet is used by IMS Connector for Java.

The user ID, password, and group name are placed in the OTMA message sent by IMS Connector for Java to the host component, IMS Connect. IMS Connect then calls the host's *Security Authorization Facility* (SAF) under control of the IMS Connect *SETRACF* command.

Synchronization Level

Currently, all IMS Connector for Java interactions use the OTMA protocol *Commit Mode 1*, also referred to as send-then-commit. Under this protocol, if the synchronization level is Confirm, IMS sends the output message to the client and then waits for a response from the client. It is the responsibility of the client to respond to IMS. If the synchronization level is None, IMS commits any changes made by the IMS application without waiting for a response from the client.

For *Synchronization level none*, the transaction runs and IMS sends the output message to the client. Any database changes are then committed. IMS does not require that the client send a message in response to the transaction output message in order to commit the database changes. Synchronization level None is typically used for Java applications and servlets that run IMS transactions that browse or query host databases.

For Synchronization level confirm, the transaction runs and IMS sends the output message to the client without committing any database changes. IMS does not complete the transaction until the client responds to the transaction output message by sending a positive or negative acknowledgment to IMS. If the client is satisfied with the transaction output, it responds by sending a positive acknowledgment. IMS then completes the transaction by committing the database changes, if necessary. If the client is not satisfied with the transaction output (or does not want to continue with the transaction for any reason), it responds by sending a negative acknowledgment. IMS then rolls back any changes to the database.

Connection Management

Connection pooling is key to enhancing the performance of Java applications or servlets that access IMS transactions. This connection management feature is provided by the IBM *Common Connector Framework* (CCF). CCF is a set of Java APIs that provides infrastructure services like connection management, transaction services, security, and tracing facilities to Java applications and servlets.

IMS Conversations

IMS Connector for Java Conversational Support enables customers to build Java applications and Web applications to access IMS conversational transactions. A conversational IMS transaction is a transaction that is defined to IMS as being conversational, meaning that it can process transactions made up of several individual steps. An IMS transaction is made up of a connected series of client-to-program-to-client interactions. The IMS conversational program receives messages from the client, processes the requests, and replies to the client. It also saves the intermediate data from the transaction in the *scratch pad area* (SPA). When the user enters more data from the client, the program has the data it saved from the last message in the SPA, and thus can continue processing the request without having the user enter the data again. When the client sends a message to initiate the next iteration of the conversation, the program uses the data in the new message along with the data it saved in the SPA at the end of the last iteration of the conversation as its input. In more complex conversations, different transactions can be invoked using an immediate or deferred program switch.

In Summary

IBM has provided the mainframe Java programmer the tools to access two important and commonly used system software packages: IMS and CICS. With these tools, Java programmers have access to existing mainframe data and applications.

Java and DB2

As part of IBM's "Java Everywhere" strategy, IBM has provided the OS/390 Java programmer with two access mechanisms to access DB2 data. This chapter discusses two mechanisms: using Java Database Connectivity, or JDBC, and using SQLJ. In addition, the Java programmer can use either mechanism to access DB2 data by calling DB2-stored procedures.

The chapter starts by providing an overview of Java with DB2 in the OS/390 environment. Next, the chapter covers how the OS/390 Java programmer can access DB2 data by using JDBC, SQLJ, and stored procedures. The reader will see code snippets illustrating each access mechanism. A comparison of the strengths and weaknesses of JDBC versus SQLJ follow.

Overview of Java and DB2 for OS/390

Figure 19.1 shows the major components that make up a Java/DB2 environment for OS/390. The programmer can access DB2 data by including static DB2 in their Java source (SQLJ), dynamic DB2 (JDBC), or both. Also, the programmer can access DB2 data by having their Java programs access DB2 stored procedures.

If the Java programmer uses either SQLJ or stored procedures, they must call a DB2 preprocessor called the SQLJ translator. This translator provides the same function as the DB2 preprocessor for translating static SQL embedded in COBOL, PL/I, or C programs. After a successful SQLJ translation, it's business as usual with the production of

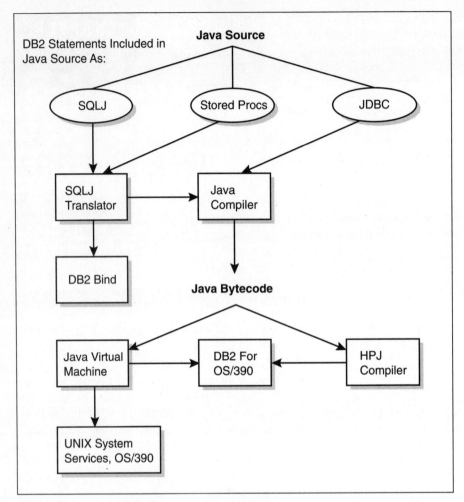

Figure 19.1 Java/DB2 environment for OS/390

a DBRM and a plan or package bind. The Java programmer using JDBC for dynamic SQL skips these DBRM/plan or package bind steps.

The OS/390 Java DB2 programmer can use a mixture of static (including stored procedures) and dynamic SQL statements like the COBOL DB2 programmer. Whatever the combination of SQL statement types used, the code gets to the Java compiler where the compiler produces industry-standard Java Bytecode. From here, the Bytecode can get passed to the *Java Virtual Machine* (JVM) for program execution or to IBM's *High Performance Java* (HPJ) compiler.

The HPJ compiler accepts Bytecode as input and produces OS/390 native code as output. Java's cross-platform execution by using standard Bytecode formats comes at a price. Bytecode execution is interpretive and therefore slow when compared to traditional compiled and linked languages like COBOL or C. To address the needs of customers who want the advantages of Java application development (cross-platform source code or the use of object-oriented techniques, for example) without the execution performance degradation common with interpretive languages, IBM offers the HPJ compiler. As Figure 19.1 shows, the same source code that gets compiled and sent to the Java Virtual Machine can be sent to the HPJ.

Java Database Connectivity (JDBC)

JDBC is an industry-standard SQL API that enables the Java programmer to access most relational databases, including DB2. The programmer should include the java.sql package to use JDBC. This package includes the following class and abstract interfaces:

- **DriverManager.** This *class* is used to load the DB2 driver code needed to create database connections.

- **Connection.** This *interface* enables a programmer to connect and disconnect to a named data source.

- **Statement.** This *interface* is used to execute SQL statements. Included with the Statement interface are two interfaces:

  - **PreparedStatement.** Executes SQL statements containing input parameters.

  - **CallableStatement.** Invokes a DB2 stored procedure.

- **ResultSet.** This *interface* is used to retrieve the data in the results set of a previously executed SQL statement.

These classes and interfaces are not unique to the OS/390 environment; any Java programmer wanting to access relational database data with Java would use these classes and interfaces.

Using JDBC

Here are the steps a Java programmer takes to access DB2 data with JDBC (with code snippets):

1. Import the JDBC package java.sql by coding:

```
import java.sql.* ;
```

2. Load the DB2 driver using DriverManager:

```
String ibmDriver = "ibm.sql.DB2Driver" ;

try { Class.forName( ibmDriver ) ; }
catch ( ClassNotFoundException exception) {
   exception.printStackTrace() ;
}
```

The method Class.forName automatically creates an instance of a driver object. A benefit of using the class method from class Class (quite the tongue twister) is that the forName() method automatically *registers* the driver with the Java runtime. Notice that you need not assign the results of the invocation of forName() to any object. It's all part of the Java magic.

3. Declare and connect to a named data source (database):

```
String db2URL = "jdbc:db2os390:mydb2db" ;
  Connection myCon ;


try { myCon = DriverManager.getConnection( myURL ) ; }
catch ( SQLException exception ) {
  exception.PrintStackTrace() ;
}
```

The named data source identifies the database that will be queried or updated. The form of the string is a *URL*. The DBA responsible for maintaining the DB2 catalog should associate the URL with some DB2 access object, such as a table, database, or view. In particular, for OS/390, JDBC identifies a data source for connection by accepting a database URL in the following format:

jdbc:db2os390:<locationname>

where <locationname> is the DB2 LOCATION found in the DB2 catalog table SYSIBM.LOCATIONS.

Once the data source is identified to the Java program, the program must make a *connection* to the named access object. The *getConnection()* method in class *DriverManager* does this. If the method invocation is successful, the program has a *connection object*, which the program uses to issue SQL and process results.

4. Execute one or more SQL statements by creating a Statement object, associating the statement(s) with an active connection, and executing the statement using the appropriate method.

For SQL SELECT statements, the appropriate method is executeQuery(). For SQL statements that modify or create tables, the appropriate method is executeUpdate(). The following code shows a Java program issuing an SQL DELETE statement. Step 5 shows a Java program issuing an SQL SELECT statement.

```
Statement deleteStmt = myCon.createStatement() ;   //myCon is the active
connection
String deleteSQL = "DELETE FROM EMP WHERE UNIT = 'A001'" ;
deleteStmt.executeUpdate( deleteSQL ) ;                //Execute Statement
```

SQL statements may be constructed by using the full arsenal of String methods and operators. The previous code snippet shows a static string. However, you may construct the string by concatenating arguments and String objects. The following is valid in the world of Java and JDBC:

```
String tabKeyForDelete = "'A001'" ;
String deleteSQL = "DELETE FROM EMP WHERE UNIT = " + tabKeyForDelete ;
```

Notice the inclusion of the *single quotes* for string data. DB2 recognizes both single and double quotes as long as you are consistent. If you omitted the single quotes surrounding the value of UNIT in the previous example, your code would generate an SQLException.

5. Retrieve the data returned by a SELECT statement by creating a ResultSet object and accessing the rows of this ResultSet, usually with a loop construct.

```
Statement selectStmt = myCon.createStatement() ;
ResultSet selectResults =
selectStmt.executeQuery( "SELECT NAME, SALARY, UNIT FROM EMP") ;
//Loop through selectResults to access each row of the //ResultSet
object
while( selectResults.next() ) {
String javaName   = selectResults.getString( 1 ) ;
float javaSalary = selectResults.getBigDecimal( 2,2 ).floatValue() ;
    String javaUnit      = selectResults.getString("UNIT") ;
  }
```

The next() method of an instance of ResultSet advances the cursor to the next row. The cursor is initially above the first row; hence, the first call to next() advances to the first row in the ResultSet. Next() returns false when no following row exists in the ResultSet.

Class ResultSet contains get???? methods, where ???? is a Java primitive data type or class that corresponds to a SQL data type. A program could use a method to access the DB2 data but could get unexpected results. For example, a program accessing a DECIMAL type as FLOAT could result in a loss of precision. Table 19.1 shows what get???? methods of class ResultSet are recommended to get DB2 data. Note that the recommended method to access a DB2 FLOAT data type is getDouble(), not getFloat(). The generic getObject() method could be used to access data of any type, but the returned results could be unpredictable.

Only SQL statements create result sets. SQL INSERT, DELETE, and UPDATE statements do not.

JDBC enables two ways to identify a column in the results set: by position and by name. Note the first call to getString() in the previous code snippet:

```
String javaName      = selectResults.getString( 1 ) ;
```

The second call uses the name of the table column, "UNIT":

```
String javaUnit      = selectResults.getString("UNIT") ;
```

The author is not aware of any advantages one method of identification has over the other.

As you know, most indexed entities in Java have indices that start with zero. For example, to access the first element of a Java array, you access element 0. However, with indexed entities returned by JDBC calls, the index starts with 1, not 0. The call to getString() earlier accesses the *first column* in the result set. Were you to code

```
String javaName      = selectResults.getString(0) ;
```

the Java compiler would not catch the error because the method signature states that the method requires an argument of type *int* (or String). Upon execution, your program would throw an *SQLException*.

You may use the *PreparedStatement* interface to issue SQL statements. The Prepared-Statement interface is used to issue *precompiled* SQL. The ideal is that DB2 can perform some optimizations on the SQL statement. This is not quite the same thing as preprocessing your SQL statement by creating a *plan*.

Here's a code snippet for issuing SQL with the PreparedStatement interface:

```
String SQLString = "SELECT NAME, SALARY, UNIT FROM EMP WHERE NAME = ?
and SALARY > ?" ;
```

Table 19.1 Recommended Access Methods According to DB2 Data Type

DB2 DATA TYPE	RECOMMENDED ACCESS METHOD
TINYINT	getByte()
SMALLINT	getShort()
INTEGER	getInt()
BIGINT	getLong()
REAL	getFloat()
FLOAT	getDouble()
DOUBLE	getDouble()
DECIMAL	getBigDecimal()
NUMERIC	getBigDecimal()
BIT	getBoolean()
CHAR	getString()
VARCHAR	getString()
LONGVARCHAR	getAsciiStream(), getUnicodeStream()
BINARY	getBytes()
VARBINARY	getBytes()
LONGVARBINARY	getBinaryStream()
DATE	getDate()
TIME	getTime()
TIMESTAMP	getTimeStamp()

```
PreparedStatement myStmt = myCon.prepareStatement( SQLString ) ;
//Recall that myCon Is the active connection
//Set parameters
myStmt.setString( 1, "Lou Marco") ;
myStmt.setDouble( 2, 234567.89 ) ;
//No parameter to the executeQuery() method
ResultSet selectResults = selectStmt.executeQuery( );
//Loop through selectResults to access each row of the //ResultSet
object
while( selectResults.next() ) {
String javaName      = selectResults.getString( 1 ) ;
float javaSalary = selectResults.getBigDecimal( 2,2 ).floatValue() ;
     String javaUnit       = selectResults.getString("UNIT") ;
}
```

The question marks in the SQL string are placeholders. The *setString()* and *setDouble()* methods are used to fill in the placeholders. You must know the data types of the DB2 columns you want to access. You may replace the word "get" with the word "set" with the method names shown in Table 19.1 to set SQL predicate values for SQL issued with the PreparedStatement interface.

Notice that when using the Statement interface, the SQL string is passed to the *executeQuery()* method, whereas with the PreparedStatement interface, the SQL string is not. If you forget and code a string argument, don't fret. The Java compiler will stop you in your tracks.

The technique used to access the result set is the same whether you use the Statement interface or the PreparedStatement interface.

6. Clean up by closing the statement and closing the connection from the database:

```
selectStmt.close() ;      //Close the statement
selectResults.close();//Close the result set
myCon.close()      ;       //Close the connection
```

The application should have code that closes the statement(s), the result set, and the active connection when the application encounters an unrecoverable error. Many Java programmers place the calls to the close() methods within a *finally* block. When enclosed within a finally block, the close() methods are *guaranteed* to execute even if no exceptions are thrown.

The structure of Java code that issues SQL resembles

```
try{
//load driver, create connection, Issue SQL, process results
}
catch (SQLException sqlE) {
//report any errors arising from SQL execution
}
finally {
//Close statement(s), result sets (If any) and connection(s)

}
```

JDBC use, with DB2 under OS/390, is not different than JDBC use with other relational database products under different operating systems. The only DB2-specific code is the loading and registering of the DB2 driver by using the *Class.forName()* method. The creation of statements using the Statement or PreparedStatement interfaces is the same.

Java and SQLJ

SQLJ is a standard way of embedding static SQL statements in Java programs. The overall methodology is similar to embedding SQL in COBOL or PL/I programs. A Java program can use both SQLJ and JDBC to access DB2 data.

The SQLJ standard includes three parts: the embedded SQL, the SQLJ translator, and a SQLJ runtime environment. The programmer embeds SQL in SQLJ programs by preceding the SQL statement with the #sql token. SQLJ programs can contain any data manipulation SQL, DB2 table DDL, COMMIT/ROLLBACK, searched and positioned UPDATE and DELETE, CALL to access stored procedures, and SET for host variables. SQLJ files containing Java and embedded SQLJ must have a sqlj extension.

The SQLJ translator produces Java source containing embedded SQL into Java source files. Put another way, the SQLJ translator is similar to the DB2 preprocessor used by the COBOL, PL/I, or C programmer accessing DB2 data. The SQLJ translator also produces profiles that provide the runtime with various details on the database schema. These profiles are used to create DBRMS that are bound to packages or plans.

The SQLJ runtime environment executes SQL using, in part, the information found in the previously generated profile(s). Typically, the runtime SQL implementation is done through JDBC.

Using SQLJ

Here are the steps a programmer takes to create a Java/DB2 program using SQLJ.

1. Import the java.sql and sqlj.runtime.ref packages by coding:

```
import java.sql.* ;
import sqlj.runtime.ref.* ;
```

2. Declare and establish a connection context. A connection context is the SQLJ equivalent of a database connection. In JavaSpeak, a connection context is an instance of a connection context class. Here's how an SQLJ program declares a connection context:

```
#sql      context myCtx ;
```

Once the program knows the connection context, the programmer has a choice of two DB2 connection methods. The first is to invoke the constructor for the class created by the previous declaration using the location of the DB2 data source as an argument. Here is an example:

```
//Note difference in second qualifier
//from JDBC location name
String     db2URL = "jdbc:db2os390sqlj:mydb2db" ;


myCtx      myCon = new myCtx( db2URL ) ;
```

The second method is to invoke the constructor for the context connection class using the JDBC connection returned by DriverManager.getConnection(). For example,

```
Connection myJDBCCon     = DriverManager.getConnection( db2URL ) ;
myCtx            myCon         = new mtCtx( myJDBCCon ) ;
```

3. Load a DB2 driver as shown in the section *"Using JDBC."*

4. Declare result set iterators. A result set iterator is similar to the ResultSet object discussed earlier. In the language of static SQL, a result set iterator is like a cursor. Like a cursor, the iterator declaration identifies the columns of a DB2 table or join to be accessed. One interesting feature of iterators not shared by their cousins, the cursors, is that iterators can be passed to methods as arguments (like other Java objects), whereas cursors cannot.

SQLJ iterators come in two flavors: positioned iterators and named iterators. A positioned iterator associates the columns in the results table with the columns referenced in the iterator in left-to-right order. A named iterator associates these columns by the name of the column in the DB2 table.

The programmer declares the iterator classes corresponding to those SQL statements that produce result set tables having more than one row. The programmer declares objects of the iterator classes. Here are some examples:

```
//By Position iterator showing data type of
//result set column.
#sql     iterator       ByposUnitIter ( String ) ;


//By Name iterator showing data type
//and name of result set column
#sql     iterator       BynameNameIter( String unit ) ;
```

It is important to remember that the previous #sql statements declare Java classes and that the DB2 program works with objects created from these classes.

5. Execute the SQL statement(s). If the SQL statements access more than one row, the SQL statement may refer to a previously declared iterator. Here is an example:

```
//Declare an object of Class ByposUnitIter
ByposUnitIter     aniterByPos ;
//Construct the iterator object and execute statement
#sql  (myCon)     aniterByPos =
      {SELECT UNIT FROM EMP WHERE EMPID=23790 } ;
```

```
//Do the FETCH, loop down the iterator
#sql  (myCon)     { FETCH :aniterByPos   INTO    :javaUnit } ;
while (!aniterByPos.endFetch() ) {
/* Do Stuff With The Retrieved Data*/
#sql  (myCon)     { FETCH :aniterByPos   INTO    :javaUnit } ;
}
```

Like embedding SQL in a COBOL or PL/I program, the Java programmer passes data between the Java program and DB2 by using *host expressions*. A Java host expression could be a Java identifier, like the previous FETCH statement shows, or a Java expression that evaluates to a value, preceded by a colon. Java identifiers, therefore host expressions, are case-sensitive.

Here's an example of some Java code that uses a named iterator:

```
//Declare an object of Class BynameNameIter
//Construct the iterator object and execute statement
BynameNameIter  aniterByName;
#sql (myCon) aniterByName =
     {SELECT NAME FROM EMP WHERE UNIT='A001'} ;
//Get the data, loop down the iterator
while (aniterByName.next() )  {
/* Do stuff with the retrieved data */
javaName = aniterByName.Unit() ;
}
```

Note the name of the accessor method provided to the program from the iterator class: `aniterByName.Unit()`. SQLJ generates an accessor method for every column named in the iterator. For those cases where the DB2 column name is not a valid Java identifier, the programmer could use the AS feature of the SELECT statement. For example,

```
//Declare named iterator Class
#sql      iterator      aNameIter      ByName( String MyCol ) ;
//Declare iterator from Class
aNameIter myIter ;
#sql      myIter =
          {SELECT "GOOD DB2 BAD JAVA NAME" AS MYCOL FROM ATABLE};
```

6. Commit any changes by invoking the commit() method of the Connection object with code that resembles the following:

```
myCon.commit() ;
```

7. Finally, close any iterators and close (disconnect) from the database:

```
myIter.close() ;
myCon.close() ;
```

As with a JDBC connection, the program should disconnect from the database when the program encounters an unrecoverable error.

Comparing JDBC to SQLJ

Java programs that access DB2 data may use both JDBC and SQLJ. However, if a Java program needs to issue dynamic SQL, that program must use JDBC only. The dynamic nature of JDBC has an impact on security. DBAs can grant users access to tables; a user can either change a table or not. In contrast, a program that uses SQLJ uses a previously bound package or plan. The DBA can grant users execution authority to the package or plans.

Of course, the old argument of execution speed still applies. Programs that use statically bound SQL statements execute quicker than programs that use dynamically bound SQL statements. In addition, the access paths contained in the DBRMs can be analyzed and tweaked, yielding further performance gains.

The JDBC program cannot check that the SQL data types match the Java primitive types or classes until runtime. In programs that use SQLJ, type checking is done at the translator (precompiler) stage.

On the flip side, using SQLJ limits the portability of the application. Each vendor could provide their SQLJ translator, which would be different for different products. Also, the SQLJ development process is more complex owing to the need for translation (precompilation) and binding.

If Java/DB2 development parallels DB2 development in COBOL, PL/I, or C, it is a safe bet to assume that most Java/DB2 programs would use static SQL more than dynamic SQL.

The mainframe DB2 programmer is used to precompiling their SQL and producing plans. There are no facilities in Java that assist the programmer in creating plans. You, the Java DB2 programmer, will continue to use the operating system products from IBM that precompile SQL, bind plans, and (optionally) create packages.

In Summary

The Java programmer has access to IBM's flagship database product DB2. Because DB2 is available on every IBM platform, the promise of Java, "Write once, run everywhere," is closer to reality in the IBM world.

CHAPTER 20

The Training Department Class Scheduler System Revisited

We revisit the training department scheduler shown in Chapter 13, "The Training Department Class Scheduler System." In this chapter, you'll see a function of the system done with DB2 database calls as opposed to using native Java File I/O.

The chapter starts by describing the implemented feature and shows a mainframe solution. Next, we present a Java solution that implements the feature. We do not repeat the descriptions of the data; we leave it to the reader to refer to Chapter 13 for such details. We conclude the chapter with a summary of the key issues addressed in the chapter.

The Application Feature Defined

The feature we'll show here is to access three tables with an SQL join to create a list of classes offered later than a date input parameter. The SQL will reference table names so you can see where the columns are coming from. All data represented in the tables are strings.

The SQL Used in the Example

Listing 20.1 shown here is the SQL that will retrieve the needed data.

The quantity ENTEREDDATE is the date parameter used to qualify the class list. Of course, the same SQL will be used in the procedural language and the Java language solution.

```
select classinfo.classid, courseinfo.coursetopic,
       instructorinfo.instructorfirstname || " " ||
       instructorinfo.instructorlastname,
       classinfo.dateoffered, classinfo.roomnumber
from courseinfo, instructorinfo, classinfo
where courseinfo.courseid = substr( classinfo.classid, 1, 5) and
      classinfo.instructorid = instructorinfo.instructorid   and
      classinfo.dateoffered > ENTEREDDATE
```

Listing 20.1   SQL to retrieve data.

A Procedural Language Solution for "Display Class List Later Than Entered Date" Option

Listing 20.2 shown here is a COBOL module that performs the following tasks:

- Accepts a date parameter
- Creates an ISPF table to display the outputs
- Issues the SQL shown in Listing 20.1, reformatted to fit COBOL's column coding requirements
- Fetches a row retrieved from the query and adds the row's data to an ISPF table
- Saves return codes to send back to the calling routine

Comments on the COBOL Solution

The COBOL module handles the SQL execution and the creation of the structure (an ISPF table) that will display the output. The module could have been coded to pass the data retrieved by the SQL query back to the calling module, leaving the calling module to build the ISPF table. However, COBOL's lack of support for all but the most elementary data structures makes such an approach awkward.

Given the procedural nature of mainframe programming languages, including COBOL, the approach is centered around the *process*. The code shown in Listing 20.2 flows naturally. However, there is no real hope of reusability aside from copying and pasting code from one dataset to another.

```
IDENTIFICATION DIVISION.

    PROGRAM-ID.  CBLEX.
    ENVIRONMENT DIVISION.
    CONFIGURATION SECTION.
    SOURCE-COMPUTER. IBM-OS390.
    OBJECT-COMPUTER. IBM-OS390.
    INPUT-OUTPUT SECTION.

    FILE-CONTROL.
        SELECT PRINTFILE ASSIGN TO PRINTER-QPRINT
           ORGANIZATION IS SEQUENTIAL.

    DATA DIVISION.

    FILE SECTION.

    FD  PRINTFILE
        BLOCK CONTAINS 1 RECORDS
        LABEL RECORDS ARE OMITTED.
    01  PRINT-RECORD PIC X(132).

    WORKING-STORAGE SECTION.
    *********************************************************************
    *  This string holds the ISPF Table Commands to add data,       *
    *  create, and display the ISPF Output table.                   *
    *********************************************************************
    01  TABLECOMMANDS.
        05  TBADD     PIC X(15)
            VALUE "TBADD DTELATER".
        05  TBCREATE  PIC X(72)
          VALUE "TBCREATE DTELATER NAMES(CLASSID,CTOPIC,INSTNAME,
    -DOFFERED, ROOMNUM)".
        05  TBDISPL   PIC X(17) VALUE "TBDISPL DTELATER".
    *********************************************************************
    *  Return Code from ISPF                                         *
    *********************************************************************
    01  ISPFRC        PIC S9(4) COMP.


    *********************************************************************
    *  Structure that holds data resulting from SQL Join            *
    *********************************************************************

    01  SQLJOINDATA.
        05  CLASSID      PIC X(8).
        05  CTOPIC       PIC X(15).
```

Listing 20.2 A COBOL solution.

```
    05   INSTNAME      PIC X(10).
    05   DOFFERED      PIC 99/99/9999.
    05   ROOMNUM       PIC X(5).
***************************************************************
*  The SQL Communications Area                                *
***************************************************************
    EXEC SQL
        INCLUDE SQLCA
    END-EXEC.
***************************************************************
* The linkage section contains return codes returned to the  *
* calling routine and the date for the query.                *
***************************************************************

LINKAGE SECTION.

01   ENTDATE        PIC 99/99/9999.
01   ISPFRETURN     PIC S9(4) COMP.
01   SQLCODERETURN  PIC S9(4) COMP.

PROCEDURE DIVISION.

A000-MAIN.

***************************************************************
* Issue the SQL Join. Report on any errors.                   *
*                                                             *
***************************************************************


    EXEC SQL
        WHENEVER SQLERROR GO TO E000-SET-RETURN-CODES.
    END-EXEC.


***************************************************************
*  Issue the SQL that generates a result set containing rows  *
*  with data for classes offered later than the passed date.  *
***************************************************************
    exec sql
        declare c1 cursor for
            SELECT ClassID, CourseTopic, InstFName || " " ||
                  InstLname, DateOffered, RoomNum
            from CourseInfo, ClassInfo, InstructorInfo
            where DateOffered > :ENTDATE and
                  ClassInfo.InstID = InstructorInfo.InstID and
                  CourseID = Substr( ClassID, 1, 5 )
    end-exec.
```

Listing 20.2   A COBOL solution. (*continued*)

```
       EXEC SQL
            OPEN C1
       END-EXEC.

       CALL 'ISPEXEC' USING TBCREATE, ISPFRC.
       IF ISPFRC > 0
           PERFORM E000-SET-RETURN-CODES THRU
                   EOOO-SET-RETURN-CODES-EXIT.

       PERFORM B000-ADD-ROWS-TO-OUTPUT-SCREEN THRU
               B000-ADD-ROWS-TO-OUTPUT-SCREEN-EXIT.
           UNTIL SQLCODE NOT EQUAL TO ZERO.


   A100-DONE.
       EXEC SQL
            CLOSE C1
       END-EXEC.


**********************************************************************
*  All done. Set Return codes and split.                            *
**********************************************************************


   A900-MAIN-EXIT.
       PERFORM E000-SET-RETURN-CODES THRU
               E000-SET-RETURN-CODES-EXIT.
       EXIT.


**********************************************************************
*  Fetch and add row to ISPF table                                  *
*********************************************************************s*


   B000-ADD-ROWS-TO-OUTPUT-SCREEN.
       EXEC SQL
           WHENEVER NOT FOUND GO TO A100-DONE
       END-EXEC.
       EXEC SQL
           FETCH C1 INTO :CLASSID,
                         :CTOPIC, :INSTNAME,
                         :DOFFERED, :ROOMNUM
       END-EXEC.

       CALL "ISPEXEC" USING TBADD, ISPFRC.
       IF ISPFRC > 0
           PERFORM E000-REPORT-ERROR THRU
                   EOOO-REPORT-ERROR-EXIT.
```

Listing 20.2 A COBOL solution. (*continued*)

```
B000-ADD-ROWS-TO-OUTPUT-SCREEN-EXIT.
    EXIT.


*********************************************************************
*   Error occurred while issuing SQL. Set SQL and ISPF return   *
*   codes to return values and split.                          *
*********************************************************************


E000-SET-RETURN-CODES.
    MOVE SQLCODE TO SQLCODERETURN.
    MOVE ISPFRC  TO ISPFRETURN.
E000-SET-RETURN-CODES-EXIT.
    EXIT.
```

Listing 20.2   A COBOL solution. (*continued*)

A Java Language Solution for "Display Class List Later Than Entered Date" Option

The code listings that soon follow show Java classes that contain methods that issue SQL to capture class offerings that start after the entered date. We present code for four Java classes. Each class contains methods for a set of related tasks.

The Code for a Single Class Retrieved from the Database

Listing 20.3 shows the Java code that models the information relevant to a single class. Each instance of the class shown will be an element of another class that contains all classes offered later than the entered date. The instance variables are not declared private; you could declare the instance variables private and code get/set methods to retrieve or change the values as the need arises.

Listing 20.4 shows a Java class, *sqlClass*, with limited but important responsibilities. Class sqlClass has methods that establish a database connection and disconnect from the database. With a bit of polish, class sqlClass could make an excellent utility. In particular, we'd need a mechanism to obtain the driver information and the database (URL) name from parameters.

Class *queryClass*, shown in Listing 20.5, has methods that issue the query and return a value corresponding to a single column in the result set. Class queryClass contains the sql query as a string. However, the query string could be passed as a parameter.

```
public class CourseOfferedLaterThan {
    String classID ;
    String courseTopic ;
    String instructorName ;
    String dateOffered ;
    String roomNumber ;
    public CourseOfferedLaterThan( String cID, String cTopic,
                                   String iName, string dOff,
                                   String roomNum ) {

        classID = cID ;
        courseTopic = cTopic ;
        instructorName = iName ;
        dateOffered = dOff ;
        roomNumber = roomNum ;

    }
}
```

Listing 20.3   Java code for a single class.

```
import java.sql.*;
import java.io.*;
public class sqlClass
   {
  private String myDriver = "ibm.sql.DB2Driver";
  private String myURL = "jdbc:db2os390:classdb";
  protected Connection myConn;
  public sqlClass() {}
  public void makeConnection() throws  Exception
    {
    Class.forName( myDriver);
    myConn = DriverManager.getConnection(myURL);
    }
  public void disconnectFromDB() throws Exception
    {
    myConn.close();
    }
  }
```

Listing 20.4   Java code for the sqlClass class.

```
import java.sql.*;
import java.io.*;
public class queryClass extends sqlClass
  {
  String mySelectQuery =
        "SELECT ClassID, CourseTopic, InstFName || " " || " +
                  "InstLname, DateOffered, RoomNum " +
              "from CourseInfo, ClassInfo, InstructorInfo " +
              "where ClassInfo.InstID = InstructorInfo.InstID " +
                  "and CourseID = Substr( ClassID, 1, 5 ) " +
                  "and DateOffered > " ;



  ResultSet myResultSet = null;
  public queryClass() {super();}
  public boolean getCourses(String enteredDate) throws Exception
    {
    String myQuery = mySelectQuery + enteredDate;
    Statement stmt = myConn.createStatement();
    myResultSet = stmt.executeQuery(myQuery);
    return (myResultSet != null);
    }
  public boolean getNextCourse() throws Exception
    {
    return myResultSet.next();
    }


  public String getColumn( String inCol) throws Exception
    {
    return myResultSet.getString(inCol);
    }
  }
```

Listing 20.5 Java code for the queryClass class.

Notice that queryClass extends the sqlClass. That's why the reference to *myConn*, an object of class Connection, is understood in queryClass, although myConn is not declared in queryClass.

Class *CoursesLaterThanOutput,* shown in Listing 20.6, models a list of classes that are offered later than a specified date. The class contains a constructor that invokes all the needed methods from classes sqlClass and queryClass. Since queryClass extends sql-Class, the constructor can invoke the *disconnectFromDB()* method defined in sqlClass by referencing an object of class queryClass.

```
public class CoursesLaterThanOutput {
   //The only instance variable in the class
   private Vector coursesLater ;
   //The constructor for the courses can handle all the necessary
   //work.
   public CoursesLaterThanOutput ( String dateForQuery ) {
    queryClass myQuery = new queryClass();
    try
      {
      myQuery.makeConnection();
      myQuery.getCourses(dateForQuery);
      while (myQuery.getNextCourse())
      {
        CourseOfferedLaterThan aCourse =
          new CourseOfferedLaterThan(
                    myQuery.getColumn("classid"),
                    myQuery.getColumn("coursetopic"),
                    myQuery.getColumn("instructorname"),
                    myQuery.getColumn("dateoffered"),
                    myQuery.getColumn("roomnumber"));
        //Add new course to vector
        aCourse.coursesLater.addElement ( aCourse ) ;
      }
      myQuery.disconnectFromDB();
      }
    catch (Exception e)
      { e.printStackTrace(); }
   }
}
```

Listing 20.6 Java code to hold information for the classes later than entered date.

In Summary

The COBOL solution, at first glance, may appear simpler and more straightforward than the offered Java solution. The COBOL solution accomplishes the goal within the confines of a single module, whereas the Java solution uses four classes. However, thinking of a solution as simple because the code required for implementation is short may be narrow-minded. The issues of code reuse and maintenance should also be considered as well.

The Java classes shown in this chapter that connect and disconnect from the database, and issue the query and return the results, could be changed to be reusable.

Java: Above and Beyond Other Programming Languages

Applets

Before you read this book, you may have thought of Java as the "applet language of the Internet." In case you don't know, an *applet* is a Java program that runs within the context of a Web browser. This chapter provides you with information on coding Java applets.

We'll start by providing a bit of background followed by the key methods you must code for an applet to *be* an applet. Next, you'll see some short examples. The chapter concludes with some comments on the future of applet development.

A Bit of Background

You'll see that you already *know* how to code Java applets. In other words, you write Java if/else statements, while loops, assignment statements, and method calls as you've been doing up to now. All you need do is code a few required methods and voila! You've got an applet.

Of course, you should have an understanding of how an applet differs from an application, how to code a Web page that can use an applet, and how an applet executes on the user's machine. So, let's get started.

Applications versus Applets

As mentioned earlier, an applet is a Java executable that runs within a Web page. You may also run applets in the Java SDK utility *appletviewer* as explained in Chapter 2. Java applications run within the context of the *Java Virtual Machine* (JVM). The JVM is usually invoked from a command prompt or from some program that accepts operating system commands.

Applications must contain a main() method with the often-seen signature:

```
public static void main( String[] args )
```

Applets do not *require* a main() method. If an applet contains a main() method, the method is not automatically invoked as with applications. Applets have their own '"magic" methods that are invoked by the Java runtime.

Applications do not come with a standard graphics context. If you want GUI elements in your Java application, you need to create at least one container and take it from there (see Chapter 22). For applets, you have a graphics context; every applet has a container of class *Panel* (or *JPanel*) immediately available.

Coding the Web Page that Uses the Applet

You can use the *applet* tag within an HTML page to cause the browser to download the applet into the browser. Here's a bare-bones example:

```
<applet code=AnApplet.class width=400 height=400>
</applet>
```

The applet tag names the class file containing the applet and provides a size for the initial graphics context. The size parameters, width, and height are in pixels.

You may code other parameters in the applet tag that specify the border to draw around the graphics panel. Because this chapter is on applet coding, not HTML coding, let's forgo the subtleties of the applet tag. When you code applets, you'll probably spend most of your time using the appletviewer program, which is more full-featured than using a Web page.

As an aside, you cannot change the size of the panel within your applet that you code on the HTML page within the applet tag.

How an Applet Executes

As earlier mentioned, applets have their own magic methods. Table 21.1 describes these methods.

You do not invoke any of the methods in Table 21.1 directly (by name). These methods are invoked by the Java runtime within the browser when the runtime deems it necessary.

When the user clicks on a Web page containing an applet tag, the browser downloads the file cited in the code= parameter into a panel of size coded in the applet tag. Once the download completes, the *init()* method executes. After init() executes, the applet's *start()* method executes. At this point, you may imagine the user is interacting with the applet, at which point methods *that you code* are usually invoked. If the user

Table 21.1 Magic Applet Methods

METHOD SIGNATURE	DESCRIPTION
void init()	Invoked when the applet is initially loaded into memory.
void start()	Invoked each time the user visits the Web page containing the applet.
void stop()	Invoked when the user leaves the Web page containing the applet.
void paint(Graphics g)	Invoked by the graphics environment when a component (or container) needs to be redisplayed.
void destroy()	Invoked when the user closes the Web page containing the applet.

takes any action that causes a component to be redrawn, the applet's *paint()* method is invoked by the runtime (not by your code).

If the user clicks on another Web page, thereby deactivating the page containing the applet, the applet's *stop()* method is invoked. When the user clicks on the Web page again, the applet's *start()* method is invoked. Finally, when the user has had enough and closes the Web page, the runtime invokes the *destroy()* method.

One important point: All the magic methods cited previously are not required. You do not have to code these methods. However, if you do not code a paint() method, you'll not see anything.

A Minimal Applet

Here's an example of a pretty minimal applet:

```
public class MinApplet extends javax.swing.JApplet {
    public void paint( javax.awt.Graphics g ) {
        g.drawString("Hello World", 15, 15 ) ;
    }

}
```

Yes, the previous code is a bona fide applet that will draw the phrase "Hello World" in the graphics panel. Figure 21.1 shows the result of running this applet in appletviewer.

The HTML that may be used to invoke this applet within a Web page may be:

```
<applet code=MinApplet.class height=400 width=400>
</applet>
```

Figure 21.1   A minimal applet output.

Another Pretty Minimal Example

This applet shows the invocations of the init(), start(), and destroy() methods. Listing 21.1 shows the code.

The applet displays as before (see Figure 21.1); the println() methods *do not write to the graphics pane*. The appletviewer program directs standard output to a command window; a browser has its own Java log that may be used to record standard output messages. Figure 21.2 shows the command window.

Notice the line of code in the methods:

```
repaint()
```

The *repaint()* method forces the Java runtime to invoke the paint() method. That's why you see calls to paint() throughout the execution of the applet. Although you do not call paint() yourself, you may force a call to paint() by calling repaint().

The calls to start() were caused by the user minimizing and then restoring the applet window. Finally, the call to destroy() shows up as the last line to be written to the standard output.

```
import javax.swing.* ;
import java.awt.* ;
public class MinApplet extends JApplet {

    String messageStr = "Hello World" ;
    int xPos = 15,  yPos = 15 ;
    public void init() {

        System.out.println( "Invoking init()" ) ;
        repaint() ;
    }
    public void start() {
        System.out.println( "Invoking start()" ) ;
            messageStr = "Invoking Start()" ;
            xPos =+50 ;
            yPos =+50 ;
            repaint() ;



    }
    public void destroy() {
        System.out.println( "Invoking destroy()" ) ;


    }
    public void paint( Graphics g ) {
        System.out.println("Invoking Paint") ;
        g.drawString(messageStr, xPos, yPos ) ;
    }

}
```

Listing 21.1   Showing the init(), start(), and destroy() method invocations

Objects that you want to access inside the magic applet methods must be declared outside any method; the objects *cannot be local to any method*. The signatures of the magic methods are cast in stone. For all but paint(), the methods take no arguments. You cannot pass any objects as parameters to the magic methods. The message string and the position of the message to be drawn are declared outside any method. Ergo, these objects are accessible within any method.

One more point: The paint() method *redraws the entire panel*. The display of the applet in Listing 21.1 is the string "Invoking start()." Actually, if you are from Krypton, you'd notice the message displayed in the applet window changing from "Hello World" to "Invoking Start()." Because the paint() method redraws the entire container, you'll see the results of the last redraw operation.

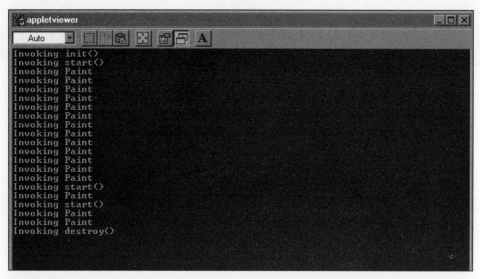

Figure 21.2   Showing the init(), start(), and destroy() method invocations.

Applet Odds and Ends

Before we close this chapter, here are some odds and ends about applets.

Applet code may be bundled with images, sounds, or other resources into a *jar* file. Chapter 2 has some information on the Sun JDK utility program jar. Jar is short for *Java Archive*. Think of a jar file as a compressed version of one or more files, of which one is usually a Java class. Because applet code is downloaded to the browser, it makes sense to minimize download activity. Compressing the class file(s) helps, of course, However, if the applet uses other files, combining these files with the applet class into one file means the browser needs only one download session to fetch required files.

You may pass parameters to applets. Within the applet tag, you have the option of coding one or more *param* tags. For example:

```
<applet code=AnApplet.class height=300 width=300>
  <param name=param1 value="This Is the value for Param1">
  <param name=anotherparam value="another Value">
</applet>
```

Within the applet, you would code the *getParameter()* method as follows:

```
String valParam1 = getParameter("param1") ;
String valParam2 = getParameter("anotherparam") ;
```

In Summary

Applets are a time-honored way of presenting the user with a more robust user interface than with garden variety HTML. In addition, applets enable the Web page developer to bring the power of Java to their pages. This is, of course, a good thing.

However, another side is there to be told. When Java first made the Web scene in the mid-1990s, Web developers had few options in providing their customers with robust, animated Web pages. Today, Web developers have a host of tools that can provide what applets once did without having to use Java. In addition, the enterprise is learning that other Java technologies, such as Java Servlets and JavaServer Pages, can provide more effective access to corporate data than applets while providing customers with a professional look. As the enterprise moves toward using enterprise Java technologies, applet use may dwindle.

CHAPTER 22

Java User Interface Basics

Java supports the creation and manipulation of the traditional GUI elements. Here, you'll get some exposure to the "Java way" of creating front ends for applications.

The topic of user interfaces is sizeable and entire books have been written on Java GUI alone. The intent of this chapter is to provide you, the mainframe Java programmer, with the fundamentals of Java GUI programming. We'll start the chapter with some information on Java GUI packages and a review of the standard GUI components, and describe the Java mechanism for representing these components. Next, you'll read about Java containers and Java layout managers. Along the way, you'll see a few examples of Java GUI component creation and manipulation. The chapter closes with some comments on Java GUI usage in the enterprise.

Java GUI Component Libraries

You have two packages at your disposal when creating Java GUIs: the *Abstract Windowing Toolkit* (AWT) package and the *Java Foundation Classes* package. The AWT contains more than GUI component *Application Programming Interfaces* (APIs). The AWT package includes support for Java *events* (refer to Chapter 11) as well as miscellaneous Java functions, such as printing.

The Java Foundation Classes package contains the *Swing* component set. Swing replaces one piece of the AWT, namely the GUI component construction piece.

YOU WILL NOT CODE MUCH JAVA NATIVE GUI INTERFACES

You, the Java programmer, are far too valuable a commodity to be spending time coding GUIs. These days, GUIs are developed using screen-building tools, which are similar to Visual Basic form builders and the like. Also, the days of the graphical Java application are coming to a quick close. Java has found a home with server-side and enterprise technologies. The new application model is to have a front layer represented by a client running a browser, one or more middle layers representing business logic, and a data layer housing permanent data stores.

Having said that, you should have a basic understanding of the Java GUI mechanism. You may be called upon to rewrite old (four years old?) Java applications with Java GUIs. Two possibilities for a modern facelift are Java server-side programs called *servlets* that generate HTML pages for display or *JavaServer pages*, which are a combination of HTML and Java scripting code.

Standard GUI Components

Table 22.1 describes some standard GUI components. The first column is the AWT component name, the second column is the Swing name, and the third is a short description. Figure 22.1 shows a screen shot with these components.

Soon, you'll see the Java code for the creation of this display. First, however, you need to read some background on how Java implements GUI components.

Java Containers

In Java, a *container* is an object that holds one or more graphical components, including other containers. The Java class *Container* is abstract; you cannot create container objects directly. You usually create one of two popular subclasses of class Container: the Panel (for applets) and Frame (for windows and dialogs) subclasses.

Here's the short story on how to create a Java user interface:

- First, create a container using an object from a Java container class.

- Second, decide on a *layout manager* for the container. You'll read more about layout managers soon. For now, a layout manager is an overall scheme for placing components within a container.

- Third, create your components using initialization parameters that are peculiar to the component.

- Fourth, place components (the items listed in Table 22.1, among others) inside the container. The layout manager decides how to place the components within the container.

Table 22.1 Some Standard GUI Components

AWT NAME	SWING NAME	DESCRIPTION
Label	JLabel	Text describing another component or providing instructions
Button	JButton	Component that triggers a user action
Checkbox	JCheckbox	Component that offers a user an *on* or *off* choice
CheckboxGroup	ButtonGroup	Radio buttons where one and only one of the group must be selected
Choice	JCombobox	A list where the user may select one or more entities
List	JListbox	A Choice with more than one entity visible
TextField	JTextField	Enables the user to enter a line of text
TextArea	JTextArea	Enables the user to enter multiple lines of text
ScrollBar	JScrollbar	Enables the user to bring in previously hidden portions of a component

- Fifth, attach a *listener* to the components. You will recall from Chapter 11 on event handling, that Java uses the event delegation model to capture and process events.

Listing 22.1 shows a piece of code that creates a small window with two text entry fields. The example uses AWT components with comments on using Swing components. As you'll see, little difference exists between the coding of the two components. Here is the code that corresponds to the previous steps.

1. **Create a container using an object from a Java container class.** The call to the constructor and the constructor code creates the container:

```
AWTEntryScreen1 myES = new AWTEntryScreen1() ;
super("Enter Name and Employee ID") ;
```

The class statement clarifies that the object of class AWTEntryScreen1 is a child class of class Frame; the constructor invocation using the keyword *super* gives AWTEntryScreen1 objects the characteristics of the Frame superclass.

Think of a Frame as a window. Although Java has a Window class, the Window class is not what you might think. A Java Window object is a piece of screen area without a border, a title bar, or open or close buttons. You'd use the Frame class to create "Windows." By the way, Frame is a subclass of Window.

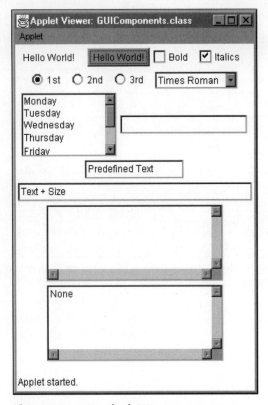

Figure 22.1   Standard GUI components.

```
//java.awt.* Is for the user Interface components
//java.awt.event Is for the event handling
//You would Import java.swing.* for swing components.
//You still need java.awt.events because swing components use
//awt events.
import java.awt.* ;
import java.awt.event.* ;
//Swing: extends JFrame
//The ActionListener Interface Is for event capture and
//processing
public class AWTEntryScreen1 extends Frame implements ActionListener{
    //String objects to hold what the user enters
    private   String userName = null ;
```

Listing 22.1   Create a window with two text fields and a button with AWT components.

```
private    String userID   = null ;
//AWT Text field components
//Swing:  JTextField userNameTF = new JTextField( 20 )
TextField userNameTF = new TextField( 20 ) ;
TextField userIDTF   = new TextField(  6 ) ;

public AWTEntryScreen1() {
   //Create a Frame object with the title In quotes.
   //See text below for comments on the getContentPane() call
   super("Enter Name and Employee ID") ;
   //Swing: this.getContentPane().setLayout( new GridLayout(3,2) )

   //See the text below for commentws on the setLayout call
   this.setLayout (new GridLayout( 3, 2) ) ;
   //Swing: JLabel userNameLabel = new JLabel( "Name    ") ;
   Label  userNameLabel = new Label( "Name          " ) ;
   Label  userIDLabel   = new Label( "Employee ID " ) ;
   //Swing: JButton submitBtn = new JButton(" Submit" ) ;
   Button    submitBtn  = new Button(" Submit" ) ;
   submitBtn.addActionListener(this) ;
   //Swing: this.getContentPane().add(Ö)
   this.add( userNameLabel ) ;
   this.add( userNameTF) ;
   this.add( userIDLabel ) ;
   this.add( userIDTF ) ;
   this.add( submitBtn ) ;
   //This Is the action listener that allows the user to
   //close the window. See Chapter 11 for details.
   this.addWindowListener (new WindowAdapter() {
        public void windowClosing( WindowEvent we ) {
             System.exit( 0 ) ;
         }
    } ) ;


}
//This Is the callback that the Java runtime Invokes
//when the user clicks on the button
public void actionPerformed (ActionEvent aev ) {
    userName = userNameTF.getText() ;
    userID   = userIDTF.getText() ;

    System.out.println( userName + "   " + userID ) ;

}

public static void main( String[] a ) {
```

Listing 22.1 Create a window with two text fields and a button with AWT components.
(*continued*)

```
        AWTEntryScreen1 myES = new AWTEntryScreen1() ;


        myES.pack() ;
        myES.show() ;
    }


}
```

Listing 22.1   Create a window with two text fields and a button with AWT components. (*continued*)

2. **Decide on a *layout manager* for the container.** A layout manager is a Java object that describes the overall look of a container. The choices are a *GridLayout*, a *FlowLayout*, a *BoxLayout*, a *GridbagLayout*, and a custom layout. You have the option of using absolute component placement within the container, but real Java programmers frown on absolute placement (although absolute placement comes in handy when developing custom layouts).

   In our example, we've chosen to use GridLayout. Imagine that the frame is divided into a grid of so many cells wide by so many cells tall. Each component placed within the frame occupies a grid position. The GridLayout adds components in left to right order. The GridLayout is the default layout for Frame (or JFrame) components.

   A FlowLayout adds components using directions: north, south, east, west, and center. You may add a component by specifying a direction, or add components and let FlowLayout take care of placement. FlowLayout is the default for *Panel* (or JPanel) components.

   The BoxLayout adds components either left to right or top to bottom, depending on initialization parameters.

   The GridbagLayout is similar to the GridLayout without the restriction of each component occupying only one cell. With a GridbagLayout, a component may span multiple cells. However, the complexity of the GridbagLayout has left many users with less hair than when they started. GridbagLayout is not for the squeamish.

   Here's the code that adds the layout manager to the Frame component:

   ```
   this.setLayout (new GridLayout( 3, 2) ) ;
   ```

   As an aside, use of the keyword *this* in the previous example is not required.

3. **Create your components using initialization parameters that are peculiar to the component.** We create five components: two *Labels*, two *TextField*, and a *Button*. Here's the code that creates the components:

```
TextField userNameTF = new TextField( 20 ) ;
TextField userIDTF  = new TextField( 6 ) ;
Label     userNameLabel = new Label( "Name        " ) ;
Label     userIDLabel   = new Label( "Employee ID " ) ;
Button    submitBtn = new Button(" Submit" ) ;
```

Notice that the two text field components are created *outside* the constructor because we'll need to access these text fields outside the constructor.

4. **Place components (the items listed in Table 22.1, among others) inside the container.** As previously mentioned, the layout manager decides how to place the components within the container. The code that places the components inside the container is

```
this.add( userNameLabel ) ;
this.add( userNameTF) ;
this.add( userIDLabel ) ;
this.add( userIDTF ) ;
this.add( submitBtn ) ;
```

The GridLayout adds the components in left to right, top to bottom order. Again, use of the keyword *this* is optional.

5. **Attach a *listener* to the components.** We could attach a listener to every component except the *Label* component (Label does not generate events). However, for this example, we'll attach an event listener to the *Button* and the *Frame*. We want to know when the button is clicked and we want to be able to *close the window*.

Here's the code that attaches the listener to the Button:

```
submitBtn.addActionListener(this) ;
```

When the user clicks the button, the Java runtime looks for a method named *actionPerformed()* with the following signature:

```
public void actionPerformed (ActionEvent aev )
```

Notice that no code actually invokes the actionPerformed() method; no code invokes the method directly.

The code for the actionPerformed() method fetches the text from the two TextFields and writes the field contents to the default output stream. This is why the text field components were not declared within the constructor. If they were, the code could not access the components outside the constructor to gain access to the entered text.

```
public void actionPerformed (ActionEvent aev ) {
    userName = userNameTF.getText() ;
    userID  = userIDTF.getText() ;

    System.out.println( userName + "   " + userID ) ;
}
```

Here is the code that attaches the window listener so the user can close the window, thereby quitting the application:

```
this.addWindowListener (new WindowAdapter() {
    public void windowClosing( WindowEvent we ) {
  System.exit( 0 ) ;
}
} ) ;
```

The technique used in this code is known in Java circles as using an *anonymous inner class*. The *addWindowListener()* method is attached to the *this* object, which is AWTEntryScreen1, the subclass of Frame. The class name is *WindowAdapter*, which contains stub methods for catching window-related events, like moving, resizing, or closing a window. The body of the method invokes the *exit()* method, which quits the application. Using anonymous inner classes to exit windowed applications is common; the previous code is a Java idiom that is found everywhere.

Notice that we did not attach a listener to the text entry fields. The use of event listeners is optional. You may gain access to a component's contents without using a listener, as we did in the previous example. If you want to perform some input validation as the user is entering text, you could attach a listener to fetch characters as the user enters them.

The main() method creates and displays a windowed object. If this object was part of an application, the windowed object would be created as part of the application workflow.

Another Example

Next, let's take a look at the code that generates the screen shown in Figure 22.1. Listing 22.2 shows this code.

The code creates an applet (see Chapter 21) that contains a host of GUI components. As with the previous example, let's examine the code according to the formula cited earlier.

```
import java.awt.*;
import java.applet.*;
import java.awt.event.*;
//For swing, Import java.swing.* ;

// This is an AWT implementation of the code that generates
// the "all components" screen shot.
//For swing, extend class JApplet.
public class GUIComponents
    extends Applet
```

Listing 22.2   The code that generates Figure 22.1.

```
implements ActionListener, ItemListener
{
Label greeting;                    //JLabel
Button aButton;                    //JButton ;
Checkbox bBox, iBox;               //JCheckbox
Checkbox cBox1, cBox2, cBox3;
CheckboxGroup cbGroup;
Choice chooser;                    //JCombobox
List lstDays;                          //JListBox
TextField txt1, txt2, txt3;//JTextField
TextArea sendText, recvText;       //JTextArea

public void init()
    {
    //Remember, for Swing, to add components to the
    //content pane, accessible by a call to getContentPane()
    greeting = new Label( "Hello World!" );
    add( greeting );

    aButton = new Button( "Hello World!" );
    aButton.addActionListener (this);
    add( aButton );

    bBox = new Checkbox ("Bold");
    iBox = new Checkbox ("Italics", true);
    bBox.addItemListener (this);
    iBox.addItemListener (this);
    add (bBox);
    add (iBox);

    cbGroup = new CheckboxGroup();
    cBox1 = new Checkbox( "1st", cbGroup, true );
    cBox2 = new Checkbox( "2nd", cbGroup, false );
    cBox3 = new Checkbox( "3rd", cbGroup, false );
    cBox1.addItemListener (this);
    cBox2.addItemListener (this);
    cBox3.addItemListener (this);
    add( cBox1 );
    add( cBox2 );
    add( cBox3 );

    chooser = new Choice();
    chooser.addItem( "Times Roman" );
    chooser.addItem( "Helvetica" );
    chooser.addItem( "Courier" );
    chooser.addItemListener (this);
    add( chooser );
```

Listing 22.2   The code that generates Figure 22.1. (continued)

```java
        int howMany = 5;
        boolean multiSelect = true;
        lstDays = new List( howMany, multiSelect );
        lstDays.addItem( "Monday" );
        lstDays.addItem( "Tuesday" );
        lstDays.addItem( "Wednesday" );
        add( lstDays );
        lstDays.addItem( "Thursday" );
        lstDays.addItem( "Friday" );
        lstDays.addItem( "Saturday" );
        lstDays.addItem( "Sunday" );
        lstDays.addActionListener (this);
        lstDays.addItemListener (this);

        txt1 = new TextField( 20 );
        txt2 = new TextField( "Predefined Text" );
        txt3 = new TextField( "Text + Size", 40 );
        txt1.addActionListener (this);
        txt2.addActionListener (this);
        txt3.addActionListener (this);
        add( txt1 );
        add( txt2 );
        add( txt3 );

        int rows = 5, cols = 30;
        sendText = new TextArea( rows, cols );
        recvText = new TextArea( "None", rows, cols );
        add( sendText );
        add( recvText );
        }

    public void actionPerformed (ActionEvent e)
        {
        if (e.getSource() == aButton)
            { System.out.println ("Hello World Button"); }
        if (e.getSource() == lstDays)
            { System.out.println ("List double clicked"); }
        if (e.getSource() instanceof TextField )
            { System.out.println ( ((TextField)e.getSource()).getText()
); }
        }

    public void itemStateChanged (ItemEvent e)
        {
        if (e.getSource() instanceof Checkbox )
            {
```

Listing 22.2 The code that generates Figure 22.1. (*continued*)

```
            Checkbox c = (Checkbox) e.getSource();
            System.out.println (c.getLabel() + c.getState() );
            }
        else
        if (e.getSource() == chooser)
            {
            System.out.println ("Font is " + chooser.getSelectedItem() );
            }
        if (e.getSource() == lstDays)
            {
            System.out.println ("Day selected is " +
              lstDays.getSelectedItem() );
            }


        }
    }
```

Listing 22.2   The code that generates Figure 22.1. (*continued*)

1. **Create a container using an object from a Java container class.** For applets, you do not need to explicitly create a container; applets come ready-made with a container. Applets (and JApplets) extend the Panel container. Hence, the Java runtime already provides applets with a container to play in.

2. **Decide on a *layout manager* for the container.** The default layout manager for objects of class Panel (and hence, applets) is the *FlowLayout*. Our example does not attach a flow manager to the Panel. Nonetheless, the layout manager exists. When components are added to the container, they will be added in flow layout order.

3. **Create your components using initialization parameters that are peculiar to the component.** Here is some code that creates GUI components. This is a button:

```
aButton = new Button( "Hello World!" );
```

Here's a choice.

```
chooser = new Choice();
chooser.addItem( "Times Roman" );
chooser.addItem( "Helvetica" );
chooser.addItem( "Courier" );
```

Here's a TextField:

```
txt1 = new TextField( 20 );
```

The rest of the components are created with constructors that are peculiar to the component.

4. **Place components inside the container.** Components are placed in a container with the *add()* method, as shown:

```
add( aButton );     //Add the button to the Panel container
add (chooser) ;     //Add the Choice object
add( txt1) ;        //Add the TextField
```

For swing components, the add() method invocations could resemble the following:

```
getContentPane().add( aButton );      //Add the button to the Panel
container
getContentPane().add (chooser) ;      //Add the Choice object
getContentPane().add( txt1) ;         //Add the TextField
```

5. **Attach a *listener* to the components.** Here is the code that "listens" for events on these components with their respective listener methods.

```
//Attach the listener for the button
aButton.addActionListener (this);
//Attach the listener for the text field
txt1.addActionListener (this);
//Here's the callback
public void actionPerformed (ActionEvent e)
{
    if (e.getSource() == aButton)
       { System.out.println ("Hello World Button"); }
    if (e.getSource() == lstDays)
       { System.out.println ("List double clicked"); }
    if (e.getSource() instanceof TextField )
       { System.out.println ( ((TextField)e.getSource()).getText() ); }
}
}
```

You may attach the same listener to multiple components. The Java event handling API specifies which component types should be attached to which listener methods. Buttons, lists, and text fields may be listened to by catching an *ActionEvent*.

When one listener is attached to multiple components, your program needs a way of distinguishing which component is the source of the event. The *getSource()* method of class Event (and known to all subclasses of class Event) can identify the event source. A sequence of if/else statements may be used to hone in on the event source component.

Here's the code for attaching the listener and the callback for handling events that arise from selecting an item from a Choice object.

```
//Attach the listener
chooser.addItemListener (this);
//Here's the callback
public void itemStateChanged (ItemEvent e)
{
    if (e.getSource() instanceof Checkbox )
        {
        Checkbox c = (Checkbox) e.getSource();
        System.out.println (c.getLabel() + c.getState() );
        }
    else
    if (e.getSource() == chooser)
        {
        System.out.println ("Font is " + chooser.getSelectedItem() );
        }
    if (e.getSource() == lstDays)
        {
        System.out.println ("Day selected is " + lstDays.getSelectedItem()
);
        }


}
```

Components that contain lists have their events captured by item events.

Something worth mentioning is that you may attach more than one event class to a component. For example, the list of a *days* component, a multiselect list object, has an ActionEvent and an ItemEvent attached to it. In Java, you can attach events to components in a somewhat arbitrary fashion, depending on what makes sense for your application.

In Summary

Java provides the programmer with extensive facilities to create robust GUI front ends. The Java GUI mechanism integrates nicely with Java event delegation, enabling a clean separation of user interaction processing and user presentation. However, most of us in the Java world rely on tools to create user interfaces or are delving into Java enterprise technologies, leaving the user interface issues to HTML or XML screen generation.

Java File I/O

Every programming language needs a mechanism for reading and writing data to and from permanent storage: a disk file. This short chapter describes the basics of native file I/O in Java. Here, we do not discuss the IBM package JRIO as we did in Chapter 17. Instead, you'll read about some of the methods in the package *java.io*. You'll also see how Java file I/O stacks up against I/O in COBOL and PL/I.

The chapter starts with a discussion of a file in Java, followed by the concept of a *stream*. The chapter continues with covering how to read and write bytes and primitive data types to and from files. You'll see sample programs throughout the chapter illustrating the concepts. You'll read about the Java implementation of random file access and see how this stacks up against procedural, mainframe programming languages.

YOU WILL NOT CODE MUCH JAVA NATIVE FILE I/O

As you'll read, Java native file I/O is similar to using ACCEPT/DISPLAY statements in COBOL or GET/PUT LIST statements in PL/I. Most mainframe programmers do not use these statements in their programs. Most mainframe programs use record I/O or perform database calls with SQL, or work in a transaction monitor like CICS. Likewise, Java programmers make database calls using JDBC, like in Chapter 18, or get user inputs by way of a visual presentation component, such as an applet or HTML screen. That said, you, the mainframe Java programmer, should have a bit of exposure to native Java file I/O, which this chapter provides.

The File

Think of the file as an entity that holds related sets of data, known to the operating system by a single name. Now, each operating system has a set of naming rules used to construct file names. Also, one or more files may be grouped together to form higher-level data storage structures, such as databases. Here, we are concerned with accessing data kept in storage structures represented by catalog (MVS) or directory (other) listings.

Files (Datasets) in COBOL, PL/I

The term *file* as used by MVS mainframe programmers usually means a reference to a data store used in an application program; the actual data store is called a *dataset*. An application program written in COBOL, PL/I, or another MVS mainframe programming language references the *filename*. The filename must be previously associated with a dataset name prior to program execution. Typically, the association lasts for the duration of a program or job step execution. The common term for a filename associated with a dataset for the duration of a program or job step is a *DDName*.

The previous association of a filename and a dataset name, or allocating a dataset to a DDName, is usually done statically in a JCL jobstream for batch programs, or by the execution of a TSO ALLOCATE statement in a REXX EXEC or TSO CLIST. Listing 23.1 shows a REXX EXEC that associates a filename with a dataset name; it then invokes a program that uses that dataset, and it also shows a COBOL code snippet that may read the dataset.

Listing 23.1 shows that the filename is a further abstraction of the dataset name, or an abstraction of the data store as known to the operating system. The program knows the dataset by the filename, not the dataset name. The obvious advantage of associating filenames with dataset names in programs is that the data used by the program may be changed without changing the program. For example, changing the line in the REXX EXEC shown in Listing 23.1 to

```
"Allocate Da( 'TX12345.SalesDta.Feb2000.Data') Fi(SalesDta) Shr Reu"
```

causes the COBOL program to use February's sales data, not January's. The application developer does not recompile the COBOL program. Actually, the COBOL program has no real knowledge of the name of the dataset; the association of the dataset name with the filename is made by the operating system.

A file allocation, or association between a filename and a dataset name, does not guarantee that a program will use the data. Listing 23.2 shows a JCL job stream that makes two datasets available to a program, and a PL/I code segment that conditionally uses one of the two datasets.

For the most part, MVS application programs know little about the characteristics of datasets. The dataset name is hidden from the application as are other dataset attributes, such as blocksize or where the dataset resides. The file allocation mechanism does not require that application programs know most dataset attributes in order for the programs to use the data.

```
/* Execute program MAKRPT using January data */
Address TSO
"Allocate Da( 'TX12345.SalesDta.Jan2000.Data') Fi(SalesDta) Shr Reu"
If RC > 0 Then
   Call Display_Allocate_Error
"Call 'TX12345.SalesPgm.Load(MakRpt)'"
/** Other Rexx Code May Follow **/

* Here Is a possible COBOL code snippet
  FILE SECTION.
  FD  SALESDTA
      RECORD CONTAINS 120 CHARACTERS.
  01  SALES-REPORT-INPUT-RECORD.
      05  SALES-AREA-ID          PIC 'X(3)'.
* Other Fields In This Record Follow
* WORKING-STORAGE section Follows

  PROCEDURE DIVISION.
  A100-MAIN.
      OPEN INPUT SALESDTA
           OUTPUT ANOUTFLE
      PERFORM UNTIL NO-MO-RECORDS
           READ SALESDTA
* Process Records, etc.
```

Listing 23.1   Making a dataset known in a COBOL program.

Files in Java

Files in Java are, of course, instances of the *File* class. File objects in Java do not permit a Java program to do any I/O on a file. The class File enables a Java program to glean information (attributes) about a file. Methods in class File enable a Java program to

Determine whether or not a file can be read from or written to

```
boolean canRead(), boolean canWrite()
```

Determine whether a File object is a file or a directory

```
boolean isFile, boolean isDirectory()
```

Get the size of a file in bytes

```
long length()
```

Delete a file or directory

```
boolean delete()
```

```
//AX12345A JOB(ACCTINFO),OTHER JOB CARD PARMS
//*
//RUNPGM    EXEC PGM=MAKRPT,PARM='SUMMARY'
//STEPLIB  DD    DSN=AX12345.REPORT.LOADLIB,DISP=SHR
//SUMRY    DD    DSN=RT98765.SALESDTA.JANSUMRY,DISP=SHR
//DETAIL   DD    DSN=RT98765.SALESDTA.JANDETAL,DISP=SHR
//SYSOUT   DD    SYSOUT=*
//SYSUDUMP DD    SYSOUT=*
//*** Other Job steps may follow

MakRpt: Proc( Summary_Detail_Parm ) Options( Main )
        Reorder ;
    Dcl    Summary_Report_Desired     Bit( 01 ) Aligned
           Init( Input_Parm_For_Summary( Summary_Detail_Parm ) ) ;
    Dcl    Mo_Data                     Bit( 01 ) Aligned Init('1'B);


    Dcl    SaleDta File Variable;


    Dcl    Sumry   File Input Record ;
    Dcl    01  Sumry_Input_Record,
               05   Field_A        Fixed Bin( 31 ),
               /* Other Fields For This record Follow */

    Dcl    Detail  File Input Record ;
    Dcl    01  Detail_Input_Record,
               05   Field_A        Fixed Bin( 31 ),
               /* Other Fields For This record Follow */
   /** Use the Summary or Detail File Based on the Runtime Input Parm
**/
   If Summary_Report_Desired Then
      SaleDta = Sumry ;
   Else
      SaleDta = Detail ;


   Call Process_Sales_Data ;
   /** And so on **/
```

Listing 23.2   Conditionally using a file in PL/I.

Make a directory

```
boolean mkdir()
```

The previous list of methods in class File is not exhaustive. You can see that, in Java, class File denotes objects that are files and directories.

Listing 23.3 shows some of the methods in the File class in use.

```
import java.io.* ;
import java.util.* ;

public class FileTest {

public static void main( String[] a ) {
    //Make a new File Object
    String      fName = "classinfo.dat" ;
    File aFile = new File( fName ) ;
    //Does the file exist?
    System.out.println( fName + " exists is a " +
          aFile.exists() + " statement" ) ;
    //Is this a file or a directory? (could use the isFile()
    // method as well)
    System.out.println( fName + " is a directory is a "
              + aFile.isDirectory() + " statement" ) ;
    //Where is this file located?
    System.out.println( aFile + " is located at " +
              aFile.getAbsolutePath() ) ;
    //How big is the file?
    System.out.println( aFile + " is " + aFile.length()
              + " bytes." ) ;
    //Can we read from or write to this file?
    System.out.println( "You may write to " + aFile + " is a "
              + aFile.canWrite() + " statement") ;
    //When was this file last modified?
    System.out.println( aFile + " was modified on " +
                new Date(aFile.lastModified()) ) ;
  }
}
```

Listing 23.3   Some methods in class File in use.

A few comments about the code are in order. First, the constructor does not create a new file. That is, by constructing a new File object, you do not create a new file on disk. The File constructor provides your Java program with a *reference* to an existing file (assuming the file exists). Hence, the statements

```
//File aFile = new File( "classinfo.dat" ) ; works here, too
String   fName = "classinfo.dat" ;
File     aFile = new File( fName ) ;
```

enable your program to determine the attributes of a file *in the current directory* named classinfo.dat.

Notice that some of the println statements use the character string representation of the filename (String fName), while others use the File object (File aFile). We can get away with using the File object because the magic of the println statement causes the *toString()* method of class File to be invoked.

Listing 23.4 shows the output of the code in Listing 23.3.

We've seen that a major use of a file in the mainframe world is to associate a file with a dataset, thereby enabling an application program to perform I/O operations on that dataset. Does an object of class File provide the Java programmer with similar functionality? Is an object of class File a DDName of sorts for the Java program? The short answer is yes; the long answer is included in the next section.

The Concept of a Stream

A file, or dataset, is one of a number of data sources for a program. A program can get data from the keyboard, a Web page, a network socket, or a file. To accommodate the idea of an abstract data source, Java and other programming languages support the concept of a *stream*. In this section, you'll read about streams in mainframe programming languages and in Java.

Streams in COBOL and PL/I

MVS programmers do not speak of COBOL, PL/I, and other procedural mainframe languages supporting streams. Rather, MVS programmers speak of programming language support for stream I/O and record I/O. In the MVS world, you get data into a program by using stream I/O facilities and record I/O facilities.

COBOL and PL/I support stream I/O with input and output statements that are part of the programming language, whereas, in Java, every I/O statement deals with a stream in one form or another. Put another way, stream I/O is a feature or function of an MVS programming language, whereas the stream is the very heart and soul of Java I/O.

In mainframe programming languages and in Java, the concept of system-defined streams is used. Let's take a look at system-defined streams in COBOL and PL/I.

```
classinfo.dat exists is a true statement
classinfo.dat is a directory is a false statement
classinfo.dat is located at D:\Lous Folder\Java MF Book\Book
Chapters\Java File IO\Code\classinfo.dat
classinfo.dat is 9772 bytes.
You may write to classinfo.dat is a true statement
classinfo.dat was modified on Sat Feb 17 14:28:50 CST 2001
```

Listing 23.4   The output from code in Listing 23.3.

System-Defined Streams in COBOL and PL/I

The system-defined streams of the MVS world are known by two filenames: SYSIN and SYSOUT. If you do not tell your program any differently, your program assumes your input source is allocated to (or associated with) DDName SYSIN, and your output destination is allocated to DDName SYSOUT.

You would use different I/O statements in COBOL for stream I/O than in record I/O. COBOL supports the ACCEPT statement that may fetch input from the keyboard and the DISPLAY statement for output to the terminal. PL/I supports the GET and PUT statements for keyboard I/O. The record I/O statements for COBOL are READ, WRITE, and REWRITE; for PL/I, the record I/O statements are READ INTO, WRITE FROM, REWRITE, and LOCATE.

For example, the short code snippet shown in Listing 23.5 gets a line of input from the terminal and assigns the input line to a variable called *Customer-Name* in COBOL and PL/I.

```
* COBOL example
* Environment Division, et. al. is coded here
  Configuration Section.
  Special-Names.
    Console is Terminal-Input.
* More Statements follow
  Working-Storage section.
    01 Customer-Name  Pic X(80).
* More Statements Follow
  Procedure-Division.
* More Statements follow
    Accept Customer-Name From Terminal-Input.
  Display "You Entered " Customer-Name "From the Terminal".
* End of COBOL Example

/** PL/I Example **/
Ex: Proc Options( Main ) ;
   /** Statements follow **/
   Dcl   Customer_Name    Char( 80 ) Varying Init( '' ) ;
   /** More Statements **/
   Get Skip List( Customer_Name ) ;
   Put Skip List( "You Entered " || Customer_Name || " From The
Terminal" ) ;
```

Listing 23.5 Reading characters from and writing characters to the default I/O streams.

Streams in Java

Think of a stream in Java as any data source that holds a series of bytes that can be read or written. Such a series may be stored on a file or kept in memory, or the series is accessible over a network port. The essence of an object-oriented programming language like Java is to express accessing such a series of bytes the same way, regardless of its source or destination.

All I/O in Java is done through a stream. Java defines a library of stream classes in the *java.io* package. Here we'll take a look at some of the methods in the java.io package as well as some methods from java.lang.System that define some streams.

System-Defined Streams in Java

The class *java.lang.System* defines three streams available from any and all Java programs:

- System.in: Reads bytes from the keyboard.
- System.out: Writes bytes out to the screen.
- System.err: Writes error text to the screen.

You've already seen `System.out.println()` statements a zillion times, right?

```java
import java.io.* ;

public class KeybdIO {

public static void main( String[] a ) {
  char aCharRead ;
  try {
   aCharRead = (char) System.in.read() ;
   while ( aCharRead != (char) -1 ) {
      System.out.println( "Here's a char read ==> " + aCharRead ) ;
      aCharRead = (char) System.in.read() ;


  }
  System.out.println( "You never see this statement" ) ;
  }
     catch( IOException ioe) {
             System.out.println("IO Error " + ioe ) ;
   }

 }

 }
```

Listing 23.6   Reading characters from the keyboard.

Reading and Writing a Stream of Bytes–Java

How do you read characters from the keyboard? Listing 23.6 shows you one way.
The statement

```
aCharRead = (char) System.in.read();
```

is responsible for fetching a single character from the keyboard. Oddly, the read()
method reads an *int* that usually gets cast to a char. The value ñ1 signals end of file; on
the PC, press Control+Z.

The println() statement outside the while loop never gets executed; the only way to
stop the input loop is to stop the program.

As far as writing characters to the screen is concerned, you've seen and done Sys-
tem.out.println() many times, right? The default output stream *out* has the println()
method, which you use to write characters to the stream.

Java file I/O is done within a try/catch block. The methods in the various stream
classes throw an exception of class IOException, which your code must deal with.

To read characters from a file, you may create a file object and assign that file object
to a file, not unlike using a DD statement in a JCL job stream. Once done, you use a
mechanism similar to the one shown in Listing 23.6. Listing 23.7 shows how to read
characters from a file.

The program in Listing 23.7 detects the end of file and eventually lists the phrase,
"You see this statement at end of file."

You could have constructed the FileReader object with the following constructor:

```
FileReader  myReader  = new FileReader( "afile.dat" ) ;
```

and not use the constructor for the File object.

Listing 23.8 shows a small program that captures keyboard inputs and writes the
inputs to a file.

Notice the use of a Java class called *FileWriter*. Java uses *reader* and *writer* classes to
reference file streams. Also, notice that in Java, you do not *open* streams, but you should
close them. In Listing 23.7, if you did not close the stream, your outputs (via the
myWriter.write() statement) would not stick.

So much for character IO. What if you want to read and write ints, floats, or other
primitive types? The next section sheds some light.

Reading and Writing Primitive Data Types–Java

We consider two categories of IO here. The first is performing I/O on Java primitive
types so the result is human-readable text. That is, we want to write primitive types as
characters (no, you don't convert the primitive types to characters first!). Next, we'll
consider doing I/O on primitive types as is, not in human-readable form.

You use a *PrintWriter* stream to write Java primitive types to a stream in character
form. Listing 23.9 shows an example:

Here, we require the use of the *PrintWriter* class. PrintWriter objects take a FileWriter
object as an argument for its constructor. Notice that the output stream object myWriter
should be closed.

```
import java.io.* ;

public class FileRead {


public static void main( String[] a ) {
  char aCharRead ;
  try {
      File       myFile   = new File("afile.dat") ;
      FileReader myReader = new FileReader( myFile ) ;
   aCharRead = (char) myReader.read() ;
   while ( aCharRead != (char) -1 ) {
      System.out.println( "Here's a char read ==> " + aCharRead ) ;
      aCharRead = (char) myReader.read() ;

  }
  myReader.close() ;
  System.out.println( "You see this statement at end of file" ) ;
  }
    catch( IOException ioe) {
            System.out.println("IO Error " + ioe ) ;
  }

}


}
```

Listing 23.7   Reading text from a file.

Next, we'll look at writing Java primitive types to files as is, in binary format. We'll use methods in the Java class *DataOutputStream* for this task. Listing 23.10 provides an illustrative example.

Notice that we use objects of class *FileOutputStream* and *DataOutputStream* in Listing 23.10. The rule is, for character I/O, use *reader/writer* classes, such as FileWriter. For binary I/O, use *InputStream/OutputStream* classes, such as DataOutputStream.

Reading and Writing Objects–Java

Java supports the reading and writing of entire objects. The Java term for the process of writing an object is to *serialize* the object. When an object is serialized, all properties of that object, including other objects, may be written to disk.

The Java keyword *transient* marks object properties as not worth saving. That is, an instance variable coded with the transient modifier will *not* be saved upon serialization.

```
import java.io.* ;

public class FileWrite {

public static void main( String[] a ) {
  char anInputChar ;

  try {
      FileWriter  myWriter  =
                 new FileWriter( "anewoutfile.dat" ) ;
      anInputChar = (char)System.in.read() ;
      while ( anInputChar != (char) -1 ) {
         myWriter.write( anInputChar ) ;
         anInputChar = (char) System.in.read() ;
      }
      myWriter.close() ;

  }

    catch( IOException ioe) {
             System.out.println("IO Error " + ioe ) ;
    }

:}

}
```

Listing 23.8   Writing characters to a file.

Listing 23.11 shows the writing of an object to a disk file and reading that object in.

The serializable interface contains no methods (in JavaSpeak, it's called a *marker* interface). Notice that the methods in the ObjectInputStream class throw a *ClassNot-Found* exception that your code must catch.

The object property *notSaved* is just that, not saved, because the property is coded with the *transient* modifier.

In Summary

Java release 1.3 contains 75 classes in the java.io package. Here you've seen a bit of Java file I/O capabilities. Java exploits the concept of a stream, which is an abstraction for a data source or data output destination. You use reader and writer stream classes to perform character I/O, and InputStream and OutputStream stream classes to perform native Java primitive type I/O. Java also supports the direct input and output of objects through a process called serialization.

```
import java.io.* ;

public class UsePrintWriter {

public static void main( String[] fname ) {
  int      anInt   = 12345 ;
  double   aDouble = 123.45 ;
  boolean  aBool   = true ;

  try {
      FileWriter   myFW       = new FileWriter( fname[ 0 ] ) ;
      PrintWriter  myWriter  = new PrintWriter( myFW ) ;
      myWriter.print( anInt ) ;
      myWriter.print( aDouble ) ;
      myWriter.print( aBool ) ;
      myWriter.close() ;

  }
    catch( IOException ioe) {
            System.out.println("IO Error " + ioe ) ;
  }

}

}
```

Listing 23.9   Writing Java primitive types to a file as characters.

```
import java.io.* ;

public class UseDataOutputStream {

public static void main( String[] fname ) {
  int      anInt   = 12345 ;
  double   aDouble = 123.45 ;
  boolean  aBool   = true ;

  try {
      FileOutputStream   myFOS      =
                         new FileOutputStream( fname[ 0 ] ) ;
      DataOutputStream  myWriter =
                         . new DataOutputStream( myFOS ) ;
      myWriter.writeInt( anInt ) ;
      myWriter.writeDouble( aDouble ) ;
      myWriter.writeBoolean( aBool ) ;
      myWriter.close() ;

  }

    catch( IOException ioe) {
              System.out.println("IO Error " + ioe ) ;
    }

}

}
```

Listing 23.10   Writing Java primitive types as binary data.

```java
import java.io.* ;

public class ObjIOExample implements Serializable {

  int    intprop1 = 12345;
  double doubprop2= 321.65 ;
  transient char  notSaved = 'K' ;
  String strprop3 = "This is an example of Object serialization";

public static void main( String[] fname ) {


  try {

      FileOutputStream   myFOS      =
                       new FileOutputStream( fname[ 0 ] ) ;
      ObjectOutputStream  myWriter  =
                       new ObjectOutputStream( myFOS ) ;

      ObjectInputStream   myReader  =
           new ObjectInputStream(
           new FileInputStream( fname[0] ) ) ;
    ObjIOExample obj1 = new ObjIOExample() ;
    ObjIOExample obj2 ;

     myWriter.writeObject( obj1 ) ;

     myWriter.close() ;

     obj2 = (ObjIOExample) myReader.readObject( ) ;
     System.out.println( obj2.strprop3 ) ;

  }
    catch( IOException ioe) {
            System.out.println("IO Error " + ioe ) ;
    }
    catch( ClassNotFoundException cnfe) {
            System.out.println("Class not found " + cnfe ) ;
    }

}

}
```

Listing 23.11   Writing and reading Java objects.

CHAPTER 24

The Java 2 Enterprise
Edition Libraries

J2EE, the *Java 2 Enterprise Edition* platform is a collection of about a dozen application programming interfaces (APIs) for developing enterprise applications. These APIs define a complete set of services that software engineers use to develop software in 100 percent Java that is scalable, fault-tolerant, distributed, and secure. This chapter discusses the J2EE APIs.

What Is J2EE?

Depending on your point of view, J2EE is a *set of APIs* that gives the Java programmer the additional capabilities of writing enterprise-class applications. J2EE can also be viewed as a *product*. You can download the J2EE software development kit from the Sun site, which certainly lends the impression that J2EE is a product. However, the J2EE "product" does little in and of itself. It is a means by which a team of software developers may develop a large, multi-user Java application.

Up to now, you've been reading about the Java 2 platform, Standard Edition (J2SE). It serves as the foundation for Java technologies. You might say that J2EE includes J2SE, plus a set of extra APIs. Whereas J2SE deals with writing application programs and applets on the client, the J2EE APIs deal with writing Java *on the server*.

Java on the Server

J2EE assists the Java application development team by providing a foundation for server-side software development. Let's face it—using Java solely on the client raises some issues. Java is interpretive, which translates into slow. How many REXX (an immensely popular IBM mainframe scripting language, in case you don't know) production applications do you see in your mainframe environment?

Also, Java being interpretive means that every box that runs Java requires a separate Java Virtual Machine (JVM), or Java runtime. That's one more piece of maintenance requiring attention. In addition to distributing new releases of productivity tools, such as word processors and the like, the company must attend to distributing new JVMs. Isn't the hassle of software maintenance on the client one reason why the enterprise is spending fortunes on developing N-tier applications?

Turns out that Java makes for a pretty darn good platform for server-side software development. As you've seen, using an object-oriented language *greatly* aids you, the application developer, in your appointed task (whether you're writing client or server software). Java, with full support for object-oriented software development *and* a rich set of classes available for use, enables powerful software development.

The fact that Java is interpretive does not impact server-side applications much. Although Java code does not execute as quickly as code written in compiled languages, Java code executes quickly enough for the server. The real bottleneck in N-tier applications is not the speed of the code per se; the bottlenecks arise from poor application design, including the failing to engineer software to be scalable to thousands of users in a distributed environment. Besides, enterprise applications dealing with distributed components and data stores running over networks can only be as fast as the underlying network. Java code has no problem executing faster than the network's capability to move around data and code.

Actually, the interpretive nature of Java may serve as a benefit in the server environment. The Java environment has the capability to dynamically load Java classes when needed. A static executable may require that all needed software be resident at the moment of execution, whereas a Java server-side application may load Java classes as needed and remove them when not needed. The dynamic loading and purging of software components (loosely speaking, Java classes) help servers to maximize resources, such as memory, storage, and database connections. The J2EE specification (apart from the API specifications) published for draft release 1.3 is 161 pages.

The J2EE APIs enable you, the Java developer, to write your application without having to worry about the dynamic loading and purging of class files. Actually, the J2EE APIs enable you to write software without worrying about a number of server-side application issues, such as network communications or transaction integrity and security. You may concentrate on solving your problem without dealing with the mundane but necessary details involved in writing enterprise-wide, distributed server applications. Let's look at the J2EE components next and see just what services J2EE provides you, the Java server-side application developer.

J2EE APIs

Here is a list of the J2EE APIs with a brief description. Please understand that most of these J2EE APIs are worthy of a separate book. Sun has published specifications for these APIs, often running into hundreds of pages for each specification. Of course, you may freely download any of these specifications from the Sun Web site.

JavaServer Pages (JSPs)

JavaServer Pages enable developers to dynamically generate Web pages with HTML, XML, and Java code. Some call JSPs the front door to enterprise applications, and with good reason. The thrust of JSPs is to help the enterprise application developer separate presentation code from business logic code on the server. The theory is that by separating the presentation into its own layer, the application developer can make changes to the presentation (Web pages) without impacting the code that implements the business logic, and vice versa.

You create a JSP using a text or HTML building tool and store the JSP on the server. The user invokes a JSP by entering the name of the JSP in the location bar of his or her browser or clicking on an HTML form containing the JSP as the target of the *ACTION* attribute.

Listing 24.1 shows a JSP page that displays "Hello <Your name here>" on a Web page.

JSPs use *tags* to send commands to a JSP translator. The JSP tags are shown in italics. We assume that some previously displayed Web page had a form with an entry field named *you*, making this value known to the server during the session.

Notice the previous JSP page has a mixture of HTML and Java code. The HTML is coded as you'd expect; the Java code is sandwiched between <% and %> tag markups.

```
<html>
<head><title>The Hello JSP</title></head>
<body>
<%@ page language="java" %>
<p> Hello
<% String you = session.getParameter("you");
out.println(you); %>

</body>
</html>
```

Listing 24.1 Hello <your name here> JSP.

The latest version of JavaServer Pages, version 1.2, is in the final specification phase, meaning that unless some organization with clout involved in JSP development says otherwise, the version becomes official. The JSP specification for release 1.2 is 243 pages.

Java Servlets

Like JSP, servlets enable developers to dynamically create Web content as well as provide additional functionality to a Web server. As we'll see later, a JSP is actually translated into a Java servlet, which resides on the Web server.

Listing 24.2 shows a Java servlet that does the same thing as the JSP shown in Listing 24.1.

Notice how the servlet constructs HTML by using println statements. The servlet has the full features of the Java programming language available to construct whatever HTML (or XML or text) is desired.

Actually, JavaServer Pages get translated into Java servlets. When a client requests a JavaServer Page (by entering the JSP name in the location bar of a browser, for example), the browser sends a request to the Java-enabled server. The server determines if a servlet corresponding to the requested JSP page is present; if not, the server translates the JSP into a servlet and executes the servlet. Subsequent invocation of the JSP page results in the server executing the previously-generated servlet. Figure 24.1 shows the process.

You can do everything with a servlet that you could do with a JSP. Looking at Listings 24.1 (JSP) and 24.2 (servlet), most will agree that the JSP is smaller than the servlet. Most will agree that the JSP is easier to understand and maintain than the servlet. Most

```java
import java.io.*;
import javax.servlet.*;
public class HeyItsYou extends HttpServlet {
  public void doPost(HttpServletRequest req,
    HttpServletResponse res) throws ServletException, IOException {
    res.setContentType("text/html");
    PrintWriter out = res.getWriter();
    String you = session.getParameter("you">) ;
    out.println("<html>");
    out.println("<head><title>The Hello JSP</title></head>");
    out.println("<body>");
    out.println("<p> Hello," + you );
    out.println("</p>");
    out.println("</body>");
    out.println("</html>");
  }
}
```

Listing 24.2 The Hello <your name here> servlet.

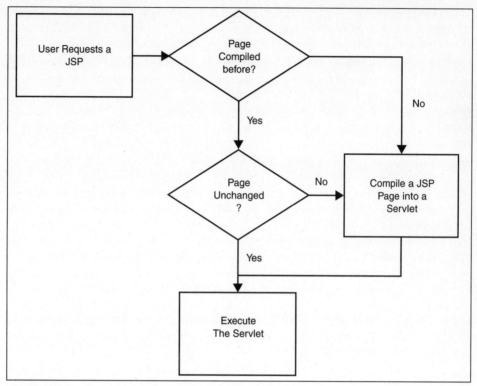

Figure 24.1 JSP-to-servlet translation process.

will also agree that writing out HTML (or XML, of course) by way of out.println() statements is a major drag. A large page could have hundreds of out.println statements!

However, servlets have a place in the J2EE world. Some server-side tasks are pretty awkward by using JSPs alone. Also, recall that JSPs were developed to help the application developer separate business logic from presentation logic, not to replace business logic. Servlets are best used to implement business logic, whereas JSPs are best used to deal with presentation details. The Java servlet specification for release 2.3 is 267 pages.

Java Messaging Services (JMS)

JMS is a set of APIs that invokes asynchronous messaging services like broadcast and point-to-point (client-to-client) messages. JMS is an API for using networked messaging services. A messaging system accepts messages from "producer" clients and delivers them to "consumer" clients. Data sent in a message is often intended as a sort of event notification.

In a synchronous messaging service, the producer sends a message and then waits for verification from the consumer that the message was received and understood. This waiting can cause severe bottlenecks. In an asynchronous messaging system, the producer sends the message and delegates the responsibility of delivery and verification to the messaging service. The producer is free to continue without waiting for the verification of message delivery by the consumer. The messaging service tends to the messy details. The specification for the current version of JMS, release 1.0.2, is 112 pages.

Java Transaction API (JTA)

JTA provides developers with a mechanism for handling the commit and the rollback of transactions as well as insuring the Atomicity, Consistency, Isolation, and Durability (ACID) properties of a transaction.

JTA is used for managing distributed transactions (such as updates to multiple databases that must be handled in a single transaction). JTA is a low-level API and associated coding is complex and error-prone. Fortunately, other J2EE technologies, such as Enterprise JavaBeans, and application servers provide transaction support, which means that rarely, if ever, an application programmer makes calls to the JTA API. Transaction support is one of the many services provided to the enterprise application developer using the J2EE family of APIs. The specification for the current version of JTA, release 1.0.1, is 60 pages.

Java Transaction Services

Java Transaction Services (JTS) provides developers with a means of communicating with transaction monitors and other transaction-oriented resources. Of course, JTS provides high-level support for JTA, as well as other transaction services.

JTS plays the role of an intermediary for all the constituent components of the EJB architecture. In JTS terminology, the director is called the transaction manager. The participants in the transaction that implement transaction-protected resources, such as relational databases, are called resource managers. When an application begins a transaction, it creates a transaction object that represents the transaction. You would use JNDI to access this transaction object. The application then invokes the resource managers to perform the work of the transaction. As the transaction progresses, the transaction manager keeps track of each of the resource managers enlisted in the transaction. Often, JTS assists in managing the activities involved in a two-phase commit. The specification for the current version of JTS, release 1.0, is 17 pages.

Enterprise JavaBeans

Enterprise JavaBeans (EJB) defines an *architecture* that enables developers to create reusable, server-side components. EJBs typically reside on the application server or may have their own dedicated server. These components are the heart and soul of the enterprise application. Although the long list of J2EE APIs is necessary for any substantial enterprise or N-tier application, most of the API sets define interfaces to support services and external resources that are required for EJB usage. EJB is *the* API that deals with creating application components and how these components interact with the other J2EE APIs.

A key feature of the EJB architecture is the construction of applications from software components (enterprise beans). The EBJ architecture defines *what* the enterprise beans are, what enterprise beans are made of, and what classes and interfaces enterprise beans extend or implement. The EJB architecture does not define *how* a vendor constructs enterprise beans; the vendor is free to use whatever tools and technologies are at their disposal. The vision is one of a rich marketplace of vendors creating reusable server-side distributed components and an industry of customers mixing and matching different vendor offerings, secure in the knowledge that the developed enterprise beans will work according to the EJB architecture.

If you plan to develop Java-distributed applications, plan on using EJB. The specification for the final draft version of EBJ, release 2.0, is 558 pages.

JavaMail

The JavaMail API offers a standard Java extension API to talk to all your favorite standard Internet mail protocols. The API provides a platform-independent and protocol-independent framework to build Java technology-based mail and messaging applications. Put differently, JavaMail represents a standardized, extensible platform for communicating, presenting, and manipulating all current and future Multimedia Internet Mail Extension (MIME) types. The JavaMail API is implemented as a Java platform standard extension.

Say goodbye to writing your own classes for talking to mail protocols. Say goodbye to learning yet another unique third-party or in-house class library for dealing with e-mail or newsgroups. JavaMail was designed to communicate with popular protocols and mime types. The specification for the current version of JavaMail, release 1.2, is 104 pages.

Java Naming and Directory Service (JNDI)

JNDI provides an interface for accessing name and directory services, such as LDAP directory services and Domain Name Service (DNS). JNDI enables Java programs to use name servers and directory servers to look up objects or data by name. This important feature enables a client object to locate a remote server object or data.

JNDI is a generic API that can work with any name or directory service. As such, JNDI was not designed to replace existing technology; instead, it provides a common interface to existing naming services. For example, JNDI provides methods to bind a name to an object, allowing that object to be located, regardless of its location on the network.

Server providers have been implemented for many common protocols (such as NIS, LDAP, and NDS) and for CORBA object registries. Of particular interest to users of J2EE, JNDI is used to locate EJB components on the network.

Again, the thrust of J2EE technology is to provide enterprise application developers with much-needed services in the distributed realm. It's hard to think of a more invaluable service than a naming service. JNDI provides the Java application developer with this much-needed service. The specification for the current version of JNDI, including the API documentation, release 1.2, is 76 pages.

JDBC

Java Database Connectivity (JDBC) provides the J2EE application a standard interface to databases (usually relational databases). You've seen JDBC in Chapter 19, "Java and DB2." However, the latest releases of JDBC have additional capabilities not yet supported in the IBM environment.

Sun offers two versions of JDBC: one version for client-side development and the other for server-side. If your needs are to issue SQL statements, either version will work. The server-side JDBC package provides additional transaction support, using JTA and JTS, which you'll need in a distributed environment. The specification for the alpha draft version of JDBC, release 3.0, is 190 pages.

Java Interface Definition Language (Java IDL)

By using the Java Interface Definition Language (IDL), the Java programmer has access to CORBA objects. The Java programmer can use the IDL-to-Java compiler, called idlj, to generate Java code to interact with CORBA objects.

CORBA, the Common Object Request Broker Architecture, defines a standard for creating distributed object request systems. The CORBA standard is the result of the collaboration of well over a hundred companies. The end result is a standard that is language-, platform-, and vendor-neutral.

CORBA enables the enterprise to use existing software by providing features that developers can use to wrap existing software as CORBA objects. With CORBA, applications written in several languages can happily coexist and communicate. By using Java IDL, the Java enterprise application developer can tap into the CORBA world.

In Summary

As you can see, J2EE is a robust framework that covers much ground and provides numerous, vitally important services to the enterprise application developer. J2EE is an evolving technology. As industry participants, in collaboration with Sun, use J2EE, we can expect the specifications of the J2EE APIs to change in the future.

The previous (and other) J2EE APIs do not stand in isolation. When developing a distributed, enterprise application in Java, you'll need to write code that uses several of the mentioned APIs. Fortunately, you need not deal with several underlying issues; the J2EE APIs tend to many of the details, leaving you free to bust code to solve your problems.

CHAPTER 25

Remote Method Invocation

Java gives you, the programmer, the interesting capability to invoke Java methods that live on different machines, or JVMs. Now, what makes this capability interesting is that the invocations appear, for the most part, to work on methods on the *same* machine. This capability, or feature, is called *Remote Method Invocation* (RMI).

This chapter describes how you would code RMI method invocations. We start by describing the requirements for Java RMI, followed by the code for a pair of classes that execute on the same JVM. Continuing, we split this pair by placing one class in one JVM, the other in another JVM, and coding the RMI constructs required to invoke the methods remotely.

What Is Java RMI?

Java RMI is an API that enables you to invoke methods residing on different Java Virtual Machines as if these methods were available locally. The RMI mechanism will send parameters across the network and tend to values (if any) that return to the calling method.

RMI is a completely 100 percent Java solution to the problem of accessing distributed objects on the network. Now, RMI is not the only distributed object technology available. Non-Java environments could use a similar technology called *Remote Procedure calls* (RPC), which is very similar to RMI. Also, implementations of the CORBA standard address accessing remote objects across a network. For now, let's limit our discussion to RMI.

NOTE Because mainframe environments are rarely 100 percent Java, RMI may not address all of the issues involved in accessing distributed objects in a mainframe environment. The CORBA standard was developed to address distributed objects in a heterogeneous distributed environment. Also, RMI is not the only Java solution to distributed objects. Enterprise JavaBeans also addresses this issue and applies to environments that are not 100 percent pure Java. That said, the concepts underlying RMI will serve as a basis for CORBA and Enterprise JavaBeans, should your shop decide to pursue one of those routes.

Before we start, a bit of terminology is in order. We call the method residing on the distant JVM the *remote method*. We call the object invoking the remote method the *client*; we call the object naming the remote method the *server*.

Please understand that the client/server pairing is only for the duration of a single remote-method invocation. The same object may serve as a client for one method invocation and a server for a subsequent invocation.

Also, understand that when your RMI program invokes a remote method, it *executes on the server*. Don't think that RMI is copying the method over from the server to the client JVM before executing the method. That's why RMI is called *Remote Method Invocation*, not Remote Method Copying.

Java RMI Mechanics

The basic idea behind Java RMI and all remote method or distributed object referencing technologies is to create understandable constructs for the client and the server; however, they are not what they appear to be. For this feat of Java magic to work, a few details must be taken care of.

First, we need a way of invoking the remote method with the appearance of invoking a local method. Next, we will want the capability to address the second detail mentioned.

Second, your client Java object needs a way to locate this remote method. Remember that the remote object may be on any server on the network. In addition, you don't want to hard code some particular server reference; you want to access the remote object wherever it may be today. If the remote object moves to another server tomorrow, *you don't want to be forced into changing your client code*.

Third, your client needs a way of sending parameters over the network and accepting returned values, if any, back from the remote method. Recall that the method is invoked locally from the client, but executed on the server. Hence, any data returned via a return statement originates in the server JVM.

Fourth, because you are sending and receiving data over the network, you may have security considerations. We'll not cover the nitty gritty of Java's security features. You'll see what you have to code in order for your RMI programs to pass the muster.

The next section addresses the first issue of concern: invoking the remote method like it is a local method.

The RMI Stub

In RMISpeak, you create an object accessed locally by the RMI client that the RMI server understands. When the client accesses this local object, the magic of RMI performs network tasks, which include locating remote objects, sending parameters, and invoking the remote object.

The local object cited in the preceding paragraph is called a *stub*. The stub is implemented as a Java class like everything else in Java, right? Think of the stub as a dummy routine that looks similar to the remote method (it has the same signature and return value type).

Part of the magic of RMI is that the stub tends to collect all the parameters, ready the parameters for network transport, and send the parameters over the network. In RMISpeak, the process of collecting and readying the parameters is called *marshalling* the parameters.

You don't need to be a rocket scientist to figure out what happens on the server side. The parameters are fetched from the network and made ready for the remote method by a process called *unmarshalling*.

Of course, all this marshalling and unmarshalling is totally transparent to the Java program or Java programmer. You, the Java programmer, merely code your application as RMI-ready; the Java runtime takes care of the messy details. The marshalling and unmarshalling of parameters and returned values answers the third detail previously cited. How nice that you don't have to tend to the sticky networking details!

You may wonder what this stub looks like or how you can create it. The short story is that you use a Sun-supplied JDK tool called *rmic* to create the stub. Before we show you how, we need one more piece to fully respond to the first detail.

The RMI Interface

We can't get a stub class because we need to tell the stub what it should look like. In other words, we need to tell the stub what the remote method looks like. The method used by RMI is to rely on a Java interface that describes the remote method implemented by the server class. Ergo, when the client calls the stub, the stub knows what the server method looks like because the server class implements the interface; the interface describes the remote method.

Yes, it already sounds confusing, right? Soon, we'll take a look at an example that will show you how the interface ties with the server class, which ties with the stub, which ties with the client object.

Let's address the second detail: locating the remote method.

The rmiregistry Program

Although the interface describes the remote method and the stub is aware of the interface, your client still needs a way to locate a *remote object* so the client can invoke the remote method. Once your client has a reference to the remote object, your client invokes the method by the old and familiar object.method() invocation syntax.

The RMI way of locating remote objects is by using a JDK tool called *rmiregistry*. The rmiregistry program loads a Java *registry* with a symbolic name (that's a fancy phrase for a string) paired with a remote object. Your server program creates a remote object, invokes a method in the rmi API to associate the name with the remote object, and the rmiregistry program loads the pair into the registry. Your client program accesses the registry using a method from the rmi API and invokes the remote method using object.method() syntax.

Think of the registry as a small table resident on every JVM. You don't need to know anything more about the registry in order to use it. If you are privy to the registry on Windows operating systems, you have a good understanding of the Java registry.

On to the fourth detail: the issue of security.

Security Considerations

Because RMI sends data to and from different JVMs, security concerns should be addressed. Every time data comes into a JVM from an outside source, that data may be corrupted by omission or commission. Prudence is called for, especially in these perilous times.

We will not delve into the specifics of Java security in this section. You'll read enough to get kick-started on using RMI. What we need to do is tell the JVM(s) that the client, server, or both, have permission to connect, accept, and receive network connections.

We do this by passing an option to the Java runtime when we execute our client (or server) RMI programs. We code the relevant permissions into a *policy file* and make that policy file known to the client or server. Later, you'll see an example of a policy file used in our up-and-coming example.

Time for an Example

The next several sections show a pair of classes that reside in a single Java VM that we'll break up. We'll make one class the client, the other the server, and "RMIize" the classes. Along the way, we'll provide commentary.

Refer to listing 25.1 for the Java source for the two classes.

After the compile, you'll see two Java classes. Figure 25.1 shows the output when running the RMIExample class.

Our mission is to convert the class RMIExample into the RMI client and the class RemoteMethodLocal into the RMI server. We'll do this one step at a time. As we progress through the steps, we'll encounter RMI requirements and explain them en route.

Step 1: Create the RMI Interface

The interface has to show a description of the remote method. In our case, the method *rollDice()* is the method in question. Listing 25.2 shows the code for our RMI interface.

```
public class RMIExample {

    public static void main( String[] a ) {

        RemoteMethodLocal myEx = new RemoteMethodLocal() ;

        String rolledValue = myEx.rollDice() ;
        System.out.println( rolledValue ) ;
    }


}
class RemoteMethodLocal {

    public String rollDice() {

        int dieValue1 = (int) (5 * Math.random() ) + 1 ;
        int dieValue2 = (int) (5 * Math.random() ) + 1 ;
        return "You rolled a " + dieValue1 + " and a " + dieValue2 ;
    }
```

Listing 25.1 Two Java classes in one JVM.

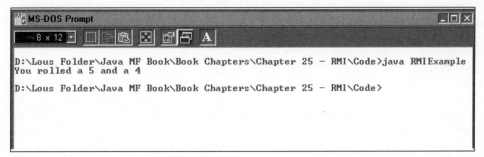

Figure 25.1 Running the RMIExample class.

This interface shows some RMI requirements. First, the interface *must extend the Remote interface*. The Remote interface is part of the java.rmi package shown imported in this interface. Second, *all remote methods must have a throws clause, throwing RemoteException*. That is all for the RMI interface.

```
import java.rmi.* ;

public interface RMIInterface extends Remote {

    public String rollDice() throws RemoteException ;

}
```

Listing 25.2   The RMI Interface that describes the remote method.

Step 2: Code the Client Class

You could code the server class here if you like—it doesn't really matter. Anyway, Listing 25.3 shows code for the client class.

Let's examine Listing 25.3 for differences from class RMIExample in Listing 25.1. First, the code is sandwiched between a try/catch block. Every time you do any RMI, you *must be prepared to catch exceptions.* Here, we are merely printing out the text that accompanies the caught exception.

Although the catching of exceptions is a requirement for RMI programming, catching exceptions is not "RMIish." However, the following two lines are definitely "RMI-Ish:"

```
Remote        remObj       = Naming.lookup("//localhost/RMIExample" ) ;
RMIInterface serverObject = (RMIInterface) remObj ;
```

The *Naming* class of (you guessed it) the java.rmi package contains methods to load into and retrieve data from the rmi registry. Because this is our client program, we need a reference to the remote object; the *Naming.lookup()* method provides this referencing service.

The method Naming.lookup() returns an object of class *Remote.* In order for our client program to use this remote object, we must cast it. The second line casts the reference to the remote object to that of the *RMI interface* coded in Listing 25.2.

In our example, we used the special name *//localhost.* This name refers to the same host, but not necessarily the same JVM. When you run RMI on a network, your argument to Naming.lookup() will resemble

```
rmi://yourservername.com/namefromNaming.rebind()
```

where namefromNaming.rebind() is the symbolic name paired with the remote object in the RMI server class.

How do we know that the cast will be valid? We know the cast is valid because when we code the server, we take pains to *have the server class implement the interface.* Next we will take a look at the server code.

```
import java.rmi.* ;

public class RMIExampleClient {

    public static void main( String[] a ) {

      try {
        Remote remObj = Naming.lookup("//localhost/RMIExample" ) ;
        RMIInterface serverObject = (RMIInterface) remObj ;

        String whatYouRolled = serverObject.rollDice() ;
        System.out.println( whatYouRolled ) ;
      }
      catch (Exception exc) {
          System.out.println(exc.getMessage() ) ;
      }


    }

}
```

Listing 25.3 The RMI client class that invokes the remote method.

Step 3: Code the Server Class

Listing 25.4 shows the code for the server class.

It looks like the server class has additional RMI constructs and requirements. The first is that the server class *must extend java.rmi.UnicastRemoteObject*. For now, the only class supported by the server-side of Java RMI is the UnicastRemoteObject. People are talking about Sun developing a class for MulticastRemoteObject, but that's for tomorrow.

The second RMI requirement is that the server class *must implement the RMI interface*. You read this in the previous section on the client code. With the server implementing the interface, the client can access the remote object as if it were a local object. Of course, it doesn't matter where on network the remote class resides—that's the magic of RMI.

The third RMI requirement is that the *default constructor throws RemoteException*. As a rule, every method invoked remotely must throw RemoteException. However, is the constructor invoked remotely? Well, the client program invokes the Naming.lookup() method, which accesses the rmi registry for a name/remote object pair. At this time, a reference to the remote object is made available to the client program.

The fourth requirement is not strictly an RMI requirement, but you follow it because of RMI. Your remote method must *match the signature of the interface description*.

```
import java.rmi.* ;
import java.rmi.server.* ;

public class RMIExampleServer extends UnicastRemoteObject
                             implements RMIInterface {

   public RMIExampleServer() throws RemoteException {
       super() ;
   }

   public String rollDice() throws RemoteException {

       int dieValue1 = (int) (5 * Math.random() ) + 1 ;
       int dieValue2 = (int) (5 * Math.random() ) + 1 ;
       return "You rolled a " + dieValue1 + " and a "
               + dieValue2 ;
   }

   public static void main( String[] a ) {
       System.setSecurityManager( new RMISecurityManager() ) ;
       try {
          RMIExampleServer myExObj = new RMIExampleServer() ;
          Naming.rebind("/RMIExample", myExObj ) ;

       }
       catch (Exception exc ) {
           System.out.println( exc.getMessage() ) ;
       }

   }

}
```

Listing 25.4 The RMI server class that contains the remote method.

Of course, that is part and parcel of why you use interfaces. However, the requirement that all remote methods throw RemoteException comes into play here.

The fifth requirement is not a hard-and-fast RMI requirement, but we show an example because it deals with security. The following line of code,

```
System.setSecurityManager( new RMISecurityManager() ) ;
```

shows the *implementing of a Java security manager*. Here, we show the *RMISecurity-Manager* being "installed" in the server. Again, this is not an RMI requirement;

however, you may have to code a security manager because of shop standards (remember them?) or overly paranoid management.

The fifth requirement is that your server RMI code must be sandwiched in a try/catch block.

The next two lines highlight the seventh requirement:

```
RMIExampleServer myExObj = new RMIExampleServer() ;
Naming.rebind("/RMIExample", myExObj ) ;
```

The first line merely creates an object of the server class. Nothing terribly "RMIish" about that; however, the client programs need an object to "hang" the remote method on.

The second line invokes the *Naming.rebind()* method to associate the remote object with a string (name). Note the name string */RMIExample* is very similar to the name used in the client program's invocation of the *Naming.lookup()* method.

That's it. We've seen the code for the interface that makes the remote method look like a local method and the code for the RMI client and RMI server programs. Now, let's continue our steps and get our RMI example up and running.

Step 4: Compile the Interface, then the Server, and Then the Client Classes

Easy enough, right? Put all three source files in one directory and compile them with the Java compiler. Compile the interface first because the server and the client require knowledge of the interface.

Step 5: Generate the Stub with the rmic Program

Run the *rmic* program with the server class file as an argument. Figure 25.2 shows a successful rmic execution and a listing of the class files.

Notice the last file shown in the directory listing: *RMIExampleServer_Stub.class*. This is the infamous stub file we've been talking about. Again, part of RMI magic is causing the client to reference the stub, which looks like the server method, giving the appearance that the remote method invocation is local.

Step 6: Place the Stub Class File where the Client and the Server Classes can Find Them

You would copy the stub class file to a common directory in the *classpath* of both the client and the server. For our example here, the current directory will suffice.

```
MS-DOS Prompt                                               _ □ ×

  8 x 12

D:\Lous Folder\Java MF Book\Book Chapters\Chapter 25 - RMI\Code>rmic -v1.2 RMIEx
ampleServer

D:\Lous Folder\Java MF Book\Book Chapters\Chapter 25 - RMI\Code>dir *.class

 Volume in drive D is FAT MAN
 Volume Serial Number is 106D-1703
 Directory of D:\Lous Folder\Java MF Book\Book Chapters\Chapter 25 - RMI\Code

RMIEXA~1 CLA          500  02-04-01   2:43p RMIExample.class
RMIEXA~2 CLA        1,231  02-04-01   1:40p RMIExampleServer.class
RMIINT~1 CLA          223  02-04-01   1:39p RMIInterface.class
RMIEXA~3 CLA          718  02-04-01   1:40p RMIExampleClient.class
REMOTE~1 CLA          578  02-04-01   2:43p RemoteMethodLocal.class
RMIEXA~4 CLA        1,652  02-04-01   3:45p RMIExampleServer_Stub.class
       6 file(s)           4,902 bytes
       0 dir(s)       12,292.30 MB free

D:\Lous Folder\Java MF Book\Book Chapters\Chapter 25 - RMI\Code>_
```

Figure 25.2   Results of a successful execution of rmic.

Step 7: Start the rmi Registry

You may start the rmi registry by running the Sun JDK tool, *rimregistry*. However, in our example, we want to run rmiregistry in a *separate window* because the rmiregistry program continues to run until stopped.

Create a new command shell by entering *start* in an existing command window. Enter *rmiregistry*. Your command shell window will remain open. You stop the rmiregistry program by issuing an interrupt (Ctrl-C).

Step 8: Create a Policy File

The policy file describes the permissions available to the client, server, or both. The policy file will be used as an argument to the Java runtime interpreter (that's step 9). Listing 25.5 shows what our policy file looks like.

Each line in the policy file grants a network permission on the stated host over a range of ports. For now, you should know that the host identifier (here, we're using an *IP address*) 127.0.0.1 refers to the same machine (not the same JVM); the expression 1023-65535 means being on any network post in the range 1,023 to 65,535. As an aside, the default RMI port is 1, 099.

You could use the same policy file for the client, server, or both. However, as the code in Listing 25.4 shows, we installed a security manager only in the server class. You may use a text editor to create this file; don't use a word processor. You might save formatting characters in the file, which would cause the Java policy file parser to choke. We named this file *rmiexample.policy*.

```
grant {
  permission java.net.SocketPermission "127.0.0.1:1023-65535",
"connect" ;
  permission java.net.SocketPermission "127.0.0.1:1023-65535",
"accept" ;
  permission java.net.SocketPermission "127.0.0.1:1023-65535",
"resolve" ;

} ;
```

Listing 25.5 A Java policy file showing network permissions.

Step 9: Execute the Server Class

Open a new command window (with the start command) and enter the following:

```
java -Djava.security.policy=rmiexample RMIExampleServer
```

Figure 25.3 shows the result of the server execution.

Yes, the server program just sits there, waiting. What does it wait for? The client, of course. Speaking of which, we've come to the end of the line with the last step.

Step 10: Execute the Client Class (Invoke the Remote Method)

All you do here is get a command window you can type in (remember the window running rmiregistry and the server class are blocked from further inputs) and enter

```
java RMIExampleClient
```

Figure 25.4 shows the command and the output.

Because we didn't install a security manager in the client, we do not need to pass the policy file to the Java runtime with the -D option.

Summary of RMI Steps

We close with a list of the previous steps for your convenient reference.

Step 1: Create the RMI Interface.

Step 2: Code the Client Class.

Step 3: Code the Server Class.

Step 4: Compile the Interface, then the server, and then the client classes.

Step 5: Generate the stub with the rmic program.

Figure 25.3 Executing the RMI server program with the Java policy file.

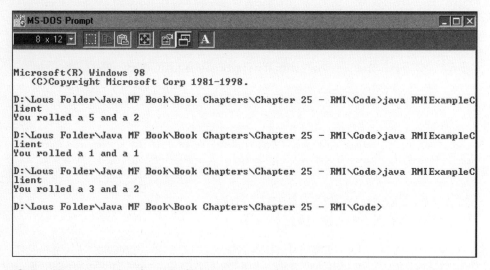

Figure 25.4 Executing the RMI client program and accessing the remote method.

Step 6: Place the stub class file where the client and the server classes can find them.

Step 7: Start the rmi registry.

Step 8: Create a policy file.

Step 9: Execute the server class.

Step 10: Execute the client class (invoke the remote method).

Perhaps you should try this out in your spare time. Although it looks intimidating, if you walk through the steps a couple of times, you'll get the hang of it.

In Summary

The techniques used in RMI may seem overly complicated at first. However, stop and think about what RMI allows you to do. With the ability to invoke Java methods that reside on different machines, the world of Java distributed processing opens up. Also, the technique of using stubs to describe and interface to other methods is the cornerstone of other distributed Java technologies, such as Enterprise JavaBeans.

Glossary

Accessor Methods   A series of methods used to retrieve and set object property values. Also called get/set methods.

Aggregate Data Structure   A declared variable that consists of more than one piece of data: arrays and record structures.

API   Application Programming Interface. A set of specifications and libraries that enables a programmer to write application code that communicates with another system (usually a system-level package, such as a windowing system or a DBMS).

Appletviewer   Sun JDK tool that lets you run an applet in a window outside of a browser.

ASCII   An 8-bit encoding scheme used by most all operating systems (notably, not used by IBM's MVS operating system).

AWT   Abstract Windowing Toolkit. A set of Java libraries that enables a Java programmer to use platform-independent windowing, printing, GUI construction and event handling, and other utilities. AWT relies heavily on the underlying operating system's graphics-rendering routines.

Behavior   A characteristic of an object; how an object acts. An object method implements that object's behavior.

BXBATCH   An MVS utility that enables you to execute a UNIX command or executable in batch. Used often to compile and run Java programs in MVS batch.

Bytecode   The output from the Java compiler. Bytecode is a platform-independent representation of a Java software object.

Casting   The act of temporarily changing the type of a variable for use in a single expression.

Checked Exceptions   Exceptions that should be handled by Java code, usually with Java's try/catch/finally constructs.

Class   A template for object creation. All objects derived, or instantiated, from a class share the methods defined in the class.

Class Variable, Method   A variable or method declared with the static modifier; a variable or method that is not attached to a single instance of a class. Class variables and methods are known to and are the same (have the same value) for all instances of a class. Contrast to instance variables and methods.

Classpath   A collection of directories and jar files containing the classes used by the Java runtime.

Conditional Compilation   Describes the activities of a preprocessor in conditionally generating code. Basically, the preprocessor directives are if/else statements of some sort that cause the source to be conditionally generated. Java does not support conditional compilation.

Constructor   A method that creates an instance of a class.

CTG   CICS Transaction Gateway. The CTG provides access from Web browsers and network computers to applications running on a CICS Transaction Server in a two-tier configuration.

Data Hiding   A property of object systems where the inner workings, or details of the object's behavior, and representation of an object's properties are hidden from other objects.

Doc Comment   A special Java comment that starts with /** and ends with */. The Java utility javadoc uses doc comments to generate documentation.

EBCDIC   An 8-bit data encoding scheme used by IBM for its MVS operating system.

Encapsulation   A property of object systems where an object is packaged such that other objects interact with the object by means of a well-defined interface.

Enterprise JavaBeans (EJB)   Enterprise JavaBeans (EJB) defines an *architecture* that enables developers to create reusable, server-side components.

Error   An object of class Error.

Escape Sequence   A series of characters that enables a Java programmer to output certain nonprintable characters.

Event   An object of class java.util.EventObject or one of its subclasses; an encapsulation of a state that usually requires a programmed response.

Event Delegation   The term used to describe Java's event-handling model. Events are assigned listeners. When the event occurs, the Java runtime listener delegates the event to its assigned listener.

Exception   An object of class Exception or a subclass; a direct subclass of class Throwable; a condition in a program that may demand attention.

extcheck   JDK tool that checks if a Java Archive (jar) file conflicts with other jar files.

Finalizer Method   A method that executes between the time the garbage collector recognizes an object as garbage and the garbage collector reclaims the memory.

Garbage Collector   A part of the Java runtime that recognizes unused objects as such and automatically reclaims the object's memory. Garbage collection frees the programmer from having to manage memory.

Get Methods   A set of methods that retrieves the values of object properties. The properties have the private visibility modifier; the get method has the public visibility modifier. Sometimes called Accessor methods.

Header, Method   The part of a method that consists of the visibility and other modifiers, the returned type (or void), the method name, the argument list, and its optional throws clause. The method header is contained in Java interfaces.

HFS   Hierarchical File System. A UNIX-based file system used with IBM's OS/390 operating system.

HPC   High Performance Compiler. An IBM Java compiler that generates native OS/390 instructions as opposed to generating bytecode.

IMS Connector for Java   An IBM product that enables Java applications to access IMS transactions.

Inheritance   A property of object-oriented systems where one class (the subclass) automatically knows, and can use, the properties and behaviors of another class (the superclass).

Inheritance, Multiple   A property of object environments (C++, in particular) where a subclass may have more than one superclass.

Inheritance, Single   A property of object environments (Java, in particular) where a subclass may have, at most, one superclass.

Inner Class   A class wholly contained within another class.

Instance Variables, Methods   A variable, object, or method that is known to and usually has a unique value for each instance of a class. Contrast with Class variables and methods.

Interface   A collection of abstract behaviors, coded as method headers, that will be implemented by a class. When a class implements an interface, the class is responsible for providing concrete method bodies for all the method headers declared in the interface.

IOException   An object of class IOException or a subclass; an exception thrown by a condition dealing with IO, such as FileNotFoundException. Also called checked exceptions.

J2EE   Java 2, Enterprise Edition. The specification, written by Sun Microsystems, that describes a collection of APIs that enable programmers to develop enterprise-class applications in Java.

J2ME   Java 2, Micro Edition. The specification, written by Sun Microsystems, that describes a collection of APIs that enable programmers to develop Java applications that run on small machines and embedded devices.

J2SE   Java 2, Standard Edition. The specification, written by Sun Microsystems, that describes a collection of APIs that enable programmers to develop client applications in Java. Considered the core of the Java language.

jar   JDK tool that combines multiple files into a Java Archive file.

java   JDK tool that runs compiled Java programs.

Java Applet   A Java software object that executes within the context of a browser. Applets have a different structure than applications and usually have different security requirements as well.

Java Application   A Java software object containing a main() method and is executed by invoking the main() method. Sometimes called a client application.

JavaBeans   An architecture for developing software components, mostly used to create custom user interface components.

javac   JDK tool that compiles Java source code.

javadoc   JDK tool that generates documentation for Java programs in HTML format.

javah   JDK tool that generates C header files for use in writing native C code methods.

JavaMail   A Java extension API that can communicate with standard Internet mail protocols.

Java Messaging Service (JMS)   JMS is a set of APIs that invokes asynchronous messaging services like broadcast and point-to-point (client-to-client) messages.

Java Naming and Directory Service (JNDI)   JNDI provides an interface for accessing name and directory services, such as LDAP directory services and Domain Name Service (DNS), to locate distributed objects by name (not location).

javap   JDK tool that disassembles Java source from class files.

Java Runtime   See JVM.

JavaServer Pages (JSP)   A JSP is a combination of HTML (or XML) and Java scripting code that can dynamically generate HTML (or XML).

Java Servlet   A Java software object that executes on a Web server, additionally providing that server with increased functionality.

Java Transaction API (JTA)   JTA provides developers with a mechanism for handling the commit and the rollback of transactions as well as insuring the Atomicity, Consistency, Isolation, and Durability (ACID) properties of a transaction.

Java Transaction Services (JTS)   JTS provides developers with a means of communicating with transaction monitors and other transaction-oriented resources.

jdb   JDK line-oriented Java debugging tool.

JDBC   Java Database Connectivity (not an acronym, but often used as such). A Java API that enables Java programs to access data stored in relational databases and enables Java programs to issue SQL statements.

JDK   Java Development Kit. A set of software tools and utilities supplied by Sun Microsystems.

JFC   Java Foundation Classes. A set of Java classes that contains Swing user interface classes.

jni   Java Native Interface. An API that enables programmers to interface C programs with Java methods

JRIO   Java Record Input/Output. A set of proprietary IBM classes that enables the Java programmer to perform record I/O on traditional MVS datasets.

JVM   Java Virtual Machine. The environment in which Java software objects execute in. Also called a Java Runtime.

Layout Manager   An object of class LayoutManager; an abstraction used by Java GUI programmers to define the overall layout of GUI components in the interface.

Listener   A Java object assigned the task of reporting on certain classes of events. The listener reports the event to the appropriate system manager, which invokes a callback to handle the event.

Method   The term used to describe the code that implements some behavior of an object.

Modifier   A keyword placed before a variable or object type or method return value that provides additional information about the variable, object, or method.

Multithreading   The practice of coding programs (Java or otherwise) that may create multiple threads of control.

MVS   IBM's operating system that runs on mainframe-class computers. MVS is being phased out in favor of IBM's OS/390, although many MVS shops are still in existence.

OS/390 UNIX   A flavor of UNIX that runs with OS/390.

Object Oriented Programming   A view of software where software is constructed by creating objects, which is a combination of properties and behaviors (as opposed to separate data and processes).

OS/390   IBM's operating system used on mainframe-class computers. OS/390 combines features of UNIX and MVS.

Overloading, Methods   The coding of two or more methods with the same name, but different argument lists. Often done when coding multiple constructors for a single class.

Overriding, Methods   The coding of a method in a subclass with the same signature as a method in the superclass.

Package   A collection of classes used together and referenced by a name. The package name mirrors the directory structure that specifies its location.

Pass by Reference   When passing an argument to a method, the JVM passes a reference (pointer or address) of the argument to the method. Reference types are passed by reference. Contrast with pass by value below.

Pass by Value   When passing an argument to a method, the JVM generates a copy of the argument and passes the copy to the method. Primitive types are passed by value. Contrast with pass by reference above.

Polymorphism   A property of object systems where behaviors of the same name may be used in different contexts.

Preprocessor   A piece of software that generates source code based on directives coded within a source code file. Java does not support preprocessors.

Primitive Type   A piece of data declared in a Java software object that is not derived from a class. Primitive types correspond to declared types in non-object languages and closely parallel variables declared in C programs.

Reference Data Types   A class, array, or a string type, as opposed to primitive types.

Representative Typing   Declared variable types mirror the underlying data representation. COBOL and PL/I are representatively typed.

RMI   Remote Method Invocation. A Java technology that enables a Java program executing in one JVM to invoke methods from an object residing in another JVM.

RuntimeException   An object of class RuntimeException; an exception thrown in a Java program usually as a result of poorly written code, such as a zerodivide or array out of bounds.

Set Methods   Methods used to assign values to the properties of an object. The object properties are typically declared with the private visibility modifier; the set methods are typically declared public. Sometimes called Accessor methods or Mutator methods.

Signature, Method   The part of a method header containing the name and the argument list.

SQLJ A library (not Java-specific but a Java binding is available) that enables Java programs to issue SQL statements to access relational databases. Similar in function to JDBC.

Stream A data source or destination abstraction that Java uses to define input/output resources. Java IO is done on streams that may be defined as disk files, network sockets, or URLs.

Strong Typing The language does not enable the programmer to use variables of different data types in the same expression. Pascal is an example of a strongly typed language.

Structured Programming A view of software as separate process models and data models. The process model describes processes as sets of related processes.

Subclass A class that automatically knows properties and methods of the classes' superclass. A subclass may override superclass methods and properties or provide additional methods and properties to distinguish itself from its superclass.

super A Java keyword that refers to an instance of the object's superclass, used to reference superclass methods.

Superclass A class that contains methods and properties that are automatically known by the classes' subclass.

Swing A set of Java libraries that enables the Java programmer to develop platform-independent user interfaces. Swing does not depend on the underlying operating system's graphics rendering like AWT does.

this A Java keyword that refers to the current object.

Thread An object of class Thread or a subclass; a flow of control in a Java program; short for Thread of Control.

throw Java keyword that, when used in a program, introduces an object of class Throwable (or a direct subclass) into the JVM.

Throwable Superclass of exceptions and errors.

Unicode A 16-bit data encoding scheme used by Java. The first 8 bits are ASCII.

URL Uniform Resource Locator. A naming scheme that enables a directory service to locate a resource on a network; commonly used to reference Web pages.

Variable Scope The locations in a program where a declared variable is known and can be used. Globally declared variables, such as those used in COBOL, can be used throughout the compile unit containing the variable. Locally declared variables, such as those declared inside a PL/I procedure or a Java method, can be used only within the declared procedure or method.

Variable Typing How the language runtime compares the attributes of a variable to other variables in the same expressions. See strong typing, weak typing, and representative typing.

Variable Visibility See variable scope.

Visibility Modifier A modifier that defines the visibility of a declared variable, object, or method.

Visual Age IBM's Java integrated software development environment (IDE).

void Java keyword coded before a method name that indicates that the method does not return a value to the calling method.

VSAM Virtual Storage Access Method. A data structure used on OS/MVS to implement direct and random access data access.

Weak Typing   The language enables the programmer to use variables of different data types in the same expression (within certain bounds). Taken to the extreme, some weakly typed programming languages (REXX is an example) do not even permit declaring variables with a data type.

Bibliography

"E-business Application Solutions on OS/390 Using Java." *IBM Redbooks.* SG24-5342-00

"E-business Application Solutions on OS/390 Using Java: Samples." *IBM Redbooks.* SG24-5365-00

"Experiences Moving a Java Application to OS/390." *IBM Redbooks.* SG24-5620-00

Flanagan, David, et. al. *Java in a Nutshell, Deluxe Edition.* O'Reilly. ISBN 1-56392-304-9

"IBM OS/390 Introduction and Release Guide, Release 10." *IBM Redbooks.* GC28-1725-09

"IMS Connect Guide and Reference." *IBM Redbooks.* SC27-0946-00

"Integrating Java with Existing Data and Applications on OS/390." *IBM Redbooks.* SG24-5142-00

"Java Application Development for CICS." *IBM Redbooks.* SG24-5275-01

"Java Programming Guide for OS/390." *IBM Redbooks.*

"JRIO API User's Guide." IBM Redbooks.

"OS/390 UNIX System Services User's Guide." *IBM Redbooks.* SC28-1891-10

"Programming with the Host Access APIs." *IBM Redbooks.* SG24-5856-00

Roman, Ed. *Enterprise JavaBeans and the Java 2 Platform Enterprise Edition.* John Wiley & Sons. ISBN 0-471-33229-1

Index